INTRODUCTION TO LITERARY CONTEXT

English Literature

INTRODUCTION TO LITERARY CONTEXT

English Literature

SALEM PRESS

A Division of EBSCO Information Services, Inc.
Ipswich, Massachusetts

GREY HOUSE PUBLISHING

Publisher's Cataloging-In-Publication Data

Introduction to literary context. English literature / [edited by Salem Press].

 pages : illustrations; cm

 Includes bibliographical references and index.
 ISBN: 978-1-61925-485-5

 1. English literature–History and criticism. I. Salem Press. II. Title: English literature

PR99.I587 2014
820.9

First Printing

PRINTED IN THE UNITED STATES OF AMERICA

CONTENTS

PUBLISHER'S NOTE

Introduction to Literary Context: English Literature is the third title in *Salem's Introduction to Literary Context* series. It follows *American Post-Modernist Novels* and *American Short Fiction.* A fourth title in the series is *World Literature.*

This series is designed to introduce students to the world's greatest works of literature—including novels, short fictions, novellas, and poems – not only placing them in the historical, societal, scientific and religious context of their time, but illuminating key concepts and vocabulary that students are likely to encounter. A great starting point from which to embark on further research, *Introduction to Literary Context* is a perfect foundation for *Critical Insights,* Salem's acclaimed series of critical analysis written to deepen the basic understanding of literature via close reading and original criticism. Both series – *Introduction to Literary Context* and *Critical Insights* – cover authors, works and themes that are addressed in core reading lists at the undergraduate level.

Scope and Coverage

English Literature covers 31 works – novels, short stories, and poems—written by English authors, published between 1516 and 2003. The authors in this collection – 6 women and 18 men – represent a variety of ages, life styles, and political beliefs, including those whose work has been banned, burned, and revered. Their stories are based on real life experiences and struggles, as individuals and members of a group. A major theme in English literature, and thus in this collection, is alienation, with science, nature and religion popular refrains.

With in depth analysis of works by the likes of Charles Dickens, Charlotte Brontë, H. G. Wells, Salman Rushdie, J. K. Rowling, Rudyard Kipling and Roald Dahl, *Introduction to Literary Context: English Literature* offers students the tools to grasp more firmly and dig deeper into the meanings of not only the works covered here, but English literature as a whole.

Organization and Format

The essays in *English Literature* appear alphabetical by title of the work. Each is 6–8 pages in length and includes the following sections:

- Content Synopsis – summarizes the plot of the work, describing the main points and prominent characters in concise language.
- Historical Context – describes the relevance to the story of the moods, attitudes and conditions that existed during the time period that the novel took place.
- Societal Context – describes the role that society played within the work, from the acceptance of traditional gender roles to dealing with mental illness.
- Religious Context – explains how religion— of the author specifically, or a group generally, influenced the novel.
- Scientific & Technological Context—analyzes to what extent scientific and/or technological progress has affected the story.
- Biographical Context – offers biographical details of the author's life, which often helps students to make sense of the story.
- Discussion Questions – a list of 8–10 thoughtful questions that are designed to develop stimulating and productive classroom discussions.
- Essay Ideas – a valuable list of ideas that will encourage students to explore themes, writing techniques, and character traits.
- Works Cited

Introduction to Literary Context: English Literture ends with a general Bibliography and subject Index.

ABOUT THIS VOLUME

Although the great volumes analyzed in the span of this collection differ vastly in plot, a surprising number feature the common thread of characters who are out of place in society for a variety of reasons; some are self exiles, others have been driven out, and some are excluded simply for being different. The Monster in *Frankenstein*, the mad scientist in *The Island of Dr. Moreau*, Dr. Jekyll and his alter ego Mr. Hyde on up to Harry Potter could not seem any more opposite from one another, yet all are literally and figuratively orphans—characters set apart from their fellows. Alienation is a major theme throughout much of English and, indeed, world literature. Science, nature, religion, and the classes—some individually and others in relation to each other—also play a pivotal role in many of these works. Let's take a closer look.

Playing God

First published in 1818, *Frankenstein* is the story of the ultimate do-it-yourselfer and considered by most critics to be the progenitor of science fiction. The epistolary novel unfurls second hand through the letters of Robert Walton, captain of a vessel trapped in the ice of the North Pole. The ship, a man made creation, threatened by nature (the ice) immediately establishes a parallel that follows throughout the action of the novel. Walton has come to the frozen wastes of the North seeking fame as a trailblazer of science and discovery. Victor Frankenstein, the novel's true protagonist, has followed a similar course, but within the confines of a laboratory, and his handmade creation becomes the vessel of his destruction. Both men venture forth without fully having considered the risks involved not only to themselves but to those around them. This myopic vision costs Victor not only his own life, but, ultimately, the lives of his innocent loved ones. Like Walton who ignores the effects of his actions on his crew, Victor's desires blind him to the high price that others might pay for his foolishness. Through Victor, Walton realizes his folly and, suppressing his pride and vanity, decides to abandon his quest in order to spare his own life and those of his men. For Victor, however, it is far too late and he pays the ultimate price.

Author Mary Shelley offers an excellent example of location used as a metaphor for the story's action. The isolation of the frozen North perfectly reflects the loneliness and sense of disconnection experienced by Victor's creature. *Frankenstein* includes the popular literary motifs of both science and religion and, arguably, pits one against the other. As Tracy M. Caldwell states:

> Victor is a man over whom religion seems to hold no sway. He, in fact, actively seeks to become a God; to create life, perhaps to live forever. In a reading in which Victor stands as an uncaring and abandoning 'father,' he would symbolize that God, which people believe created man only to leave him to his own devices, the result of which is, in many people, though certainly not all, a murderous and vengeful instinct.

Victor uses science in order to create human life and become godlike but abandons his creation and refuses to answers his creature's prayers when confronted by the monster with the request to build him a mate. Victor initially agrees but later destroys the female version before the spark of life is instilled in its dormant limbs and organs. This action shows that Victor finally has learned from his mistakes and is unwilling to repeat them. Although he might have learned from his past errors, he still does not take responsibility for them and again abandons his creation, although this time symbolically. The tug of war between science, religion, and nature also is addressed in the element of the novel in which a human is created through unnatural means. Shelley was pregnant when writing the story, so childbirth was ever present in her thoughts. Caldwell points out that:

> The possibility of a birthing process taken over by men, which is arguably, at least partly a reflection of the increase in male physicians' interest in women and birthing, duties that had previously been performed only by midwives, is explored in *Frankenstein*. Scientific [and/or medical] study devoid of women's research and involvement is shown to yield terrible results in this text, as much as the literary texts exploring this idea today. The text engages with some of the more specious sciences of the day, including the writing of Cornelius Agrippa who believed God and the universe could be understood via magic. Paracelsus is also a man Victor studies, an alchemist; he represents the scientific theory falling out of favor at the time. The combination in Victor's courses of study, of both magical and 'scientific' theory proves fruitful, if dangerous.

Born To Be Wild

Several of the themes and even circumstances employed in *Frankenstein*, coincidentally (or not), also are present in H. G. Wells' 1896 novel *The Island of Dr. Moreau*. Like Shelley, Wells offers a cautionary tale of a scientist who desires to mimic god and create human life. Wells' Dr. Moreau, however, takes a different tack than Victor Frankenstein by using surgery to convert live animals into human-like beings. Like *Frankenstein*, this story, also science fiction, unfurls through a text written by the book's protagonist, Edward Prendick, and begins aboard a ship. The icebound waters of *Frankenstein*'s frozen North are replaced by the tropic swells of the South Pacific. Prendick is a shipwrecked sailor rescued by a vessel headed for Moreau's island home. Like Victor, Prendick is plucked from certain death by a ship. Along with a menagerie of animals, among the vessel's odd inventory are a man named Montgomery and his silent companion, the feral M'Ling. Like Frankenstein's creature, M'ling's is revealed to be a manmade man. Whereas Victor produced a lone creation, Dr. Moreau's lab has sired numerous beings cobbled together from animal parts.

Unlike Victor, however, Moreau's foray into playing god goes deeper than simply bestowing life. Whereas Victor fled in horror from his creation who is cast out and left to fend for himself, Moreau keeps a watchful eye on his population and has provided them with "the Law," a set of commandments that must be obeyed. The Law provides a moral code for the Beast People to adopt in order to be more human and civilized. Anyone violating the Law is severely punished in the House of Pain (Moreau's surgery). Although Moreau has defined rules for his Beast People, he, ironically, rejects the ethics concerning their creation.

As Anita R. Rose points out, Wells' novel functions on several levels. Wells was well known to be anti-colonial, and critics have read that stance into several of his leading works. Says Rose:

> The morality and even the efficacy of Empire were being questioned in the late nineteenth century. In general, there were two distinct ways of thinking about Empire: it was a means to pursue and acquire wealth for England or it was an opportunity to civilize the savage and "unchristian" (usually brown or black) races who occupied colonial holdings. Some critics have suggested that *The Island of Dr. Moreau* can be read as a parody of this latter attitude. The Beast People are described as racially different, often dark as well as bestial. In trying to make these beasts men, Moreau has only drawn out their unsavory qualities,

taken them far away from what nature has made them, and given them an empty religion that is the mere chanting of the "Law" with no real understanding or faith. For many in Great Britain, this could also be a description of the effects of imperialism on indigenous people through the British empire, Prendick's repeated comparison of the Beast People to "savages" he has encountered only serves to reinforce this connection.

In addition to its religious elements, scholars have attached evolutionary meaning to the novel. While on the surface it might appear that Moreau is playing god with his creations, another perspective is that he is hastening the evolutionary process. Darwin's theory was roughly 25 years old and still controversial at the time of the *Dr. Moreau*'s publication. Even though Wells might have accepted the theory of evolution as truth, he didn't necessarily view it as positive. As Rice observes:

Wells' conviction that evolution doesn't necessarily mean improvement or progress set him apart from many others of his era who wanted, even needed, to believe that all of the suffering and loss implied in evolutionary theory had a purpose, and that purpose was to raise up the species. Rather, evolution simply means change, and adaptation to the environment is not necessarily a noble, clean, or enlightened thing. This premise is perhaps most clearly evident in Wells' *The Time Machine* (1895), in which humanity has evolved into two separate species, one industrious, misshapen, and cannibalistic, the other beautiful, slothful, and essentially useless.

Inside Out

Robert Louis Stevenson built his literary reputation on youthful adventure stories like *Treasure Island*. *The Strange Case of Dr. Jekyll and Mr. Hyde* presents a broad departure from his typical fare. Like the authors discussed above, Stevenson uses this story to comment on society and science. Published in 1886, Stevenson examines the lower and middle classes by presenting a single character encompassing both. As a physician, Jekyll occupies a respected place in the middle class; he is educated and sophisticated yet must work for his living. He, however, employs members of the lower class as servants in his household. The dreaded Hyde, however, is strictly lower-class even although he possesses all of Jekyll's knowledge and loftier interests. As Calum A. Kerr observes:

Having seen the life of these characters so clearly displayed, the degeneracy of Hyde comes to act as a commentary on them. Although ultimately a part of the very middle-class Jekyll, Hyde decides to take his lodgings in the lower-class area of Soho, thereby associating himself with this other section of society. In this way we can see Stevenson commenting that it is at least as likely for higher members of society to succumb to perversion and degeneracy as for the lower members. And this commentary is emphasized when Hyde's rooms in Soho are found to contain wine, silver plates and other fineries, marking him as a gentlemen with base tastes rather than the lower-class figure that might have been presumed. This is a figure who would have been quite familiar to readers of the time thanks to other characters such as Duc Jean Floressas des Esseintes (*A Rebours* by J. K. Huysmans, 1884) and Dorian Gray (*The Picture of Dorian Gray* by Oscar Wilde, 1890), both also rich and decadent.

Science and religion also come into focus. Jekyll is a scientist whose studies should be limited to the physical, but he ponders the nature of the moral and psychological. His physical and mental alteration from the moral Jekyll to the immoral

Hyde, however, comes through the ingestion of chemicals. He does not start out as a good man who suffers the ravages of poverty and disadvantage to emerge a villain, but rather employs science to corrupt himself into an evil being. The concoction not only alters his body but his mind and soul as well. Hyde is a man without morals who lives only for his pleasures. He has stepped outside of society by casting off the yoke of its rules. This proposes an interesting element: those who do good because it's right and those who only do it because it's the law. Once there is no entity to enforce the law, several of these characters discussed in this collection revert, like Hyde, back to savagery.

King Me

Wells and Kipling both had anti-colonial streaks. Wells stories asserts that technologically-superior might does not equal the right to dominate another nation and its people. Kipling, while very pro-England, also openly criticized his country's colonization of India. Scholars have asserted that Kipling's stance on England and India is the reason he was never knighted despite being the first English-language writer awarded the Nobel prize for literature. Kipling's *The Man Who Would Be King* (1888) finds Danny Dravot and Peachy Carnehan, two former British army regulars, who tire of performing a high-risk job for low wages, setting off for the wilds of Kafiristan (Afghanistan) to become kings. Having fought for the Empire in a number of lands where the locals were dismissed by them as no better than savages who often are locked in petty feuds with their neighbors, Danny and Peachy believe that two experienced and industrious lads like themselves can easily subjugate one of the warring factions by assisting them to defeat their enemies by applying the military skills they acquired serving the crown.

Kipling's story is different from the previous tales in that science plays no direct role, while it also is similar, as Dravot eventually establishes

himself not merely as a king but as a deity. Again we have the "civilized" attempting to dominate the "uncivilized," with disastrous results. Like Dr. Moreau being slain by his Beast People subjects, Dravot eventually is flung into a ravine and killed by those he has tried to rule after they discover that he is merely a man and not divine. Once again the "savages" have rejected the interference of an advanced culture and returned to their nature. Carnehan miraculously survives crucifixion and is released only to relate the amazing tale in a long flashback to a newspaper reporter like Captain Walton in *Frankenstein*.

Do You Believe in Magic?

While the titles above are all products of the nineteenth century, spring boarding into modern literature reveals that the themes that dominated English literature a century-plus ago still endure among today's writers. Debuting in 1981 with *Harry Potter and the Philosopher's Stone* (or *Sorcerer's Stone* on U.S. shores), author J. K. Rowling's series became the last great publishing sensation of the twentieth century. While Harry Potter might seem far removed from *Frankenstein's* murdering monster and the sinister Mr. Hyde, the fledgling wizard shares the same attributes as the characters discussed above: he is alone and apart from society; an orphan both literally (his parents are dead) and figuratively. Harry being a wizard immediately sets him apart from the non-magic "muggles," but even amongst his fellow magic folk he is unique: he alone bears the lightning streak scar and is the lead target of Voldemort, the series' villain.

Rowling presents a world consisting of two distinct societies: the magical and the nonmagical. As Jen Cadwallader's essay on *Harry Potter and the Order of the Phoenix* states:

> Rowling focuses on society in two ways in the novel. Within the confines of Privet Drive we see a glimpse of British suburbia, and

the picture Rowling presents is not flattering. Middle-class Britain is obsessed with the notion of "keeping up with the Jones's." Whose lawn is nicest or who has the newest car seems to be the extent of people's interest in one another. At the start of the novel, we see a bleak day for Privet drive due to drought — the neighborhood has been "deprived of [its] usual car-washing and lawn-mowing pursuits." At the same time, the Dursleys believe that conformity—looking, thinking, and acting like everyone else—is the only way to gain social acceptance. All of the houses on Privet Drive look identical, and similar cars sit in every driveway. One of the Dursleys' greatest fears is that someone will discover they have "freaks" like Harry in their family. Further, Rowling's muggles are technology driven while the magic folk reject technology and rely on their special powers.

Continues Cadwallader:

Rowling does deal with modern technology in the glimpses she gives us of the Muggle world. In *Harry Potter and the Sorcerer's Stone*, Rowling is critical of the impact technology has on children. Dudley, who "was very fat and hated exercise," receives for his birthday a computer with sixteen games, a second television, a video camera, a remote control airplane, and a VCR (20). In *Order of the Phoenix*, Muggles are presented as technology-obsessed. As Harry is walking toward St. Mungo's, he is almost run down by "a gaggle of shoppers plainly intent on nothing but making it into a nearby shop full of electrical gadgets" (483). Rowling's use of the term "gaggle" implies that the shoppers are a sort of mindless herd, buying up new technology simply because it is there.

Status in society also comes into play in Harry's world. Cadwallader notes that, "The prejudices of nineteenth-century England are apparent in the wizarding world as well. Status is still based, in the eyes of many, on wealth and birth ('pureblood' versus 'mudblood')."

However, where several of the previous titles depicted characters working against society, Rowling is refreshing in that Potter, although singular, must align himself with others in order to succeed. Orphan Harry has found a new adopted family among fellow wizards although in some ways he remains an outsider even to them. Among his own kind, Potter often is, as Cadwallader notes, "purposely kept in the dark about the goings-on in the wizard world."

The religious aspects of the Potter series are tricky. While the mere existence of wizards and practitioners of magic arguably constitutes a religion unto itself, the characters celebrate Christmas and believe in the afterlife.

As you read further into the essays included in this collection on such volumes ranging as wide as the classics – Charles Dickens' *Oliver Twist* and Henry Fielding's *Tom Jones* – to 20th-century fare like Salman Rushdie's *Midnight's Children* and Philip Pullman's *The Golden Compass*, you will find other similarities in their themes and actions despite differences in character and plot. Hopefully this introduction will serve as a stepping stone to identifying them.

Michael Rogers
Freelance writer and former
Senior Editor, *Library Journal*

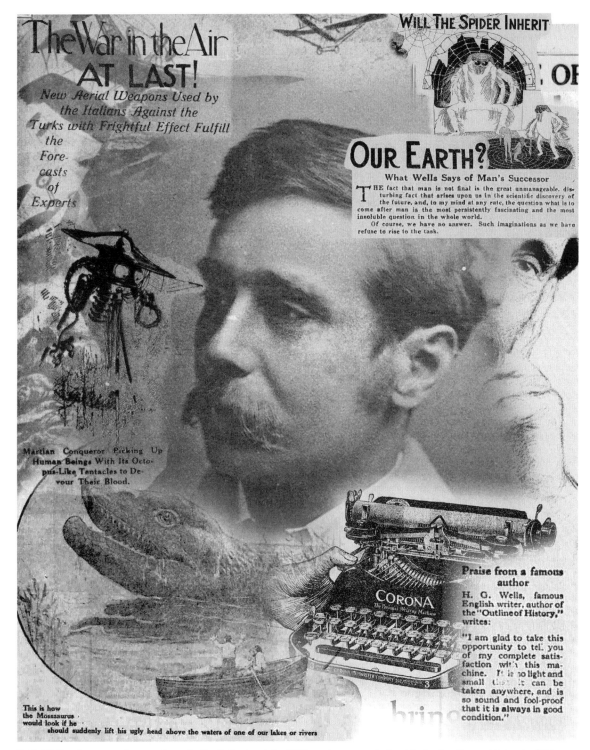

The War in the Air AT LAST!

New Aerial Weapons Used by the Italians Against the Turks with Frightful Effect Fulfill the Forecasts of Experts

WILL THE SPIDER INHERIT

OUR EARTH?

What Wells Says of Man's Successor

THE fact that man is not final is the great unmanageable, disturbing fact that arises upon us in the scientific discovery of the future, and, to my mind at any rate, the question what is to come after man is the most persistently fascinating and the most insoluble question in the whole world.

Of course, we have no answer. Such imaginations as we have refuse to rise to the task.

Martian Conqueror Picking Up Human Beings With Its Octopus-Like Tentacles to Devour Their Blood.

CORONA
The Personal Writing Machine

Praise from a famous author

H. G. Wells, famous English writer, author of the "Outline of History," writes:

"I am glad to take this opportunity to tell you of my complete satisfaction with this machine. It is so light and small that it can be taken anywhere, and is so sound and fool-proof that it is always in good condition."

This is how the Mosasaurus would look if he should suddenly lift his ugly head above the waters of one of our lakes or rivers

H. G. Wells, above, center, was born in Kent, England, in 1866, and won a scholarship to the Normal School of Science in London, where he was influenced by the teachings of T. H. Huxley. Wells won acclaim with the classic, *The Time Machine;* this volume analyzes these three works: *The County of the Blind,* page 41; *The Door in the Wall,* page 47; *The Island of Dr. Moreau,* page 111. Photo: Designed by Jim DuPlessis with images from Library of Congress.

The Amber Spyglass

by Philip Pullman

"And she herself was partly Shadow-matter. Part of her was subject to this tide that was moving through the cosmos. And so were the Mulefa, and so were human beings in every world, and every kind of conscious creature, wherever they were. And unless she found out what was happening, they might all find themselves drifting away to oblivion, every one."

—Philip Pullman, *The Amber Spyglass*

Content Synopsis

The volume preceding "The Amber Spyglass" in Philip Pullman's "His Dark Materials" sequence of novels, "The Subtle Knife," ended with Will Parry, bearer of the subtle knife that can cut windows between worlds, having both found and lost his missing father in a few terrible moments. He returns to camp to find his witch-allies attacked by the soul-draining Specters, and his newfound friend and partner in adventure, Lyra, gone. Lyra has clearly been abducted, since she has left behind her most precious possession, the truth-telling alethiometer (the "Golden Compass" of the first volume.) Will is so shocked by this new loss that he barely registers the presence in the camp of two figures: angels.

"The Amber Spyglass" opens in a cave in a secluded valley high in the Himalayan Mountains of Lyra's world. Lyra has been taken by her mother, Mrs. Coulter. Having learned that Lyra's destiny is to disobey the church and become a new Eve, Mrs. Coulter knows that she should turn her daughter over to the Church she serves, but instead she is keeping Lyra with her in a drugged sleep.

The two angels Will meets, Balthamos and Baruch, are wise and of great age, but not omniscient. Nor are they gentle, shiningly virtuous entities; Balthamos can be acerbic, sarcastic, petulant and impatient. They plan to take to Lord Asriel, (Lyra's father and leader of a rebel army) a secret they have learned that will help him in his challenge to "The Authority." "The Authority" has given himself many names: "God, the Creator, the Lord, Yahweh, El, Adonai, the King, the Father, the Almighty," but he is not the creator; he was the first angel, condensed out of Dust. Dust, the central idea of the series, "is only a name for what happens when matter begins to understand itself. Matter loves matter. It seeks to know more about itself, and Dust is formed" (33). It represents conscious thought, self-awareness, independent thought, and the intellect. "The Authority" told those who came after him that he created them. One exercised independent thought, found out the truth, and was banished. The rebel angels serve her. Balthamos and Baruch do not name their leader, but we suspect that she is one of the Eves—the women whose intellect and courage have led to the "Fall" in so many different worlds. The angels want Will to go with them, taking the subtle knife, the only weapon that will work against "The Authority." Will refuses to go, however, until the angels have helped him to find Lyra. They decide that Baruch will take the secret to Asriel while Will and Balthamos will go on to rescue Lyra.

Baruch reaches Asriel but is mortally wounded. Before he dies, he reveals that "The Authority" has retired to an inner crystal chamber. "The Regent," an angel called Metatron, who was once Baruch's brother Enoch, is the real power of the Kingdom. He and "The Authority" have decided that conscious beings have learned to think for themselves more than is desirable (which is why there has been so much Dust in the worlds). They plan to intervene and restore their own absolute authority and power. "The Authority" is to be moved into a permanent citadel, and the Chariot is to become an engine of war. An inquisition will be set up in every world, and the republic Asriel hopes to build will be destroyed.

Back in the mountains, a local girl, Ama, obtains herbs from a Holy man to counteract Mrs. Coulter's potion, and wake Lyra, but meanwhile the Church's Consistorial Court has sent a priest, Father Gomez, to find and assassinate Lyra. Gomez is to find her by looking for "the Tempter," who will be a woman from another world. In our world, Dr. Mary Malone, the scientist who had found a way to talk to angels, and had been told by them to follow Lyra, acting like "the serpent," finds her way from our Oxford to a new world. This new domain is populated by extraordinary beings, the Mulefa, who exist in perfect harmony with their environment. She finds that this world too has Dust, or "scraf" as the Mulefa call it, and that it has been in their world since their species became self-aware thirty-three thousand years ago. She finds a way of making scraf visible, using two translucent sheets of amber enamel to make a spyglass. As Mary learns to communicate with the Mulefa, she learns that their world is changing; the balance of nature has been altered; the trees on which the Mulefa depend are sickening, and Dust is flowing away.

While Lyra sleeps, short italicized sections of narrative that intercut with Will's story show that she is dreaming. In her dream, she meets Roger, the Jordan College boy who had been her friend and who died because Lyra took him to her father. Roger is in a grey place full of grey shadows of people who have given up all hope. Lyra decides it is the world of the dead. Only Roger has hope, which springs from his utter confidence in Lyra.

Will meets Iorek Byrnison, the bear-king; just as he is leading his people away from their thawing, Arctic homeland to the icy regions of the highest mountain ranges, Will joins their group. A party sent by Asriel also reaches the Himalayas, including two Gallivespian spies, small, fierce, dragonfly riders, the Chevalier Tialys and Lady Salmakia. So too do the zeppelins of the Consistorial Court converge at the spot, bringing the Church's Swiss Guard. In the cave, Lyra wakes, and Will tries to use the subtle knife to cut a way out of that world before she is taken by either side, but the knife breaks. The Gallivespians assist Will and Lyra in their escape, and an uneasy alliance is formed. They find Iorek Byrnison, who mends the subtle knife physically as Will mends it mentally.

Lyra is determined to find Roger in the land of the dead, and Will is equally determined to find his father. They cut a way into a world where the dead are visible, and follow them along a road to a miserable, polluted, shantytown on the edge of a lake, the transit port of the dead. There, they have to wait. Everyone here has a companion who follows them everywhere—their death. The deaths tell the living when it is time to die, and cross the lake. Lyra and the others can no longer keep their deaths at bay as in their own worlds, but must each call up their deaths and face them. With great courage, Lyra faces her death, but a harder thing is to come: the hardest thing of her life so far. All of them will leave a part of themselves behind; Lyra's is visible, her demon. She must leave Pan: "And then for the first time Lyra truly realized what she was doing. This was a real consequence. She stood aghast trembling, and clutched her dear demon so tightly that he whimpered in pain" (295).

Torn apart by pain physical and emotional, the four arrive at a desolate wasteland. The land of the dead is presided over by dreadful ancient harpies to whom "The Authority" has given the power to see the worst in everyone who arrives in their domain. Lyra tries to get past their leader, "No-Name," by offering a story of the kind she has used many times in the trilogy—fantastic, impossible, but diverting, but the harpy screams "Liar" and dives at her, gouging a deep wound in her scalp. Will treats the wound, but Lyra, in shock, has lost much of her confidence and fire. The harpies torment and terrify the dead, preying on their secret shames and worst fears. Lyra finds Roger and becomes the focus of the ghosts' attention when she speaks about the living world. They plead for more and she tells them the story of her adventures in Oxford. They are spellbound, and so are the harpies. Having had nothing to feed on for thousands of years but wickedness, cruelty, pettiness, and greed, the harpies find nourishment in hearing about sun, wind, rain, and the narrative of lives with a purpose. A bargain is made: the harpies will remain guardians of the land of the dead; they will escort the dead from the landing place to the window Will is going to cut into the outer world. In exchange, the dead must tell the harpies their stories. If the dead lie or hold anything back, the harpies have the right to refuse to guide them. In return for the story of Lyra and Will's adventures, the harpies guide them to the part of the land of the dead that lies closest to the upper world. Once outside, the particles that make up the dead will fly apart, and they will cease to

have any physical integrity, but they will become part of all that is. Some ghosts, devout believers in the Church, refuse to believe Lyra, but most follow her, in an almost unending column, into the passage.

Mrs. Coulter has been taken by Asriel's forces and is held captive. She escapes in a stolen "intention craft," a new invention, but a Gallivespian, Lord Roke, manages to slip onboard with her. She returns to the President of the Church, but is no longer trusted because of her failure to deliver her daughter, and she is put under arrest. One of the priests steals Mrs. Coulter's locket, which contains a lock of Lyra's hair. The hair is used to make a bomb whose effects will be directed to wherever Lyra is. Although she has been unscrupulous and ruthless throughout the trilogy, Mrs. Coulter loves her daughter and is willing to fight to the death to avert this danger from Lyra, but in a last-minute struggle, the President wins by cutting the bond between himself and his demon, providing the energy needed to detonate the bomb. Lord Roke is killed, but Asriel arrives in time to take Mrs. Coulter away.

In the underworld, the ghost of Will's father, the shaman Grumman, or John Parry, tells Will to find the strand of Lyra's hair that is shorter than the rest, cut it off to the scalp, and put every piece into another world. The detonation does not kill Lyra, but it causes violent tremors and rock falls in the underworld, and a seemingly bottomless pit opens at the edge of the precarious ledge along which the children have to lead the dead. Will knows that it is worse than a chasm in rock; it is a window into a world, perhaps an eternity, of blackness. Lyra falls. No-Name, the harpy, swoops down to rescue Lyra, and restores her to Will. They reach the end, and Will cuts a way through. Lyra gives No-Name a name: Gracious Wings, and bids her farewell until her real death, which she no longer fears. Some of the ghosts, led by John Parry and Lee Scoresby, hold back from the dissolution they long for to help fight Metatron, because the spirit-sucking Specters used by Metatron's army can't hurt them. Lyra and Will go out into a raging storm and a raging battle.

Mrs. Coulter, piloting the intention craft again, finds the Clouded Mountain and Metatron, whom she tricks into believing she will betray Asriel and Lyra. She lures him to Asriel, and together they take Metatron over with them into the pit. Metatron has sent "The Authority" to a place of safety, but with only a small guard, which is attacked by cliff-ghosts. After a fight in which Tialys dies, Lyra and Will find "The Authority" alone in his crystal litter/prison. "The Authority" is ancient, terrified, and demented. Once in the air, his fragile form disintegrates. The God of Lyra's world, and others, is dead.

When Will and Lyra are reunited with their demons, Will finds that in this world he has a visible demon, Kirjava, who is in the same shape as Pantalaimon now often takes. To save the demons from Specters, he cuts into the Mulefa world. Because Lyra and Will are almost grown up, Dust is beginning to be attracted to them. In the battle, they began not only to feel the effects of the Specters but also to see each other in ways other than as friends. As they come together in an idyllic clearing, Father Gomez, the priest sent to kill Lyra, is tracking them, but as he raises his rifle, he is stopped by Balthamos the angel, ashamed of having failed the children in the battle back in Lyra's home world, and determined to protect them now. He kills Father Gomez, but then dies himself. Dr. Malone learns that Dust began to flow away at the same time the subtle knife was created; the knife has created wounds in nature through which Dust is lost into the abyss. As Lyra and Will return from the clearing hand-in-hand, radiant with love, she realizes that the tide has turned; Dust is flowing back to that world. But it isn't enough. Dust is escaping into the abyss through every window cut by the knife, and every time a window is opened a Specter, a sliver of the abyss, emerges.

Lyra cannot live in Will's world, nor he in hers for more than a short period, which means that once apart they will never meet again. Except—they learn that Dust is not constant; it can be renewed by thinking, feeling, and gaining wisdom. If each of the adventurers in each of their worlds encouraged their people to learn and understand, one window could be kept open. For a moment Lyra and Will have hope, then they realize: one window must be kept open to release the dead. They make the choice.

Before Lyra returns to her world and Will smashes the subtle knife, they go to Oxford's Botanic Garden, and locate a bench that exists in both worlds. Every year of their lives, at midday on Midsummer's Day, they will both sit on the bench in their parallel worlds, and remember.

Historical Context
"The Amber Spyglass" was first published in 2000, three years after "The Subtle Knife," and too long for many fans of the series, some of whom took to writing to the author demanding the next episode, and posting spoof reviews of the next volume on the web. The novel's cosmic upheavals and metaphysical debates were congruent with preoccupations of the millennium, but no specific date is given for the events of the stories.

Societal Context
The Mulefa live in harmony with their environment and are largely a pastoral community, but they do use some low-level technology which, in being peaceful and ecologically sound, could be a lesson to the other societies depicted in the series, such as our own, which are dependent on ecologically expensive and wasteful high technology. In a recent message on his website, Philip Pullman put the case for action to protect the environment in our world:

> The great entrepreneurs who set the Industrial Revolution going couldn't have known, when they invented their steam engines and

burnt vast amounts of coal, what the results would be two hundred years later; the inventors of the internal combustion engine and the automobile, the Henry Fords, couldn't have known. But it's what they did to set up the way the world works now, and it's what we've done to keep it going, that is going to destroy human civilization unless we wake up very soon.

In "The Amber Spyglass," he shows the consequences of such actions, implicitly warning every member of society that if we continue to do nothing we shall be culpable, since, unlike our ancestors, we are informed of the impending catastrophe. In Lyra's world, Asriel's hugely wasteful method of going between worlds has caused an environmental catastrophe; the magnetic field of the world has altered, the northern polar ice cap is melting, we assume that low-lying lands are flooded, and we see the Arctic bears migrating south in a vain search for new hunting grounds.

Religious Context

Unlike the other volumes in the trilogy, "The Amber Spyglass" doesn't have illustrations by Philip Pullman. Instead, each chapter is headed by a quotation, many from Milton and Blake. One, from the Gospel of St. John is "And ye shall know the truth, and the truth shall make you free" (321). "The Amber Spyglass" makes explicit and overt the major theme of the sequence: the dangerousness of fundamentalist, authoritarian religion and the need for freedom of thought, open-mindedness, tolerance, and simple kindness rather than imposed rigid codes of morality.

When Nicolas Hytner's adaptation of "His Dark Materials" was staged at the British National Theatre, the Archbishop of Canterbury, Rowan Williams, surprised many church-goers by expressing admiration for the series. A conversation between the two men on the subject of religious education, the representation of religion, and Pullman's books took place at the theater and is available on the Internet. Philip Pullman said that the figure of "The Authority" in the series is "one of the metaphors I use. In the passage I wrote about his description, he was as light as paper—in other words he has a reality which is only symbolic. It's not real, and the last expression on his face is that of profound and exhausted relief." Of the theme of the Fall in "The Amber Spyglass," Pullman said that he saw it not as something that happened only one time, but repeatedly: "The Fall is something that happens to all of us when we move from childhood through adolescence to adulthood and I wanted to find a way of presenting it as something natural and good, and to be welcomed, and, you know, celebrated, rather than deplored" (http://www.telegraph.co.uk).

In Christian culture, the Fall begins with Eve's succumbing to the temptation of the serpent and in turn tempting Adam to eat the fruit of the tree of knowledge. In Pullman's worlds, this stands for coming into consciousness, self-awareness, and desire for knowledge. We see that every world has had an Eve. Mary's Mulefa friend, Atal, tells her that a female "creature" first learned to use the seed-pod wheel and the Dust-laden oil, thirty-three thousand years ago. Atal uses a metaphor of a snake in the hole of a seed pod, which asks, "What do you know? What do you remember? What do you see ahead?" to which the creature replies "Nothing, nothing, nothing." Then the hitherto unnamed female put her foot in the hole of the pod, and became the first to learn to devise the Mulefa's ingenious method of traveling: "She and her mate took pods and they knew that they were Mulefa" (236–7), i.e. gained self-awareness.

Scientific & Technological Context

The Mulefa have little metal, though they do work in wood, stone, and cord, and do produce ornamental as well as functional things. Their means of transport is rolling along natural highways of basalt using giant seed pods and a naturally produced lubricating oil, and they have bone spurs, perfectly adapted for the purpose, to connect them to the pods. The environmental benefit is that the seed pods are too hard to split from normal bio-degrading, but eventually crack from wear on the roads, so the Mulefa are part of the life-cycle of the trees.

In Lyra's world, both the Church and the rebel army have invested much of their effort and ingenuity into developing weapons and methods of transport and communication to serve the military forces. Their technology is part-scientific, part metaphysical. The Church has modified the "inter-cision" mechanism of separating child from demon seen in "The Golden Compass" to produce energy enough to launch a remote bomb. Lord Asriel has an "intention craft," a silent and almost invisible flying machine that is directed by its pilot's intentions but can only be flown by beings that have demons, since it is powered by a current flowing between a helmet worn by the person and a cable held by the demon. The Gallivespians can communicate between worlds via a "lodestone resonator," which has had its particles entangled and has then been split, so that when one half is played by a bow, the other will reproduce the sounds.

Biographical Context

Philip Pullman studied English at Exeter College, Oxford, on which he loosely based his Jordan College. While writing the trilogy, he was living in Oxford, and working in a shed at the back of his garden, though he has since moved to a village elsewhere in Oxfordshire. Before becoming a full-time writer, he was a school teacher for a number of years and later taught trainee teachers at West-minster College, also in Oxford. He was therefore very well acquainted with contemporary and clas-sic children's literature before he began writing it.

He has been awarded several prizes, including the Carnegie Medal, the Guardian Children's Book Award, the Astrid Lindgren Award (with illustra-tor Ryoji Arai), the *Publishers' Weekly* best Book of the Year Award, and the Whitbread Book of the Year Award (for "The Amber Spyglass," the third in the "His Dark Materials" trilogy), in the first instance of that prize going to a book classified for children (though read by many adults). Pullman produced illustrations for the first two volumes of the trilogy and small pictures as running heads for the second, to indicate which world the characters are in at the time. These were not printed in the first U.S. editions of the novels, but are present in the 2002 editions published by Knopf.

Philip Pullman has a web site that contains biographical and background material as well as his illustrations for his novels and a FAQ section. His acknowledgements pages in "The Amber Spyglass" also point to a third (in addition to Milton's "Paradise Lost" and the poetry and engravings of William Blake) source of inspiration for the novel and the series, an essay by Heinrich von Kleist, "On the Marionette Theatre" (1810), which Pullman first encountered in translation in *The Times Literary Supplement* in 1978 (550). The essay, a conversation between two men, discusses, among other things, the relationship between grace and innocence, or between affectation and the loss of innocence with its acquisition of self-consciousness.

With the completion of the "His Dark Materials" trilogy, Pullman's work attracted a great deal of critical interest, ranging from many fan websites to in-depth critical analysis. Two of the most interesting full-length publications are "His Dark Materials" Illuminated: Critical Essays On Philip Pullman's Trilogy" edited by Millicent Lenz and Carole Scott, and Claire Squires' "Philip Pullman's "His Dark Materials" Trilogy: A Reader's Guide."

Sandie Byrne

Works Cited

Lenz, Millicent and Carole Scott, eds, *His Dark Materials Illuminated: Critical Essays On Philip Pullman's Trilogy*. Wayne State University Press, 2005.

Pullman, Philip. *The Amber Spyglass*. London: Scholastic/David Fickling Books, 2000.

——. *Home page*. 20 Dec. 2005. <http://www.philip-pullman.com>

——. *Interview titled "I am of the devil's party with Helena de Bertodano. Arts-Telegraph.* 29 Jan 2002. <http://www.telegraph.co.uk/arts/main.jhtml?xml=/arts/2002/01/29/bopull227.xml>

Squires, Claire. Philip Pullman's "His Dark Materials" Trilogy: A Reader's Guide. *Continuum Contemporaries Series*, Continuum, 2003.

von Kleist, Heinrich. On the Marionette Theatre (1810). Translated by Idris Parry, online from *The Southern Cross Review* <http://www.southerncrossreview.org/9/kleist.htm>

Discussion Questions

1. Is the amber spyglass as essential and central to this novel as the "golden compass" (alethiometer) and the subtle knife are to their respective novels? If not, why might the author have used it for the title of this volume?

2. How do you respond to the short quotations that preface the chapters of "The Amber Spyglass"?

3. To what extent do we believe Mrs. Coulter when she first declares her maternal feelings for Lyra?

4. What purpose does Mary Malone find in life to replace the religious purpose she once had?

5. How closely does the representation of the world of the dead follow conventional ideas about an afterlife?

6. Are there signs of Will and Lyra's maturation before they acknowledge their love for one another?

7. What do you think will happen to Iorek Byrnison and his bears after the close of the story?

8. What is the republic of heaven?

9. What do you think will happen to Will back in his own world?

10. Are possibilities left in "The Amber Spyglass" for a sequel? What kinds of direction might the story take?

Essay Ideas

1. To what extent does Lord Asriel correspond to a Miltonic Satan figure or to a Blakean leader of rebel angels?

2. Discuss the number of coincidences and last-minute rescues in "The Amber Spyglass"?

3. Write an essay about the Mulefa, their home world, and their significance in "The Amber Spyglass." Compare the ways in which Mary Malone learns about the Mulefa with the ways in which Ransome learns about the inhabitants of Mars in C.S. Lewis' "Out of the Silent Planet."

4. Discuss the significance of the relationship between Metatron and "The Authority" and of their deaths.

5. Heinrich von Kleist's fictional puppet master argues that "Grace appears most purely in that human form which either has no consciousness or an infinite consciousness. That is, in the puppet or in the god." (http://www.southerncrossreview.org/9/kleist.htm). How might this idea have influenced Philip Pullman's construction of the "His Dark materials" series?

The Bloody Chamber

by Angela Carter

Content Synopsis

"The Bloody Chamber" (1979) is a series of short stories that rewrite fairy tales, including several collected by Charles Perrault in 1697. The first and eponymous story is based on Perrault's "Bluebeard." In Perrault's version, a nobleman named Bluebeard gives his wife the keys to every room in his castle, and tells her she may enter all of them but one. In his absence, she enters the forbidden room only to find the dead bodies of Bluebeard's previous wives. Upon his return, Bluebeard sees blood stains on the room's key and knows his wife has disobeyed him. He threatens to behead her on the spot, but she is saved by the fortuitous arrival of her brothers, who slay Bluebeard. The plot is much the same in Carter's "The Bloody Chamber," except that it is set in twentieth-century France and is told from the first-person perspective of Bluebeard's wife. As the story begins, this nameless narrator describes her courtship and honeymoon with the noble, worldly, and monocle-wearing Marquis. She is a seventeen-year-old piano player, much younger and poorer than her suitor. Despite her mother's quiet disapproval, she has been wooed by his gifts of fine furs and expensive outings, and agrees to marry him. He then gives her the most precious gift of all, a choker of rubies "bright as arterial blood" (11) and designed to mimic the cut of the guillotine. Before the narrator is taken away to her new husband's castle, we learn that the Marquis has been married before, and that his previous wives are all dead. We are also forewarned that the Marquis is a sexual predator, since he watches the narrator "with the assessing eye of a connoisseur inspecting horseflesh" and a "sheer carnal avarice" (11).

After marrying, the couple retires to the Marquis's seaside castle, where he undresses his bride for the first time. In the bedroom's many mirrors, the narrator sees "the living image" of a pornographic sketch he had shown her: "the child with her sticklike limbs" and "the old, monocled lecher who examined her" (15). However, the Marquis postpones their first sexual encounter, leaving the narrator to wander into his library. She discovers its shelves are filled with sadistic pornography. Excited by her exposure to this material, the Marquis takes her to the bedroom once more; there, a "dozen husbands impaled a dozen brides" in the many mirrors (17). This marks the end of a brief honeymoon; as per the "Bluebeard" formula, the Marquis must leave the castle on business. He gives the narrator his keys and extracts her promise that she will not enter one of the rooms. In his absence, she uses the keys to explore the castle, hoping for a glimpse into the Marquis's heart, but finds nothing that satisfies her curiosity: she "wanted to know still more" (26). When she accidentally scatters the keys over the floor, the first key she picks up is the key to the forbidden room.

This coincidence prompts her to follow the passageway to the Marquis's secret den, where she hopes to "find a little of his soul" (27). Within, of course, she finds the bodies of her predecessors. Here, Carter's rewriting renders the sadomasochistic undertones of the original "Bluebeard" story explicit. As the narrator, herself, points out:

> "There is a striking resemblance between the act of love and the ministrations of a torturer," opined my husband's favorite poet; I had learned something of the nature of that similarity on my marriage bed (27–28).

The Marquis's former wives have all been subjected to torture; the blood of the latest wife is still seeping from a spike-lined cage known as the "Iron Maiden." The narrator drops the key into this blood, giving it the telltale stain that will not wash off.

Going to the piano to calm herself, she is joined by the new piano tuner, a young blind man named Jean-Yves. Overwhelmed by his "lovely, blind humanity" (32), she confides in him. However, they soon realize the Marquis has returned to the castle, and try to pretend nothing has happened. The Marquis sees the stained key, however, and knows his wife has broken her promise. Her punishment will be death by beheading, just as her ruby choker foretold. As the narrator prepares for her execution, she sees a figure on horseback, racing toward the castle. It is her mother, who arrives at the last moment to shoot the Marquis. Thus, Carter offers a revised happy ending: the narrator inherits the Marquis's estate, marries Jean-Yves, and transforms the castle into a school for the blind.

Carter's next two stories are versions of the French fairy tale "Beauty and the Beast." Carter's "The Courtship of Mr. Lyon" reproduces the original plot in a modern setting. A man in financial difficulty is returning from a meeting with lawyers when his car stalls in the middle of a storm. He is granted use of the telephone at the nearest house, without ever meeting the owner. On his way out, he plucks a white rose from the garden, because he had promised to bring one home for his daughter Beauty. He is immediately accosted by a "leonine apparition" (44): this is "the Beast" and the master of the house. The man explains to the Beast why he took the rose, and the Beast lets him leave on the condition that he bring Beauty to dinner. Over this meal, the Beast promises to help her father's case; in exchange, Beauty must live at the Beast's house. During her stay, she forms a polite friendship with her host but cannot overcome her "indescribable shock" at his animal form (47). When Beauty's father is solvent once more, Beauty is allowed to leave, but promises the Beast she will return of her own accord before the winter ends. At home again, Beauty is so distracted by her father's new wealth that she forgets about her promise until the Beast's terrier appears at her door. She realizes at once that spring has arrived and she has broken her promise. She returns to the Beast at once, only to see he is dying. However, her tears of compassion and her promise to stay with the Beast revive him. He is transformed into human form, and the story ends with a view of Mr. and Mrs. Lyon walking in the garden.

"The Tiger's Bride" is set in Italy, and narrated by the unnamed daughter of a Russian nobleman. He has just bet and lost all his possessions and his daughter while playing cards with The Beast, the masked grand seigneur of the city. After her father leaves, a monkey-like valet presents the narrator to The Beast and informs her that if she will allow The Beast to look just once at her naked body, he will return her and her family's lost fortunes to her father. The narrator replies with a different offer, intended to shame The Beast: she will allow him to have sex with her as if she were a prostitute, so long as her face remains covered. The Beast is embarrassed by this reply, and the valet takes the narrator away to her room. There, she is attended by an automaton designed to look like a maid for, as the valet admits: "Nothing human lives here" (59). The valet returns to this room a few more times, plying the narrator with gifts from The Beast and repetitions of his request. Finally, the narrator is asked to go riding with The Beast. When they stop at a river, the valet tells her that because she will not submit herself to The Beast's gaze, she must look upon his unmasked, undressed form. Once she sees his true form as a tiger, she undresses herself and lets The Beast look upon her. She is then left alone for a while. Momentarily out of her father's and The Beast's care, she feels "at liberty for the first time in [her] life" (64). Back at The Beast's home, she realizes she is to be returned to her father. However, she sees her father in her maid's magic mirror and is disgusted with him. She decides to dress up her mechanical maid in her own clothes, and return the automaton in her place. The narrator herself goes to The Beast's room, where she sheds her clothing once more and draws him toward her; he licks her hand, and she feels him licking away "skin after successive skin," leaving her covered with "beautiful fur" (67).

Four rewritings of different tales follow. "Puss-in-Boots" is a version of Perrault's "Puss in Boots," in which the cat tricks a king into marrying off his daughter to Puss' master, a lowly miller's son. Carter's tale is also narrated by the cat Puss, and depicts Puss' conspiracy to advance his master's love affair with the young wife of Signore Pantele-one, who is guarded by an elderly but strict chaperone. Puss and his master disguise themselves as rat-catchers to sneak into the lady's bedroom, while Puss plots with kitchen tabby to trip Pantele-one on the stairs, and so enable the young lovers to marry and enjoy his wealth.

The next story, "The Erl-King" may allude to Goethe's poem of the same name, in which a child hears the promises of the fearful, invisible "Erl-King," and dies as a result. In Carter's story, a young girl visits the Erl-King, who appears to have tamed the flora and fauna of the forest. She enters his garden "where all the flowers were birds and beasts," and is enticed by his embraces. However, their strange relationship has undertones of vampirism and sadism. The Erl-King sinks his teeth into her neck, and the narrator describes being undressed as being skinned like a rabbit. As autumn nears, the narrator becomes aware that all the Erl-King's birds are caged, and she sees the cage he is building for her. One day, when he rests his head in her lap, she makes braids with his hair, intending to strangle him with them. The story ends with a vision of what will happen next: when the narrator lets the birds free, they will all turn into young girls, and the Erl-King's fiddle, strung with his own hair, will sing "Mother, mother, you have murdered me!" (91).

The very short "The Snow Child" alludes to the description of Snow White in the Brothers Grimm tale. On a midwinter horse ride, a Count wishes for a girl "as white as snow," "as red as blood," "as black as a raven's feather" (91). Suddenly, "the child of his desire" appears: a naked, white-skinned, red-lipped, and black-haired girl. Jealous, his wife the Countess is desperate to "be rid of her" (92). She asks the girl to fetch a dropped glove, and then a brooch flung into the lake. Each time, the Count prevents the girl from doing so, and the wife's clothing flies off her and onto the girl's body, leaving the Countess shivering in the cold. Finally, the Count permits the girl to pluck a red rose for his wife. When the girl pricks her finger on a thorn and dies, the Count "got off his horse, unfastened his breeches, and thrust his virile member into the dead girl" (92). The girl's body immediately melts into a feather and bloodstained snow. When the Count gives his wife the red rose, she drops it, exclaiming, "It bites!" (92).

"The Lady of the House of Love" draws on Perrault's "Sleeping Beauty." In Carter's tale, the sleeping princess is replaced by the Countess, a beautiful vampire living in a dilapidated chateau in an abandoned Romanian village. The Countess is cared for by an elderly governess, who brings travelers using the village fountain back to the chateau. Although she feeds on these hapless victims, the Countess detests her nature: "Everything about this beautiful and ghastly lady is as it should be, queen of the night, queen of terror—except her horrible reluctance for the role" (95). When a young British soldier on bicycle (significantly, a virgin) stops at the fountain one evening, the Countess falls in love with him. She reluctantly lures him to her bedroom, using her familiar pretense of seduction to draw him toward his death. She drops the protective glasses she wears over her sensitive eyes, and the shattering glass startles and stops her: "She has fumbled the ritual, it is no longer inexorable" (105). Mistaking her shaken state for the hysteria of a sheltered, inbred, and unhealthy girl, the soldier takes pity on her. He sees she has cut her hand, and he kisses the wound: "A single kiss woke up the Sleeping Beauty of the Wood" (97). This moment of tenderness and the sight of her own blood marks a change in the Countess: "How can she bear the pain of becoming human?" (106) The soldier puts her to bed and falls asleep on the floor. When he awakens, he sees she had flung open the curtains and is sitting, dead, in the sunlight. However, she has left him a flower, "the dark, fanged rose I plucked from between my thighs, like a flower laid on a grave" (107). The soldier returns to his regiment, and much later discovers the faded rose in his pocket. When he puts it in a glass of water, it revives in all its "corrupt, brilliant, baleful splendour" (108).

Two versions of Perrault's "Little Red Riding Hood" follow. "The Werewolf" is a very short story set in a primitive village whose inhabitants fear vampires and witches. A child is told to go through the woods to her ailing grandmother's cottage, to bring her some food. On the way, she fights a wolf,

cutting off its forepaw with her father's hunting knife. She puts the paw in her basket and continues on her path. When she arrives at the cottage, she discovers that the paw has turned into a hand, and she sees that the cause of her grandmother's fever is the wound from her missing arm. The girl's cries bring in the villagers, who stone the grandmother to death; the girl inherits her grandmother's house and prospers. "The Company of Wolves" has a similar setting and begins by outlining various tales about men turned into wolves, and vice versa. Despite the warning stories, a young, strong-willed girl dons her red cloak and insists on going through the woods to visit her grandmother. On the way, she meets a young man. Charmed by his flirtatious manner, she walks with him for a while. He shows her his compass but the girl refuses to believe it will guide them through the woods. The man laughs, and bets that he can beat her to her grandmother's house. If so, the girl will give him a kiss. They go their separate ways, and the young man does arrive first. He pretends to be the girl, fooling the grandmother into letting him in. He undresses and reveals he is a wolf, "carnivore incarnate" (116). He eats the grandmother and burns her inedible hair in the fireplace. When the girl arrives, she sees this hair and realizes she is "in danger of death," and that "the worst wolves are hairy on the inside" (117). A pack of wolves surround the house, but the girl realizes that her fear will not save her. Instead of cowering before the young man, she flings her clothes into the fire. When he says his large teeth are "all the better to eat you with," she laughs: "she knew she was nobody's meat" (118). She joins him in the bed, and the wolves and the rising blizzard outside become quiet. When the clock strikes midnight, ringing in Christmas Day, the girl is sleeping "sweet and sound" in her grandmother's bed, "between the paws of the tender wolf" (118).

The last story in the collection is "Wolf-Alice." This tale alludes to several fairy tale motifs and is about a girl raised among wolves. When her wolf mother is shot by hunters, the girl is discovered and brought to a convent. The nuns train her to complete menial tasks but cannot convert her from her wolf-like ways, so they eventually leave her at the castle of the ancient Duke. The Duke is a body snatcher and cannibal who does not cast a reflection, and stirs trouble in the village for robbing the grave of a young bride, but he leaves Wolf-Alice alone. For some time, she lives with the Duke in an animal state of mind, "amongst things she could neither name nor perceive" (122). It is only when she begins to menstruate that she feels the "first stirrings of surmise" (122). Her menstrual cycle initiates "a punctuality" on her "vague grip on time," and prompts a rudimentary system of hygiene based on habits the nuns taught her. She begins paying more attention to her body and to her reflection in the Duke's mirror, and in this way experiences a growing human sentience. One night, she experimentally puts on an old dress and walks outside, only to be caught in the middle of a chase. The husband of the young bride has come after the Duke, and is shooting silver bullets at him. Both the Duke and Wolf-Alice run back to the castle, where Wolf-Alice succumbs to her sense of pity for the wounded Duke. As she licks his wounds clean, the moonlit mirror catches both her and the Duke's reflections, as if her compassion has transformed them both from monsters into humans.

Historical Context

Many of the stories in "The Bloody Chamber" are based on French fairy tales. It was fashionable among the literary salons and royal courts of seventeenth- and eighteenth-century France to adapt common folk tales into entertaining, elegant, and moralizing stories (Carter, Perrault 13–15). Charles Perrault's collection, "Contes de ma Mére l'Oye" ("Mother Goose's Tales," 1697), is the source of several of Carter's stories. (Carter published an English translation of Perrault's fairy tales in 1977, although his stories had infiltrated the English-speaking world,

and Western culture at large, long before. See Carter, Perrault, 13.) However, at least one story, "The Snow Child," alludes to a later collection of fairy tales from Germany. Jacob Ludwig Karl and Wilhem Karl Grimm were German professors who published several editions of collected fairy tales. Their first volume, "Children's and Household Tales," was published in 1812; a second volume and new editions followed, and the stories are generally known as "Grimm's Fairy Tales." Like Perrault's tales, the Grimms' stories were didactic, sanitized adaptations of the folk tales on which they were based, but they functioned as cautionary tales for children rather than elegant entertainment for a literary audience. Carter's "The Courtship of Mr. Lyon" and "The Tiger's Bride" are also based on a later story; "Beauty and the Beast" is a French fairy tale that was published in different versions in the eighteenth century.

National background aside, all of Carter's fairy tale sources originate in an oral folk tradition. Figures such as the Grimm Brothers and Perrault collected and adapted popular folk tales and presented them in written form, thereby stabilizing stories whose content had previously changed as they were passed from one teller to another. While fairy tales may seem universal and timeless, they are not. Fairy tales reflect the social values of a given time, and have a cautionary and/or didactic function for their audience; they therefore transmit expectations about appropriate behavior, including gender-, age-, and class-appropriate conduct (Bottingheimer xii). When European fairy tales were collected and written down in the seventeen and eighteenth centuries, they reflected the values of those times. These written tales, rather than the changing oral versions, persisted and have become the fairy tales known to modern Western culture (Zipes 5–17). (Disney, for example, has made many of the Perrault and Grimm tales into popular animated movies.) Recent scholarship has investigated the folk roots and social history of fairy tales, but in the popular imagination, they are still often viewed as harmless entertainment for children. In his study "The Uses of Enchantment" (1976), the psychoanalyst Bruno Bettelheim even speculated that fairy tales provide a safe way for children to learn conflict resolution and achieve a sense of independence.

Societal Context

Despite, and perhaps because of, the prevalence and popularity of fairy tales, some feminist writers have challenged the idea that they represent universal values or teach helpful moral lessons, and have raised questions about their representations of women. In her own retelling of fairy tales, Carter also challenges their outmoded representation of gender roles and sexuality. The stories in "The Bloody Chamber" typically abandon the conventional omniscient narration of their source texts in favor of a first-person perspective. This has the effect of transforming the one-dimensional stock characters of fairy tales into fully developed subjects, and allows Carter to explore the encounter between conventional female roles (the princess, the helpless wife, and the victimized daughter) and contemporary female subjectivity. Carter also rewrites fairy tales from previously marginalized viewpoints, reverses the traditional gender of active and passive roles, and subverts expectations about characters' sexuality. All of these strategies enable Carter to depict familiar female characters as active and sexually confident rather than passive, victimized, or naïve. However, some literary critics have criticized "The Bloody Chamber," insisting that it upholds rather than resists the problematic gender roles of the fairy tale. Patricia Duncker has argued that Carter's heroines are still defined by the "straitjacket" of their fairy-tale fates, and that the erotic element of her tales reproduces "women's sensuality simply as a response to male arousal." This is problematic, Duncker emphasizes, because "male sexuality has too long, too tenaciously been linked with power and possession, the capture, breaking and ownership of women" (Duncker 6–7). However, an alternative reading, such as that promoted by Margaret Atwood, views Carter's project as a subversion of the very way we define gender and sexual desire. Atwood reads "The Bloody Chamber" as a "writing against" the pornographic writings of the Marquis de Sade—the subject of Carter's study "The Sadeian Woman," published in the same year as "The Bloody Chamber." Atwood argues that "[p]redator and prey, master and slave, are the only two categories" de Sade "can acknowledge," but that Carter's tales destabilize binary divisions such as aggressor/victim, passive/active, and animal/human: "in this respect, Carter's arrangements are much more subject to mutability than are de Sade's" and her text "celebrates relativity and metamorphosis" (Atwood 120–22). If we accept Atwood's reading, the stories in "The Bloody Chamber" represent identity as something fluid rather than fixed, and work against preconceptions about "acceptable" or "unacceptable" sexual behavior and desire.

Feminist rewritings of fairy tales and myths do not offer new stories so much as participate in the evolving history and transmission of fairy tales; to this end, "The Bloody Chamber" both questions problematic representations of women in existing narratives and calls attention to the contextual nature of stories we take for granted. As Patricia Brooke puts it, "Carter reveals the false universalizing inherent in many so-called master narratives of the Western literary tradition" (Brooke 67). In rewriting fairy tales, Carter recalls and participates in an oral tradition in which stories were not fixed authoritative texts, but changed from teller to teller. Carter's attention to this history signifies a postmodern awareness of the constructed and intertextual nature of fiction . The writer John Barth defined postmodern fiction as "the literature of replenishment": "literature can never be exhausted, if only because no single literary text can ever be exhausted—its 'meaning' residing as it does in is transactions with individual readers over time, space, and language" (432). In keeping with this perspective, Carter's text is a blend of genres and intertexts. While Carter's primary sources are fairy tales, she also recycles the sexually charged, castle-strewn landscapes of the gothic novel and employs the imperative of magic realism, which dictates that unreal and improbable events are treated as normal. Carter also alludes to specific texts. In "The Bloody Chamber," the Marquis' first wife died in a mysterious boat accident that recalls Daphne du Maurier's "Rebecca" (1956); in that novel, a similarly young and nameless narrator marries a wealthy man, and finds herself metaphorically haunted by his previous wife. In "The Erl-King," Carter reproduces the themes, and even paraphrases some of the lines, from Christina Rossetti's "Goblin Market" (1862), a verse fairy tale in which a young girl falls prey to the temptations of the goblins.

Religious Context

Religion and spirituality are not significant features in Carter's stories, but this is in keeping with the fairy tales they rewrite, in which figures of authority and power are usually members of the landed nobility, rather than members of the clergy. There are a few direct references to religion, but these have little bearing on the meaning of the stories in question. In "The Company of Wolves," the grandmother cries out to Jesus Christ before the wolf devours her, and in "Wolf-Alice," the narrator is temporarily cared for by nuns. These allusions to Christianity suggest that the religion has penetrated village culture, but the presence of werewolves and cannibals shows that superstition and legend still dominate the villagers' beliefs. The world of fairy tales exists outside the reach of scientific, rational, and even religious discourse; and Carter's tales return us to these realms of the magical and profane.

Scientific & Technological Context

The presence of certain technologies situates some of Carter's stories in the twentieth century. The narrator in "The Bloody Chamber" travels to the Marquis' castle by train, for instance, while cars and telephones feature in "The Bloody Chamber" and "The Courtship of Mr. Lyon." These small details confirm a modern and sometimes urban or suburban milieu, marking a departure from the conventionally timeless atmosphere and rural settings of fairy tales. Carter's subtle emphasis on the contemporary stresses the fact that her characters are modern women struggling to fit into, or break out of, outdated roles. It also suggests a clash between progressive, modern cultures and the superstitions of the old world. In "The Lady of the House of Love," for instance, takes place on the cusp of World War I, but is set in a rural Romanian village. The young soldier, "rooted in change and time, is about to collide with the timeless Gothic eternity of vampires" (97). The later stories in the collection have a less specific timeframe, and their settings are more like the ahistorical settings of the fairy tale. "The Werewolf," "The Company of Wolves," and "Wolf-Alice," for instance, are all set in rural, primitive villages. In the absence of scientific discourse and modern technology, superstitions thrive: the villagers stone witches, use garlic to ward off vampires, and shoot werewolves with silver bullets.

Biographical Context

Angela Carter was born as Angela Stalker in Eastbourne, Sussex in 1940. At the age of eighteen, she worked as a reporter for the *Croydon Advertiser* before marrying Paul Carter in 1960. The couple moved to Bristol the same year, where Carter studied English at the University of Bristol, specializing in medieval literature. She received her degree in 1965. Her writing career began in 1966, with the publication of her novel "Shadow Dance" (published under the title "Honeybuzzard" in the United States). "Shadow Dance" was followed by "The Magic Toyshop" in 1967, which was awarded the John Llewellyn Rhys prize. "Several Perceptions" was published the next year, and "Love" in 1971. These two novels, along with "Shadow Dance," form Carter's "Bristol Trilogy."

In 1969, Carter separated from her husband and used the proceeds from a Somerset Maugham Travel Award to relocate to Japan, where she lived for two years. When she returned to Britain in 1972, she wrote "The Infernal Desire Machines of Doctor Hoffman" (1972), "Fireworks: Nine Profane Pieces" (1974), and "The Passion of New Eve" (1977). However, her work from the 1970s failed to gain the positive reception of her earliest novels. This changed with the publication of "The Bloody Chamber" in 1979, which received good reviews in newspapers, and caught the attention of academic critics. In the same year, Carter published "The Sadeian Woman," a study of the Marquis de Sade's erotic writings. Carter continued producing short stories, journalism, and non-fiction throughout the 1980s, and by the time "Nights at the Circus" was published in 1984, she was an established figure in the British literary scene. She had also developed a career as a teacher of writing. From 1976–78 she was an Arts Council Fellow in Creative Writing at Sheffield University; this was followed by writer-in-residence posts at Brown University in the United States in 1980–81 and at the University of Adelaide in Australia in 1984. From 1984–87, she contributed to the Master's program in Writing at the University of East Anglia.

In 1991, Carter's last novel, "Wise Children," was published. This is considered one of her best works, but preceded her untimely death from cancer in 1992. Obituaries written by well-known writers and scholars, including Salman Rushdie, Marina Warner, and Margaret Atwood, lauded Carter's work. Soon after her death, Rushdie edited the collection of Carter's short stories,

"Burning Your Boats" (1995). Her dramatic works were collected in "The Curious Room: Collected Dramatic Works" in 1996, and her non-fictional writings in "Shaking a Leg: Collected Journalism and Writings" in 1997. Since her death, Carter's work has been the focus of several academic studies. Critical discourse on "The Bloody Chamber" and "The Sadeian Woman" in particular has raised productive questions about Carter's representations of sexuality and her rewriting of cultural master narratives; as she herself put it, "I'm in the demythologizing business" (Carter, "Shaking a Leg" 38).

Jennifer Dunn

Works Cited

Atwood, Margaret, ed. *Running with the Tigers. Flesh and the Mirror: Essays on the Art of Angela Carter*, Lorna Sage. London: Virago, 1994. 117–35.

Bettelheim, Bruno. *The Uses of Enchantment: The Meaning and Importance of Fairy Tales*. New York: Knopf, 1976.

Bottingheimer, Ruth B., ed. *Fairy Tales and Society: Illusion, Allusion, and Paradigm*. Philadelphia: U of Pennsylvania P, 1986.

Brooke, Patricia. "Lyons and Tigers and Wolves-Oh My! Revisionary Fairy Tales in the Work of Angela Carter" *Critical Survey*. 16.1 (2004) 67–88.

Carter, Angela. *The Bloody Chamber*. London: Penguin, 1981, repr. 1987 (c. 1979).

———. *Shaking a Leg: Collected Journalism and Writings*. London: Chatto & Windus, 1997.

Carter, Angela, translator. *The Fairy Tales of Charles Perrault*. Illustrator. Martin Ware. London: Victor Gollancz, 1977.

Duncker, Patricia. Re-Imagining the Fairy Tales: Angela Carter's Bloody Chambers." *Literature and History 10.1* (1984) 3–14.

Gamble, Sarah. *Angela Carter: Writing from the Front Line*. Edinburgh: Edinburgh UP, 1997.

Hoffman, Michael J. and Patrick D. Murphy, eds. *John Barth. The Literature of Replenishment. Essentials of the Theory of Fiction*, Durham and London: Duke UP, 1988. 273–86.

Sage, Lorna. *Angela Carter*. Plymouth, Northcote, 1994.

Zipes, Jack. *Breaking the Magic Spell: Radical Theories of Folk and Fairy Tales*. London: Heinemann, 1979.

Discussion Questions

1. "The Bloody Chamber" subverts "Bluebeard" by problematizing its objectification of women in sexual fantasy and in the marriage market. Does the narrator's "happy ending" in marriage mean the text ultimately succumbs to the very fairy tale form it criticizes? Alternatively, does this conclusion retain an aspect of subversion?

2. Other than its modern setting, how does "The Courtship of Mr. Lyon" differ from the original "Beauty and the Beast" tale? What is the effect of exploring Beauty's perspective more fully?

3. In "The Tiger's Bride," why does the daughter stay with the Beast?

4. "Puss-in-Boots" is highly stylized, with a light-hearted tone. How does this different story fit in with the others in the collection?

5. How do you interpret the last line of "The Erl-King?" Why does the Erl-King cry out against his mother, who has not appeared in the text before?

6. What is the significance of the rose that "bites" in "The Snow Child?"

7. "The Lady of the House of Love" is primarily a rewriting of "Sleeping Beauty." What other motifs or stories does the text allude to?

8. Unlike the other stories in the collection, "The Snow Child" and "The Werewolf" are very short, with very little character development. What are they about? Do they challenge the fairy tales to which they allude? How?

9. Some critics have derided the way Carter represents female sexuality in "The Company of Wolves." Does the story's conclusion suggests a subversion of the wolf's aggressive sexual desire, or a submission to it?

10. What different fairy tales, legends, and motifs are combined in the last story, "Wolf-Alice"? What is the effect of placing this story last in the collection?

Essay Ideas

1. Analyze Carter's use of animal imagery in the stories.

2. How do the stories in "The Bloody Chamber" relate to Carter's study of the Marquis de Sade, "The Sadeian Woman"?

3. Compare and discuss narrative devices in the different stories.

4. Are fairy tales especially subject to literary revisions? Why? Discuss in relation to Carter and at least one other writer.

5. Discuss the role of magic, the supernatural, and/or the improbable in the stories. What relation does Carter's fantastical style have to the text's political agenda?

The Castle of Otranto

by Horace Walpole

Content Synopsis

"The Castle of Otranto" takes place in the principality of Otranto, ruled by the prince Manfred. Manfred's castle is inhabited by his wife Hippolita, their daughter Matilda, and their sickly son Conrad. Conrad is about to be wed to Isabella, the daughter of Frederic, Count of Vicenza. Manfred is eager for this wedding, since Hippolita can no longer produce male heirs and he desires to secure his family's rule over Otranto through a grandson. However, the servants also believe that Manfred's urgency is due to a prophecy: "That the castle and lordship of Otranto should pass from the present family, whenever the real owner should be grown too large to inhabit it" (17). This preoccupation with property (and, correspondingly, with the integrity of ancestral lines) manifests itself throughout the novel, and became a recurrent trope in later Gothic fiction.

Before the wedding can occur, a harbinger of the prophecy's fulfillment appears when a giant helmet falls from the sky and crashes into the courtyard, killing Conrad. This event initiates two scenes that reveal both Manfred's character and Walpole's mechanism for generating terror. First, while Hippolita and Matilda grieve for Conrad, Manfred is preoccupied with the helmet: "The horror of the spectacle, the ignorance of all around how this misfortune happened, and above all, the tremendous phenomenon before him, took away the prince's

speech" (19). He shows no concern for his family members, but instead asks that Isabella be looked after. When an unknown peasant wanders into the scene, remarking that the helmet resembles that on the statue of Alfonso the Good—the former ruler of Otranto—an outraged Manfred imprisons him under the helmet. Second, Manfred summons Isabella and proposes to her: "Since I cannot give you my son, I offer you myself" (25). In his desperation to secure an heir, Manfred plots to divorce Hippolita and marry Isabella in Conrad's place. Isabella had no fondness for Conrad, because their marriage was one of arrangement, not love. However, she finds marriage to Manfred even less appealing, and she recoils from him.

The incestuous overtones of this second scene are overlaid with the suggestion of (sexual) violence as Manfred ignores Isabella's protests and seizes her hands. The tension of this encounter is heightened by its setting. Isabella, "half-dead with fright and horror," pulls away; as Manfred pursues her, the moon "gleamed in at the opposite casement [and] presented to his sight the plumes of the fatal helmet, which rose to the height of the windows, waving backwards and forwards in a tempestuous manner" (25). The moonlight, the empty castle corridor, and the huge and threatening proportions of supernatural helmet contribute to the different terrors felt by Isabella and Manfred. The effect of this Gothic fear is physical. During Manfred's proposal, Isabella's hands are cold; a moment later, on viewing the helmet, Manfred is speechless. Similar somatic effects characterize scenes of fear throughout the novel: women faint, characters are rendered speechless or breathless, and blood runs cold. These physical effects are described to induce similar sensations in the audience, transferring terror from character to reader. At the same time, certain tropes are associated with these effects—such as darkness, or immensity.

Isabella flees Manfred only to find herself in another typically Gothic setting: the murky cavern below the castle courtyard. There, she encounters a young man who helps her escape through a trapdoor. As she follows a secret passage to the nearby convent, the young man delays Manfred and is revealed to be the peasant, who has escaped from beneath the helmet. Suspicious of the peasant's connections with Isabella, Manfred is nonetheless impressed by his noble and brave manner. He sends him to a room for the night and, in a ploy to catch Isabella, orders his guards to let no one leave the castle.

As dawn approaches, Matilda, and her servant Bianca discuss courtship. Bianca tells her about the peasant and his resemblance to the portrait of Alfonso that Matilda so admires. Suddenly, they hear him in a nearby room. Through the window, they speak with him and learn of Isabella's flight. Matilda is intrigued by the man's presence and possible affection for Isabella. Meanwhile, the friar, Jerome, arrives from the convent. He has taken in Isabella and approaches Manfred about her plight. As the men talk, Manfred suspects a love affair between the peasant and Isabella, and orders the young man's execution. The youth, who introduces himself as Theodore, is hardly given the opportunity to defend himself. However, as he kneels to be executed, Jerome sees a mark on his shoulder and joyfully claims him as his son.

In the ensuing confusion, a herald arrives at the castle. He claims that the "knight of the gigantic sabre" has arrived, representing Frederic, Isabella's father, and challenging Manfred as "the usurper" of Otranto (61). The knight accuses Manfred of bribing Isabella's guardians for her hand in marriage to Conrad and demands that he abdicate his seat at Otranto. Here, the history of Otranto is revealed: Alfonso, ruler of Otranto, had died without issue, leaving Frederic's and Manfred's ancestors in dispute over its ownership. Manfred's more powerful ancestors had won, but in arranging Isabella's marriage to Conrad—and in hoping to gain her as his own bride—Manfred had planned to unite the warring lines. To earn Frederic's approval of this plan, Manfred invites the knight in. An enormous retinue—including "an hundred gentlemen bearing an enormous sword"—enters, laying the giant weapon next to the helmet (65). These giant objects are harbingers of the prophecy, but also emphasize the problem of inheritance at the heart of the story, and the supernatural forces intervening to establish rightful ownership.

Meanwhile, Isabella has disappeared from the convent, and Matilda frees Theodore from a chamber in the castle. Upon setting eyes on each other, the two fall in love, but Matilda gives him a suit of armor and convinces him to flee. In the nearby woods, Theodore encounters Isabella and mistakenly defends her from the knight of the gigantic saber, who has gone looking for her. Theodore attacks him, only to learn he is Frederic himself in disguise. The two men make amends and return to the castle with Isabella. There, Frederic tells of a dream warning him about Isabella's safety, and his encounter with a hermit who directed him to the gigantic saber. It is inscribed with a cryptic message about Isabella being rescued by "Alfonso's blood" (82).

All parties retire for the night, and Isabella and Matilda discuss their mutual interest in Theodore. Hippolita interrupts their conversation to inform them that Manfred has promised Matilda to Frederic. Both of the young women are dismayed, and

Isabella reacts to the news by divulging Manfred's secret plan to divorce Hippolita. Hippolita immediately goes to Jerome for counsel. At Alfonso's tomb, they discuss Manfred's plan for a double marriage, which Jerome opposes. There is a statue of Alfonso at the tomb, and this suddenly and ominously begins to drip blood. Jerome interprets this as a sign that the blood of Alfonso's line will not mix with that of Manfred's.

Manfred continues to suspect a love affair between Theodore and Isabella, and questions Bianca about Isabella's affections. She cannot carry out his request for spy work, however, because she sees a giant hand at the bottom of the castle stairs. Frederic, accused by an increasingly paranoid Manfred of conspiring against him, refuses to agree with the proposed double marriage. Yet, he still feels lust for Matilda. Entering the castle chapel, he sees a figure in robes. It turns on him to reveal "the fleshless jaws and empty sockets of a skeleton" (106): it is the ghost of the hermit from the woods. The figure admonishes Frederic for allowing his desire for Matilda to distract him from the sabre's message.

Meanwhile, Manfred is informed that Theodore is alone with a woman at the convent chapel. Thinking it is Isabella, he steals upon them and stabs the woman—who turns out to be Matilda. Overwhelmed with regret, he tries to kill himself. He is prevented, and all return to the castle. There, as everyone grieves over the dying Matilda, Theodore and Jerome reveal that Theodore is the direct descendant of Alfonso. Manfred, in turn, admits that his grandfather, Ricardo, poisoned Alfonso and inherited Otranto through a fraudulent will. In exchange for founding a church and two convents, St. Nicholas allowed Ricardo to retain his rule in keeping with the conditions of the prophecy. As soon as Matilda dies, the castle walls fall, and the giant figure of Alfonso appears to pronounce Theodore the rightful heir to Otranto. The prophecy fulfilled, Manfred and Hippolita retire to nearby convents, leaving Otranto to Theodore, who, after a time of grieving over Matilda, enters a happy marriage with Isabella.

Historical Context

William Marshal, Gent, originally published "The Castle of Otranto" in 1764 as the translation of a medieval Italian tale. This first edition included a preface describing "English Baron" (1778), "Otranto's" self-proclaimed "literary offspring." In 1765, a second edition was published, with a new preface and the initials "H. W." While these additions revealed the text was fiction, perhaps the most significant change was the new subtitle: "A Gothic Story." This provided a name for a literary genre Walpole described in his second preface as a "blend" of the older romance and the contemporary novel (9). In contrast to the positive reception of the first edition, this second edition was derided as a ruse (see, *Monthly Review* 32 (1765): 97–99, 394). However, Walpole's slim novel spawned a long line of imitators, beginning with Clara Reeve's "Old English Baron."

The British eighteenth century was shaped by the Enlightenment, the intellectual movement emphasizing rational thought as a means of progress beyond the superstitions and insular traditions of the past. Enlightenment thought influenced the ideologies behind the French and American revolutions, which in turn had an impact on Britain's national identity, challenging Britain's power as an empire and calling into question the validity of its social organization—class divisions based on a feudal system of land ownership and inheritance. Walpole's theme of property passing into the wrong hands is in keeping with this historical context. As E. J. Clery notes, the novel is set in the feudal past, but addresses the "live issue" of property inheritance, illustrating the tensions between the rising middle classes and the established landed ones, as well as the philosophical "conflict between aristocratic and bourgeois ideals of social being"

(Walpole xxxi). These conflicts, and in particular the question of the divine rights of kings, drove the revolutions in France and America. Because Walpole's plot ultimately upholds the principle of primogeniture, restoring Otranto to Alfonso's closest heir and ousting Manfred as an upstart usurper, it can be read as a conservative reaction to these changes. At the same time, however, it can also be understood "as a study of revolutionary politics: it celebrates the overthrow of a tyrant, after all" (Ellis 34). Perhaps the most compelling reading of the novel, however, emphasizes not its politics but its theme of terror in portraying "the nightmarish collapse of a system of power that contains the seeds of its own destruction" (Walpole xxxii–xxxiii). The fear so central to this Gothic novel could reflect the anxieties stirred up by a long century of turbulence and uncertainty.

Societal Context

Walpole's generation of fear is clearly linked to certain tropes, such as the landscape (the gleaming moon), darkness (murky passageways), and size (the immense helmet). This is in keeping with the aesthetic principle of the sublime, which was defined in 1757 by Edmund Burke, as "the strongest emotion the mind is capable of feeling" (Burke 36). Whereas beauty stimulates feelings of pleasure, the sublime finds its source in "whatever is fitted in any sort to excite the ideas of pain," or "operates in a manner analogous to terror" (Burke 36). Although Burke names awe or "astonishment" as the primary quality of the sublime, he emphasizes that this awe is necessarily tinged with fear or "terror" (Burke 53). Thus, whatever suggests a sense of power and force—such as the grandeur of mountains—is a source of the sublime. In using many of the sources named by Burke, such as "obscurity" and "magnitude," Walpole stimulates awe in the reader in order to create the sense of being overwhelmed or overpowered—in short, to create fear. Many of Burke's other sources of the

sublime, such as power, privation, pain, difficulty, and physical sensation, are clearly central to Walpole's plot, and recur in later Gothic novels. The supernatural, a distinguishing characteristic of Gothic novels, is also used to stimulate fear-tinged awe. As a sign of overwhelming, unknown forces, the supernatural is also a source of the sublime.

Accordingly, the discourse of the sublime shaped Gothic conventions, although it was employed for different purposes by different authors. In its heyday in the 1790s, the Gothic novel was transformed by Ann Radcliffe, whose deliberate use of sublime landscapes was "partly a desire to exploit contemporary aesthetic fashions and partly an attempt to pitch [her] work toward the high end of the literary market, for sublimity and terror were associated with tragedy and epic, the two most prestigious literary forms" (Miles 43). Although Radcliffe's Gothic novels mark a departure from Walpole's sensational and heavy-handed plot, they also reveal how his "blend" of different literary traditions set many of the conventions for a definable genre. Gothic novels were best-sellers in the last decades of the eighteenth century; they shaped the publishing industry and reading public, influenced the literature of the nineteenth, twentieth and twenty-first centuries, and generated a lively and ongoing critical discourse, one that generally credits Walpole's text as the first Gothic novel.

Religious Context

Religion represents protection, justice, and revelation in Walpole's plot. Characters find peace and safe haven in convents and seek counsel from friars. Jerome provides guidance and protection for innocents, but more importantly, he holds the information needed for the plot's resolution. Jerome is privy to the hidden history of Alfonso's line, persistently referring to the prophecy that will be Manfred's undoing, and ultimately reveals why Theodore is Otranto's true ruler. (It is another religious figure, St. Nicholas, who sets the prophecy in motion in the first place, and who appears at the end of the story to show that justice has been done.) It is unclear if this representation of religious figures as benevolent authorities is ironic or not, given Walpole's two prefaces. While the first disdainfully suggests the tale was written by a priest seeking to "confirm the populace" of the dark ages "in their ancient errors and superstitions" (5), the second reveals that the tale and "William Marshal" are counterfeits. In any case, Walpole's representation of a dark age shaped by religious superstition is in keeping with an eighteenth-century Gothic revival—an interest in the ornate architecture and imaginative literature of the Middle Ages (Walpole x). The text's double-edged tone might reflect the double-edged attitude toward more "barbaric" times: "on the one hand, a growing enthusiasm for the superstitious fancies of the past; and on the other, a sense that this kind of imaginative freedom was forbidden, or simply impossible, for writers of the enlightened present" (Walpole xi).

Scientific & Technological Context

Science and technology do not play an explicit role in the story; although the text is medieval, the setting is in keeping with the eighteenth-century Gothic revival. In this respect, the text could be read as a reaction to the scientific advances and empiricism of the Enlightenment, or as a critique of the superstitions—the lack of scientific rationalism and progress—of the past.

Biographical Context

Horace Walpole (1717–97) was born Horatio Walpole in London, and educated at Eton and Cambridge. As a young man he was friends with the poet Thomas Gray, and the pair completed the Grand Tour of Italy and France in 1739–41. During this trip, Walpole was elected to a place in Parliament, representing a borough in Cornwall. His father, Sir Robert Walpole, is considered the First Prime Minister of England. Sir Robert's retired from politics in 1742, and was given the title of Earl of Orford. His son Horace continued to be a Member of Parliament for twenty-five years, and became the fourth Earl of Orford in 1791.

In addition to his political career, Horace Walpole was also an active writer, antiquarian, and social commentator. In 1749, he purchased the villa Strawberry Hill near Twickenham, and refurbished the building in the style of, an extravagant neo-Gothic villa. Strawberry Hill embodied Walpole's particular interest in Gothic architecture. This building influenced the Gothic revival of the eighteenth century and was also a tourist attraction. It was there, he claimed, he had the dream that inspired his Gothic novel:

> "I had thought myself in an ancient castle (a very natural dream for a head filled like mine with Gothic story) and that on the uppermost banister of a great staircase I saw a gigantic hand in armour. In the evening I sat down and began to write. . . " (Gray 8).

Walpole established a printing press at Strawberry Hill, where he published "The Castle of Otranto." He also wrote the Gothic drama "The Mysterious Mother" (1768), and published several volumes on painting and catalogues of major collections of art and antiques. He began writing his memoirs in 1751, while living at Strawberry Hill, and continued writing them until 1791. These writings, and Walpole's many letters to his contemporaries, provide a first-account of Georgian politics and society. His last publication, in 1768, was about King Richard III. In the same year, he retired from Parliament.

Despite a successful and multi-faceted career, Walpole's life was affected by sensationalism and scandal. He was known for being effeminate, wrote pamphlets and historical accounts that outraged politicians and historians alike, and was (wrongly) implicated in the suicide of Thomas Chatterton in 1770. He suffered gout for much of his life, and died without in 1797.

Jennifer Dunn

Works Cited

Botting, Fred. Gothic. London and New York: Routledge, 1996.

Edmund, Adam Phillips, ed. Burke. A Philosophical Enquiry. Oxford: OUP, 1990.

Gray, Jennie. "Horace Walpole." "Horace Walpole and William Beckford: Pioneers of the Gothic Revisited." Gothic Society Monograph Series. Chislehurst, Kent: Gargoyle's Head, 1994).

Markman, Ellis. The History of Gothic Fiction. Edinburgh: Edinburgh UP, 2000.

Miles, Robert. "The 1790s: The Effulgence of the Gothic." "The Cambridge Companion to the Gothic," Jerrold E. Hogle, ed. Cambridge: Cambridge UP, 2002. 41–62. Monthly Review 32 (1765). 97–99.

Punter, David. The Literature of Terror: The Gothic Tradition. 2 vols. 2nd ed. London and New York: Longman, 1996.

Reeve, Clara. The Old English Baron. James Trainer, ed. Intr. James Watt. Oxford and New York: OUP, 2003.

Walpole, Horace. The Castle of Otranto. W. S. Lewis ed. Intr. E. J. Clery. Oxford and New York: OUP, 1998.

For Further Study

Butler, Marilyn. Romantics, Rebels and Reactionaries: English Literature and It's Background, 1760–1830. New York and Oxford: OUP, 1982.

Clery, E. J. The Rise of Supernatural Fiction 1762–1800. Cambridge: Cambridge UP, 1995

———. The Genesis of 'Gothic' Fiction. The Cambridge Companion to the Gothic, Jerrold E. Hogle, ed. Cambridge: Cambridge UP, 2002. 21–40.

Hogle, Jerrold E. ed. The Cambridge Companion to Gothic Fiction. Cambridge: Cambridge UP, 2002.

Kilgour, Maggie. The Rise of the Gothic Novel. London: Routledge, 1995.

Miles, Robert. Gothic Writing, 1750–1820: A Genealogy. London: Routledge, 1993.

Richter, Norton. ed. Gothic Readings: The First Wave, 1764–1840. London and New York: Leicester UP, 2000.

Sedgwick, Eve Kosofsky. The Coherence of Gothic Conventions. New York and London: Methuen, 1986.

Watt, James. Contesting the Gothic: Fiction, Genre, and Cultural Conflict, 1764–1832. Cambridge: CUP, 1999.

Discussion Questions

1. Why does Walpole represent Manfred as having two sides—tyrannical and aggressive on the one hand, and rational and repentant on the other?
2. Gothic novels were often criticized for their lurid and sensational content. Would you consider Walpole's story sensational? What effect does sensationalism have on the reader, and how is this related to Gothic terror?
3. Is this story believable? Do the supernatural events, plot twists, and surprising revelations strain credulity, or does Walpole successfully suspend the reader's disbelief?
4. Gothic novels may seem less terrifying to today's readers than to an eighteenth-century audience. Yet, they have attracted sustained critical attention for their undertones of anxiety, transgression, and excess. What anxieties does Walpole's text hint at or produce?
5. Read Burke's theory of the sublime and discuss how instances of the sublime are used to generate fear in "The Castle of Otranto."
6. How do fears and desires of/for revolution appear in the story?
7. Can you recognize any of Walpole's themes and/or tropes in contemporary Gothic genres, such as the literary thriller, the ghost story, or the horror film?
8. The Gothic novel was derided for being escapist, and critics feared its influence on female readers. Do you think the Gothic novel in general, and Walpole's in particular, is more escapist than realistic? On the same note, is the story moralizing or didactic in any way, or purely an exercise in entertainment?
9. What is the effect of setting the story in a foreign time and place?
10. How do you interpret Hippolita's role in the story? Is she victimized by Manfred's selfish desires? Does she become a strong maternal figure?

Essay Ideas

1. Discuss the role of doubles in the text.
2. Examine the role of women in the story. Are Hippolita, Matilda, and Isabella merely tokens of exchange between men, or do they have some power over the story's outcome and their own fates? Why?
3. What role does religion, or religious figures, play in the narrative?
4. Compare Walpole's novel to its successor, Reeve's "The Old English Baron." How has Reeve altered Walpole's Gothic conventions, and to what end?
5. Compare Walpole's settings to Mary Shelley's in "Frankenstein" or Charlotte Bronte's in "Jane Eyre." How have these later authors reshaped the Gothic castle, the convent, and the Italian landscape? How do their transformations affect the generation of fear?

Clarissa

by Samuel Richardson

I WILL write!—No man shall write for me—no woman shall hinder me from writing.

(Richardson, 58)

Nothing that we know of Richardson's life or of his character and nothing we find in his letters or his earlier books adequately prepares us for "Clarissa."

(Eaves and Kimpel, 235)

Content Synopsis

Like Richardson's first novel "Pamela" (1740), "Clarissa; Or the History of a Young Lady" (1747–48) is an epistolary narrative, told in a series of letters between the characters. In this respect "Clarissa" is similar to Richardson's earlier work—in others, however, it represents a transcendence of "Pamela's" arguably limited moral vision. Vast, intricate, occasionally claustrophobia-inducing, psychologically intense, and harrowing, it is regarded as a seminal work in eighteenth-century literature. It is also an extended meditation on duty, free will, sex, power, and the survival of the self in a hostile world. The novel takes the form of two parallel, but separate, correspondences between two pairs of friends: the beautiful, virtuous, and talented Clarissa Harlowe and the lively, witty Anna Howe are set against the scheming, brilliant, seductive rake Robert Lovelace and his less sparkling, but more humane friend John Belford.

"Clarissa's" story is fairly simple. It begins with Clarissa, a young woman from an upper-middle-class family, writing to her best friend Anna and explaining the recent tumults in the Harlowe household that have taken place just before the opening of the novel. Clarissa, the youngest child and everyone's favorite, has been left an estate by her grandfather which would otherwise, by right of primogeniture, have descended to her older brother, James. Both James and Arabella, Clarissa's older sister, are jealous of the bequest and of Clarissa's place as the family favorite. To make matters worse, Clarissa is being courted by the aristocratic rake Lovelace, who had previously paid attention to Arabella but then manipulated her into refusing him so that he could legitimately woo her younger sister. Lovelace's insulting preference of Clarissa over Arabella is exacerbated in the family's eyes by the fact that Lovelace and Clarissa's brother James are old college rivals. At one point, James and Lovelace even have an altercation in which James is wounded. Clarissa tries to defuse the situation by voluntarily handing over control of her newly inherited estate to her father and by voluntarily promising not to see Lovelace. However, her siblings are unsatisfied: in the face of all the perceived provocation, Arabella and James conspire against their younger sister by persuading the family (their parents and Clarissa's paternal uncles and maternal aunt) to command her to marry a loathsome but very rich man, Roger Solmes. They represent this as being for the family good, but in reality, it is largely to punish Clarissa: if she gives in to the match, she will be miserable, and if she does not, she will incur the wrath of their father. Solmes desires Clarissa for her beauty, but she has never given him serious consideration because he is miserly, ill educated, and self-centered. As the novel opens, however, Clarissa has just returned from a short visit to Anna's to find her family determined that she will marry Solmes. Her initial demurrals are construed by her irascible, domineering father as attempts to duck her filial duty, and her brother and sister play skillfully on his temper, inciting him to insist on Clarissa's obedience.

In this difficult situation, Clarissa, who has an exacting sense of what she owes her family, tries to be as dutiful as she possibly can. But a further complication is introduced when Lovelace (who has been banned from the house) begins to write to her secretly. Previously, he had written to her as a family friend, but since his fight with James he has been shunned by the Harlowes generally. Clarissa has already given up contact with him as a means of calming her family, but Lovelace manipulatively insists that if she does not correspond with him, he will deliberately provoke her family, probably leading to a duel with her brother. Knowing that this may well result in James being seriously injured and in more trouble for herself, Clarissa agrees to continue to write to Lovelace. Initially, this is with her mother's knowledge, although Mrs. Harlowe will not stand up for Clarissa against the rest of the family. She has a warm relationship with her daughter and believes that Clarissa can defuse the situation. As things escalate, however, Mrs. Harlowe begins to disapprove of the correspondence. Intensely aware of the (particularly male) familial pressure on her and Clarissa, she forbids her daughter to keep writing.

Yet as Clarissa's family increases their pressure, Lovelace becomes correspondingly more demanding, wanting her to agree to sneak out of the house and meet him at the gate of the family's vast gardens. When her family finally tells her that they have set a wedding day for her with Solmes, Clarissa—in a moment of weakness—agrees to meet Lovelace to discuss running away with him. She believes if she does this that Lovelace will marry her, but she is still reluctant because such an act would be a major blot on her character and because she doesn't wish to completely sever ties with her family. The reality, however, is worse than she knows: Lovelace wants her to run away with him, but he does not plan to marry her. Instead, he wants to "try" her, to see if he can get her to agree to have sex with him and cohabit with him, after which he may or may not marry her. He is confident of his power over women and believes that any woman can be brought to agree to this sort of arrangement, even though in the eighteenth century this would have meant becoming a virtual social pariah and running the risk of significant financial disadvantage. He has already "ruined" many women this way, and feels that ordinary conquests no longer represent a real challenge for him. Clarissa, on the other hand, is the most strictly virtuous woman Lovelace has ever met and so he wishes to see if she can be made to participate in such a relationship like other women. Clarissa, of course, knows nothing of this; however, before she can meet Lovelace, she has second thoughts for other reasons and decides to meet him to tell him that she will not run away with him after all. Lovelace, though, has been prepared for such an eventuality. He conspires with one of the Harlowe household servants, Joseph Leman, to make a commotion in the garden during their secret meeting, making Clarissa believe that they have been discovered and that her outraged father and brother are running through the gardens, armed, seeking Lovelace's life. Terrified, bewildered, and desperate to avoid bloodshed, Clarissa panics and allows Lovelace to bundle her into the chariot he has waiting in the lane behind the house.

Lovelace first takes them to St. Albans, where Clarissa receives a letter from her sister Arabella, informing her that because of her flight, their father has disowned Clarissa and has cursed her to be punished "both here and hereafter" (509). It is at this point that Clarissa becomes truly cut off from her family and falls more deeply into Lovelace's power. Moved by her grief at her father's curse, he offers to marry her but she is too upset at the time to think clearly, and her opportunity passes. Instead, Lovelace convinces her to start going by his name, calling herself "Mrs. Lovelace" even though they are not married. This, he says, is for the sake of her reputation. In reality, it is a first step towards persuading Clarissa into unmarried cohabitation with him, pretending to be married was a common dodge for unwed lovers, and Lovelace believes that by convincing Clarissa to lie, he is sullying her perfect moral character and encouraging her to make the first motions towards what she would regard as a much greater sin.

The next step in Lovelace's elaborate plans comes when he moves their lodgings to Mrs. Sinclair's house in London. Clarissa believes that Mrs. Sinclair is a respectable matron, but in fact she is a brothel-keeper and her house is a whorehouse. Lovelace has deliberately inveigled Clarissa into living in such a place because he believes it will be easier to seduce her in such an environment. Clarissa herself, of course, has no idea of her danger. She believes that the members of the household are just what they seem. In reality, they are prostitutes. Additionally, Lovelace tells Clarissa that Dorcas, the new maid he has hired for her, is illiterate (this would not have been unusual in the eighteenth century). In fact, Dorcas can read perfectly well; but Clarissa becomes careless, leaving her letters around because she believes they cannot be read. This means that Lovelace often has access to their contents through the maid, who is really in Mrs. Sinclair's employ and frequently rifles through Clarissa's papers when Clarissa is absent. Having secured Clarissa where she cannot access the help of "respectable" people, controlling all her movements and reading her letters, Lovelace tries increasingly desperate ruses to persuade Clarissa to have sex with him, including pretending that the house is on fire and that he must come into her room when she is partially dressed. Equally, he introduces her to a group of his rakish friends, including his close confidante Belford, to whom he has been revealing details of his plans all along. His friends are prepared to meet a silly girl (Clarissa is only nineteen), but instead they are confronted with a self-possessed, intelligent young woman who will not pander to Lovelace's ego in spite of all his efforts to bring her completely into his power. Dramatic tension is created in the novel as Lovelace's correspondent, Belford, begins to have increasing misgivings about Lovelace's plans for this impressive and unusual young woman. Throughout this part of the novel, we see Lovelace's unwilling respect and affection for Clarissa combating with his desire to control her, possess her, and bend her to his will. Clarissa, meanwhile, is torn between trusting Lovelace (who is intelligent, attractive, and generous) and escaping from what she is beginning to feel is a dangerous situation.

By this time, Clarissa has noticed that Lovelace does not seem to be making any progress towards marrying her; also, she is becoming suspicious of his motives and of his friends and the women who keep the house. (In the eighteenth century, it would have been highly inappropriate and humiliating for a woman of Clarissa's class to initiate discussion of marriage with a man, and Lovelace takes advantage of this fact). Finally, Clarissa decides to run away one day when Lovelace is out. Lovelace pursues her frantically, eventually locating her at Hampstead. Here, he goes through a series of elaborate maneuvers designed to get her back, including dressing as an old man to gain access to her room at the inn where she is staying. He also hires actresses to play his aristocratic female relatives who ostensibly offer Clarissa shelter for the sake of her safety and reputation. Clarissa falls for this last trick, traveling with the "ladies" back to London, and, inevitably, to Mrs. Sinclair's house. Lovelace claims that he has to go inside simply to collect some necessaries before they proceed to his relatives' town-house, and Clarissa is bullied into entering against her better judgment. Once inside, she is fed tea laced with sedatives and, once she is unconscious, Lovelace rapes her. This is the only way in which he can stake his sexual claim in her, but it is, as he realizes, a poor substitute for the willing consent to a relationship he had once hoped to gain.

After the rape, Clarissa becomes delirious for a time, and it is here that the reader sees her "mad papers," in which she incoherently laments ever having trusted Lovelace. She returns to her senses soon enough, however, and manages to run away, once again, from Mrs. Sinclair's. From here, her life enters a downward spiral: Mrs. Sinclair's whores, eager to please Lovelace and to drag the beautiful and virtuous Clarissa down to their level, find her and conspire to have her arrested for debt. In the eighteenth century, people who did not pay their debts could be imprisoned; the whores claim that while she was living at Mrs. Sinclair's, she ought to have been paying rent, but that she has not done so. On this pretense, they have her locked up in a private jail, thinking that this horror will convince her to return voluntarily to Lovelace's and to be his mistress. They have not reckoned with Clarissa's strength of mind, however. Once she realizes the extent of Lovelace's betrayal and of his moral depravity, she determines to do anything sooner than be his mistress or even his wife. At this point, Belford finds her and buys her out of jail, but instead of returning to Lovelace, Clarissa now takes lodgings of her own, selling her few clothes and jewels in order to survive and refusing to accept money or undue favors from anybody. Slowly, it becomes clear that she is dying. It is not obvious why: critics have speculated that she pines to death of a broken heart, that she is pregnant, or that she has some type of consumption. Generally, the first option is the most commonly accepted explanation. To the end, her family refuses to be reconciled to her, and Clarissa will neither marry Lovelace nor prosecute him. She does not wish for the shame she feels a public trial would bring her; equally, in contradiction to the dictates of her culture, she will not believe that Lovelace owns her because he has had sex with her. She refuses to spend her life with someone who could commit rape. Finally, she dies; her family realizes their error too late. Clarissa's cousin Morden, who had previously been living abroad, hears of her fate and hunts Lovelace down in revenge. The story ends with Morden having killed Lovelace in a duel. Subsequently, Clarissa's will and letters relating to her burial and distribution of effects are attached, and we learn that Belford has been chosen to collate her papers, which we have just finished reading.

Historical Context

We know from the epilogue to Richardson's last novel, "Sir Charles Grandison" (1753–54) that "Clarissa" is supposed to be set about twenty years before the date of its publication in 1747–48 ("Grandison," 7:467). In spite of this historical remove, the novel engages not only with debates current at the time of its setting but also at the time of its publication. Particularly, it is important in this context to consider cultural conversations on the role of the family and the public in determining marriage.

The full title of Richardson's second novel, as printed on the title page of the first edition, is as follows: "Clarissa. Or, the History of a Young Lady: Comprehending the Most Important Concerns of Private Life. And Particularly Shewing, the Distresses that May Attend the Misconduct Both of Parents and Children, in Relation to Marriage." The novel itself is largely concerned with exploring the value of marriage and who should make decisions about it. In this respect, it is part of a wider debate about what the primary motivations for marriage should be and whether sentiment or economics should prevail in this matter. Throughout the eighteenth century, marriage was a way in which people could raise money, buy themselves into advantageous alliances, and secure places for themselves in the world. Additionally, increasingly, estates were concentrated on one heir—typically the eldest son—consolidating the family wealth so as to augment the family's social influence. This meant that "portions" (or marriage settlements) for sisters decreased over the period; similarly, younger brothers often had to make their own way in the world (either through taking up a profession or trade or through marriage) because all the family's wealth had been given to the eldest son. For these reasons, marriage was often a relatively mercenary matter; marriage settlements, in some ways similar to modern prenuptial agreements, were the norm among wealthy families. These settlements stipulated what money the wife would have during her marriage, as well as what she would get if she became a widow. In this sense, economics were a real driving factor in middle- and upper-class marriages.

Equally, however, the mid-eighteenth century saw the emergence of a new cultural discourse of sentimentalism. As is probably clear from the name, this placed more emphasis on feeling and on the emotions as guides to judgment and action. Frequently, mid-eighteenth-century marriage was conceived of in "sentimental" terms; that is, the opinion that people should marry for love was often overtly accepted. However, sentimentalism is not so simple as it sounds: as the critic Ruth Perry

has recently argued, in the eighteenth century "sentiment" itself often concealed a "calculating motivation that is moving beyond the reach of feeling" (Perry, 209). In other words, the rhetoric of love, attachment, and emotive or altruistic motivations were often used, consciously or not, to cover up more rational or scheming impetuses. When we as twenty-first-century readers look at eighteenth-century fiction, it can often seem unreal in terms of the violent or easily visible emotions that characters display—think, for example, of all Lovelace's kneeling, his poetic vows, and exclamations about Clarissa's beauty, and so forth. These become easier to understand if we say that to an extent, they are part of a cultural vocabulary of gestures, phrases, and social stances that are used partially to help achieve certain desired ends. For instance, in Lovelace's case, he often wants to flatter or cajole Clarissa into doing something (running away with him, going by his name, remaining at Mrs. Sinclair's). This is important for reading the major theme of marriage in "Clarissa" because one thing the novel seeks to do is to expose the cruelty and hypocrisy often inherent in both the mercenary and sentimental positions. Clarissa's father is deluded by her siblings into marrying her off to the rich Solmes because of Mr. Harlowe's inherent greed. Similarly, a large part of the reason that James in particular is so ill-disposed to Clarissa is that she has inherited their grandfather's estate. James, who is already promised their father's estate, expects to be given both his paternal uncles' estates, and has recently come into land in Scotland, as well. As the eldest son, however, he has expected to inherit all the family's land, and so his grandfather's bequest in favor of Clarissa comes as a nasty shock. James is used in part to discredit the misogyny inherent in the mercenary position on marriage: at one point, he says arrogantly that daughters are "chickens brought up for the tables of other men," referring to the fact that a daughter will bring with her a dowry from her family's estate (77). This will benefit her new conjugal family but will detract from the wealth of her birth family.

At the same time, "Clarissa" is not an overly romantic novel; Clarissa herself is quite clear that if a parent seriously proposes a reasonable match, a child should endeavor to concur even if the child is not in love with the potential spouse. So, for instance, Clarissa continually urges Anna to marry her long-time suitor Mr. Hickman, whom Mrs. Howe supports and who is, unlike Lovelace, a good and steady man. Anna rebels because she is not in love with Mr. Hickman and often finds his awkwardness ridiculous, but Clarissa encourages her to put such feelings aside, as they are immaterial when set against Mr. Hickman's genuine affection for Anna, the solid home he is able to offer her, and his impeccable moral character. In terms of such debates, "Clarissa" is perhaps best set in the context of the mid-eighteenth-century marriage controversy, which surrounded the passing of the Marriage Act in 1753 (just five years after "Clarissa's" publication). This act prevented people in England who were under the age of twenty-one from marrying without their parents' consent. The idea behind it was to prevent thoughtless, runaway marriages—had this act been in place when Clarissa ran away with Lovelace, she would have been unable to marry legally him, as she is only nineteen in the novel. The act was criticized, however, because many people believed that the legal requirement for parental consent would lead to the thwarting of healthy relationships between young people and would encourage parents to abuse their newfound power by insisting on mercenary marriages in order to increase the family wealth. In many ways, Clarissa's story dramatizes the conflicts this act would later seek to resolve and forms part of a mid-century body of literature on the subject (this would include such less-distinguished novelists as John Shebbeare and Sophia Briscoe).

Whilst this has been hinted at above, it is also worth mentioning the changing valuations of kinship in the period, as these inform "Clarissa's" plot. A body of recent research (including Ruth Perry's work, cited above), suggests that over the eighteenth century, it became more important for women to prioritize the families they married into, as opposed to their original or birth families. This was part of a larger trend of changing inheritance patterns, according to which families increasingly passed property onto the eldest son alone, leaving other siblings to fend for themselves. If a woman would be taken care of by the family she married into, her birth family did not have such an obligation to support her. This meant that often, tensions were created between brothers and sisters: sisters wanted brothers to provide dowries out of the family estate so that they could marry well. Brothers, on the other hand, were concerned with preserving their own inheritances and would quite conceivably go to court to do so. In "Clarissa," the grandfather's will says explicitly that the bequest to Clarissa is unusual and may not be exactly "conformable to law" (53–4). Here, he is asking the senior male members of Clarissa's family not to sue to recover the property, but to respect his last wishes. The fact that he must ask this, however, shows how odd it would have been for a younger daughter like Clarissa to have inherited a productive estate.

Other historical contexts which may usefully be considered in relation to "Clarissa" include Lovelace's identity as a rake. The rake was an iconic figure in eighteenth-century culture—he normally took the form of an urbane, wealthy, and sexually predatory, aristocratic male. Richardson developed Lovelace's character after studying the published correspondence of John Wilmot, Earl of Rochester (1647–1680), the legendary court wit and poet of the Restoration. Lovelace's characteristic energy, willfulness, humor, and sexual conquests are all reminiscent of Rochester. Lovelace is also usually seen as part of a debate about the possibility of reforming rakes. With the emergence of "sentimentalism," discussed briefly above, there came the idea that a virtuous young woman should be able to change a man's behavior through her beauty and her dogged espousal of moral concepts. This idea was contentious and was widely debated at the time. Part of the rationale for writing a character like Lovelace was to promote Richardson's view that one could not change a person who had imbibed truly wicked or immoral ideas. Richardson believed that the notion that someone as selfish and pleasure-oriented as a rake could be magically transformed to fall in love with virtue was highly unlikely and, indeed, dangerous, in as much as it encouraged young women to throw themselves away on flashy, improvident rakes who would only harm them. For all Clarissa's sense and prudence, she is young, and she does believe for a time that Lovelace's affection for her will prove transformative. In the end, of course, she is disappointed.

"Clarissa" also touches on a range of other cultural debates; perhaps one of the most important to mention is that on motherhood and maternal authority. It is noteworthy that this novel is full of inefficacious (if loving) mothers: Mrs. Harlowe fails to protect Clarissa from the machinations of her son, husband, and brothers-in-law, Mrs. Howe is largely ignored by her daughter, and Lovelace roundly blames his own mother for spoiling him. All of these mothers are loving and well-intentioned, but they lack the authority to discipline and to ensure that their children follow morally desirable paths in life. Clarissa must fend for herself (with tragic consequences) because she is unprotected at home; Anna pays no attention to her mother's often sensible comments and only agrees to marry Mr. Hickman because of Clarissa's dying wish that she do so. Lovelace's mother never disciplined him and so he is immature and able to "bear no controul" (1431). In part, this is Richardson's comment on what he perceived as mothers' responsibility for their children's moral education; also, however, it is reflective of the fact that mothers at the time really did not have a lot of control over their children. For example, from the late seventeenth century to 1839 (when the first Custody of Infants Act was passed), women who were widowed or separated from their husbands were not considered to be the legal guardians of their children, even if they had the full approval of their husbands (Foyster, 131). Instead, a male guardian had to be found. This resulted in situations in which families were broken up on the death of a father, and in children being removed from the care of their mother.

Societal Context
As is probably clear by now, "Clarissa" is a novel that concerns itself to a significant extent with cultural comment and critique. As well as the issues of changing perceptions of familial relationships and inheritance discussed above, other social issues that should be mentioned include class, publicity, and the boundaries between different sorts of societally categorized women.

Clarissa is born to a very wealthy family, but they have gained their riches relatively recently through successful trade. Although Clarissa is raised as a lady, her family's claim to gentility is questionable, and she is the only member of her family to adopt successfully upper-class manners. Lovelace, of course, is heir to his uncle, Lord M., and thus born into aristocratic life. He displays many of the vices traditionally associated with the aristocracy: sexual predation, arrogance, and general loose-living. Richardson's novel, however, does not uncomplicatedly valorize the mores of middle-class tradesmen as opposed to those of the upper classes. The Harlowes, after all, are greedy and rapacious, and seek to use their money to increase their influence and possibly even purchase a peerage. At the time, the government would often allow very wealthy businessmen to buy titles for themselves as a way of increasing state revenue. Richardson satirizes both the vulgarity of the newly rich and the self-importance and cruelty of the aristocracy. In so doing, he creates a society in which the individual self is hedged around with threats and in which ethical living is nearly impossible.

The uncertain morality of this society is one reason why Clarissa refuses to prosecute Lovelace after the rape. It is, perhaps, a modern truism that a woman who has been sexually assaulted ought to prosecute her assailant because this will help prevent future attacks he might make on other women. Clarissa, however, does not do this. How does this square with her representation in the novel as an ethical paragon? We can understand this in part by pointing to the eighteenth-century notional division between public and private. Traditionally, and perhaps simplistically, the public sphere was inhabited by men and comprised party-political and governmental structures as well as places of public resort such as inns, fairs, coffee-houses, and so forth. The private sphere, by contrast, was supposed to be women's domain. Obviously this generalization is untenable in real terms: men spent time at home and women did, of course, go to inns and fairs and plays. However, the presence of upper-class or genteel women in particular at public places was a source of anxiety at the time. Countless newspaper editorials, conduct books, sermons, and other forms of cultural commentary lament the supposedly increased tendency of contemporaneous women to "gad"—that is, to go about in public or to be seen often at public places. Women who were seen frequently in public risked cheapening themselves, or even, in extreme cases, being equated with prostitutes. For example, in Frances Burney's novel "Evelina" (1778), the innocent heroine, a young gentlewoman, is mistaken in a public park for a prostitute because she is there alone (having become separated from her friends). In another of Richardson's novels, "Sir Charles Grandison," the rascally Sir Thomas threatens to parade his daughters around in public places and sell them to the highest bidder (2: 340–1). Here, and at many other points in eighteenth-century

culture, publicity or being in a public place automatically takes on shameful sexual meanings for a woman. It is in this context that we can understand Clarissa's reluctance to expose herself in a public courtroom. Additionally, as she herself points out, there is no guarantee that he will be convicted if she does prosecute. Once again, we can glimpse the unreliability of Richardson's legal system: there is no point in taking someone to court because one cannot rely on justice being done.

Clarissa treads a line between refusing to be cowed by Lovelace's abuse of her and deciding not to publicize herself. The dignity that she gains as a result marks her out as virtuous. The danger that she could spill over into sin, however, is ever-present. She herself remarks that perhaps it is good that she is dying so young, as she will never now be exposed to the temptations that come with living in the world (1376). Clarissa maintains the dividing line between herself and Lovelace's whores, but the novel seems fascinated by the proximity between the two types of women. Clarissa lives in a brothel, of course, and loses her virginity there. One of the main moral arguments of the novel is that she is different from the whores; but the distinction between the two is constantly played with. At one point, Sally Martin, who became a prostitute after Lovelace seduced and abandoned her, mimics Clarissa in front of him. Lovelace is astonished to find that this "fallen woman" can imitate Clarissa's mannerisms and speech almost exactly (1217). Lovelace is tempted to believe that this is because there is no real difference between them: underneath, all women are the same. In a similar vein, Lovelace forges a letter to Clarissa which imitates the style and handwriting of Anne Howe; Clarissa is fooled. How does one tell the difference between a rake or whore and a virtuous young woman? Once again, the answer is that it is not mannerisms or speech patterns or physical virginity, all external signs, that reveal true virtue. This must be brought to light eventually through trial and repeated tests of moral worth. Lovelace fails to understand this until it is too late.

Religious Context

Clarissa's interpretation of, and commitment to, her religion are some of the most striking and important aspects of her character. Her particular brand of High-Anglican Protestantism places emphasis on the responsibility of the individual to behave in a morally acceptable fashion. Increasingly throughout the story, Clarissa is isolated from those who might help her: first and most obviously her family, then Lovelace as he betrays her, and then her friends Anna and Mrs. Norton, who are not able to come to her in London when she is dying. Finally, she is denied even the comfort of a last familial blessing, which she has requested by letter. As Clarissa herself remarks, "God almighty would not let me depend for comfort upon any but himself" (1356). Clarissa's life is a struggle to make the right moral choice as informed by religion: she tries to avoid marriage to Solmes in part because it will involve making a false vow (of love) before God. Similarly, she refuses to consider becoming Lovelace's mistress because this would be a sin against God, and finally, she decides not to marry Lovelace because she doesn't wish to unite herself to someone capable of committing the sort of crime of which he is guilty. If her life is a series of almost-impossible moral choices, Clarissa's death is an exemplary Christian one. Having forgiven all those who have harmed her, she gradually withdraws mentally from the world and then peacefully passes on to heaven. While today it may be difficult initially to appreciate the rationale behind Clarissa's death, the scene is constructed to reflect the beauty of Clarissa's self-abdication and acceptance of God.

Conversely and paradoxically, Clarissa's apparent self-denial is part of a religious outlook which prioritizes a self-affirming individual choice and interpretation (as well as moderation—Richardson did not condone extremist sects). For example, the novel debates the issue of the location and quality of "virtue." When Clarissa is raped, her family and friends want her to either prosecute or marry Lovelace as a way of recovering her honor. Clarissa refuses to do either: she will not put herself through the humiliation of a public trial, but equally, she does not believe that marrying Lovelace will restore her virtue. After having been put through the ultimate trial of rape, she is still able to behave in an exemplary manner; she has not, in fact, lost her virtue at all. Part of the moral argument of "Clarissa" is that a woman's honor and worth is not simply vested in a physical state of virginity, but rather in the choices she makes and in the tenor of her mind. In taking this position, Richardson aligns himself with a number of contemporaneous moralists and theologians. Perhaps two of the most suggestive for this particular novel, however, are the proto-feminists Damaris Cudworth Masham (1659–1708) and Mary Astell (1668–1731). Masham was an intimate of the late-seventeenth-century thinker John Locke and was a philosopher in her own right. She participated in heated exchanges with other noted philosophers of the time, including Astell. Richardson's (and Clarissa's) knowledge of these philosophers' writings is evident: Anna smuggles money to Clarissa in London using Clarissa's copy of the work of John Norris, a well-known devotional writer of the time and correspondent of Astell. Astell published jointly with Norris and also wrote "A Serious Proposal to the Ladies" (1694) and "Some Reflections upon Marriage" (1700), both of which urged women to value themselves and to educate themselves accordingly. Astell's writings, in general, encourage women to consider themselves separately from men, and not to simply conceive of themselves as adjuncts to their male relatives and husbands. In a similar vein, Masham's "Discourse Concerning the Love of God" (1696) reacted against the traditional equation of women's bodies, sex and sin, and promoted female virtue as something distinct from the body. In "Clarissa," we can see such ideas playing out: Clarissa does not place her moral and personal worth in her virginity (important as that is to her). By refusing to accept that her mind has been soiled and dishonored by the rape, she enables her now-damaged self to seek a destiny acceptable to her. It may seem odd to modern readers that this comes to mean her death, but in many ways her decline can be viewed as the ultimate act of self-assertion: she will do what she wants with her own body, including dying.

Finally and briefly, it is important to note Richardson's continued criticisms of what he perceives as the abuses of religion by people entrusted with the care of others. Early in the novel, Clarissa is cursed to damnation by her father after she runs away from home. The violence of his response and the fact that he extends it to the afterlife make it a completely inappropriate overreaction; Mr. Harlowe, having driven Clarissa to disobedience, now execrates her in terms which, for his religious daughter, are the worst he could possibly use. As her father, he should be supporting and protecting her. In similar terms, the novel's two clergymen, Dr. Brand and Dr. Lewen, are contrasted by their differing approaches to their religious duties. Dr. Lewen will not interfere in family matters, but he is humane and provides sensible advice to Clarissa in her time of need. Elias Brand, by contrast, is sent to watch Clarissa when she is alone in London and report back to her family. He writes back to them with a series of half-truths and misrepresentations which mean that she is not reconciled to them before her death. Brand is concerned only with furthering his own career by ingratiating himself with a powerful family; his failure to perform his pastoral duties of care and forgiveness mark him out as someone unfit to be a clergyman.

Scientific & Technological Context

Richardson's work is not generally notable for its engagement with scientific issues of the day, but one major medical question that arises in the course of this novel is: why does Clarissa die?

After the rape, Clarissa loses her senses for a time; in her famous "mad papers," found in her room and transcribed by her treacherous servant Dorcas, she reveals the mental torment and self-blame engendered by having trusted Lovelace. The shock of the rape causes her health to decline somewhat, but she is still sufficiently energetic to plan and execute an escape afterwards. Subsequently, of course, she is jailed at the instance of Mrs. Sinclair's whores, Polly Horton and Sally Martin. The trauma of being publicly arrested and carried away, coupled with the unhealthy environment of the prison, kills Clarissa's appetite and it is at this point, arguably, that her decline begins in earnest. When Belford, Lovelace's confidante, goes to see her, she is significantly weakened and begs for a cup of cold water. Later, however, she is liberated from the jail and goes to lodge at Mrs. Lovick's, where she has medical attention and friendly care. Why she continues to worsen at this point is unclear; as Lovelace says, Clarissa's doctor "deserves the utmost contempt for suffering this charming clock to run down so low" (1343). Some critics have advanced the view that Clarissa is pregnant; in fact, Clarissa's uncle John and Lovelace himself both believe that she is. (Lovelace rather hopes that she is because he thinks this would persuade her to marry him.) In any case, though, it is not immediately clear why the bare fact of pregnancy would prove fatal. It is also possible that Clarissa simply loses the will to live, although she is careful to maintain that she does nothing to hasten her own death, as this would be sinful. Essentially, Clarissa's death is left deliberately mysterious; the reader is evidently supposed to understand it as an effect of the rape and the lack of familial care. It may be explainable by her period in jail, but it is more probably an artistic device used to underline Lovelace's guilt and Clarissa's own triumphant ascension into heaven.

Rather more prosaically, it also goes to emphasize the frequent unreliability of eighteenth-century medicine. Clarissa's apparently slight ill-health rapidly turns into a fatal decline; similarly, Clarissa's servant Hannah suddenly becomes very sick in the early stages of the book, Mrs. Norton's son falls gravely ill, Mr. Harlowe is perennially plagued with tormenting gout, and both the brothel mistress, Mrs. Sinclair and Lovelace's friend, Belton, die in horrible agonies of illnesses that would today be curable. Lovelace himself dies of wounds which, in those days, could not be cleaned effectively or stitched in the same way they might be today. The terrifying reality of disease is constantly in the background in this novel; in an age without antibiotics or proper sterilization, a seemingly trivial complaint could turn suddenly into a life-threatening illness. Accidents such as the one Mrs. Sinclair has, in which she breaks her leg falling down a flight of stairs, could also prove fatal. In Mrs. Sinclair's case, the doctors cannot reset her broken leg, which becomes infected and induces a fever. The doctors consider amputating her leg, but as they do not have proper anesthetics or sterilization techniques, it is likely that this will result in her death anyway. Eventually, she is left to die of the fever and the infection in her leg.

As well as documenting the inefficacy of contemporary medicine, Richardson's depictions of doctors highlight the importance of their engaging humanely with their patients. The quack doctors who attend Mrs. Sinclair seem to regard her rather as a potential vivisection experiment than as a person needing care, and use the opportunity to preen and air their medical vocabulary in front of the impressionable whores. By contrast, Clarissa's doctor refuses her fees and acts as a genuine friend to her. As with his depictions of clergymen, here Richardson tries to emphasize the responsibilities of those entrusted with the care of others.

Biographical Context

Richardson's surviving correspondence during the years he worked on "Clarissa" is almost entirely dominated by the novel. Richardson had a wide circle of correspondents by this time, many gained after "Pamela's" almost unprecedented success. His letters frequently solicit advice from friends and acquaintances on how the work should progress—most notably, the now-forgotten poet Aaron Hill and the theologian and poet Edward Young, author of "Night Thoughts" (1741). As "Clarissa" was published intermittently in volumes, readers had the chance to engage with the characters and to imagine what might happen next. Because of this and because of Richardson's readiness to engage in correspondence about his own work, he received a massive number of suggestions as to how the plot should play out. Richardson, however, had a definite vision of what he wanted to do with his novel, and ended up rejecting the vast bulk of the advice he got. At times, his distaste for other people's suggestions led to friction in his relationships with friends, especially when he had solicited their comments in the first place. Others were not so easily rebuffed: Lady Echlin, for example, the sister of Richardson's most famous correspondent, Lady Bradshaigh, disliked "Clarissa's" tragic ending and wrote her own happy one. Even those readers who complained about Clarissa's early death (or Lovelace's loose morals, or the Harlowes' unrealistic degree of cruelty, etc) had to admit Richardson's achievement, however. "Clarissa" was the crown of his writing career and ensured his fame in his own day in England and throughout Europe (both "Pamela" and "Clarissa" were translated into French and were widely admired). Even so, Richardson often felt the need to tinker with his masterpiece.

"Clarissa" went through many editions, but probably the third edition of 1751 was the most contentious. In this version, Richardson attempted to evade what he construed as the misreading of many readers who either blamed Clarissa for running away from home, or who thought Lovelace was not so bad, after all. Richardson changed the original text, adding pointed footnotes and changing some of Lovelace's letters, to make Clarissa seem even more persecuted at home and Lovelace's character even blacker. In this edition, Richardson in his guise as "editor" is present to a much greater degree than in the first edition of 1747–8.

For reasons like this, it is often tempting to read Richardson's work biographically. He does seem, after all, to make an effort to interject his own voice into his novels. Partially, this is due to his strong moral vision for his work. It is, however, misleading to equate Richardson-the-textual-presence with Richardson-the-historical-figure. Richardson did experience sorrow and trial in his own life (six of his children died as infants or toddlers, and he was widowed and then remarried), and such biographical facts probably do inform his work to an extent.

Bonnie Latimer

Works Cited

Buickerood, James G. Ed. In *Masham, Lady Damaris Cudworth. The Philosophical Works*. Bristol: Thoemmes Continuum, 2004.

Cornford, Stephen. Ed. Young, Edward. *Night Thoughts (1741)*. Cambridge: Cambridge University Press, 1989.

Eaves, T. C. Duncan and Ben D. Kimpel. *Samuel Richardson: A Biography*. Oxford: Clarendon, 1971.

Foyster, Elizabeth. *Marital Violence: An English Family History*, 1660–1857. Cambridge: Cambridge University Press, 2005.

Norris, John and Mary Astell. *Letters Concerning the Love of God (1695)*. Ed. by E. Derek Taylor and Melyn New. Aldershot: Ashgate, 2005.

Perry, Ruth. *Novel Relations: The Transformation of Kinship in English Literature and* Culture, 1748–1818. Cambridge: Cambridge University Press, 2004.

Richardson, Samuel. *Clarissa. Or, the History of a Young Lady. . . (8 vols)*. London: S. Richardson, 3rd ed., 1750–51.

_____. *The History of Sir Charles Grandison (1753–54)*, 7 vols. Ed. by Jocelyn Harris. Oxford: Oxford University Press, 1972, rpt 1986.

Ross, Angus. Ed. Samuel Richardson. *Clarissa or the History of a Young Lady* (1747–8). Ed. by. London: Penguin, 1st ed., 1985.

Springborg, Patricia. Ed. *Mary Astell. A Serious Proposal to the Ladies (1694)*. Peterborough, Ont.: Broadview Press, 2002.

_____. *Some Reflections upon Marriage*. London: John Nutt, 1700.

Discussion Questions

1. Think about the structure of "Clarissa": most of the text consists of two threads of correspondence that cross one another. How does this affect a reader's perception of events? What kinds of ironies or juxtapositions does it generate?

2. How are familial and psychological pressures used in "Clarissa"? Clarissa herself is often accused by her embittered siblings of being too moving, even manipulative. How good do you think Clarissa is at exerting psychological advantage?

3. There is evidence that Lovelace's name would have been pronounced "loveless" in eighteenth-century British English. Does Lovelace really love Clarissa? Or is he utterly heartless?

4. Clarissa repeatedly blames herself for "one false step." Do you think this step invalidates her as a moral authority, or does the experience of having judged wrongly and suffered increase her stature?

5. After having read "Clarissa," what kinds of meanings do you think rape has in this text? Attempted ownership? Frustrated affection? Crude violation? Punishment? Any others?

6. The critical debate over whether or not Clarissa conceived during the rape has produced some interesting readings of the text. Do you think Clarissa is pregnant when she dies? How does this affect how you think about her death?

7. Think about the theme of trial in this text. Who has the right to try whom? Why?

8. Lovelace prides himself on his ability to impersonate and parody other people's voices. How is impersonation a wider theme in this text? Who else impersonates others?

9. Read the various deathbed scenes in this novel (Belton's, Mrs. Sinclair's, Clarissa's, Lovelace's). What conclusions is the reader supposed to draw from them, do you think? Are these conclusions flawed?

10. Many of Richardson's readers, when the novel was first published, wanted a happy ending, with Clarissa living, forgiving Lovelace, and marrying him. Would this ever have worked? Can you imagine a happy ending to this text that would be as effective as the actual tragic one? Is the real ending tragic at all?

Essay Ideas

1. Analyze the importance of the idea of duty in this novel.

2. Analyze Clarissa as an unreliable narrator. Can the reader always trust Clarissa's version of events?

3. Examine how the ability to write or speak well reflect on the credibility of individual characters in "Clarissa."

4. Examine the qualities that are necessary for a character to succeed in the world of "Clarissa."

5. Analyze the ways in which being a woman is an obstacle in "Clarissa."

The Country of the Blind

by H. G. Wells

Content Synopsis

H. G. Wells' short story "The Country of the Blind" relates the adventures of an explorer, Nunez, who accidentally stumbles across a mysterious valley in the Andes. Nunez comes into the valley after being separated from his mountaineering party and finds a settled little community with one marked characteristic: every individual is blind. Nunez realizes that this is the "Country of the Blind" whose existence has often been rumored in the region. Except for this one affliction however, the people lead very settled and contented lives in their rich and fertile valley. Having been blind for generations, they have adapted so well to their handicap that their state of blindness has become completely normal to them. Furthermore, they have been enclosed in their own little valley for so long that they have forgotten the outer world, to the extent that they refuse to believe that anything outside the valley even exists.

As the one seeing man amongst the blind people, Nunez is at first supremely confident that he can enlighten them about the actual state of things and so become their leader, reminding himself of the old proverb, "in the country of the blind the one-eyed man is king" (Wells 634). However, things do not go at all according to plan. The blind people are incapable of assimilating anything that he tells them about the world of sight and the existence of a world outside their valley, and accuse him of blasphemy. When he tries to assert his superiority over them in physical terms, he is equally unsuccessful and for a short time flees outside the valley. A lack of food and shelter eventually compels him to return and beg their forgiveness. They condescend to take him in on the condition that he accept their way of life and teachings unreservedly. He becomes the servant of one of their number, Yacob, and performs his duties accordingly, no longer daring to question the community's ways.

In due course, Nunez falls in love with Yacob's daughter Medina-Saroté who appears particularly attractive to him as her eyelids are less red and shrunken than those of the others' (although amongst her own people this is counted as a defect). She loves him in return, but Yacob is shocked at the idea of marrying his daughter to Nunez, whom the blind people have decided is of extremely low intelligence. Being pressed by Medina-Saroté, however, he consults the village elders. Following an examination by doctors, it is decided to remove Nunez's eyes, as it is believed that these 'irritant bodies' are putting pressure on his brain and thus affecting his mental function. Nunez is initially persuaded by Medina-Saroté to agree to the operation, but later reconsiders and resolves to leave her and the Valley of the Blind altogether. In trying to climb back to the outer world, he dies.

Wells re-wrote the ending to the story several years after the story's original completion. In this revised version, as he leaves the valley, Nunez realizes that a landslide is about to occur, and hastens back to the blind people to warn them. As before, they categorically refuse to heed him and cast him out. When Medina-Saroté comes to him, he persuades her to flee with him and they make good their escape as the landslide buries the valley. Thus, the blind people perish, but Nunez and Medina-Sarote start a new life in Quito and raise a family.

Superficially, "The Country of the Blind" reads like an adventure story; but on a deeper level, it is intended as an allegory. Wells uses literal blindness to represent the metaphorical blindness of a self-sufficient, close-knit little community that has, essentially, stagnated and become unreceptive to all outside influences to the point of absolute xenophobia. The story is also intended to be symbolic of the human race at large, which goes about its daily affairs wholly oblivious of the larger scheme of things and entirely dismissive of the warnings and prophecies of visionary individuals.

Historical Context

The two versions of "The Country of the Blind," with their significantly different endings, illustrate important historical developments during Wells' lifetime. In the original version of the story, which first appeared in 1904, Wells is concerned solely with showing how a self-sufficient community treats an outsider, resulting in his expulsion and death. The second version, which came out in 1939, depicts the wholesale destruction of that community and the powerlessness of the man who could have saved it. Wells alludes to the world situation of his time in his introduction to the second version:

> In 1904, the stress is upon the spiritual isolation of those who see more keenly than their fellows the tragedy of their incommunicable appreciation of life. The visionary dies, a worthless outcast, finding no other escape from his gift but death, and the blind world goes on, invincibly self-satisfied and secure. But, in the later story vision becomes something altogether more tragic; it is no longer a story of disregarded loveliness and release; the visionary sees destruction sweeping down upon the whole blind world he has come to endure and even to love; he sees it plain, and he can do nothing to save it from its fate (Wells 880).

Beginning with his forward-looking, non-fictional work "Anticipations" in 1901, Wells increasingly looked to the world's future and saw many dangers inherent in the political and social set-up of his day, predicting that they would lead to catastrophe. World War I eminently justified his fears, and the second version of "The Country of the Blind" takes on an added poignancy when one remembers that it was published on the eve of the even greater cataclysm of World War II. Wells might well have felt that his warnings, like those of Nunez, had been emphatically ignored. (See also Biographical Context.)

Societal Context

Society, as depicted in "The Country of the Blind," takes on chilling overtones. The community of the blind people runs along extremely efficient lines and they lead simple and seemingly very contented lives. Yet their closed mentality, their refusal and indeed inability to entertain any new idea or thought that runs contrary to their own beliefs and habits, is disconcerting. This is, in fact, a totalitarian society to some degree, which does not tolerate dissent amongst its members. The blind people have no hesitation in deeming Nunez, the nonconformist who comes among them, as being wholly inferior and indeed deranged, and he only narrowly escapes having his eyes put out. What makes this particularly frightening is that this act of removing Nunez's 'irritant bodies' is not even counted as a repressive action by these people, but rather as a necessary action to allow him to fit in with their society. This kind of cold-blooded reasoning underlies many a grim vision in literature of perfectly organized societies which operate with ruthless efficacy, from Wells' own 1899 novel, "When the Sleeper Wakes" to George Orwell's "Nineteen Eighty-Four." In such a world, the individual who sees differently and more clearly cannot remain without seriously compromising his/her own ideals and convictions. Such individuals are ultimately faced with a stark choice: passive submission or outright rebellion.

Religious Context

Never a Christian believer, Wells takes the opportunity in "The Country of the Blind" to satirize established religion. The blind people believe firmly in what they call the "Wisdom Above," a cavernous roof overarching the rocks that mark the edge of the valley and, for them, the literal end of the world. According to their scheme, there is no larger world (far less a universe) outside the valley. They have upheld this extremely limited world-view for generations, and for someone to question it, as Nunez does in talking of distant cities and civilizations and sun, moon and stars, is sheer blasphemy. Wells thus equates uncritical belief with a narrowness of intellect and meanness of spirit likely to culminate in ruthless repression.

The blind people's faith can be taken as representative of orthodox Christianity, which for hundreds of years stated that that the earth was the absolute centre of the universe and that creation had taken place in precisely 4004 BC, and often took reprisals against those who challenged this doctrine until mounting scientific evidence to the contrary could no longer be ignored. (See also Scientific & Technological Context.)

Scientific & Technological Context

Cocooned in their little valley and restricted (although they no longer know it) by their lack of sight, the blind people lead a primitive way of life. They are, luckily, blessed with an abundance of natural resources which they make good use of, but they appear to have little or no technology. In addition, they cling unthinkingly to their old tradition of the "Wisdom Above" and the belief that nothing exists outside their valley, in much the same way that for centuries, before advances in astronomy and other scientific fields, people remained unaware that the earth is only a tiny speck in an unimaginably vast universe. The blind people utterly reject the enlightenment that a modern critical and scientific attitude could have vouchsafed to them, choosing instead to remain willfully in their own dark age.

Biographical Context

"The Country of the Blind" reflects Wells' abiding concern with the workings of society. He first gained success as a writer of scientific romances such as "The Time Machine," and it is for these that he remains best-known, but even the scientific romances, although primarily viewed as entertainment, contain many incisive observations about the development (actual and potential) of society and the world. "The Time Machine," for instance, portrays a future in which the class divisions of the late Victorian period are taken to extremes.

Wells' social and political concerns became more pronounced in the later stages of his career as he knowingly cast himself in the role of scientific and social prophet, rightly predicting such developments as globalization, the mass growth of cities and super-highways as well as destructive forces such as tanks ("The Land Ironclads") and the atom bomb ("The World Set Free"). However, he continually articulated his fears about the failure of human intellect to keep pace with technological progress and feared it would all end in disaster.

Several of his books portray the destruction of the world and envisage a new Utopian order arising slowly from the ashes, conducted along strictly regimented socialist and scientific principles, and resembling Plato's ideal state as described in "The Republic." It has frequently been noted that his utopian worlds inevitably include some distasteful elements, most notably the stifling of individuality which, ironically, he critiques in "The Country of the Blind." However, he sincerely believed that the kind of world order that he envisioned was the only one that could benefit the human race in the long run. His dream was to engage others in his ideas for social regeneration and world salvation, but his final book, "Mind at the End of its Tether," which appeared in 1945 (just a year before his death) ends on a wholly pessimistic note, with a vision of human extinction. Like Nunez attempting to broaden the minds of the blind people, he took it upon himself to educate his fellow human beings, but without much success.

Gurdip Panesar, Ph.D.

Works Cited

Bergonzi, Bernard. *The Early H. G. Wells: A Study of the Scientific Romances.* Manchester, England: Manchester University Press, 1961.

Hammond, J. R. *H. G. Wells and the Short Story.* Basingstoke, England: Palgrave Macmillan, 1992.

Wells, H. G. *The Complete Short Stories of H. G. Wells.* London: Phoenix Press, 1998.

Discussion Questions

1. Do you think that "The Country of the Blind" works well as an allegory? Why or why not?
2. In what ways does "The Country of the Blind" read like a typical adventure story?
3. Which (if any) of the characters in this story do you feel are well realized? Why?
4. Do you think that Nunez could have done anything more to bring the blind people around to his way of thinking? Why or why not?
5. Why does Wells spend so much time in describing how the country of the blind came into existence? Do you feel this is necessary to the story? Why or why not?
6. Discuss the positive and negative aspects of the kind of society presented in this story.
7. To what degree do you sympathize with Nunez or with the blind people, or both? Explain your answer.
8. What kind of tone is employed in this story? How does it affect your response as a reader?

Essay Ideas

1. Examine the theme of social and political repression in relation to "The Country of the Blind."
2. Analyze the notion of the visionary in "The Country of the Blind."
3. Analyze Wells' allegorical approach in "The Country of the Blind."

Robert Louis Stevenson, pictured above, was born in 1850 in Edinburgh, Scotland. He had his first major literary success in 1883 with the publication of *Treasure Island*. *The Strange Case of Dr. Jekyll and Mr. Hyde*, featured on page 187 of this volume, was published in 1886. Photo: Collection of Jim DuPlessis.

The Door in the Wall

by H. G. Wells

Content Synopsis

"The Door in the Wall," one of H. G. Wells' most admired short stories, features Lionel Wallace, a high-ranking politician in late Victorian England who harbors a precious secret. He reveals this secret in full one night over dinner to his friend Redmond (who is also the overall narrator of the story). As a little boy, when once wandering through the London streets, he unexpectedly came upon a green door in a white wall that strangely attracted him. Going through, he found himself in a beautiful garden, seemingly far removed from the everyday world, and all manner of playmates and friendly animals. The place filled him with inexpressible delight; when he suddenly found himself back in the dreary London streets, he was overcome with misery. He then came upon the door a second time, several years later, when on the way to school, but this time did not enter, and when he returned to look for it—with a party of disbelieving schoolmates—it was not there. In later years, the door appeared to him on several more occasions, always unexpectedly, and at crucial moments in his life: once when he was on the way to winning an Oxford scholarship, another time when his father was dying, and finally, at a highly critical time in his political career. Each time he resisted the temptation to drop all his worldly cares and enter which has left him, as he now confesses to Redmond, with "inappeasable regrets" (Wells 583). Wallace vows that if the door ever appears to him again, he will definitely enter. However, he fears he has lost his chance for good.

Redmond recollects the whole story three months later, when news comes of the discovery of Wallace's body at a railway excavation site. It seems that when walking home the night before, Wallace took a detour through a door in the hoarding temporarily erected around the excavation and fell to his death. Redmond speculates whether he had been misled into thinking that it was his own special door leading to his cherished secret garden. The story ends on this doubtful, questing note, with Redmond continuing to wonder about the nature of Wallace's death and the door and garden of which he had spoke.

Historical Context

Although the main character of "The Door in the Wall" is a politician, nothing is shown of the political and social issues of the time in which the story was written. Instead, it is very much Wallace's own personal tale, the account of his private dream, alongside which his illustrious political career comes to appear merely incidental. However, in focussing upon individual dreams and desires, the story reflects contemporary interest in the science of psychology; this was the time of Sigmund Freud and Carl Jung. (For more, see Scientific & Technological Context.)

One interesting aspect of the story is the reference to the "North-West Passage," which is the name of a schoolboy game of trying to find alternative routes to school (and which leads Wallace to the door in the wall for the second time in his life). The North-West Passage was the sea route around North America from the Atlantic to the Pacific, which had been sought for centuries by European and American explorers and was eventually devised by Roald Amundsen (the Norwegian who also was the first man to reach the South Pole) in the early years of the twentieth century. This reference serves as a reminder that this was still the time of worldwide exploration and discovery, with the British Empire at its height and covering almost a quarter of the globe and other European nations similarly vying for territorial expansion. It is interesting to apply this to the case of Lionel Wallace. His particular voyage of discovery through the London streets appears to lead him to another world altogether, an unsuspected realm as far removed as can be from the concerns of everyday life.

Societal Context

Lionel Wallace, having made his way to the top of the career ladder, is clearly comfortably off and lives the life of the privileged upper classes. What is also clear, however, is his sense of loneliness and isolation despite all his social success. This surely stems at least partly from his childhood—the early loss of his mother and the emotional neglect of his father. His father, in fact, appears very much the stereotypical Victorian patriarch—stern and distant. It is easy—perhaps too easy—to link this lack of parental affection with his vision of the garden, in which he finds all the delight that he never seems to experience in any other part of his life; he gains social recognition but social recognition does not bring happiness. Indeed, the reverse is true: he comes to regard his success as merely a "vulgar, tawdry, irksome, envied thing" (Wells 583) without which he would be far better off.

Scientific & Technological Context

On one level, the story appears to invite a straightforward interpretation in psychological terms. Psychology as a science had been developing rapidly all through the nineteenth century and was reaching new heights by the dawn of the twentieth with the work of Sigmund Freud. A Freudian explanation of Wallace's vision is certainly tempting, with its emphasis on the importance of early-life experiences and the power of the unconscious mind. According to this scheme, Wallace conjures up the vision of the door and garden and the playmates he finds there as compensation for the lack of love in his real life, and particularly the loss of his mother who, we are told, died when he was only two. The vision of the door and the garden beyond in large measure reads like a classic escapist fantasy. It is significant that whenever the door appears to Wallace after childhood, it always does so at moments of high pressure in his everyday life. The whole thing might well be a product of his unconscious mind devised as an outlet from the stresses and strains of ordinary living—a means of escape to which he finally yields. Such an explanation is perhaps rather too neat, however. There surely remains for most readers (as for Redmond) an intriguing sense of mystery about the whole affair, and the persuasion that the door and garden do, after all, represent more than just an hallucination or willful daydreaming on Wallace's part.

Religious Context

Wallace's secret garden is notable for its sense of unearthly beauty and joy:

> There was something in the very air of it that exhilarated, that gave one a sense of lightness and good happening and well-being; there was something in the sight of it that made all its colour clean and perfect and subtly luminous. In the instant of coming into it, one was exquisitely glad—as only in rare moments,

and when one is young and joyful one can be glad in this world (Wells 576).

The garden appears a veritable Eden, a paradisal otherworld, Wallace's own private heaven, which perhaps, he regains following his death. Wells was certainly no orthodox religious believer but he entertained utopian visions of beautified future worlds brought about through the application of socialist and scientific principles in which he, along with many other writers of the time, fervently believed. This yearning for beautiful and joyous otherworlds also informs many of his other short stories, for example "Mr. Skelmersdale in Fairyland." Wells may have wholly repudiated Christianity and all its trappings, but nevertheless retained a strongly religious sense of otherworldly beauty, happiness, and true fulfillment.

Biographical Context

The wistfulness and delicacy that underlies such a story as "The Door in the Wall" may come as a surprise to readers who may know Wells only as the writer behind pessimistic (and often violent) works of science fiction like "The Time Machine." Born in Kent in 1866 of lower-middle class parentage, he won a scholarship to the Normal School of Science in London in 1883 that, critically, exposed him to the teachings of the famous biologist T. H. Huxley. This proved to be a lasting influence on his life and thought. He became interested in the possibility of social reform and also began to write, and composed a number of short stories before winning acclaim with "The Time Machine," the first of his self-styled "scientific romances," which also included "The Island of Dr. Moreau," "The Invisible Man" and "The War of

the Worlds." In all of these and in many of his short stories, he displays an uncommon gift for combining imaginative flights of fancy (arising from the scientific and technological possibilities of his age) with the most believable, down-to-earth realism. In "The Door in the Wall," for instance, we are given a minute description of the everyday and quite dull surroundings among which the door first manifests itself: "a number of mean dirty shops . . . a plumber and decorator with a dusty disorder of earthenware pipes, sheet lead, ball taps, pattern books of wallpaper, and tins of enamel" (Wells 573).

Wells also wrote novels of social commentary dealing with many vexing issues of the age, like marriage in "Ann Veronica" and rampant commercialism in "Tono-Bungay." In later years, and up to his death in 1946, he became more pre-occupied with composing copious works of social and scientific prophecy which argued strenuously for the need for world co-operation and a complete reorganization of society along socialist-scientific lines. He came to regard these works as being by far his most important. However, it is owing to his early scientific romances and short stories such as the lyrical "The Door in the Wall" that his fame as a writer endures.

Gurdip Panesar, Ph.D.

Works Cited

Batchelor, John. *H. G. Wells.* Cambridge University Press: Cambridge, 1985.

Huntington, John. *The Logic of Fantasy: H. G. Wells and Science Fiction.* New York: Columbia University Press, 1982.

Wells, H. G. *The Complete Short Stories of H. G. Wells.* London: Phoenix Press, 1998.

Discussion Questions

1. Do you think that Wallace is something of a weak character? Why or why not?
2. What kind of attitude does Redmond, the overall narrator of the story, adopt towards Wallace, and how does this affect the story as a whole?
3. What kind of impression does the garden leave on Wallace? How does this compare to his everyday life?
4. Do you think that the door and garden might be purely imaginary or hallucinatory? Why or why not?
5. Can it be said that the door is ultimately of greater significance than the garden which lies beyond? Why or why not?
6. Do you find Wallace's account convincing? Why or why not?
7. Do you think that the vision of the door and garden proves to be a blessing or a curse? Explain your answer.
8. Do you feel that the ending of the story is unsatisfactory? Why or why not?

Essay Ideas

1. Analyze Wells' use of imagery in "The Door on the Wall."
2. Consider the usefulness of a psychoanalytical approach to "The Door in the Wall."
3. Examine the theme of conflict in "The Door in the Wall."
4. Analyze Wells' narrative technique in "The Door in the Wall."

Frankenstein; Or, the Modern Prometheus

by Mary Shelley

Content Synopsis

The story of Victor Frankenstein and his creation is told entirely via letters Robert Walton, the frame narrator, sends his sister during a sea voyage to the North Pole, in search of glory. Thirsty for fame, Walton serves as one of several characters whose life, desires or aspirations parallel Victor's. While trapped in the ice, the crew of Walton's ship encounters both a looming figure in the distance on a sledge and a second man who approaches the trapped vessel, also on a sledge, seeking refuge. The second man is Victor Frankenstein, who is rescued by Walton and his crew. The first figure is his "creature." As he slowly recovers on the boat, Victor bonds with Walton and shares his story from beginning to end.

Victor's story begins in Geneva where he was raised with an adopted sister (Elizabeth) who later becomes his love interest. After leaving home to study chemistry and natural philosophy at Ingolstat University in Germany, Victor studies under M. Krempe and M. Waldman who shape his philosophical education. Eventually, almost by accident, by combining both abandoned and new beliefs about science, Victor discovers the secrets of life and death. The knowledge prompts him to reanimate a corpse, an act of which he never logically considers the result, including the fate of the 'creation' he animates. At first exultant at his success, Victor is soon both disgusted and fearful of his monstrous creation. After seeking his friend Clerval, the two find that the monster has escaped the laboratory and is at large. Victor falls ill and returns to his family at which time his younger brother is found murdered and Justine, an adopted member of the household, is convicted of the crime. Although Victor suspects that his monster killed William, he does not speak up in Justine's defense and she is executed.

The monster, alone and outcast from society, manages to stay alive by hiding in a lean-to adjacent to a cottage, where he begins to learn to speak and read by watching the family through a chink in the wall. Some of his early reading material includes Plutarch's "Lives," "Sorrows of Young Werther," and most significantly, "Paradise Lost," the text with which he most identifies and which is the generative force behind his desire for an Eve. He is forced to flee the family once they see him in all his monstrous glory, even though he has provided necessary goods to them like firewood.

While walking in the mountains some time later, Victor is confronted by his creation who, lonely, frustrated, and abandoned by his maker, explains that he killed William in an effort to get back at Victor. The monster asks only one thing of Victor—that he create a mate with whom he may spend the rest of his miserable days, an Eve to his Adam; one like himself, monstrous and outcast. During his plea to Victor, the monster is ironically characterized as both more human and more civilized than his maker is. He is both convincing and eloquent in his arguments.

The idea of isolation, imposed by self or society, is extended as Victor agrees to the monster's request, and goes into seclusion to recreate his first experiment and make the creature a wife. While Victor slaves to recreate his first experiment, he suddenly realizes that if he creates a female for the creature, they might breed a monstrous race together. As a result, he destroys the female he is in the process of reanimating. The monster watches Victor's actions from a window and rages at the betrayal, taking revenge by murdering Victor's future bride, Elizabeth. Victor's father then dies of grief over Elizabeth's murder. By the end of the tale, the civilized scientist Victor Frankenstein has been indirectly responsible for the death of almost every character in the book.

As Victor becomes obsessed with exacting retribution for Elizabeth's murder, both characters appear more parallel than ever, each one vowing revenge over the destruction of their love. After several thwarted attempts to capture the monster, Victor finally tracks him north where he runs into Walton and his crew. Ironically, because Victor endowed his creation with incredible strength, he is easily able to outstrip Victor who falls ill. Victor becomes progressively sicker, and dies on Walton's boat after finishing his story. The monster comes to see Victor's dead body over which he weeps and then decides that he can die, as he has no partner and nothing left upon which to take revenge.

The idea that the monster and the scientist are "antithetical halves of the same being" (Bloom 1) is a concept firmly established in literary criticism from the publication of Shelley's most famous work through the present day. Another parallel exists between Walton and Victor, one of whom attempts to tame nature by penetrating it via exploration and the other through usurping its power. Some of the themes Frankenstein addresses include the monstrous potential of human creative power when severed from moral and social concerns, the power of nature versus science, the responsibility of society towards those it treats poorly, relationships between men and women, and the idea that one can be both moral and destructive at the same time.

Historical Context

In the summer of 1816, Mary Shelley and a group of friends, including her husband Percy Shelley, Lord Byron, Claire Claremont, and John Polidori, vacationed on Lake Geneva at Villa Deodati. Because of inclement weather, they spent a significant portion of their stay reading. The majority of this reading material was comprised of ghost stories. One stormy night, Byron challenged each member of the group to write a supernatural story to share. While most of them tried, only Mary and John ultimately kept with it, each publishing their results: Shelley's "Frankenstein" and Polidori's "The Vampyre." Mary was not yet twenty when she wrote the story.

This novel is characterized as both Romantic and Gothic. Gothic literature arose following the 1764 publication of Horace Walpole's "The Castle of Otranto." Some of the characteristics of this type of fiction include the dark, the mysterious, and the supernatural. The text also represents the ideas of literary Romanticism in which "the shadow or double of the self is a constant conceptual image" (Bloom 2).

In many ways, Frankenstein reflects the frustration and disillusionment felt in the wake of the French Revolution, which was initially supported by most, if not all, Romantic writers. At the outset, the French revolution was lauded by those who stood in opposition to oppression and identified with struggle of the lower and working class. The turn of events at the end of the revolution, however, soured even its staunchest supporters. According to George Levine, the "metaphoric" nature of the tale addresses "some of the fundamental dualisms, the social, moral political and metaphysical crisis of western history since the French Revolution" (Schoene-Harwood 21).

Societal Context

The social outcast is a figure explored in depth in this story. Outcasts and their dangerous potential to disrupt the very social order that relegated them to the fringes have been explored since the time of Beowulf's Grendel. In Shelley's story, both Frankenstein and his monster suffer the effects of being cast out of society either by choice or by compulsion. The impact of outward appearance on social reception is greatly emphasized in the text, from the physical attractiveness, or lack thereof, of Victor's teachers at Ingolstat, to the reactions to the creature in civilized society. The dangers of social maltreatment in the text were explored by Percy Shelley himself who stated, "Treat a person ill, and he will become wicked . . . divide him, a social being, from society, and you impose upon him the irresistible obligations—malevolence and selfishness" (Schoene-Harwood).

A long-standing debate among sociologists, the question of whether nature or nurture is the primary influence on personality development is addressed within the text, but never satisfactorily or definitively answered. Rousseau's theories about human intellectual potential are visible in the creature who is clearly a "tabula rasa," or blank slate, when he comes into existence and whose worldview is influenced primarily by his education.

The creature is a good "man," as far as one can tell, until he is treated unfairly and poorly by members of society. The people the creature encounters, however, only react because of ingrained social norms, customs, and fears. Thus, they both are and are not truly culpable for the creature's turn to monstrous doings. It is the creature's "father" himself who is primarily responsible for his life and well-being, and it is his "father" who abandons him. The dangerous, often fatal, effects of abandonment and orphan hood are subjects close to Mary Shelley's heart. Making this point more emphatically, in "Frankenstein," as Gilbert and Gubar point out, "all the major and most of the minor characters in "Frankenstein" are [orphans]" including Victor, Walton, Elizabeth, and Justine (55).

The lack of power women possessed during the time in which the story is set is exemplified in the characters of Justine and Elizabeth, each of whom relies upon male intervention and agency to save them. Margaret, Walton's sister, clearly takes issue with some of his decisions, yet is never given her own voice with which to do so.

Malchow suggests that Shelley's text not only engages with revolutionary and gendered experiences, but also with "contemporary attitudes toward nonwhites." Malchow illustrates that it is possible to see the monster as a representation of racism in action. Malchow begins his argument by exploring the ways in which the creature is described physically, citing his complexion, size, strength and his "apelike" ability to scamper up mountainsides and his endurance of temperatures that European man would find intolerable" (18–19). Mary Shelley wrote her text after the abolition of the British slave trade in 1807. In opposition to the still prevalent racist ideology of her time, Shelley's creature is "different," "uncivilized" and vilified as Other in the text, but he quickly learns and "evolves" before the very eyes of the reader, eventually becoming, arguably more civilized than the master of his fate, Victor.

Religious Context

Both mythic and Biblical references appear in the story. Prometheus is seen by Harold Bloom as "the mythic figure who best suits the uses of Romantic poetry, for no other traditional being has in him the full range of Romantic moral sensibility and the full Romantic capacity for creation and destruction" (Bloom 2). Prometheus can also be seen as representative of the Biblical Lucifer who was cast out of heaven. Harold Bloom notes, however, there is a resemblance between the protagonist of Shelley's novel and the protagonist of Samuel Taylor Coleridge's poem "The Ancient Mariner." According to Bloom, "Coleridge's Mariner is of the line of Cain, and the irony of Frankenstein's fate is that he too is a Cain, involuntarily murdering all his loved ones through the agency of his creature" (6). Lowrey Nelson Jr. asserts that one important dimension of the rise of Gothic writing and Romantic sensibility, was that it precipitated a "trans-valuation of values [in which] Cain becomes a sympathetic figure, unjustly cursed by a vengeful God and incapable of ever purging his guilt . . . at worst he is twisted by circumstances into a monster of inhumanity" (32).

In the story itself, Victor is a man over whom religion seems to hold no sway. He, in fact, actively seeks to become a God, to create life, perhaps to live forever. In a reading in which Victor stands as an uncaring and abandoning "father," he would symbolize that God which people believe created man only to leave him to his own devices, the result of which is, in many people, though certainly not all, a murderous and vengeful instinct.

Scientific & Technological Context

The text's exploration of the relationship between nature and science is exemplified in a conversation Victor has with Walton, warning him: "Learn from me, if not by my precepts, at least by my example, how dangerous is the acquirement of knowledge, and how much happier that man is who believes his native town to be the world, than who aspires to be greater than his nature will allow" (833).

The possibility of a birthing process taken over by men, which is arguably, at least partly a reflection of the increase in male physicians' interest in women and birthing, duties that had previously been performed only by midwives, is explored in "Frankenstein." Scientific [and/or medical] study devoid of women's research and involvement is shown to yield terrible results in this text, as much as the literary texts exploring this idea today.

The text engages with some of the more specious sciences of the day, including the writing of Cornelius Agrippa who believed that God and the universe could be understood via magic. Paracelsus is also a man Victor studies, an alchemist; he represents the scientific theory falling out of favor at the time. The combination in Victor's courses of study, of both magical and 'scientific' theory proves fruitful, if dangerous.

Biographical Context

Mary Shelley was born in 1797, the daughter of writer and social activist William Godwin and early women's rights supporter Mary Wollstonecraft. Surrounded by intellectuals, Mary Shelley received a thorough, if private, education from reading books found in the vast library at her home, an education not unlike that of Victor's creature.

In 1813, Mary ran away with the then married Percy Bysshe Shelley. The relationship was turbulent for years, and resulted in marriage, only after Percy's wife's suicide. Mary Shelley's life was a very difficult one, fraught with issues about paternity, the dangers of illegitimacy, and the conflation in her mind of love and death. Some examples of this include: her own mother's death shortly after giving birth to her; Mary and Percy having their first intimate encounter at her mother's grave; the deaths of five out of six of her children; her sister Fanny's suicide after finding out that she was illegitimate; Percy's (pregnant) first wife's suicide after he left her; and Mary's own brush with death after a miscarriage in 1822. Mary was also pregnant at the time of her writing "Frankenstein." Referred to by her as "my hideous progeny" this book was the second of Mary's "children" to not only survive but also reach near immortal status.

After her husband Percy's untimely death on 1822, (by drowning) his body was cremated.

According to witnesses, the heart would not burn. First removed from the flames by a friend of Percy, his heart was then given to Mary who kept it with her until the day she died, when it was buried with her.

Tracy M. Caldwell, Ph.D.

Works Cited

Bloom, Harold. "Introduction." *Bloom's Modern Critical Views*: *Mary* Shelley. Ed. Philadelphia: Chelsea House Publishers, 1985. 1–10.

Gilbert, Sandra M. and Susan Gubar in "Horror's Twin: *Mary Shelley's* Monstrous Eve." Bloom's Major *Literary* Characters: *Frankenstein*. Harold Bloom, ed. Philadelphia: Chelsea House Publishers, 1985. 55–74.

Lowry, Nelson R. Night Thoughts on the Gothic *Novel. Bloom's Modern Critical Views*: *Mary* Shelley, Ed. Harold Bloom. Philadelphia: Chelsea House Publishers, 1985. 31–48.

Malchow, H. L. *Gothic Images of Race in Nineteenth-Century Britain*. California: Stanford University Press, 1996.

Schoene-Harwood, Ed. *Mary* Shelley *Frankenstein*: *Essays, Articles, Reviews*. New York: Columbia University Press, 2000.

Discussion Questions

1. What makes this an enduring tale?
2. Why are there so many revisions of this story? It has inspired over 50 films.
3. What is the effect on you as a reader of the narrative layers? For example, are you always aware of how the narrative voice shifts, or becomes more complicated? At one point in particular, the reader hears from Walton's sister something from Walton that came from Victor and originated with the 'monster.' The telling, however, is often so seamless that the reader misses the layers of subjectivity. Does this matter? Do you think Shelley is just making a point about the importance and pervasiveness of storytelling, or is she commenting on the bias of any/every narrative perspective?
4. Think about and discuss, what each major 'teller' has to gain in his or her 'version' of the truth? [Walton, Victor, the Monster] How does this influence their ability to be objective? Have you ever experienced the problem of providing an objective description of something about which you have strong feelings?
5. While the text overtly vilifies men (in particular scientists), in what ways are women subtly made scapegoats in the text? Why do you think Mary makes this choice? Was she reflecting concerns of the day or making some other commentary?
6. Who do you feel is the "true" monster, Victor, his creation or both? Why?
7. One of the allusions in the text is a biblical one, referring to the story of the creation and fall of Man leading to the loss of paradise. How do these themes resonate with and repeat in the text? Which character is most aligned with God/ With Satan? Does this change? What commentary is Shelley making on the Human construction of understanding good and evil based on textual learning alone (versus experience)?
8. Another allusion is to the Myth of Prometheus. Prometheus created man out of clay and went against the Gods by giving Man fire to elevate civilization. The Gods, unhappy with the elevated status of mortals, punished Prometheus for all eternity. The subtitle for this text is, A Modern Prometheus. Victor clearly is the parallel character when comparing the myth and the story by Shelley. Do you think the 'moral' of each is the same or different? Is Victor punished for all eternity as well? What would be the equivalent of our Modern Day Prometheus? Would it be a scientist? A Political figure? Religious figure?
9. One of the important repeated 'figures' is that of the Outcast. Name the many outcasts in the story—and the circumstances around their isolation. Which have 'chosen' outcast status? Which have it thrust upon them?
10. The following characters are often seen as 'parallels' or 'foils.' Discuss what each pair has in common: Walton/Victor; Victor/Creature; Elizabeth/Creature; Victor/Eve/Pandora; Creature/Adam/Satan.

Essay Ideas

1. Research and explore the importance of Milton's "Paradise Lost" on this text.

2. Analyze the role of religion and science in the story. In what ways are they at odds? In what ways are they complementary?

3. Compare the following characters as foils for one another: Walton/Victor; Victor/Creature; Elizabeth/Creature; Victor/Eve/Pandora; Creature/Adam/Satan.

4. Compare the text of Frankenstein with one or more film adaptations, studying the alterations made to the original tale. Explore whether or not the changes reflect socio/historical shifts in cultures at the time.

5. Argue the theory that "Frankenstein" and his creature are both parts of the same personality. What traits do they share in common? When combined would they make a more 'complete' human? Is Victor exiling the creature in order to exile the parts of himself he does not like?

Wilkie Collins, pictured above, was born in 1824. He gained a reputation as one of the founders of the detective fiction genre with *Woman in White* and *The Moonstone*. *The Frozen Deep*, featured opposite, was first published in 1874. Photo: Library of Congress.

The Frozen Deep

by Wilkie Collins

Content Synopsis

"The Frozen Deep" began as a play meant for amateur production at Charles Dickens' Tavistock House. In its novel form, first published in 1874, it retains some of its theatrical aspects: short, dialogue-driven scenes involving a small number of characters, a rapidly paced plot, and sparse descriptive details. The novel opens on the eve of a two-vessel Arctic expedition around 1845 ("between twenty and thirty years ago," says the narrator) at a ball given in celebration of the upcoming voyage (3). Mrs. Lucy Crayford, one of the novel's five principal characters, is dancing with Captain Helding, who questions her about the other female lead, Clara Burnham. Over the course of the conversation, we learn that Clara is an orphan living under the Crayford's care. She is of delicate health, partly owing to some secret that has been oppressing her, and partly owing to her unusual education in the Scottish Highlands. There, Mrs. Crayford informs the captain, Clara's head was filled with all sorts of superstitious notions, chief among them the belief that she possesses the "Second Sight"—the ability to see into the future. Captain Helding is shocked by this revelation, particularly, as he says, "in these enlightened times" (5). He urges Mrs. Crayford to help her friend by becoming Clara's confidante and allowing her to unburden herself.

Mrs. Crayford takes the captain's advice and encourages Clara, who has just reacted with barely suppressed agitation to the news that a ship from Africa is due soon, to discuss the secret that is troubling her. During Mrs. Crayford's discussion with Clara, we learn of Clara's history prior to her father's death. While she was living with her invalid father in Kent, a gentleman named Richard Wardour met and fell in love with her. By Clara's account, Wardour was too bold while she was too passive, and Wardour left for Africa presuming he and Clara were engaged. Clara, who had been unable to disillusion him in person, sent him a letter explaining his erroneous belief and her intention not to marry him. Mrs. Crayford asks Clara why she is still troubled, to which Clara replies, "What I wrote required an answer, Lucy—asked for an answer. The answer has never come. What is the plain conclusion? My letter never reached him" (14).

To complicate matters further, Clara has fallen in love with young Frank Aldersley, and though Mrs. Crayford warns Clara not to engage herself to him until she has definitively broken things off with Richard Wardour, Clara cannot help but admit her love when Frank confronts her. Clara immediately realizes her error, but we are told, "It is Clara who says, 'Oh! What have I done?'—as usual, when it is too late" (18). Between Clara's inability to assert herself with Wardour and her similar inability to withhold her affection from Frank, the issue of whether Clara's weakness is to blame for subsequent events is raised. Clara, who embodies the feminine passivity idealized during the Victorian period, may represent Collins' subtle critique of this gender role.

Richard Wardour turns up in the next scene—his ship has arrived and he has come straight to the ball—and he is ready to marry Clara as he promised before he left. She informs him of his mistake, but when questioned about whether she has engaged herself to another, Clara equivocates. Wardour believes himself betrayed and leaves Clara with an ominous warning: "the man who has robbed me of you shall rue the day when you and he first met" (23).

Clara is filled with foreboding and she convinces Mrs. Crayford to go with her to see the ships off the next day. Frank, it turns out, has safely made it aboard, but the two women also discover that a new recruit has been added to the roster, none other than Richard Wardour. He and Frank are traveling to the Arctic on separate ships; however, Clara is still convinced a deadly meeting will take place between them.

The story here moves forward two years and relocates the narrative focus to the Arctic Expedition. The expedition is a complete failure: the ships have become locked in the ice, many of the men are ill, and slowly, all of the men are starving. The dark mood of the scene is slightly alleviated by his introduction of John Want, a member of the expedition whose constant grumbling during his preparation of "bone soup" provides some comic relief. It is decided that a group of the men will form an exploring party in search of aid while the others stay to care for those too weak or ill for traveling. Frank asks to be one of the party, but is told by Crayford that the men will throw dice for spots; "chance shall decide among us who goes with the expedition and who stays behind in the huts" (37). The conversation next turns to Wardour, whom Frank calls the "Bear of the Expedition" because of his surliness. The conversation makes clear that

although Frank has no liking for Wardour, the two men have yet to discover the woman they have in common.

The men all gather together to cast dice—a roll over six to go, under six to stay—and significantly, Wardour throws a six. The scene is the first in the novel where we see fate and chance so obviously collide. If Wardour is fated to confront Frank, as Clara believes, it won't matter what he rolls. Indeed, the indecisive cast of the die may be chance's way of bowing out of the situation altogether. Ultimately, Wardour ends up with a two (cast by Frank at his request), while Frank rolls an eight for himself. It seems as if the two men will be separated.

Wardour professes that he doesn't care whether he stays or goes, and Crayford questions him about his lack of spirit. In a scene that mirrors Clara's confession to Mrs. Crayford, Wardour relates his history with Clara (although without mentioning her name), and his desire for revenge upon the unknown man who stole her heart. Like Clara with her ominous premonition, Wardour is convinced that he shall one day meet this man: "it is no matter whether I stay here with the sick, or go hence with the strong. I shall live till I have met that man! There is a day of reckoning appointed between us" (47). Wardour's belief in fate has left him a passive participant in his own life. Crayford voices his disappointment with his friend's vengeful mindset, but offers to let Wardour chop up Frank's berth (for firewood) as a way to help Wardour get his mind off his troubles.

By this point in the novel, the reader has most likely noticed the appropriateness of Wardour's name. He has a war-like spirit, he will later be at war with himself, and he has more than his fair share of ardor, particularly for Clara's tastes. While Wardour is chopping up Frank's berth, we learn that this young man, too, is aptly named. His open, earnest love for Clara prompted him to carve their initials in one of the wooden beams of his berth, thus proving Frank far too frank for his own good. Wardour, seeing the initials, immediately suspects that he has discovered, in Frank Aldersley, the enemy upon which he has sworn vengeance. He confirms Frank's connection to Clara in a subsequent conversation with Frank and Crayford. Crayford also catches on that the girl Wardour loved is none other than Clara. Before Crayford has a chance to reflect on this, Captain Helding enters the cabin to inform them that a member of the exploring party has been injured and that Wardour is needed to fill his place. Thus, whether by fate or chance, Frank and Wardour will be thrown together after all.

This turn of events fills Crayford with dread and he tries to convince first Wardour and then Frank to forego the exploring party. Neither complies. Crayford is torn—he doesn't feel it is proper to say something to Frank about Wardour since Wardour hasn't actually committed any crime; however, he is worried about Frank's safety. In the end, he compromises, begging Frank "While you can stand, keep with the main body" (61).

Unfortunately, the very next scene finds Wardour and Frank alone, "alone on the Frozen Deep!" the narrator proclaims, and while a weakened Frank sleeps, Wardour struggles within himself, tempted to leave Frank to certain death and have his revenge (62). The scene cuts away before Wardour makes his decision, and the reader is returned to England where Clara and Mrs. Crayford patiently await news of the men in the Arctic. Clara slips into a trance and Mrs. Crayford watches in alarm as she cries out the same warning Crayford had given to Frank. Clara has a vision of Frank asleep and at Wardour's mercy—as we know he is from the previous scene. Clara comes out of her trance fatigued and weak, and Mrs. Crayford is left to wonder if Clara really does have the Second Sight.

The next day, news arrives that a whaling vessel has come across survivors of the Arctic expedition.

Crayford's name is on the list of survivors while Frank and Wardour are listed as "Dead or Missing." Clara sees this as confirmation that her vision was correct, while Mrs. Crayford argues that it is unchristian to give up hope. A doctor is called to treat the rapidly failing Clara, and he advises both women to journey out to meet the survivors and discover whether Frank and Wardour are, in fact, dead.

The two women sail for Newfoundland aboard, appropriately enough, the Amazon. The Crayfords are reunited, but there is still no news of Frank or Wardour. In fact, Crayford will give Clara none of the circumstances surrounding their disappearance. His wife has urged him to keep quiet on the subject because "she will accept it as positive confirmation of the faith, the miserable superstitious faith, that is in her" (86). Clara, frustrated at Crayford's guarded answers to her questions, decides to interview one of his men, Steventon, and thus learns of the events that led to the two men's disappearance. Frank, it seems, fell ill after the exploring party set out, and Wardour volunteered to remain with him while the rest went on. That was the last time they were seen.

Clara has another premonition that something "dreadful" is coming nearer, and Crayford takes her into the garden for some air. The moment after they leave, a "sinister and terrible" looking man appears at the door, begging for food. He is given some which he divides into two portions, one of which he stows in his satchel. Steventon and Mrs. Crayford question him and learn that he has been shipwrecked on the Newfoundland shore. He refuses to tell them why he saves half his food, but raves wildly about the young woman for whom he is searching.

At that moment, Crayford returns from the garden and immediately recognizes Wardour. He seizes his former friend and demands to know what has become of Frank. Hearing the two men's names, Clara also enters the cabin and Wardour, seeing her, rushes back onto the beach. He returns carrying Frank in his arms. The very weak Frank and Clara are reunited, while Wardour, his strength now used up, collapses in Crayford's arms, and relates the tale of his redemption. Clara, Frank, and Crayford gather around him as he says his final goodbyes, and with Wardour's death, the novel ends.

Historical Context

In 1856, Charles Dickens wrote from Paris to the sub-editor at his *Household Words* magazine, "Collins and I have a mighty original notion (mine in the beginning) for another Play at Tavistock House" (Ackroyd, 761). Dickens was referring to the theatrical version of "The Frozen Deep," which Collins wrote expressly for Dickens' annual "Twelfth Night" production. Both the play (which directly references it) and the subsequent novel are based on Sir John Franklin's ill-fated search for the Northwest Passage. Franklin, a popular public figure, had led two previous expeditions to the northern regions, but his 1845 voyage, consisting of two ships and over a hundred men, was to be his greatest undertaking. Search parties were sent after the expedition beginning in 1848, when the food supply would have run out, but it was not until Dr. John Rae's 1854 report that anything conclusive was known about Franklin and his men. Basing his report on interviews with Inuits in possession of artifacts from the expedition, Rae concluded that Franklin and his crew resorted to cannibalism, a charge that was hotly debated in the media. Dickens was one of Franklin's staunchest defenders, printing numerous articles in *Household Words* on the subject. Characteristic of the controversy, "an editorial writer [for the *Times*] argued that if Eskimos could live through 'starving times,' it would be 'strange indeed that the white men should not have been able to accomplish the same feat'" (Brannen 14).

The racism implicit in this statement points to the larger issue at stake in the debate: England's imperial ideology. Instead of spreading civilization's softening influence, if Franklin and his men had turned to cannibalism, they had become more savage than the native "savages." Lillian Naydor writes, "Because cannibalism was associated with the most primitive of cultures, Rae's allegations called into question the moral justification of Empire; it blurred the boundary between the savage and the civilized" (2).

Any reading of "The Frozen Deep" must consider this controversy. The complete order among the men of the Sea Mew and the Wanderer directly refutes the vision of chaos painted by Rae. The lengthy preparation of the "bone soup" would have called to the Victorian reader's mind Franklin and the charges brought against him and his men.

Societal Context

"The Frozen Deep" presents us with a typical view of Victorian society. The men in the novel go off on adventures while the women wait patiently at home. This separation of the sexes was idealized during the period (and by Wardour in his "No women!" proclamation). Women were thought to belong in the domestic sphere while men dominated the public sphere. When Clara and Mrs. Crayford step outside their domestic roles, Collins ironies the situation, having them sail aboard the Amazon as if their boldness puts them on a par with the fabled warrior women.

While it is not given much explicit attention, the novel is set against the backdrop of British imperialism—thus the mention of ships going to and from Africa, and the purpose of the Arctic expedition: to find the Northwest Passage, thought to be a potentially important trade route. Clara's dread of the returning African vessel and the failure of the Arctic expedition may be a subtle critique of the imperialist enterprise, against which Collins takes a stronger stance in "The Moonstone."

Religious Context

Collins' novel is both about a physical journey to the ends of the earth and about Richard Wardour's spiritual journey to the brink of temptation and back. In her essay on religion in "The Frozen Deep," Carolyn Oulton writes, "For Collins, the influence of religion is felt through a personal response to temptation" (158). In sending his hero to "the frozen deep" with his greatest temptation, the helpless, unconscious Frank Aldersley, Collins shows us a man stripped of all civilizing influences, with only his moral sense to guide him. Wardour's triumph over the fate both he and Clara believe in demonstrates the power of both faith and human agency.

Scientific & Technological Context

Early in "The Frozen Deep," Captain Helding refers to the novel's mid-Victorian setting as "these enlightened times," a characterization which is called into question almost immediately. While it is true that this was the period when railroads first criss-crossed the country, photography was invented, and major discoveries in geology and medicine began to shape our modern-day view of the world, it was also, as Mrs. Crayford says, a time when many "believe[d] in dancing tables, and in messages sent from the other world by spirits who can't spell" (5). Pseudo-sciences such as phrenology (the science of determining characteristics of personality based on the shape of the head) and physiognomy (the science of determining personality based on facial features), along with the spirit-rapping to which Mrs. Crayford refers, were held up alongside legitimate science, and it was a long time before the chaff was separated from the grain. Furthermore, scientific discoveries such as the extinction of species seemed, to many, to be a threat to firmly-held religious beliefs and the teachings of the Bible.

Collins seems skeptical of scientific pursuits throughout the novel. The doctor who treats Clara refers to her as his "interesting patient"—a specimen of sorts—and in his strict adherence to scientific knowledge, he is entirely dismissive of Clara's prophetic visions. Additionally, as Lillian Nayder notes, "Victorians conceived of Arctic exploration as a scientific rather than an economic undertaking" (2). In both repeating through fiction the historical failure of the expedition and in foregrounding Wardour's spiritual journey rather than his physical one, Collins leaves space in his novel for both the truths of science and the truths of spirituality to exist.

Biographical Context

Wilkie Collins (1824-1889) began his literary career with the publication of his father, the painter William Collins' biography, a work William had requested of his son shortly before his death in 1847. At the time of the biography's publication, Collins was unsure of what career path to follow. He enjoyed writing, and had already written one novel that failed to interest publishers, but he was also contemplating painting, the profession of his father and younger brother. At the same time, Collins was studying law at Lincoln's Inn, and in 1851 he became a barrister. Literature won out however, and after the 1850 publication of "Antonina," Collins dedicated himself to his literary career. His creative output marked him as one of the most prolific writers of the period. In less than forty years, he wrote twenty-three novels, fifteen plays, over fifty short stories, and more than one hundred nonfiction pieces. As Paul Lewis notes, scholars are still identifying all of his work. Chief among his novels are "The Woman in White" and "The Moonstone," works which solidified Collins' reputation as one of the founders of the detective fiction genre.

Collins owed some of his success to the encouragement and influence of his close friend, Charles Dickens. Dickens contributed ideas to the theatrical version of "The Frozen Deep," and in the Tavistock House production of the play, Dickens filled the role of Richard Wardour while Collins played Frank Aldersley. The production was a huge success, and in July of 1856, Collins and Dickens reprised their roles in a performance for Queen Victoria.

Although Collins never married, he had two long-term relationships, one with Caroline Graves (thought to be one of the sources for "The Woman in White"), and the other with Martha Rudd, with whom he had three children. Poor health due to gout and a dependency on opium led to Collins' death in September of 1889.

Jen Cadwallader

Works Cited

Ackroyd, Peter. *Dickens*. New York: Harper Collins, 1990.

Brannan, Robert Louis, ed. *Under the Management of Mr. Charles Dickens: His Production of The Frozen Deep*. Ithaca: Cornell UP, 1966.

Collins, Wilkie. *The Frozen Deep*. London: Hesperus, 2004.

Lewis, Paul. *The Wilkie Collins Pages*. 18 April 2006. http://www.wilkiecollins.com.

Naydor, Lillian. *The Cannibal, The Nurse, and The Cook in Dickens, The Frozen Deep*. Victorian Literature and Culture 19: 1–24, 1991.

Oulton, Carolyn. *A Vindication of Religion: Wilkie Collins, Charles Dickens, and The Frozen Deep*. Dickensian 97(2): 154–158, 2001.

Robinson, Kenneth. *Wilkie Collins, A Biography*. New York: MacMillan, 1952.

Discussion Questions

1. The narrative of "The Frozen Deep" shifts in and out of present tense. Is there any significance to Collins' use of the present tense? How does it affect your reading of the novel?

2. We learn of Clara first through Mrs. Crayford's opinion of her. How does this color your perception of Clara? Do you ever disagree with Mrs. Crayford's assessment of her friend?

3. Collins employs heavy foreshadowing through Wardour's threat and Clara's premonition. Is this foreshadowing ever ironic? How does it relate to the theme of fate versus chance that is so pervasive in the text?

4. Do you believe that Clara has the Second Sight, or do you agree with Mrs. Crayford's notion that Clara has been influenced by her reading material?

5. Analyze John Want's character. Why does he have a prominent role in some scenes of the novel?

6. Wardour proclaims that he likes the Arctic "because there are no women here" (40). What is the significance of the separation of the sexes in the novel?

7. Compare Wardour's account of his relationship with Clara to her account of it. Are there any significant differences? If so, what do these differences reveal about the two characters?

8. Is Crayford wrong not to warn Frank about Wardour's possible intentions toward him?

9. Has Wardour redeemed himself by the end of the novel?

10. What is the significance of Wardour's death?

Essay Ideas

1. Clara says, "[Wardour and Frank] will meet — there will be a mortal quarrel between them — and I shall be to blame" (24). Is she to blame for the conflict between the two men? Support or refute her claim using evidence from the text.

2. Analyze the way in which this novel complicates traditional notions of the literary hero.

3. Analyze the role of friendship in the novel.

4. Analyze the interplay of fate, chance, and free agency in the novel.

5. Analyze the symbolism of the Arctic in the novel.

OLIVER TWIST ASKS FOR MORE.

Representative Sereno E. Payne, who will have charge of the Tariff bill on the floor of the House, does not know whether the people declared for radical or moderate revision of the Tariff on election day. — *The Sun.*

Characters in the illustration above are borrowed from Charles Dickens' *Oliver Twist* for a Progressive-era satire in *Puck* magazine. This classic tale of class division is featured on page 153 of this volume. Dickens, the most widely read and studied of English novelists, was born in 1812, in Portsmouth, England. Photo: Library of Congress.

The Golden Compass

by Philip Pullman

"Barnard and Stokes were two [...] 'renegade' theologians who postulated the existence of numerous other worlds like this one, neither heaven nor hell, but material and sinful. They are there close by, but invisible and unreachable. The Holy Church naturally disapproved of this abominable heresy, and Barnard and Stokes were silenced."

—Philip Pullman, *The Golden Compass*

Content Synopsis

"The Golden Compass" is the first volume in a series of novels, "His Dark Materials" (a trilogy to date). Initially released by a publishing company associated with younger readers, "The Golden Compass" has proved to be "crossover" fiction, that is, suitable for and equally popular with readers of all ages.

The story is set in a world and time parallel to our own, but with important differences. The power of the Church is absolute, and articulated through a tangle of rival colleges, councils, boards, and courts. Ideas, which in our world would be explored by scientists, are in this world investigated, or suppressed, by theologians.

The story opens in a parallel Oxford, in the Hall of Jordan College. Lyra Belacqua, a twelve year-old girl who has been brought up by the male Fellows of the college, wants to see the innermost sanctum of the Fellows, their Retiring Room. Hiding in a cupboard to avoid discovery, she inadvertently sees the Master of the college poison the wine to be offered to her uncle, the arrogant and powerful Lord Asriel, an explorer who is due to give a talk at the college that evening about his latest expedition. Lyra warns her uncle, who orders her back into the cupboard, and tells her to observe the Fellows' reaction to his talk. When we meet Lyra, we also meet something inseparable from her. In this world, everyone has a demon, a creature in the form of an animal which is invisibly but closely connected to them. The demon could be interpreted as the spirit or soul, or anima/animus; in all but a very few cases males have a female demon and females a male; but it acts as an independent entity. The connection is emotional and affectionate; the actions of the demon can express the emotional state of the human, and when the person dies, the demon disappears. The demons of children shape-shift according to mood or need. Lyra's demon, Pan, short for Pantalaimon, can be a mouse and hide in her pocket, or an ermine, his favorite sleeping-form, or a bird, to fly to seek something out, or an inconspicuous moth, as when we first see him. Once the child reaches puberty, the demon begins to choose one form more and more often, and by adulthood, when the young adult's character is fully established, has fixed on one kind of animal.

Lord Asriel shows the Fellows three things during his lecture. The first is evidence of the existence of Dust and its relationship to children. Dust particles, invisible to the naked eye, come from the sky in streams. The second is some slides, taken on his expedition to the Arctic region of their world, which show what seems to be a city skyline in the middle of the Aurora Borealis, otherwise known as the Northern Lights. Lyra hears one of the scholars mention the names Barnard and Stokes in connection with this, but the reference means nothing to her. The third thing Asriel mentions is evidence of what happened to the last expedition to the Northern Lights, the scalped and trepanned head of its leader, Stanislaus Grumman.

The Master of the college had been willing to kill Lord Asriel because he had been warned of appalling consequences should Asriel's research continue—consequences that would involve Lyra. The warning comes from an alethiometer, a truth-measure, one of only six ever made. It is a complex device, and thus very difficult to interpret. The Master knows that something momentous is going to happen, that there will be a terrible betrayal, and that Lyra will be the betrayer. He wants to protect her for as long as possible, but knows that he cannot for much longer.

Lyra is by no means a typical heroine: "She was a coarse and greedy little savage" and has passed her childhood "like a half-wild cat" (37). She is graceless and unkempt, lies, boasts, and steals, but is also brave, loyal, energetic, and clear-sighted. She dislikes being cleaned up, having lessons, paying attention, sitting still, and authority. She enjoys playing on the roofs and in underground passages, crypts, and cellars of the college with her best friend, Roger, the kitchen boy, leading her gang, fighting rival gangs, and fraternizing with the Gyptians (water gypsies) on the rivers and canals of Oxford. However, the gangs are diminishing. All over the country, children are disappearing. Rumor suggests that they have been taken by the "Gobblers." One day, Roger is missing.

Shortly after Roger's disappearance, Lyra is introduced to the beautiful Mrs. Coulter and told that she is to live with her in future. Before Lyra leaves, the Master gives her the alethiometer, advising her to hide it from Mrs. Coulter. In London, Mrs. Coulter buys Lyra fine clothes, takes her to parties, and makes much of her. She also, however, shows an implacable, even cruel side. When Lyra displeases her, Mrs. Coulter's golden monkey demon hurts Pan. Lyra learns that Lord Asriel is a prisoner in the far north, that Mrs. Coulter is working for the Genera Oblation Board of the Church, which she discovers is the origin of the nickname "Gobblers," and that her work involves the capture of children. Lyra escapes Mrs. Coulter and hides in the back streets of London. Two men almost capture her, but she is rescued by one of her Gyptian friends, Tony Costa.

The Costas are on their way to join John Faa, Lord of the Western Gyptians. They take Lyra with them in their boat, hiding her from the many people searching for her. John Faa tells Lyra the true story of her birth, her 'uncle,' Lord Asriel is really her father, and her mother is a beautiful scholar, wife of the politician Edward Coulter. As a baby, Lyra was given into the care of a Gyptian woman and hidden on Lord Asriel's estates. When Edward Coulter came looking for the child, her nurse fled with her to Asriel's house, where Asriel challenged Coulter to a duel, and killed him. As a result, the courts confiscated Asriel's property and land, and ordered the child to be placed with nuns. Asriel, however, stole her back, and hid her in Jordan College, where the Gyptians have been watching over Lyra ever since. Although Asriel stipulated that Lyra's mother should never be allowed to see her, her mother's position in the machinery of the Church is now so high that she could not be stopped. Her mother, Lyra learns, is Mrs. Coulter.

The Egyptians decide to send an expedition north to rescue the children kidnapped by the "Gobblers." John Faa finds that Lyra is learning how to use the alethiometer, which could help them to find the missing children, and so reluctantly allows her to go with them.

On the journey north, they meet beautiful witches, a Texan balloon aeronaut, Lee Scoresby, an armored warrior-bear, Iorek Byrnison, and what they think at first is a ghost. The 'ghost' is alive, just (in this world an obscene, terrible, unthinkable thing) a child without a demon: "A human being with no demon was like someone without a face, or with their ribs laid open and their heart torn out" (215). The purpose of the Oblation Board becomes clear. They are the perpetrators of an unspeakable cruelty: separating children from their demons. The child, unbearably bereft, dies.

Lyra is captured by hunters and sold to the experimental station run by the Oblation Board. Roger and Billy Costa are among the children held there, and the three find both the place where children and demons are separated, and the caged and fading severed demons. Mrs. Coulter arrives at the station and the children fake a fire drill in order to release them. Lyra is caught, and she and Pan are put into the separator and prepared for "intercission." Mrs. Coulter stops the process just in time, and Lyra escapes again. She organizes the children into a gang, and they try to fight their way past the guards and their wolf demons. Just in time, witches, and Iorek Byrnison arrive, and the children escape, only to have to face a long march across the frozen Arctic. Mrs. Coulter nearly snatches Lyra and Roger, again, but a witch clan-queen, Serafina Pekkala, saves them and Lee Scoresby carries them away.

Serafina Pekkala knows that although Lyra believes she came north to find and rescue her friend, in fact she was destined to follow Roger north in order to bring something important to her father. Lyra thinks it is the alethiometer, but in fact, it is Roger. Asriel has learned how to harness the immense energy released when child and demon are separated. He wants to enter the other world he knows exists, to trace the source of Dust, which he has deduced is an elementary particle; a particle that alters its nature "when innocence becomes experience" (373). Dust, he says, is what theologians call original sin. He has come to the same conclusion as the Oblation Board, though for different reasons; Dust must be destroyed. He tells Lyra that somewhere is the origin of Dust and therefore of "all the death, the sin, the misery, the destructiveness in the world," and goes on: "[h]uman beings can't see anything without wanting to destroy it, Lyra. That's original sin. And I'm going to destroy it. Death is going to die" (377). He severs Lyra's friend Roger from his demon in order to release the energy that will open a window between worlds, killing Roger in the process. Mrs. Coulter arrives and is briefly reconciled with Asriel, but refuses to join his cause. He goes through into the other world, and Lyra, knowing that he is wrong, that if the Oblation Board believe Dust to be an evil, it must be good, follows her father.

Historical Context

The story was published in the UK in 1995 under the title "Northern Lights." When it was published in the US, an editor changed the title to "The Golden Compass." Philip Pullman did not acquiesce, but his web site reports that at the time he did not have the influence to do anything about it. The story is more or less contemporary, as we see from the next volume in the trilogy, "The Subtle Knife," which is primarily set in our own world. Though parallel in time, to readers from our world, Lyra's world seems like a mixture of periods. Her world includes an all-powerful church with complex church hierarchy belonging to the middle ages or Renaissance; regions yet to be fully explored or "discovered" by the west; early modern to eighteenth-century technology; and a few developments from the nineteenth century (such as hot air balloons).

Societal Context

The societal contexts of "The Golden Compass" are inextricably bound up with its religious and technological contexts. The society it depicts is both like and unlike our own, and could be seen as an allegory of and warning to our own society. Within Lyra's world, we are shown a number of distinct societies, each providing different ways of interpreting, ordering, and understanding life. The witches are beautiful and magical, and have great longevity, but their society is based on a clan system and driven by political conflict. The bears led by Iorek are strong and loyal, and skilled craftsmen. Their society is organized and effective, but militaristic and oppressive to all but the leaders. The Gyptians are resourceful, able to make and mend and make-do with almost nothing. Their society is family-oriented, and led by wise and experienced elders, but they are on the larger society's lower rungs. The Fellows at Jordan College are scholarly, well intentioned, and kindly, but isolated, unworldly, and ultimately ineffective. Their society has narrowed down to the confines of college and the books under their noses. The Church is highly effective, and has managed to dominate the wider society, but its own labyrinthine construction weakens it as courts and councils jockey for power, negating each other's actions.

In our own world, this volume and the sequence have received critical acclaim and become bestsellers, bought by and for both adults and children. Michael Chabon, in "Dust and Demons," suggests that much in the novels is of questionable suitability for children, including the complex character of Lyra, but adds that the ambivalent character of the stories and their crossover appeal relates to the themes of the stories themselves (5).

Religious Context

The title of the series comes from Book II of John Milton's epic poem, "Paradise Lost," and refers to the "dark materials" of God; the elements from which he has made the world and from which, if he so ordains, he will make more worlds. Milton was a Christian and a Puritan at the time of the English Civil War, Oliver Cromwell's Protectorate, and the subsequent Restoration of the monarchy in Britain. His great poem tells the story of original sin, of the choice made by Eve that led to the expulsion from Eden. It has often been said that Milton inadvertently made Satan the most interesting character in his poem; an energetic and compelling character whose rhetoric is powerful. A parallel character in "His Dark Materials" is the leader of the rebellion against religious authority, Lord Asriel.

Although "Paradise Lost" is a Christian poem, Pullman uses its themes to make the case against organized religion; suggesting that the church has used the threat of damnation and the promise of an everlasting afterlife to keep people in subjection, and that ignorance rather than innocence is the state it desires in its subjects. "His Dark Materials" depicts a parallel "fall" which involves not a choice and a loss of innocence, but rather than a sin to be deplored and expiated for all time, it is a sign of humanity's finally coming of age and abandoning the superstitions and childlike dependencies of its prolonged childhood.

Another important influence is the work of William Blake. Like Blake's poetry and engravings, Pullman's trilogy expresses a mistrust of authority, particularly self-proclaimed and absolute, unfounded authority. The God of this trilogy, "The Authority," an angel of incredible age, is like the authoritarian and aloof patriarch in Blake's poem "To Nobodaddy," an ancient, bearded old man, who has become an excuse for the exercise of earthly powers. The opponent of that God and his Regent, and thus a "Satan" figure, (though for much of the trilogy he doesn't fully understand) has a name reminiscent of one of Blake's rebel angel-type figures, Asriel. In the philosophy of the trilogy, both this God and those who use worship of him as their vehicle of power must be destroyed. Humankind must depend upon itself, not a father-figure; must cease to base its happiness on a belief in future life, and concentrate on truly living this life; must cease blindly to obey the dictates of religion, and work out a true moral code. The trilogy could be seen as a response or alternative world-view to children's fiction with an overtly Christian message, such as "The Narnia Stories" by C. S. Lewis.

In a review published in *The Times*, Erica Wager called this "remarkable writing: courageous and dangerous, as the best art should be," and asserted that: "Pullman envisions a world without God, but not without hope" (12).

Scientific & Technological Context

In Lyra's world, Enlightenment rationalism has not become the dominant mode of thought that it has in our own world, and that which in our world would be scientific or technological discourses are in this world closer to the philosophical or alchemical discourses of the eighteenth century and earlier. Technological developments have been made, but there are no internal combustion engines, no nuclear power, and no computers. There are hot air balloons and Zeppelins, but no airplanes; the Retiring Room at Jordan College is lit by lamps, and Asriel's lantern has to be hand-pumped. "Anbaric" lights are relatively rare. As well as technologically developed artifacts, there are also things that in our world would belong in the realm of the mystical, mythical, or magic: the alethiometer; the witches and their pine-cloud flying sticks; sentient bears; a "spy fly" device; and, of course, demons. Ideas and theories which we now take for granted, such as quantum mechanics, chaos theory, the divisibility of the atom, and the possible existence of multiple universes, are heresy in Lyra's world, and those who disseminate them are silenced. Nonetheless, much of the plot rests upon what we would call "real" science.

Biographical Context

Philip Pullman studied English at Exeter College, Oxford, on which he loosely based his Jordan College. While he was writing the trilogy, he was living in Oxford, working in a shed at the back of his garden. Before becoming a full-time writer, he was a schoolteacher for a number of years and later taught trainee teachers at Westminster College, also in Oxford. He was therefore very well acquainted with contemporary and classic children's literature before he began writing it. He has been the awarded several prizes, including the Carnegie Medal, the Guardian Children's Book Award, the Astrid Lindgren Award (with illustrator Ryoji Arai), the *Publishers' Weekly* Best Book of the Year Award, and the Whitbread Book of the Year Award (for "The Amber Spyglass," the third in the "His Dark Materials" trilogy), in the first instance of that prize going to a book classified as for children (though read by many adults). Pullman produced illustrations for the first two volumes of the trilogy and small pictures as running heads for the second, to indicate which world the characters are in at the time. These were not printed in the first US editions of the novels, but are present in the 2002 editions published by Knopf.

Sandie Byrne

Works Cited

Chabon, Michael, ed. *Dust and Demons. Navigating the Golden Compass: Religion, Science and Dæmonology in Philip Pullman's His Dark Materials*. Glen Yeffeth. Dallas, Texas: Benbella, 2005.

Gribbin, Mary and John Gribbin. *The Science of Philip Pullman's 'His Dark Materials.'* New York: Knopf, 2005.

Pullman, Philip, *Northern Lights*. London: Scholastic, 1995; reprint, 2001. US edition, *The Golden Compass*. New York: Knopf, 1996; reprint, Laurel Leaf, 2003.

Wagner, Erica, review of His Dark Materials, *The Times* (18 October, 2000) T2, 12.

For Further Study

Gribbin, Mary and John. *The Science of 'His Dark Materials'* http://www.randomhouse.com/features/pullman/index.html

Philip Pullman's home pages at http://www.philip-pullman.com

Discussion Questions

1. How does Philip Pullman establish sympathy for Lyra without falling into sentimentality or mawkishness?
2. How well do Philip Pullman's representations create a sense of real children in real childhoods?
3. How is Mrs. Coulter invested with a sense of menace before we know her real purpose?
4. At what point in reading the novel do we realize that it is not set in our own world, and how do we learn this?
5. What are readers' initial responses to Lord Asriel and Mrs. Coulter likely to be? Do these change later in the novel?
6. At what point in the book do readers learn about Lyra's destiny and why does she not learn of it at the same time?
7. Why is the alethiometer a better and more interesting device in the novel than another prediction device such as a crystal ball would be?
8. In what ways do Pullman's witches differ from traditional representations of the witch?
9. The UK edition of the novel is called "Northern Lights." What is the significance of the Northern Lights (Aurora Borealis) in the story?
10. Some aspects of the story might seem frightening or upsetting for younger readers. How does Philip Pullman handle these?

Essay Ideas

1. Write about Philip Pullman's creation of the demon and its importance, not as a plot device but in terms of imaginative writing.
2. Discuss moral and other ambiguities of characters in the novel.
3. How does the passage from John Milton's "Paradise Lost" set the themes of the novel?
4. How does Philip Pullman avoid the trap of sentimental anthropomorphism in his depictions of talking animals such as the armored bears?
5. Discuss the ways in which science, philosophy, and religion overlap in the novel.

Charles Dickens, pictured above, was the eldest son of a naval pay clerk who was imprisoned for debts when Dickens was 12 years old. Subsequent events let to his lasting sympathy with the poor and dispossessed and antipathy toward oppressive social systems. This volume features Dickens' *Hard Times*, opposite, and *Oliver Twist*, page 153. Photo: Designed by Jim DuPlessis with images from Library of Congress.

Hard Times

by Charles Dickens

Content Synopsis
Book 1: Sowing

The novel begins in the school owned by Mr. Gradgrind, a retired hardware merchant who is about to enter politics, and we see that in this school, education consists of filling the children with facts and limiting their imagination as much as possible. The star pupil, Bitzer, is the product of this process and he is contrasted with Sissy Jupe, who has just come to the school and who represents a natural child, for whom imagination is more important that facts.

On his way home from his model school, Gradgrind finds two of his own children, Tom and Louisa, trying to see into Sleary's circus. This is where Sissy's father works as a clown. He has discussed the situation with his friend, Josiah Bounderby, a self-made industrialist and Gradgrind decides Sissy's influence is responsible for his children's actions. She must be expelled from school. The two men go to the circus to inform Sissy's father of their decision, but they learn that he has abandoned Sissy believing that she will have a better chance in life without him. The circus people are portrayed as warm-hearted and well meaning, in contrast to the emotional coldness in Gradgrind's family and the harshness of Bounderby's attitude. Gradgrind agrees to take Sissy into his family on condition that she severs all ties with the circus. Although Louisa and Sissy do not become close friends, they are shown to be sympathetic to each other, in contrast to Tom's exploitation of Louisa's love for him.

The focus shifts to Coketown and the weaving works owned by Bounderby. We are introduced to one of the workers (or "Hands"), Stephen Blackpool, who is portrayed as a man of great integrity and kindness. He returns home after a long day's work to find a woman, whom we later discover is his alcoholic wife, in his room. She is contrasted with Stephen's friend, Rachel, whom he clearly loves but regards as unattainable because he is married. The following day, Stephen goes to his employer to find out how to get a divorce, but he is treated unsympathetically by Bounderby and his housekeeper, Mrs. Sparsit, and it is made clear to him that divorce is possible for rich people only. Bounderby is revealed as a snob and the marriage laws are shown to be unjust. As he leaves Bounderby's house, Stephen meets a mysterious old woman who shows a great deal of curiosity about his employer. He reaches his home to find Rachel looking after his drunken wife, and falling asleep in the chair, he has a troubled dream in which marriage, death, and condemnation are intermixed. He awakens as his wife is about to drink from a bottle of poison that has been used to dress her wounds. Although he does nothing to stop her, Rachel awakens in time to snatch the bottle. Stephen declares Rachel to be an angel who makes him a better man than he would otherwise be.

Time passes and we learn that Sissy is still with the Gradgrinds and is still resistant to learning the facts which pass for education, but that Tom has gone to work for Bounderby in his bank. Bounderby's proposal of marriage to Louisa is relayed to her by her father. Despite their disparity in age and the fact that she does not love him, Louisa accepts the proposal. On hearing this news, Sissy gives Louisa a look "in wonder, in pity, in sorrow" (106) but this offends Louisa, bringing the sympathy between the two young women to an end. Book 1 ends with the wedding of Louisa and Bounderby.

Book 2: Reaping

Mrs. Sparsit and Bitzer, now both residential workers in the bank, express their disapproval of the action of the factory hands in "Combining" or joining together in a trade union. They do this in terms that reveal their hypocrisy, for they approve of the union of the masters: "'It is much to be regretted,' said Mrs. Sparsit 'that the united masters allow of any such class-combinations. Being united themselves they ought one and all to set their faces against employing any man who is united with any other man'" (119). They also reveal their disapproval of Tom Gradgrind as a "dissipated, extravagant idler" (121) who is tolerated mainly because he is Bounderby's brother-in-law. James Harthouse appears with a letter of introduction from Mr. Gradgrind and is accepted into the Bounderby family circle. Clearly intrigued by Louisa, Harthouse recognizes her emotional links with Tom and sets about getting to know him, aware that this could be to his advantage.

The scene shifts once more to Bounderby's factory where the trade union leader, Slackbridge, is addressing the workers. Stephen refuses to join their action and the other Hands vote to ostracize him as a result. Stephen is called into Bounderby's presence and questioned about the action and the workers' decision to cut all ties with him. His answers being unsatisfactory, Stephen is classified as a troublemaker and loses his job. As he leaves Bounderby's house, he meets the mysterious old woman again, this time in Rachel's company. They return to Stephen's lodgings for tea, where they are visited by Louisa and Tom. Louisa offers Stephen financial help and he reluctantly borrows some money from her until he can find work. Tom draws Stephen aside and offers to do him a "good turn" (164) which involves hanging around outside the bank for an hour each night until he leaves Coketown. Stephen does this, but nothing comes of it.

Harthouse decides to engage Louisa's emotions if possible, and discovers that Tom is in debt and has been borrowing money from her. When the bank is robbed soon afterwards, Louisa half suspects Tom has been involved somehow, but everyone else believes Stephen, in league with the mysterious old woman, is the culprit. After the robbery, Mrs. Sparsit lives with the Bounderbys, and begins spying on Louisa and Harthouse as part of her strategy for estranging Louisa and Bounderby. When she hears an assignation being arranged between Harthouse and Louisa, she follows Louisa but loses her somewhere in Coketown. Louisa returns to her father's house to ask his advice in dealing with a situation for which her education in his system has left her totally unprepared. At the end of an emotionally draining meeting between father and daughter, Louisa faints.

Book 3: Garnering

Louisa awakens in her old home, overcomes her resentment of Sissy, and accepts her help in dealing with Harthouse, who is persuaded to leave Coketown immediately. In the meantime, Mrs. Sparsit has reported to Bounderby the conversation she overheard, and together they go to inform Gradgrind of his daughter's behavior but are disconcerted to find her there. Gradgrind asks that Louisa be allowed to recover in her old home for a few days, Bounderby refuses, stating that she must return to him within 24 hours or not at all. When that time has elapsed, he has all her personal belongings sent to her father's house: the marriage is over.

The focus changes again to pubic life, and when Bounderby publicly accuses Stephen of the bank robbery, the factory workers, led by Slackbridge, condemn their former colleague without giving him the right of defense. Only Rachel still believes him innocent and she writes to him, confident that he will return to clear his name. She also tells Bounderby of Louisa and Tom's visit, which Louisa confirms. Mrs. Sparsit in the meantime tracks down the old woman, and drags her into Bounderby's presence where, in the presence of many witnesses, including Rachel and Sissy, she is revealed as Bounderby's mother whom he pays to keep away. Bounderby's boasts of being an abandoned, neglected child who has made good by his own efforts are lies.

Stephen is still absent, and the following Sunday Sissy and Rachel walk out into the countryside, where they find him at the bottom of a disused mine, where he had fallen as he made his way back to Coketown at night to refute the robbery charges. He is gravely injured, but before he dies, he asks Gradgrind to clear his name for him, suggesting that Tom might know something about the robbery. When Sissy hears this, she tells Tom to escape to Sleary's circus.

Gradgrind make plans to ship Tom out of the country, before he, Louisa, and Sissy go to the circus to confront him. After some discussion with his father and sister, Tom is just about to leave when he is held by Bitzer, who, suspecting him from the beginning, had followed Gradgrind to the circus. An appeal is made to Bitzer's feelings in an attempt to release Tom, but Bitzer's education under the Gradgrindian system has eradicated all feelings. An attempt is then made to buy him off, but this also fails because as he argues, "to compound a felony, even on very high terms indeed, would not be as safe and good for me as my improved prospects at the Bank" (287). Although

Sleary seems to agree that Tom must go with Bitzer, he arranges for a successful rescue attempt and Tom escapes abroad.

Sleary tells Gradgrind of the reappearance at the circus of the dog owned by Sissy's father, and his inference from this that Jupe is dead. Further discussion between Sleary and Gradgrind, together with Sleary's refusal to take money for helping Tom, reveals to Gradgrind that some things cannot be measured and are without price: fact and reason are not at the centre of the universe after all.

"Hard Times" ends with an outline of the futures of each of the main characters: Bounderby dismisses Mrs. Sparsit from his service and dies of a fit within 5 years; Gradgrind's philosophy mellows despite the mockery of former colleagues; Rachel returns to her old job; Sissy marries and has a family, and Tom dies of fever on his way home to see Louisa. Louisa herself having "grown learned in childish lore" (297) attempts to infuse the lives of others with imagination and finds greater satisfaction and happiness in the latter part of her life.

The slight reminder here of fairy tales is no coincidence, for "Hard Times" is in part a demonstration of Dickens' belief that "in a utilitarian age, of all other times, it is a matter of grave importance that Fairy tales should be respected for a nation without fancy. . ." ("Frauds on the Fairies," 168). In "Hard Times," Dickens looks at the ways in which imagination and fancy can redeem the heartlessness of modern industrial life.

Historical Context

The Industrial Revolution of the late eighteenth and early nineteenth centuries brought massive changes: machinery speeded up manufacturing processes, increasing production and concentrating what had been widely-spread cottage working into factories built in the new industrial towns which were tightly packed with low-grade housing for the workers. Wealth no longer depended upon ownership of land, but on ownership of factories or industrial processes, leading to the development of the "noveau riche," or rich middle class.

Britain was fast emerging as a capitalist society with employment practices based on cash in return for a certain amount of work done replacing the more traditional modes of employment derived from feudalism in which the employer had certain inherited responsibilities towards the employed. This resulted in employment based on the employers' needs, and the prospect of starvation for workers during periods of recession.

The situation was made worse for the workers by the dominant laissez-faire political thought which insisted that there should be no governmental interference, such as legislation setting an acceptable level of pay, or stipulating the maximum number of hours which could be worked in a week: even factory legislation limiting the hours which could be worked by children was bitterly opposed. Coupled with laissez-faire capitalism was the socio-political doctrine of Utilitarianism, which sought the greatest good for the greatest possible number of people. Although this is exemplified in "Hard Times" by Gradgrind, with Coketown itself being the "physical and metaphorical expression of a deliberate system" (Brooks, 63) which is the result of that coupling, it is Sissy who makes the most direct comment upon Utilitarianism, for when asked to comment on the death rate if twenty five people starve to death out of a population of one million, she replies that "it must be just as hard upon those who were starved, whether the others were a million or a million million" (62).

These conditions spawned political activism, with the Chartist National Convention of 1848 drawing up a Charter to demand universal male suffrage, payment for Members of Parliament and the secret ballot, as well as factory legislation and modification of the 1834 Poor Laws which limited the types of assistance which could be offered to the unemployed and which were seen as very harsh measures. (Dickens exposes the inhumanity of these Poor Laws in the early chapters of Oliver Twist [1837].) Although Chartism was generally non-violent, many people saw it as a parallel of the revolutionary movements sweeping Europe in 1848, prompting fears of revolution in Britain.

Chartism was largely spent as a political force by 1854 when Dickens began writing "Hard Times," but industrial unrest continued, especially in the north of England. The most famous example of this was the Preston lock-out or strike when some cotton-mill owners in Preston, Lancashire, refused to reinstate a 10% reduction in the workers' wages made during the economic recession of 1847. In the summer of 1853 the workers went on strike in protest, but on 15th October 1853 the Preston Masters' Association closed the mills, effectively leaving 20,000 workers without work or any means of support except the subscriptions made by workers from mills in the surrounding area. Dickens was sympathetic to the demands for factory reform (less so to the calls for parliamentary reform) and on 28 January 1854 he traveled to Preston to see for himself what was happening. Although convinced the workers were in error, it is clear he had sympathy for them as well as for the employers, for he argued:

> [I]f it be the case that some of the highest virtues of the working people still shine through them brighter than ever in their conduct of this mistake of theirs, perhaps the fact may reasonably suggest to me—and to others beside me—that there is some little thing wanting in their relations between them and their employers, which neither political economy not Drum-head proclamation writing will altogether supply, and which we cannot too soon or too temperately unite in trying to find out (On Strike, 200).

Much of Dickens' thought on this issue can be traced on the characters and situations he created in "Hard Times," with Stephen Blackpool and

Rachel representing the best working class types, while the other workers are depicted as honest but vulnerable to manipulation by Slackbridge, the leader of the Combination, whose character is based on one of the Preston workers' leaders. Bounderby represents the factory owners, and Mrs. Sparsit is a member of the respectable classes who has come down in the world and is dependent upon the wealth of the new manufacturing class.

These historical conditions were reflected in the rise of the realist novel, in which readers are persuaded they are being shown what life was actually like in that time and place. Viewed in this way, however, "Hard Times" is strangely unsatisfactory: the characters are unconvincing, the storyline involving Stephen Blackpool's wife is poorly integrated, and the final resolution fails to merge the personal and the public storylines. In many respects, therefore, it is more satisfactory to see this work as a romance, a narrative form closer to fairy tale than to realist novel. Romance operates on its own laws, usually portraying characters less as fully rounded people than as stylized figures verging on archetypes. Sissy, for example, is a redemptive figure representing higher values (such as imagination and disinterested love) which escape the harsh philosophy embodied by Bitzer and Bounderby while Sleary's circus is a source of imagination and life always located on the edge of Coketown, unable to invade the locus of industrialization where men become part of the machine, but always representing the possibility of freedom.

The romance aspect of "Hard Times" is linked to its main theme which is the death of romance and imagination, which cannot flourish in the industrial town dedicated to making money and "getting on." This is established in the opening schoolroom scene where Sissy's endorsement of the imagination in her willingness to have a floral pattern on a carpet is overturned by the teacher's instruction that "you are not to see anywhere, what you don't see in fact; you are not to have anywhere, what you don't have in fact" (13), but it is continued in the Gradgrind family who are told "never wonder" (54) and extended even to the factory workers who are reduced to "Hands" (68), a part of the anatomy that has the facility for work, but not for wonder, imagination or thought.

Societal Context

The historical events and trends of the period had three main effects. Firstly, the move towards a capitalist society loosened the traditional bonds between employers and employed which was a feature of feudalism.

Secondly, although the Industrial Revolution enabled a few people to make fortunes, for the majority work was hard, hours were long, job security unheard of and starvation during periods of economic recession an ever-present threat. Housing needs were worked out on the principle of the greatest number of people in the smallest possible space, so living conditions were cramped and dirty, leading to periodic outbreaks of cholera and typhus. Factory owners, however, lived in large houses on the outskirts of towns, where the air was clean, and the water unpolluted.

Historical conditions, in other words, created a society in which there was an unbridgeable chasm between employers and the employed, between the "haves" and the "have-nots." This in turn led to the class antagonism which is a major theme of this work. According to one critic, "Hard Times" ostensibly proposes that "social cohesion can be achieved by changing the relationship between family and society, by introducing cooperative behavior, presumably preserved in family life, into the public realm" (Gallagher, 147). However, the Gradgrindian system of education, applied to the family no less than to society, with its emphasis on fact and reason has already destroyed the means of creating cooperative behavior, and the end of the book reveals a retreat from social concerns to the relative safety of one particular family which has been enriched and modified by the emotional values embodied by Sissy.

Finally, we could note that the interaction between laissez-faire political thought, capitalism, and Utilitarianism created a society in which people were systematically dehumanized. This is underlined in "Hard Times" by the sense of an inner life in Louisa, Stephen, and Rachel (all victims of the system) in contrast to the hollow emptiness of Bitzer, Bounderby, and Gradgrind as he is depicted in the first two books. The power of the system is suggested not only by the visual metaphor of Coketown, but by the fact that Stephen is destroyed by it, while Louisa can only escape from it by escaping from her marriage and returning to her father's home which has been softened under the influence of Sissy Jupe, a circus child whose origins lie beyond the system itself. Surely, Dickens was not just concerned with the effects capitalism and Utilitarianism had on people's living conditions, but as Chris Brooks notes, "it is System's effect upon man's sense of being that matters to Dickens" (66).

Religious Context

Religion in England during the nineteenth century was overwhelmingly Christian and predominantly Protestant, with a wide range of denominations including the Methodists, and the Evangelical Movement which eroded the sectarian division between the Anglican Church and the Dissenters (Davis, 98–107). Although Dickens had little sympathy with organized religion be it Anglican or Dissenting, his actual beliefs seemed to have differed little from those of his contemporaries.

While "Hard Times" has little to say about organized religion, religious sentiment and spiritual values have a vital role in this book. The first point to note is that religious sentiment is associated with the poor, rather than the rich, overturning the usual belief that the lower classes were godless and needed the missionary endeavors of the educated middle classes. Rachel, for example, is presented as an angel who has the power to make Stephen a better man than he otherwise would be, for as he says to her "Thou changest me from bad to good. Thou mak'st me humbly wish fo' to be more like thee and fear fo' to lose thee when this life is ower, and a' the muddle cleared awa. Thou'rt an Angel; it may be thou hast saved my soul alive" (92 and footnote, 309).

It is hardly surprising that it is the poor workers, and Stephen in particular, who most often expresses the belief that this life is "aw' a muddle" and will remain so until the afterlife, for their quality of life is much lower than that of the rich. This, however, maintains the status quo by enforcing a passivity on the characters associated with religion, so that religion becomes something to make the poor more contented with their lot, rather than providing the motivation to improve their lives, as was the case with noted Evangelicals, such as William Wilberforce who worked tirelessly to end the slave trade, and Lord Shaftesbury whose concern was to introduce factory legislation to protect workers.

The second point to note is that religious belief is used to highlight the inadequacy of political economy, for when Sissy is asked what the first principle of the science of political economy is, she replies "To do unto others that I would they should do unto me" (60)—a reference to the Catechism of the Church of England in the Book of Common Prayer (292) which is itself derived from the New Testament (Matthew 7:12).

Finally, we could note the extent to which biblical language pervades "Hard Times": the headings of the three books, "sowing," "reaping" and "garnering" which were added to the first volume edition of 1854 are an allusion to Galatians 6:7, while the title of the first chapter of the first book, "The One Thing Needful" is derived from Luke 10:42. The title of the second chapter, "Murdering the Innocents" is even more pointed for it equates the education of children under the harsh Gradgrindian system with biblical story of King Herod who had all children under the age of two years old murdered in an attempt to kill the Messiah, Jesus (Matthew 2:1–18). The biblical allusiveness reaches a climax in Stephen's vision of the star seen from the disused mine called "Old Hell Shaft" which, as Chris Books notes, is a 'specifically Christian vision of transcendence' (67).

Scientific & Technological Context

Britain's manufacturing power had been celebrated at the Great Exhibition in the Crystal Palace (itself a triumph of manufacturing design and ingenuity) in 1851, but Dickens creates a much darker vision of industry in Coketown, which might lead to the conclusion that he was in some sense against science and technology. This is not, however, the case, for Dickens was happy to use the new printing technology for his journal, *Household Words*, and especially for the illustrations for his novels by Hablot Knight Browne under the name, "Phiz".

Industrial processes had changed however, so that instead of each worker creating a small number of complete objects, each was given a small part of the process of creating a large number of objects. The work was therefore highly repetitive, without the satisfaction of creating a completed object and the work was done at a pace dictated by the machinery. In effect, workers were becoming part of their machines, and it was to this dehumanization that Dickens objected (as did, for example, Thomas Carlyle, John Ruskin and William Morris), particularly when that dehumanization furthered the dehumanization resulting from the dominant philosophy of the day.

Biographical Context

Charles Dickens was the eldest son of a naval pay clerk, but when he was 12 years old his father was imprisoned in Marshalsea Debtors' Prison and he was forced to work in blacking warehouse.

Although this has been subject to a certain amount of mythologizing by biographers, it was nevertheless a key period in Dickens' life and gave him a lasting sympathy with the poor and dispossessed and an antipathy towards oppressive social systems. In "Hard Times," this is particularly obvious in the sympathetic portrayal of Stephen and Rachel. At the same time, Dickens held back from a simple equation between poverty and virtue, for Stephen's drunken wife, like Stephen and Rachel, was a factory worker, but unlike them turned from virtue to vice.

The period of imprisonment in which Dickens as the eldest son had to attempt to make a living for the family seems to have left its mark on his fiction in the fatherlessness of the families depicted, and this is inscribed on "Hard Times" in three ways. Firstly, although Sissy Jupe's father leaves her in the belief it will be for her good, she has nevertheless been abandoned. Secondly, while Louisa and Tom are not fatherless in fact, it could be argued that they are emotionally fatherless, for Gradgrind denies emotional need in favor of reason, with disastrous consequences for them both. Finally, Stephen's action in asking Bounderby for advice on how to obtain a divorce suggests that the employer's relationship to his employee is similar to that of father to son, but like Gradgrind, Bounderby refuses to acknowledge emotional need, and finally disinherits his 'son' by dismissing him from service without cause, just as he had already disowned his own mother.

Dickens married Catherine Hogarth in 1836, but theirs was not a happy marriage, and he relied upon his sisters-in-law for the day-to-day management of his household for much of the time. The marriage itself ended in a formal separation in 1858. There are again clear parallels with his fiction, and in "Hard Times" the marriages we are shown are unhappy while Stephen's request to Bounderby for advice on how to obtain a divorce allows Dickens to reveal what he saw as the injustice of matrimonial law in Britain and the folly of forcing two unhappy people to stay together. At the same time, the supportive relationship between Sissy and Louisa shows up by contrast the exploitative aspect of the relationship between Louisa and Tom, as well as revealing the importance of siblings or near siblings, reflecting Dickens's reliance on his sisters-in-law throughout his married life.

Helen Sutherland, Ph.D.

Works Cited

Ackroyd, Peter. *Dickens*. London: Minerva, 1990.

Brooks, Chris. *Signs for the* Times. *Symbolic Realism in the Mid-Victorian World.* London: George Allen and Unwin, 1984.

Davis, Philip. "The Victorians". *The Oxford English* Literary *History.* Vol. 8 1830–1880. Oxford: Oxford UP, 2002.

Dickens, Charles. *Hard Times For These Times.* (1854). Ed. Kate Flint. London: Penguin, 1995.

Gallagher, Catherine. *The Industrial Reformation of English Fiction. Social Discourse and Narrative Form* 1827–1867. Chicago: University of Chicago Press, 1985.

Ibid. *On Strike* "Household Words," 11 February 1854). 196–210.

Lougy, Robert E. Dickens's Hard Times: The Romance as Radical Literature in *Charles Dicken's Hard Times*. Ed Harold Bloom. New York: Chelsea House, 1987.

McCullough, Dairmid. Ed. *Book of Common Prayer* (1622 version). London: Everyman, 1999.

Slater, Michael. Ed. "Frauds on the Fairies Household Words", 1 October 1853 in Dickens's *Journalism.* "'Gone Astray'" and other Papers from "Household Words" 1851–1859. London: J.M. Dent, 1998. 166–174.

Discussion Questions

1. Discuss the significance of names in "Hard Times."

2. Look at the descriptions of Coketown: how does Dickens use them?

3. What do you notice about gender roles in "Hard Times?"

4. Make a list of as many allusions to the Bible as you can find (use the notes from a scholarly edition of the text to help you). What conclusions can you draw from your list?

5. How does Dickens enlist the reader's sympathy for Louisa?

6. What do you think about Tom Gradgrind, and why?

7. What role does Harthouse play in "Hard Times?" What do you think about the way he just disappears at the end?

8. Look at the language used by Slackbridge. What does it tell you about him, or about Dickens' attitude towards trade unions?

9. What role is played by Sleary's circus and how important is it?

10. What do you think of the characterization in "Hard Times?" Are you convinced by it?

Essay Ideas

1. Write an essay about the various forms of repression you find in the text. This could include, but is not limited to, repression of the imagination; repression of childhood; sexual repression; social repression.

2. Write an essay on "Hard Times" as a critique of Utilitarianism and/or capitalism.

3. Discuss the ways Dickens builds up his characters, addressing the extent to which they are—or are not—convincing.

4. Discuss the competing claims of "Hard Times" as a Romance or as a realist novel.

5. Argue the case for "Hard Times" as a fairy tale for grown ups (hints to get you started: Louisa as enchanted princess; Gradgrind as Master Wizard; Sissy as spell-breaker; descriptions of factories as fire-breathing dragons).

Pictured above is the Divinity School in the Bodleian Library in Oxford, England. Built in the fifteenth century, here is where several scenes for the film versions of the Harry Potter books took place. J. K. Rowlings wrote seven Harry Potter books. The fifth, *Harry Potter and the Order of the Phoenix*, is featured opposite. Photo: iStockphoto.

Harry Potter and the Order of the Phoenix

by J. K. Rowling

Content Synopsis

"Harry Potter and the Order of the Phoenix," the fifth book in J.K. Rowling's "Harry Potter" series, begins, as do the previous four books, with Harry at home with his "muggle" (i.e. non-wizard) relatives, the Dursleys, during the summer. This book opens with Harry hiding in a flowerbed beneath the living room window of Number 4, Privet Drive in order to eavesdrop on the evening news. Harry, having witnessed the return of Lord Voldemort at the end of "Harry Potter and the Goblet of Fire," (Book 4) has been frustrated all summer at not learning anything further of the evil wizard's activities either in the *Daily Prophet*, a wizarding newspaper, or through muggle channels of communication.

Part of Harry's frustration stems from feeling very out of place in the "relentlessly non-magical world of Privet Drive" (37). He is barely tolerated by the Dursleys, he has no friends in Little Whinging, and his neighbors regard him with suspicion. As he wanders the streets, we are told, "Harry preferred Little Whinging by night, when the curtained windows made patches of jewel-bright colors in the darkness and he ran no danger of hearing disapproving mutters about his 'delinquent' appearance when he passed the householders" (12). Although Harry's case is extreme—he is

a wizard in a world that doesn't believe in magic— the issues he is dealing with (feeling unaccepted, alone, like an "outsider") are the common troubles of teenagers everywhere.

Harry believes that he'll fit in once he returns to the wizard world, but this turns out not to be the case. After defending himself, and his cousin Dudley against a Dementor attack, nearly being expelled from school, and finally being "rescued" by a group of wizards from the Order of the Phoenix, Harry finds himself reunited with (among others) his best friends Ron and Hermione, his godfather Sirius Black, and Arthur and Molly Weasley—the people that to Harry constitute his "real" family. While it is a relief for Harry to be among wizarding folk once again, his frustration and sense of being an outsider are not lessened when he learns that he has been purposely kept in the dark about the goings-on in the wizard world.

The Order of the Phoenix, Harry learns, is the group of people who opposed Lord Voldemort when he was last menacing the wizard world, and has now reunited to stand against him once more. They have set up headquarters at Number 12, Grimmauld Place, the ancestral home of the Black family. The Black mansion, with its obscenity-screaming portraits, elf-head decorations, and dangerous knickknacks, looks to Harry "as though it belonged to the Darkest of wizards" (62). Number 12, Grimmauld Place is important on two levels. It demonstrates that characters in the Potter-verse are not bound by the tenets of their upbringings. Sirius, for example, has overcome the teachings of his parents, and rejected their upper-class elitism in favor of supporting the more democratic Order. Grimmauld Place also helps illuminate the ideology of Voldemort and his supporters; body parts from rational creatures used as furniture and a tapestry where the names of those who have voiced dissenting opinions have been obliterated both point to a worldview very different from the one Dumbledore espouses and teaches.

While staying at Grimmauld Place, Harry must visit the Ministry of Magic to face a charge of using magic under age. Though Harry is acquitted, his trial raises a number of disturbing issues. During the trial, it becomes clear that Cornelius Fudge, the Minister of Magic, would like to discredit Harry publicly. The other issue that worries Harry is Dumbledore's behavior. While the headmaster defends Harry at the trial, he also seems to avoid any personal contact with him.

The start of the school year brings about a number of changes, but still does not help alleviate Harry's sense of isolation. Both Ron and Hermione are made prefects, leaving Harry feeling overlooked. Harry also notices the whispered attention he is attracting from his fellow students. It turns out that a majority of Hogwarts students believe the *Daily Prophet's* assertions—that Harry is a liar and an attention-seeker. This painful state of affairs is brought home to Harry when one of his dorm-mates, Seamus Finnigan, makes a similar claim.

To make matters worse, Harry's friend and the Care of Magical Creatures Professor, Rubeus Hagrid, is no where to be found. Additionally, the frequently changing position of Defense Against the Dark Arts (DADA) Professor has this year been filled by Delores Umbridge, a member of Fudge's ministry and a face frighteningly familiar to Harry

from his trial. Umbridge hints ominously at a hidden agenda during the Welcoming Feast, and soon makes her presence known around the school.

Through a series of "Educational Decrees" passed by the Ministry, Umbridge is appointed "High Inquisitor of Hogwarts." The impressive title gives Umbridge the power to inspect (and dismiss) her fellow teachers, control the formation of student organizations, and decide any student's punishment for a violation of school rules. This spells immediate trouble for Harry, as the DADA group he and Hermione were organizing stands no chance of receiving the green light from Umbridge. The group, called "Dumbledore's Army" in response to the Ministry's paranoid belief that Dumbledore is secretly trying to overthrow the government by training an army of Hogwarts students, decides to carry on in secret, using the magical Room of Requirement as a meeting place. Umbridge also uses her authority to have Harry "banned for life" from Quidditch after he has a physical altercation with Draco Malfoy. This is a terrible blow to Harry, who loves the sport.

When things look at their worst for Harry, Hagrid returns. Harry, Ron, and Hermione sneak out to his cabin to listen to the tale of his unsuccessful mission to persuade the giants to join the fight against Voldemort. Hagrid is quite a sight when he returns—a blackened eye, missing teeth, cuts and bruises everywhere—and while the trio assumes these injuries are a result of his brush with the giants, they have a suspicion that Hagrid is hiding something.

A much more pressing issue emerges when Harry has a vision of being a giant snake and attacking Arthur Weasley. Convinced that this is no mere dream, Harry raises an alarm that enables Dumbledore to get Arthur to the hospital before it is too late. Harry and the Weasley children are sent back to Grimmauld Place to await news of Arthur's condition.

While Arthur turns out to be in stable condition, Harry is worried that he was the one who actually attacked Mr. Weasley. Harry's fears that Voldemort possesses him are laid to rest after Ginny explains (based on her first year experience) what being possessed actually feels like. With his mind now at ease, Harry is able to relax and enjoy the Christmas holiday. On Christmas Day, Harry, Hermione, and the Weasley family visit Arthur in the hospital, where they run into Neville Longbottom, there to visit his parents who had been tortured into madness during the first war with Voldemort.

The spring term brings with it an unrelenting supply of homework as the fifth year students prepare for their Ordinary Wizarding Level (O.W.L.) exams—a standardized test in each school subject that qualifies students for advanced study. Harry has the additional burden of Occlumency lessons with Snape. Occlumency is the magical art of closing one's mind off from outside intrusion. The lessons are supposed to help Harry break the connection he shares with Voldemort—a connection that has allowed him access to Voldemort's thoughts and feelings. Dumbledore fears Voldemort will use the connection to harm Harry. Even more frightening is the news that ten Death Eaters, supporters of Voldemort, have escaped from Azkaban Prison.

Valentine's Day proves very eventful for Harry. He has a disastrous date with Cho Chang, but ends the day by giving an interview to Rita Skeeter regarding the events that took place at the end of "Harry Potter and the Goblet of Fire." The interview, orchestrated by Hermione, is meant to counter the Ministry's whitewashing of the recent breakout and the *Daily Prophet's* attempts to mar Harry's reputation. It turns out to be a great success. The Ministry passes an Educational Decree banning Hogwarts' students from reading the interview, much to Hermione's delight. She explains to Harry, "If [Umbridge] could have done one thing to make absolutely sure that every single person in this school will read your interview, it was banning it!" (582).

During an Occlumency lesson, Harry and Snape hear screaming coming from the Great Hall and rush upstairs to find that Umbridge has dismissed the Divination Professor, Sybil Trelawney. Trelawney, not entirely sober, creates quite a scene until Dumbledore steps in and invites her to continue living at Hogwarts. He also brings with him Firenze, a centaur, to replace her as the Divination Professor.

Shortly following this event, a DA meeting is raided by Umbridge. Harry is the only student caught, and he is promptly escorted to Dumbledore's office. Through some quick thinking on the parts of Dumbledore and Kingsley Shacklebolt, a secret member of the Order, Harry avoids getting in trouble when Dumbledore falsely admits to trying to form an army of students. He stuns the Ministry officials in his office (including Fudge) and makes his escape. Unruffled by this minor setback, Umbridge has herself declared headmistress.

During Harry's next Occlumency lesson, he takes advantage of Snape being called away to examine a memory Snape is hiding in the Pensieve. When he sees his father and Sirius cruelly bullying Snape, Harry is determined to question Sirius about the event. The Weasley twins create a diversion so that Harry can contact Sirius, and though Sirius's defense—"A lot of people are idiots at the age of fifteen. [James] grew out of it"—makes Harry feel slightly better; his beliefs about both Snape and his father have been altered (671). Harry finishes his conversation in time to see Fred and George's grand exit from Hogwarts, complete with a swamp in the hallway and a fast getaway on brooms.

Hagrid's secret is finally revealed during the last Quidditch match of the year. Harry and Hermione accompany Hagrid into the Forbidden Forest while everyone is distracted by the game to meet Hagrid's half-brother, a sixteen-foot giant named Grawp. Hagrid asks his two young friends to look after Grawp and help him with his English in the likely event that Hagrid gets sacked. Rather unwillingly, the two agree, and return to school grounds just in time to find out that Gryffindor has won the Quidditch Cup, thanks largely to Ron's first success at goal tending.

Events move quickly toward the novel's climax. The O.W.L. exams begin, and during the Astronomy practical, Harry and his classmates witness Hagrid being forcefully removed from school grounds. Minerva McGonagall is injured in the attack and sent to St. Mungo's. During Harry's History of Magic exam, he nods off and has a vision of Sirius being tortured in the Department of Mysteries by Voldemort. Hermione suspects the vision is a trap, but with no teachers left at the school to turn to for help, Harry and friends devise a plan to find out for themselves if Sirius has left Grimmauld Place. While the others are creating a diversion, Harry contacts Grimmauld Place through the fireplace in Umbridge's office and speaks with Kreacher, who tells him that Sirius has left the mansion. Before Harry can do anything about it, he and Ron, Hermione, Ginny, Luna, and Neville are caught by Umbridge and her "Inquisitorial Squad." When Umbridge decides she needs to use torture to force a confession from Harry, Hermione claims the group was trying to contact Dumbledore to tell him the "weapon" was ready. Umbridge demands to be taken to the weapon, and follows Harry and Hermione into the Forbidden Forest, where she, as an adult, is attacked by a herd of centaurs. Harry and Hermione almost find themselves in trouble with the centaurs, too, but Grawp fortuitously arrives on the scene and the two make their escape amid the ensuing chaos. Outside the Forest, they are met by the rest of their group, and all six of them travel to the Ministry building.

The six students make their way through the maze-like Department of Mysteries, encountering many fantastical magical items, but seeing no sign of Sirius. After Harry picks up a strange bauble with his name on it, the group is attacked by Death Eaters. In the battle, Sirius (who has arrived with other members of the Order) is killed by Bellatrix Lestrange, and Dumbledore arrives just in time to defend Harry from Voldemort himself. The bauble that everyone is fighting over—a prophecy concerning Harry and Voldemort—gets broken in the scuffle and no one hears it.

Harry is heartbroken over the loss of Sirius and blames himself for his godfather's death. After Dumbledore explains to Harry the significance of the lost prophecy and his decisions regarding Harry's childhood, Harry finds some comfort. The novel ends with the Ministry finally recognizing Voldemort's return and the return to normalcy at Hogwarts. Umbridge (who survived the centaurs) is ousted; Dumbledore, Hagrid and McGonagall return, and the Educational Decrees become a thing of the past. Lastly, we see Harry heading off for another summer with the Dursleys.

Symbols & Motifs

Unity is a recurring motif in the novel. From the Sorting Hat's unusual start-of-term song, to the banding together of the DA, a group composed of members from three of Hogwarts' houses, to Harry's friends' insistence on facing whatever dangers await at the Ministry building together, the novel demonstrates that obstacles are overcome, not through the heroism of one, but through the teamwork of many.

"I will not tell lies": Harry carves this line into his own skin as punishment for lying, according to Umbridge. However, by branding himself with this expression, Harry ironically affirms that he is truthful, and points to how hard it can be at times to stand up for the truth, particularly when it is unpopular.

The Fountain of Magical Brethren—At first glance, the fountain in the atrium of the Ministry Building presents a happy picture of peace and unity between witches, wizards, centaurs, goblins and house-elves. On closer inspection however, the fountain reveals a hierarchical worldview that places wizards on a pedestal and assumes that all other magical creatures rightfully worship and adore them. It suggests that wizarding kind may be blinded by its own sense of superiority. If this is the way wizards view themselves, it also points ominously to trouble ahead when wizards may need the help of other magical beings in the fight against Voldemort.

The Order of the Phoenix—The phoenix is a mythical bird said to catch fire when it dies and then be born anew out of the ashes of that fire. The Order of the Phoenix has likewise risen once again to combat Voldemort and his Death Eaters.

Historical Context

While Rowling's often-negative experiences with the press may have influenced her portrayal of journalism in the novel, the major conflict between Harry and Voldemort in "Harry Potter and the Order of the Phoenix" is not based on a particular historical event. Parallels may be drawn between Voldemort and any number of cruel leaders in history, but the basic struggle between good and evil in the novel points more toward a universal cultural myth than a specific event or time period.

Rowling's use of the terms "High Inquisitor of Hogwarts" and "Inquisitorial Squad" does carry a specific historical connotation, however. Umbridge's reign over Hogwarts brings about a time of repression for its students similar to historical periods marked by stringent government surveillance and the limitation of personal liberties such as the suspension of habeas corpus in England during the French Revolution, 1940s McCarthyism in the United States, and most recently, the controversial Patriot Act passed in the U.S. following the events of September 11, 2001. The term "inquisitor" has significance within this context. It both alludes to the Inquisition that took place in thirteenth-century Europe under Pope Innocent III, a particularly dark period in the history of the Catholic church, and to the specific meaning of "inquisition" as defined by the Church: "An ecclesiastical tribunal (officially styled the Holy Office) for the suppression of heresy and punishment of heretics" (Oxford). In this case, the heresy that needs to be suppressed is Harry's assertion that Voldemort is back.

Societal Context

Rowling focuses on society in two ways in the novel. Within the confines of Privet Drive we see a glimpse of British suburbia, and the picture Rowling presents is not flattering. Middle-class Britain is obsessed with the notion of "keeping up with the Jones's." Whose lawn is nicest or who has the newest car seems to be the extent of people's interest in one another. At the start of the novel, we see a bleak day for Privet drive due to drought—the neighborhood has been "deprived of [its] usual car-washing and lawn-mowing pursuits" (1). At the same time, the Dursleys believe that conformity—looking, thinking, and acting as everyone else—is the only way to gain social acceptance. All of the houses on Privet Drive look identical, and similar cars sit in every driveway. One of the Dursleys' greatest fears is that someone will discover they have "freaks" like Harry in their family.

Wizarding society gives us a view into England's past. The Black mansion, with its house-elf heads mounted like trophies on the wall and its troll-leg umbrella stand in the hall, recalls the age of British imperialism, when similar trophies, taken from the far reaches of the empire, graced the homes of England's upper class. The prejudices of nineteenth-century England are apparent in the wizarding world as well. Status is still based, in the eyes of many, on wealth and birth ("pureblood" versus "mudblood").

Religious Context

The "Harry Potter" novels and their religious context have a long and troubled history. Though the novels seem to espouse Christianity—all the major characters celebrate Christmas, for example—a number of Christian groups have raised objections to the novels. At issue are a number of Biblical passages denouncing witchcraft, particularly Deut. 18:10–11: "No one shall be found among you who makes a son or daughter pass through fire, or who practices divination, or is a soothsayer, or an augur, or a sorcerer, or one who casts spells. . . ." Groups calling for public banning of the novels claim that the "Harry Potter" series both endorses witchcraft and encourages readers to practice it. Rowling has adamantly denied these charges, saying, "I have yet to meet a single child who's told me that they want to be a Satanist or are particularly interested in the occult because of the book[s]" (Bridger 10).

In "The Order of the Phoenix," Rowling broaches the subject of the afterlife—a focal point of a number of belief systems. We first get a glimpse of the afterlife when Harry enters a room in the Department of Mysteries that contains a "stone archway that looked so ancient, cracked, and crumbling. . . . Unsupported by any surrounding wall, the archway was hung with a tattered black curtain or veil which, despite the complete stillness of the cold surrounding air, was fluttering very slightly as though it had just been touched" (773). The veil is a traditional icon in Christian mythology, symbolizing the separation of this world from the next. Harry is sure that he hears voices coming from the other side of the veil—perhaps a reference to Tennyson's "In Memoriam," a poem written on the loss of Tennyson's closest friend, Arthur Henry Hallam. Tennyson writes, "O for thy voice to soothe and bless! / What hope of answer, or redress? / Behind the veil, behind the veil" (56. 26–28). Harry feels similarly frustrated with the loss of Sirius, and is comforted much the same way. Luna says:

> "'And anyway, it's not as though I'll never see Mum again, is it?'
>
> 'Er—isn't it?' said Harry uncertainly.
>
> She shook her head in disbelief. 'Oh, come on. You heard them, just behind the veil, didn't you?'" (863)

Thus, in endorsing a belief that we are reunited with loved ones after death, the scene seems to align the novel with a Christian worldview.

Scientific & Technological Context

Wizards, understandably, have little use for technology—who needs a dishwasher when the whole kitchen can be cleaned with the flick of a wrist? In many ways, wizards are still getting by with technology that is a century old. Candles are used instead of electric lighting, and Hogwarts is heated with fireplaces rather than a furnace. Partly this choice on Rowling's part is necessary to create the space for magic to exist. Sending an owl to a friend would become obsolete if wizards had email.

Rowling does deal with modern technology in the glimpses she gives us of the Muggle world. In "Harry Potter and the Sorcerer's Stone," Rowling is critical of the impact technology has on children. Dudley, who "was very fat and hated exercise," receives for his birthday a computer with sixteen games, a second television, a video camera, a remote control airplane, and a VCR (20). In "Order of the Phoenix," Muggles are presented as technology-obsessed. As Harry is walking toward St. Mungo's, he is almost run down by "a gaggle of shoppers plainly intent on nothing but making it into a nearby shop full of electrical gadgets" (483). Rowling's use of the term "gaggle" implies that the shoppers are a sort of mindless herd, buying up new technology simply because it is there.

Biographical Context

The history behind Joanne Kathleen Rowling's success as a novelist seems almost as much a fairy tale as her boy hero's. The story of the single mother living on government assistance while writing her first novel, who goes on to become fabulously rich and famous is as much the stuff of legend as "The Boy Who Lived (Chapter 1 of Book 1)." Rowling did receive government aid when she was finishing her novel, but hers is not a simple rags-to-riches tale.

Rowling was born in Chipping Sodbury, outside Bristol, on July 31, 1966, and had, by her own account, a typical middle-class childhood filled with the imaginative games she played with her younger sister and other children in the neighborhood. Rowling, like Hermione, excelled in school, becoming Head Girl in her final year of high school. She attended the University of Exeter where she majored in French due to "parental pressure" to study a useful subject ("Biography").

The idea for the "Harry Potter" series first occurred to Rowling in 1990, and she worked on "Harry Potter and the Sorcerer's Stone" over a period of five years, during which time she lost her mother to multiple sclerosis, moved to Portugal where she met her first husband, and gave birth to her first child, Jessica. Following the dissolution of her marriage, Rowling returned to Britain, where she worked to finish the novel before beginning a teaching job.

Since the publication of "Harry Potter and the Sorcerer's Stone," Rowling has received numerous honors and awards.

Rowling remarried in 2001, gave birth to a son, David, in 2003, and a daughter, Mackenzie, in 2005. She and her family live in Scotland where Rowling wrote the sixth and seventh (final) novels of the series.

Jen Cadwallader

Works Cited

Bridger, Francis. *A Charmed Life: The Spirituality of Potterworld*. London: Darton, Longman and Todd, 2001.

The New Oxford Annotated Bible. New York: Oxford UP, 1989.

The Oxford English Dictionary. 5 December 2005. *http://dictionary.oed.com*.

Rowling, J. K. *Biography*. J. K. Rowling Official Site. 3 December 2005. *http://www.jkrowling.com/textonly/en/biography.cfm*.

_____. *Harry Potter* and the *Order* of the *Phoenix*. New York: Scholastic, 2003.

_____. *Harry Potter* and the Sorcerer's Stone. New York: Scholastic, 1997.

Tennyson, Alfred. *In Memoriam A.H.H. Victorian Poetry and Poetics*. Walter E. Houghton and G. Robert Stange, Eds. New York: Houghton Mifflin, 1968.

Discussion Questions

1. Harry is frustrated at the lack of important news in the *Daily Prophet* over the summer, yet he later learns of a number of crucial bits of information he missed in his hasty glance at the front-page headlines. Is this style of reading indicative of one of Harry's character traits? Does it have any repercussions later in the story?

2. Hermione and Luna have a number of heated arguments; in fact, they seem unable to hold a discussion which doesn't devolve into verbal sparring. In what way are these two characters set up as opposites? How are their opposing qualities relevant to larger concerns in the text?

3. Discuss Harry's detentions with Umbridge. Why won't he admit to being in pain? What does this reveal about his character?

4. How is racism presented in the novel?

5. Discuss the novel as a tool for discussing the issues facing teenagers in the real world.

6. Discuss the theme of fate versus choice.

7. Harry spends a great deal of time complaining about being treated like a child by the "grown-ups" (495). In what ways does Harry do his own growing up over the course of the novel?

8. Does Harry's look at Snape's memory in the Pensieve change the way you think about Snape? Does it change the way you view James or Sirius?

9. Discuss the relationship between Kreacher and Sirius. Is Kreacher responsible for his actions, or is Sirius to blame? What do you think of Dumbledore's assessment of the relationship between the two?

10. Firenze is an unusual teacher even by Hogwarts' standards. Students learn that "his priority did not seem to be to teach them what he knew, but rather to impress upon them that nothing, not even centaurs' knowledge, was foolproof" (604). How does this idea resonate in the novel?

Essay Ideas

1. Luna Lovegood is one of the new characters introduced to us in "Harry Potter and the Order of the Phoenix," and she plays a crucial role in a number of scenes. Analyze her character and importance to the novel.

2. Hermione remarks at one point about "this horrible thing wizards have of thinking they're superior to other creatures" (171). Using examples from the text, support or refute this claim.

3. Did Sirius have to die at the end of the novel? Does any of his earlier behavior make his death seem inevitable?

4. Analyze how Dolores Umbridge's character complicates notions of good and evil.

5. Analyze the novel's stance on the related issues of the "power of the press" and free speech.

Howards End

by E. M. Forster

Content Synopsis

Set in England during the first decade of the twentieth century, E[dward] M[organ] Forster's (1879-1970) "Howards End" (1910) tells the story of two sisters, Margaret and Helen Schlegel and their dealings with the Wilcox family. The half-German Schlegel sisters have active social consciences, and are enthusiastic devotees of art, literature, music, and culture, while the Wilcox family consists of practical and sometimes ruthless men of business. Forster characterizes these two views of the world in terms of "the seen" and "the unseen": the Wilcoxes deal with the "seen" world, all that is the tangible and concrete, while the Schlegel sisters are more attuned to the "unseen" world, to the spiritual, and to abstract ideas and thought. The novel's famous epigraph, "Only connect. . ." suggests the possibility of reconciling these two competing ways of understanding the world.

The novel opens, famously, with Helen's letter to her sister. Helen is staying at the family home of the Wilcoxes, Howards End. Her letter sets up the novel's key opposition between the masculine, practical Wilcox family and the feminine, artistic Schlegel sisters. Helen also announces that she is in love with the family's son, Paul. According to the social mores of the day, Margaret assumes that Helen and Paul are now engaged. The sisters' Aunt Juley, decides to travel to Howards End to encourage Helen to end the relationship, believing it to be too sudden. However, while Aunt Juley is on her way to Howards End, Margaret receives a telegram in London from Helen telling her that the engagement is off.

Aunt Juley meets Paul's brother, Charles Wilcox, at the station, and mistakes him for Paul. On the journey to Howards End, they argue over the engagement—of which Charles had no prior knowledge. Helen and Aunt Juley return to London in a state of emotional collapse, after an awkward stand-off with the Wilcox family over Helen and Paul's relationship. Helen admits to Margaret she had fallen in love with the Wilcox family, as much as with Paul. She describes the encounter with Paul as a "chance collision" (38) and expresses her disappointment at seeing how frightened he was afterwards. She also realizes that Paul's mother, the deeply intuitive Mrs. Ruth Wilcox, knew everything about the affair, though she had not been told of it.

The Schlegel sisters attend a performance of Beethoven's Fifth Symphony with Aunt Juley and their brother, Theobald, more generally known as Tibby. Helen leaves early, accidentally taking the umbrella of a young clerk, Leonard Bast, with her. The impoverished Bast becomes agitated by its loss, and accompanies Margaret back to Wickham Place, feeling ill informed and nervous, as she chatters about music and art. At the house, Helen scares Leonard off, by commenting thoughtlessly about the tattered state of his umbrella.

The grandson of agricultural laborers, Forster depicts the young Leonard Bast as intellectually and physically underfed. Bast is desperate "to come to Culture" (62), but has little time to read and little money for concerts. Leonard is envious of the Schlegels, whom he believes were "born cultured" (67). He lives with Jacky, a blowsy woman, more than ten years his senior, whom he has promised to marry once he comes of age. Described rather cruelly as "bestially stupid" (224), Jacky does not understand Leonard's interest in literature and art.

Aunt Juley discovers that the Wilcoxes are moving into new flats on the same street as the Schlegel sisters' house. Mrs. Wilcox calls on Margaret, but Margaret writes back to say they should not meet in case of any awkwardness over the incident with Paul. Mrs. Wilcox, offended, writes to say that Paul has gone abroad. Margaret and Mrs. Wilcox meet and sort out the muddle between them. Her son, Charles, has married Dolly and is spending his honeymoon in Italy. Her husband, Mr. Henry Wilcox gave him a car, a symbol of the Wilcoxes' commitment to the "seen" world of machinery and technological progress, for his wedding gift. Margaret discovers that Howards End is Mrs. Wilcox's family home.

Margaret gives a lunch for Mrs. Wilcox. However, it is not a success. Mrs. Wilcox is alarmed by the "clever talk" (84) of Margaret's friends, while Margaret's friends find Mrs. Wilcox dull and uninteresting. Margaret discovers that Mrs. Wilcox does not like to be hurried into intimacy. However, the women have another opportunity to build their friendship when they go Christmas shopping together. Mrs. Wilcox discovers on this trip that the Schlegel family must leave their house in Wickham Place in a few years when their lease runs out. She tells Margaret that she could not bear the idea of leaving Howards End. She believes the idea of being removed from one's home is "worse than dying" (93). Mrs. Wilcox invites Margaret to Howards End. Margaret, not realizing the significance of the offer, refuses and deeply offends Mrs. Wilcox. As Margaret watches Mrs. Wilcox enter her house, she realizes her mistake.

Mrs. Wilcox dies suddenly. Though they have generally "avoided the personal note in life" (101), the Wilcox family is hit hard by her death. The family discovers a hand written note from Mrs. Wilcox, bequeathing Howards End to Margaret Schlegel. The Wilcoxes, who have never understood the value of Howards End to Mrs. Wilcox, decide to ignore this bequest, which they regard as a form of treachery. Though they recognize that "mother believed so in ancestors" (108), they fail to understand that Mrs. Wilcox was actually seeking a "spiritual heir" (107) to Howards End.

Margaret reflects on her friendship with Mrs. Wilcox. She realizes that she is less disparaging of the Wilcoxes than Tibby and Helen, because unlike her siblings she does not "brood too much [. . .] on the superiority of the unseen to the seen" (112). Instead, she believes that "our business is not to contrast the two, but to reconcile them" (112), just as the spiritual and intuitive Mrs. Wilcox attempted to reconcile the two by tempering the extremely masculine, practical temperament of her family.

Two years pass and the Schlegels are still living a life of "cultured but not ignoble ease" (115), despite the fact that their lease on Wickham Place is about to expire. Helen announces the arrival of a woman looking for her husband. The sisters nickname the woman "Mrs. Lanoline" (120), but recognize that her visit is a "goblin footfall" (122), a reminder that the lives of the poor are not as easy as those of the Schlegel sisters. Leonard Bast arrives the next day to explain the situation. "Mrs. Lanoline," or Jacky as she is properly known, is his wife. She had found Margaret's card from their meeting a few years earlier and assumed he had gone to visit her. In fact, Bast had left for a walk that evening and not come back until the next day. He got lost in London, as he could not follow the stars. Then, inspired by Robert Louis Stevenson's stories, he walked through the night and into the countryside in order to see the dawn. He admits that, despite the romantic nature of his adventure, the dawn was not wonderful. He talks of the writers he has read, whom he regards mistakenly, according to the narrator, as destinations rather than signposts. The sisters greatly enjoy their meeting with Leonard, but he does not want to meet them again, claiming, "things so often get spoiled" (128).

The sisters discuss Leonard at dinner parties, where he figures in a debate about how an imaginary millionaire should deal with his money. Margaret argues that the rich should give money, not gifts to the poor. The sisters bump into Mr. Wilcox and discuss Leonard with him. He tells the sisters that Leonard's employer, the Porphyrion Fire Insurance Company, will crash before Christmas. The sisters decide it is their duty to tell Leonard this news and they write to him.

Leonard comes to tea with the sisters, and it is a failure, just as he predicted. He becomes annoyed when the sisters talk about insurance companies instead of books. He tells the sisters that he does not want their help, or patronage. Mr. Wilcox arrives unexpectedly during tea, and later asks the sisters what right they have to interfere in Leonard's life or to deem it gray. The sisters defend their actions, claiming that Leonard is "such a muddle of a man, and yet so worth pulling through" (153).

Evie Simpson invites Margaret to Simpson's restaurant with Evie's fiancé Percy Cahill. Mr. Wilcox also attends the dinner, and Margaret discusses the Schlegel family's housing situation with him. Shortly afterwards, while the sisters are visiting Aunt Juley, Margaret gets a letter from Mr. Wilcox offering his Ducie Street house to her. Margaret wonders whether Mr. Wilcox is courting her, and scolds herself for thinking like a spinster. She contrasts their ways of seeing the world. While she sees the world "whole," she believes Mr. Wilcox sees it "steadily" (165).

Margaret visits Mr. Wilcox's house on Ducie Street, where he proposes to her—much to her surprise. She promises to write to him with her answer. When Margaret tells Helen of the proposal, Helen bursts into tears. Helen complains that Mr. Wilcox belongs to the outer life of "telegrams and anger" (176). Margaret counters by arguing that people like the Wilcoxes made life in England possible.

Margaret agrees to marry Mr. Wilcox. Mr. Wilcox discusses the financial arrangements of the marriage. Margaret shocks him when she asks how much money he has. They kiss for the first time, but Margaret is disappointed, as she feels there was no tenderness. Charles and his wife, Dolly, are very suspicious of Margaret's motives, and believe she is still trying to get hold of Howards End.

Margaret hopes to reconcile the seen with the unseen in her relationship with Mr. Wilcox, or as she puts it "connect the prose and passion" (188). Her mantra is "only connect" (188), but she meets with failure, due to a quality in Mr. Wilcox that she was not prepared for: "his obtuseness" (188).

Leonard writes to Helen to tell her he is leaving the Porphyrion Fire Insurance Company. Margaret mentions the news to Mr. Wilcox, who now claims that Porphyrion is a good business. The sisters are angry, but Mr. Wilcox shows no sympathy or guilt over Leonard's situation. His attitude contributes to Helen's unhappiness over the marriage, though she believes Margaret may be able to make it work because she is "a heroine" (195).

Margaret travels to Howards End with Mr. Wilcox by motorcar. Margaret is struck by the fertility of the soil around Howards End. Howards End is dirty and unkempt, but despite this, Margaret finds Howards End beautiful. The house is explicitly contrasted with the world of the motorcar and the Wilcoxes. Though small, Margaret recovers "the sense of space which the motor had tried to rob from her" (201) in Howards End. She also meets an old woman, Mrs. Avery, inside the house. Mrs. Avery mistakes Margaret for Mrs. Wilcox, claiming that Margaret has the first Mrs. Wilcox's "way of walking" (202).

Margaret believes Howards End "transcended any simile of sex" (206), thus embodying the philosophy of "only connect." She finds the pigs' teeth in the wych-elm tree that Mrs. Wilcox had told her about. Mr. Wilcox sees the pig's teeth for the first time, and is surprised Margaret knew of them. Like her apparent resemblance to the first Mrs. Wilcox, Margaret's knowledge of the house and its grounds, indicates that she is truly Mrs. Wilcox's spiritual heir. While Margaret does not refer to Mrs. Wilcox by name, her presence still haunts the house.

Margaret and Mr. Wilcox travel on to Oniton, another of Mr. Wilcox's properties. Margaret believes Oniton will be her permanent home, and resolves "to make a lasting impression" (208). She arranges a sightseeing trip around the area by car. During the trip, the car hits a dog. Margaret wants to help the animal, but Charles insists, "the men will see to it" (212). Upset, Margaret jumps out of the moving vehicle. Charles later informs Mr. Wilcox of Margaret's behavior. He has no trouble believing Charles's story, as his rendering of Margaret's "hysteria" fits "well with their view of feminine nature" (214). Charles is still suspicious of Margaret and believes that she "means mischief" (216).

Evie and Percy get married at Oniton in a low-key ceremony. Helen arrives unexpectedly with Leonard and his wife, Jacky. Leonard had lost his new job at the bank, and Helen claims that he and Jacky are starving. Margaret asks Henry to employ Leonard, and Mr. Wilcox agrees to see him. However, the drunk Jacky recognizes Mr. Wilcox. Hen, as she calls him, had been her lover some ten years earlier. Mr. Wilcox is furious, believing Margaret brought Jacky deliberately to Oniton to embarrass him. Margaret is shocked to discover the affair, having never had to confront "life's seamy side" (230) before. However, Margaret realizes it is "not her tragedy, it was Mrs. Wilcox's" (231).

Helen talks with Leonard at his hotel. He tells her that since his marriage to Jacky, his family has cut him off financially. Since he lost his job, he realizes that his earlier romantic view of the world was flawed. Now Leonard understands that "one must have money" (235). The waiter brings letters for Helen and Leonard from Margaret. Margaret tells Leonard that Mr. Wilcox has no vacancy for him; while she advises Helen "the Basts are not at all the type we should trouble about" (239).

Tibby is now in his last year at Oxford. Helen arrives at his rooms, and asks him to tell Margaret that she is going to Germany. Tibby "has never been interested in human beings" (250) and is unconcerned by the revelation that Mr. Wilcox has had a mistress. He does not understand Helen's upset but agrees to carry out her commission. He sends the Basts a check for five thousand pounds from Helen. Leonard returns this check, despite the fact that he and Jacky have just been evicted for not paying their rent.

Wickham Place is now deserted. Mr. Wilcox offers the Schlegel family storage for their belongings at Howards End. Margaret and Mr. Wilcox marry in a quiet ceremony. They honeymoon near Innsbruck, and Margaret hopes to meet with Helen, but does not. Mr. Wilcox leases Oniton to a tenant without consulting Margaret, which upsets her, as she desires, like the first Mrs. Wilcox, a permanent residence.

After Helen has been away for eight months, Dolly informs Margaret that Mrs. Avery has been unpacking the Schlegels' cases at Howards End. Margaret goes to Howards End to repack their belongings and discovers that Miss Avery has fitted out Howards End with all the Schlegel family's possessions. Even her father's sword hangs amongst the books. Miss Avery tells her that it has been a mistake to allow the house to lie empty.

Aunt Juley develops acute pneumonia, and Helen is summoned to see her. Helen telegraphs to say that she can only visit Aunt Juley and must return to Germany as soon as she is better. Helen's prolonged absence and infrequent letters worry Margaret. She supposes Helen's behavior was prompted by the discovery of Mr. Wilcox's infidelity, but she begins to wonder whether Helen might also be losing her sanity. When Helen refuses to see her family on her trip to England, Mr. Wilcox proposes that Margaret should write to Helen, telling her that she must unpack her books at Howards End. He suggests that Margaret could then surprise her sister at Howards End.

Margaret, Mr. Wilcox, and a young doctor drive down to Howards End to meet Helen. Margaret becomes increasingly incensed by the way in which Mr. Wilcox and the doctor label Helen, describing her as "highly strung" (282). Margaret slips out of the car first, and comes upon Helen on the porch of Howards End. Helen is heavily pregnant.

Margaret decides that she is "fighting for women against men" (283). She sends the doctor and Mr. Wilcox away. She discovers that her sister is to give birth in June, and that she has been living with Monica, an Italian feminist. Helen realizes that Howards End looks like their house now. The sisters realize that the house has "wonderful powers" (293), because as Margaret claims, Howards End "kills what is dreadful and makes what is beautiful live" (293).

Mr. Wilcox demands to know the name of Helen's "seducer" (296), whom he wants to make marry Helen. Margaret asks if Helen can stay the night at Howards End. Mr. Wilcox refuses, claiming he has "the memory of my dear wife to consider" (300). This argument angers Margaret, who insists that Mr. Wilcox should see the connection between his own adulterous behavior and Helen's actions. She accuses him of being "criminally muddled" (300).

Charles and Tibby meet at Ducie Street to discuss the situation. However, the two men struggle to communicate. Tibby cares nothing for social conventions or human relations, while Charles is convinced that the Schlegels are trying to ruin the reputation of his family. Crucially, however, Tibby mentions the Basts, and Charles becomes convinced that Leonard is the father of Helen's child.

Helen tells Margaret about her sexual encounter with Leonard Bast. Loneliness and a sense of injustice drove her actions. She saw Leonard that night "not [as] a man, but a cause" (303), a symbol of Mr. Wilcox's lack of social conscience. Afterwards she experienced panic, but now her "blinding hate" (305) of the Wilcoxes has gone. Margaret and Helen talk of Mrs. Wilcox, whom they believe would have known everything and understood everything. Unlike the Schlegels or the Wilcoxes, Mrs. Wilcox had succeeded in connecting the seen and unseen. That night, both Helen and Margaret sleep at Howards End.

Leonard is troubled by remorse over his relationship with Helen. It never occurs to Leonard that Helen was to blame. Leonard is becoming increasingly unemployable and has turned to his family for financial handouts. He visits Ducie Street to call on Margaret, and Tibby tells him that she is at Howards End. Leonard travels to Howards End resolving to confess all to Margaret. However, on his arrival at the house he meets Charles who beats him with a stick. In the confusion, a book falls on top of Leonard and he dies of heart failure.

An inquest is held and Charles is committed to trial, before being sentenced to three years imprisonment. Margaret resolves to go to Germany with Helen. She tells Mr. Wilcox she is leaving, and he admits that he is finally "ended" (324). Margaret takes him, a broken man, to Howards End.

Fourteen months pass, and Helen, Margaret and Mr. Wilcox are living at Howards End, with Helen's young baby. Mr. Wilcox is presently shut up inside the house, due to his hay fever. Margaret tells Helen to love her child, admitting that she cannot love children. Margaret has now made a permanent home at Howards End, but the suburbs are creeping ever closer. Mr. Wilcox announces to his children that he is to leave Howards End to Margaret, who will pass it after her death to Helen's son, her nephew. Dolly mentions Mrs. Wilcox's scribbled bequest, and Margaret learns for the first time that Mrs. Wilcox always wanted her to have Howards End. The novel ends as Helen bursts in joyously with news that the hay has just been cut.

Historical Context

"Howards End" was written and published during the Edwardian era. While the Merchant Ivory film adaptations of Forster's novels often present this period as a halcyon interlude in British history, it was, in fact, a time of great change and upheaval, as Victorian Britain shifted into the modern age. "Howards End" addresses this transition between eras, as Forster speculates about the future of England, while examining its changing political, social, cultural, and physical landscape.

Growing national rivalries in Europe contributed to the sense of transition and change in the Edwardian era. The rise of Germany, since its unification in 1871, threatened the military and industrial dominance that Britain had attained in the Victorian era. Significantly, the Schlegel sisters are Anglo-German, and thus represent Europe's two foremost rival national powers. Although "Howards End" makes repeated reference to the growth of German nationalism, Forster explicitly connects the sisters' father to an earlier German era. Despite fighting in the Prussian wars of the mid-nineteenth century, he was a pre-nationalist German, better classed "as the countryman of Hegel and Kant, as the idealist, inclined to be dreamy, whose Imperialism was the Imperialism of the air" (42). The sisters' British Aunt Juley exhibits more a straightforward form of patriotism, and would have the sisters "English to the backbone" (23). However, Helen and Margaret reject both English and German nationalism. When Margaret was thirteen years old she remarked: "To me one of two things is very clear: either God does not know his own mind about England and Germany, or else these do not know the mind of God" (44). "Howards End's" rejection of the nationalism and patriotism that characterized the Edwardian period

is significant because it was such national rivalry that helped precipitate the First World War only four years after the publication of "Howards End."

The novel also makes frequent references to imperialism, another key feature of the period. By the early twentieth century, the British Empire was the largest in the world, with colonies in India, Australia, Canada, and many other locations around the globe. Britain had also competed for colonies in Africa alongside Germany, France and Belgium in the late nineteenth century, during what was called "the scramble for Africa." "Howards End" focuses largely on Britain's connections with African colonies. It is to Nigeria, for example, that Paul must "go to make his way" (35). Europeans conceived of colonization, particularly in Africa, as a duty. White Europeans widely assumed that it was their responsibility to civilize African "savagery," what Rudyard Kipling would refer to as famously as "the white man's burden," in his poem of that name. Crucially, even Margaret presents Paul's actions in this light. Despite coming back ill from Nigeria, he has returned "out to his duty" (119). Mouthing the Wilcox family's own justifications, Margaret claims, "He doesn't want the money, it is work he wants, though it is beastly work" (119). However, these statements are disingenuous. Mr. Wilcox's business, Imperial and West Africa Rubber Company, relies for its profits on the actions of men like his son, Paul. The map of Africa in Mr. Wilcox's office, "on which the whole continent appeared, looking like a whale marked out for blubber" (196), reveals the exploitative nature of European imperial activities in Africa.

The Schlegel family's response to imperialism is important. The sisters' father had rejected imperialism and Tibby is explicitly hostile to the concept. Margaret lacks interest in imperialism. As she tells Tibby, "Empire bores me" (119). She associates a "formlessness and vagueness" (196) with Africa and confuses Nigeria with India in a conversation with Mrs. Wilcox. Although

Margaret repeats the Wilcox family's easy plati-
tudes about Paul's activities in Africa, after visiting
Mr. Wilcox's office, she realizes "Imperialism
always had been one of her difficulties" (197).
Forster also saw "this new age of international
finance and competing nationalisms" (Caraliero
108) as a threat to the liberal values embodied by
the Schlegel sisters. Significantly, the small space
of Howards End is depicted as a defense against
empire. Margaret's visit prompts a memory of "the
map of Africa" (202) and the realization that "ten
square miles are not ten times as wonderful as one
square mile, that a thousand square miles are not
practically the same as heaven" (201).

Societal Context

"Howards End" is often described as a
"condition-of-England" novel. This term, stem-
ming from fiction of the 1840s and 50s, denotes
novels like Elizabeth Gaskell's "North and South"
and Charles Dickens' "Hard Times," which examine and critique the state of Britain. "Howards End"
explores a number of Edwardian social issues,
including English class structure, the changing role
of women and England's gradual shift from a rural
to urban society.

One side effect of the industrial revolution in
Britain was the increase in the number of people
able to live from unearned income. The rentier
class, or independent class, as the Victorians called
them, grew throughout the nineteenth century. The
Schlegel sisters belong firmly to this class, and
are able to live comfortably on the income from
their investments. Like many others members of
the rentier class during this period, the Schlegels
invest heavily in "Foreign Things" (28), which do
markedly better than Aunt Juley's British railway
stocks. Indeed, between 1855 and 1914, British
investment abroad amounted to over four billion
pounds (Delany 71). According to Paul Delany,
the impact of this overseas investment was enormous, as it allowed "the displacement of industry

overseas" (73). In other words, investment in
"Foreign Things" allowed the South of England
to reap the financial benefits of industrialization,
while preserving the rural landscape, so beloved by
Forster, a little longer.

The Utilitarian philosophy of the nineteenth
century had assumed that the growth of the
bourgeoisie would result in an improved social
order and a better standard of living for the poor
(Cavaliero 16). However, by the early twentieth
century, this idea was becoming discredited. Much
of "Howards End" focuses on bourgeois social
responsibility and the impact of financial status on
individual subjectivity. Margaret and her friends
debate such topics as how millionaires should dis-
pose of their wealth (132), and how best to help the
poor. However, "Howards End," as Forster tells us
explicitly, is "not concerned with the very poor"
(58). Instead, this novel "deals with gentlefolk or
with those who are obliged to pretend they are gentlefolk" (58). The interaction of these two classes
is seen most clearly in Leonard Bast's encounters
with the Schlegel sisters. Bast, a young clerk, is
not absolutely impoverished when he first appears
in the novel. Instead, his class is "near enough her
[Margaret's] own for its manners to vex her" (50).
Bast struggles to educate himself and is desperate
to "come to Culture" (62). However, Margaret's
encounter with Bast forces her realization that
"independent thoughts are in nine cases out of ten
the result of independent means" (134). Rather than
scorning financial security, Forster emphasizes that
money, or the lack of it, has an inestimable effect of
the intellectual and personal development of individuals. As Forster stresses, Bast is "not as courte-
ous as the average rich man, nor as intelligent, nor
as healthy, nor as lovable" (58) because he is poor.
Despite rising literacy rates, and the introduction
of mass education in the late nineteenth century,
Forster argues it is still almost impossible for the
poor to achieve as much intellectually as the rich.
Even Bast himself finally realizes that he will

never achieve his intellectual and cultural ambitions, because "one must have money" (235) to do so. Leonard's realization is also significant for the Schlegel sisters. The investments that allow them time and leisure for independent thought are possible only because of the hard work of the poor in Britain and abroad. As Forster writes of his class, the rentier class, "we did not realise that all the time we were exploiting the poor of our own country and the backward races abroad, and getting bigger profits from our investments than we should. We refused to face this unpalatable truth" (Delany 68).

The industrial revolution in Britain sparked a mass migration from the country into the city. Leonard Bast is a product of this migration. While his grandparents were agricultural laborers, Bast works as a clerk in London, but is not the better for the move. As Forster writes, "one guessed him as the third generation, grandson to the shepherd or ploughboy whom civilization had sucked into the town; as one of the thousand who have lost the life of the body and failed to reach the life of the spirit" (122). The suburbs that Forster so dislikes, also represent this migration of Britain's population into its cities, as Britain became increasingly urbanized through the nineteenth and twentieth centuries. At the time of Mrs. Wilcox's funeral, the suburbs could be seen from high ground near Howards End. At the end of the novel, they are creeping towards the house itself. Forster was extremely ambivalent about this shift in Britain's physical landscape. He had deep love of rural England, which was matched only by his suspicion of urbanization.

"Howards End" also deals with the changing role of women in the Edwardian period. The woman's suffrage movement, which campaigned for women's right to vote, gained momentum in Britain at this time. Led by Emmeline Pankhurst, the Women's Political and Social Union, or suffragette movement, began a militant campaign of action in the first decade of the twentieth century.

Though not explicitly depicted as suffragettes, both Margaret and Helen Schlegel support women's suffrage, unlike Mrs. Wilcox, who is "only too thankful not to have a vote" (87). Helen and Margaret represent what Mr. Wilcox calls "emancipated wom[e]n" (152). They are financially independent, educated and hold "progressive" ideas. Mr. Wilcox represents the conventional, conservative masculine view of women at this time. He dismisses women's equality and suffrage. To him, the Schlegel sisters are "unpractical" and vulnerable: "girls like that oughtn't to live alone in London" (153). However, both Helen and Margaret subvert Mr. Wilcox's expectations. Helen becomes pregnant outside the bounds of marriage, and does so—crucially—by seducing Leonard. This fundamentally disrupts the preconceptions of Mr. Wilcox, who is unable to conceive of a woman initiating an unsanctioned sexual encounter. Furthermore, Helen also behaves in stereotypically masculine fashion after her night with Leonard. She has no desire to see him again, and attempts to pay him off with five thousand pounds. "Howards End" also points to the double standard that characterized conventional British attitudes to sex in its depiction of Helen's relationship with Leonard. While Mr. Wilcox excuses his affair with Jacky on the grounds that "I am a man, and have lived a man's past" (230), he refuses to allow the pregnant Helen to stay at Howards End, out of respect to the memory of his first wife. Margaret calls this hypocrisy "criminally muddled" (300).

Religious Context

Increasing religious skepticism marked the late nineteenth century. Darwinism, and the work of thinkers such as philosopher Friedrich Nietzsche and psychoanalyst Sigmund Freud, threatened traditional Christian beliefs. Writers like Samuel Butler, whose novel, "The Way of All Flesh," was deeply influential on Forster's own work, satirized organized religion. Forster himself became an atheist while he was at Cambridge, and later served as president of the Humanist society.

Margaret and Helen's rejection of traditional religion reflects this increasing trend in British society. Indeed, when Leonard Bast meets Margaret he assumes she is "one of those soulless, atheistical women" (53). Margaret herself admits that she "was not a Christian in the accepted sense; she did not believe that God had ever worked amongst us as a young artisan" (91), while Helen specifically attacks Victorian notions of Christianity, which saw poverty as God's will. Helen decides to help the Basts, in order to "show up the wretchedness that lies under this luxury, this talk of impersonal forces, this cant about God doing what we're too slack to do ourselves" (223). Helen recognizes that society's assumption that God would help the poor is an abnegation of its own responsibility.

During this period, many people also began to look for alternatives to orthodox Christianity, and the early twentieth century saw a growth in interest in spiritualism and non-Judeo-Christian religions. Forster reflects this interest in "Howards End." Margaret pokes fun at the clientele of Mr. Eustace Miles', who believe in auras and astral places (158), while even Helen's references to goblins in her interpretation of Beethoven's Fifth symphony invokes a non-Christian mythology. "Howards End" also harkens back to older folklore and superstition. Mrs. Wilcox tells Margaret about the pigs' teeth in the Wych-Elm tree, the bark of which was believed to cure toothache (82).

Scientific & Technological Context

Industrialization and new technologies, such as the railway and telegraph, changed Britain rapidly throughout the nineteenth century. The first decade of the twentieth century saw a continuation of this rapid transformation. The invention of the motorcar in the late nineteenth century was beginning to make an impact on Britain. Though still the preserve of the rich, the car was gradually changing conceptions of space and movement, as well as the British landscape. The car was widely disliked during this period, in part because of the dust it raised on roads, which had not yet been tar marked (Stallybrass 11). The car is the ultimate symbol of the threat posed by the modern world in "Howards End." It is firmly associated with the "seen" world of the Wilcox family, who owns several motorcars. Forster depicts the vehicle in an intensely negative light. Charles and Aunt Juley argue in one, while Margaret jumps from a moving car that has hit a dog. It is a symbol of the upheaval and pace of modern life, in direct contrast to the permanence and peace that Forster values in this novel. Indeed, it is only in Howards End that Margaret "recaptured the sense of space which the motor had tried to rob from her" (201). The car embodies "Howards End's" deep suspicion of technology, which Forster blames for a depersonalization of human relations, and the growth of the urban, industrial landscape that threatens his beloved English countryside.

Telegrams are the other key technology in "Howards End." By 1910, the telegram was a standard form of communication, while the telephone was also becoming more widespread. Like the car, the telegram is depicted negatively. Forster deliberately contrasts the brusque brevity of the telegram with the more expressive form of the letter in the novel's opening chapters. As Margaret notes, telegrams are "cold and cryptic" (26). This form of communication is also explicitly associated with the impersonal, "seen" world of the Wilcoxes, like the motorcar. As Margaret tells Helen of the Wilcoxes, "The truth is that there is a great outer life that you and I have never touched—a life in which telegrams and anger count" (41).

There is some respite from the upheaval associated with technology at the close of the novel. The Schlegels are settled in their permanent residence, Howards End, and since the death of Leonard, we are told that "the time for telegrams and anger was over" (321). However, the encroaching suburbs serve as a final reminder that the peace the Schlegel sisters find at Howards End is only a temporary respite from the unrelenting industrialization and technological growth that characterized Britain in this period.

Biographical Context

Perhaps the most obvious connection between Forster's life and this novel is Howards End itself, which is modeled after Forster's childhood home, Rooksnest. Rooksnest, like Howards End, is an old, red brick country house situated in the county of Hertfordshire. Like Howards End, Rooksnest even has an old wych-elm tree in its grounds. Forster held the house in great affection; however his family was forced to leave Rooksnest in 1893, when their lease expired, just as the Schlegels are forced to leave Wickham Place. The creeping urbanization of the countryside around Howards End is also inspired by Rooksnest's situation, as—much to Forster's distress—the suburbs of Stevenage continued to encroach on the house through his lifetime.

Some commentators have noted other biographical connections to "Howards End." Paul Delany argues that Tibby is "a surrogate for Forster himself" (74). Both Forster and Tibby share a deep interest in art and literature, and both grew up in female dominated households. There is also a hint that Tibby is slightly effeminate and, perhaps, homosexual, like Forster himself. As the narrator tells us, Tibby handles a teapot "almost too deftly" (55). However, the rather cold and unemotional Tibby seems far less interested in human beings and their relationships, than Forster apparently was.

Whether or not Tibby is a version of the author, Forster undoubtedly shares many of the sensibilities of the Schlegel family. Like the Schlegels, he believed art and culture were of central importance to human life, claiming they are what "distinguishes us from the animals" (Lago 1). Furthermore, Forster shared the Schlegel sisters' liberal politics, recognizing that the wealth of the middle and upper classes rested on the exploitation of the poor at home and abroad. Forster also shared the sisters' apparent atheism. Having lost his religious faith while an undergraduate student at Cambridge, Forster later became president of the humanist society.

"Howards End" is a novel of oppositions, between the seen and unseen, the practical and abstract, the mechanical and the artistic. Some critics have contended that these oppositions correspond to a division in Forster's own identity. Homosexuality was not legalized in Britain until 1967, and Forster was forced to lead a double life of sorts, conducting homosexual affairs in secret. Critic Glen Cavaliero even points to the confusion over Forster's first name (registered at birth as Henry, but christened Edward) to suggest that different aspects of Forster's personality correspond to Wilcox and Schlegel qualities: "One part of him was Henry, the other Edward; one was conservative, serious, truthful and punctilious, the other was rebellious, humorous and unexpected" (1). The novel's epigraph, "Only Connect" may indicate his desire to reconcile the different aspects of his life.

Anne Longmuir, Ph.D.

Works Cited

Cavaliero, Glen. *A Reading of E. M. Forster.* London: MacMillan, 1979.

Delany, Paul. *Island of Money: Rentier Culture in Howards End.* New Casebooks: *E. M.* Forster. Jeremy Tambling, Ed. Basingstoke: MacMillan, 1995. 67–80.

Forster, *E. M. Howards End.* London: Penguin, 1973.

Lago, Mary. *E. M. Forster: A Literary Life.* Basingstoke: MacMillan, 1995.

Stallybrass, Oliver. Editor's Introduction. *Howards End.* London: Penguin, 1973. 7–17.

Discussion Questions

1. The opening of "Howards End" is famously informal. What purpose does the first chapter serve in terms of setting up the novel's themes?

2. What kinds of oppositions does Forster set up between the Wilcox and Schlegel families?

3. What do we learn about each character from their response to Beethoven's Fifth Symphony?

4. Margaret Schlegel claims, "independent thoughts are in nine cases out of ten the result of independent means" (134). Do you agree? Why? Why not?

5. What do we learn about Margaret and Mrs. Wilcox during Margaret's unsuccessful lunch party? What values does Mrs. Wilcox symbolize?

6. What is the significance of the Schlegel sisters' Anglo-German parentage?

7. What does the motorcar symbolize in this novel?

8. What is the symbolic function of Helen's sexual encounter with Leonard Bast? Is it psychologically realistic?

9. Forster calls Jacky "bestially stupid" (224) and Dolly "a rubbishy little creature" (101). Is he guilty of misogyny? Why? Why not?

10. Is the conclusion of "Howards End" optimistic? Why? Why not?

Essay Ideas

1. Analyze the symbolism of "Howards End." Consider whether it ever detracts from the psychological realism of the novel.

2. Examine the depiction of gender in "Howards End."

3. Examine the role of money and class in "Howards End."

4. "Howards End" is sometimes described as a "condition-of-England" novel. Explain whether this designation is appropriate.

5. The epigraph of "Howards End" is "Only connect…" What oppositions does Forster set up in this novel, and does he succeed in connecting them?

Charlotte Brontë's work is featured twice in this volume, *Jane Eyre* on page 119, and *Villette* on page 239. Brontë, who is pictured above, wrote under the pseudonym Bell, and was one of three sisters. By age 13, she was writing and hand sewing her own books of poetry and prose. Photo: Library of Congress.

The Interlopers

by Saki [Hector Hugh Munro]

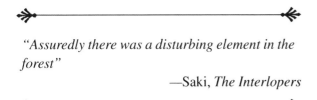

"Assuredly there was a disturbing element in the forest"

—Saki, *The Interlopers*

Content Synopsis

On a wild winter's night, a landowner, Ulrich von Gradwitz, patrols a steep, forested strip of land on the margin of his estate. Though he is a hunter, he is not looking for deer or boar, but a human quarry, his neighbor, Georg Znaeym. There has been a feud between their families for generations; since a legal ruling deposed a Znaeym from this piece of land and bestowed it upon von Gradwitz, the two men have inherited an ancestral hatred. Von Gradwitz suspects that Znaeym is poaching on his land; the roebuck are running and other creatures not usually active at night have clearly been disturbed. He posts men on the crest of a hill and goes down through the undergrowth to the valley bottom. Rounding the trunk of a huge beech tree, he comes face to face with Znaeym. For a moment, the two enemies stare at one another. Before either can shoot, the fierce wind brings down the tree. Both men are pinned to the ground, close together, alive, but badly hurt.

The prone men exchange insults and curses, and each predicts that his foresters will arrive first, and kill the other. Eventually, they fall silent, weakened by pain and cold. Von Gradwitz manages to reach his pocket flask and on an impulse offers Znaeym a drink. At first, Znaeym refuses, but von Gradwitz persists. In the face of probable imminent death, the old hatred suddenly seems unimportant. They are reconciled. If either band of foresters reaches them in time, von Gradwitz or Znaeym will order them to rescue his neighbor. The two lie silent for a while, imagining the future without the poison of the feud, when they will visit one another on feast days and invite each other to hunt over their respective estates.

The wind drops and the men cooperate for the first time in their lives on a joint venture, calling for help. Together, their voices carry further than one man's alone, and after a while, von Gradwitz can make out, though indistinctly, figures coming down the hill towards them. Each hopes that it will be his men who arrive first, so that he will be the one to demonstrate his magnanimity and nobility. Von Gradwitz notes that they are making good speed. Then he breaks off. Znaeym impatiently demands to know who they are, and von Gradwitz, with a laugh: "the idiotic chattering laugh of a man unstrung with hideous fear," replies, "Wolves" (452).

Style & Theme

"The Interlopers" has elements utterly characteristic of Saki's writing: an eastern European setting;

men familiar with the woods and the wild; wolves (a recurring motif); a twist at the end; and black humor. The style too is characteristic, ranging from the airy disdain for readers' desire for specific detail: "a forest of mixed growth" to the ironic reference to an obscure region: "one of the eastern spurs of the Carpathians" as though every reader would, of course, be familiar with the topography of the area (447). The language is quite formal, with an Edwardian cadence; there are few contractions and little use of slang. Even while severely injured and facing death at the hands of each other's partisans, the protagonists keep a certain arrogant insouciance. Zmaeym says, "Your men will find you dead under a fallen beech tree. For form's sake I shall send my condolences to your family." Von Gradwitz replies: "It is a useful hint [. . .] Only as you will have met your death poaching on my lands I don't think I can decently send any message of condolence to your family" (448).

Historical Context

The Carpathian Mountains, in present-day Romania, were once part of Transylvania, a region of Hungary. In the middle ages, the area was invaded by the expanding Turkish Ottoman empire, the defense against which was led by the infamous Prince Vlad, known as "The Impaler." In the twentieth century, the area was inhabited by a number of different nationalities: Hungarian, Polish, Romany, German, and was subject to border and boundary changes and disputes that often erupted into violent conflict. The story could be read as a satire on conflicts over useless strips of land between neighboring states that result in both sides being left crippled and vulnerable and the land being left exposed and open to opportunistic outsiders.

"The Interlopers" was written during another conflict which embraced Eastern Europe, the First World War, but Saki, born in 1870, was almost forty-four when that war was declared, and in many ways his world-view remained pre-war. The story should be read in the context of Victorian and Edwardian fiction by authors such as Oscar Wilde (whose work influenced Saki), A. A. Milne (a fan of Saki's writing), and M. R. James (most famous for the ghost story "Oh whistle and I'll come to you"), as well as more fanciful and whimsical writing by, for example, Kenneth Grahame, Ronald Firbank, Max Beerbohm and James Stephens. Saki's work could also be seen as having much in common with the colonial adventure stories of authors such as Rudyard Kipling and H. Rider Haggard. Many of the stories are fantastic or supernatural in content, but are realist in form and technique. Saki never took part in the Modernist experiments of contemporary writers such as Virginia Woolf and James Joyce.

Societal Context

Many of Saki's stories are disguised as light and frothy social comedies or decadent anecdotes narrated by youthful dandies. The suggestion is that there are no morals in these tales, and very little morality. The wonderfully spare, pointed, and polished style can cause the reader to skate over the surface and miss the real literary value of the writing, as well as its underlying message. "The Interlopers" displays some of humankind's less noble characteristics, and contrasts them with the behavior of "beasts." The story explores the opposition between the unnatural and pointless viciousness of humankind: "as boys they had thirsted for one another's blood, as men each prayed that misfortune might fall on the other"; and the natural killing instincts of animals (447). Unfortunately for the two protagonists, when they give up on one kind of bloodthirstiness they become victims of the other. Virtue is seldom rewarded in Saki's writing, and the reader is rarely allowed a sentimental or happy ending.

As in Classical Greek tragedy, "The Interlopers" shows men punished not for present but past crimes, even for the faults of their ancestors. The protagonists' repentance and reconciliation does not earn them redemption; nemesis descends regardless. The agents of nemesis, as often happens in Saki's stories, are wild animals. The message seems to be that life is not much like Aesop's "Fables," fairy stories or any other moral tales, so don't expect renunciation of your wicked ways and reformation of your life to bring about a happy ending; the wolves may still get you. The ending of "The Interlopers" threatens though it does not depict nemesis in the form of a horrible death. This is typical of the more macabre of Saki's stories. In his "The Satire of Saki: A Study of the Satiric Art of Hector H. Munro" (Exposition Press, 1963), critic George James Spears remarks: "We do not deny Munro's predilection for the ghoulish and sadistic" (51). Not all of Saki's writing was either ghoulish or sadistic; some is light, witty, and very amusing, and though the nemesis he doles out to his characters is often appalling, it is very rarely fully described. Again, as in Classical Greek drama, it is usually enacted off-stage.

Who are the interlopers of the title? From the perspective of von Gradwitz, Znaeym is an interloper, a trespasser and poacher on his land. Znaeym, who rejects the decision of the courts, sees von Gradwitz as an interloper and land-thief. Both are interlopers on nature. They are where they should not be, in the world of the wild, among high winds, running deer, and hunting wolves, and their trespass costs them their lives. The hunters become the hunted and the predators become the prey. We might think that the wolves are interlopers because Znaeym says that he and von Gradwitz will fight to the death: "you and I and our foresters, with no cursed interlopers to come between us" (449). The wolves come between; they interlope and intervene, but between the new friendships, not the old fight. In terms of the forest, the wolves are not interlopers. They are in their rightful place, going about their rightful business. To the trapped and helpless men they are terrifying, but they are not culpable.

Whatever the social message of the story, Saki was no pacifist. He enlisted in the British army when war was declared in September 1914, and in many of his stories glorifies and even romanticizes the cause of patriotism. It seems to suggest that it is natural for men to have aggressive instincts that lead them to fight, and that fighting is only dishonorable if it is not channeled into a proper cause such as the defense of one's homeland.

Religious Context

The reconciliation of von Gradwitz and Znaeym seems not to have been prompted by religious feeling. Relief at having survived the fall of the tree mingled with anger at being trapped beneath it make von Gradwitz produce "a strange medley of thank-offerings and sharp curses" (449–50), but beyond this, the men neither pray for deliverance nor make any kind of religious preparation for death. The only prayers that come to their lips are when each "prayed a private prayer that his men might be the first to arrive, so that he might be the first to show honorable attention to the enemy that had become a friend" (451). The prayer is not answered, and the revelation of exactly who (or what) has come in answer to their calls so paralyzes the men with fear that we infer they make no more prayers. It could be suggested, however, that von Gradwitz, who makes the first conciliatory move, and who persists in spite of Znaeym's rejection of it, is motivated by religious or at least moral reasoning. He says that the two have "quarreled like devils all our lives over this stupid strip of forest, where the trees can't even stand upright in a breath of wind," and continues: "Lying here tonight, thinking, I've come to think we've been rather fools; there are better things in life than getting the better of a boundary dispute." (450). That he addresses his old enemy as "Neighbor" perhaps suggests that he is thinking of the commandment "Love thy neighbor as thyself."

Scientific & Technological Context

That the setting of the story is modern is made clear by the inclusion of a rifle and the reference to the sportsman's calendar, which is an index of animals that it is permissible to hunt, and the seasons at which it is permissible to do so. We are not given a specific date for the story, other than the fairy-tale-like "one winter's night." For a modern reader, the Carpathians are likely to be associated with old Transylvania and the Dracula legends, so one feels that this could be an archetypal story, set in any period. A sparsely inhabited, mountainous, thickly forested land inhabited by wolves is a mysterious and potentially eerie place, a perfect setting for an atmospheric out-of-time fable, and apart from the mention of the rifle and the possibility that the men will shoot one another, modern science and technology play no part in the story. The law is not that of modern civilization, but of the wild.

Biographical Context

H. H. Munro (Saki) was a foreign correspondent for the *Morning Post*, a Tory (politically right wing) daily newspaper, for a number of years before returning to journalism and fiction writing in London. During that time, he visited Poland, the Balkans, Russia, and France, and remained greatly interested in the politics and history of those countries. He would have been well aware of the troubled history of the land in which "The Interlopers" is set.

Most of Saki's short stories first appeared in periodicals such as the *Morning Post*, the *Westminster Gazette*, and the *Bystander*. During his lifetime, four collections of stories were published: "Reginald," "Reginald in Russia," "The Chronicles of Clovis and Beasts" and "Super-Beasts." Two further collections were published posthumously: "The Toys of Peace" and "The Square Egg." "The Interlopers" appeared in book form in "The Toys of Peace," a disparate collection first amassed by Ethel Munro and the publisher John Lane and published by the Bodley Head in 1923, seven years after Saki's death. The collection was dedicated to his regiment, the 22nd Royal Fusiliers, and some of the stories were written in France, at the front, where he was killed by a sniper's bullet in October 1916. The story has been reprinted in many selections from Saki's work, including the Penguin "Complete Saki." When he was writing the story, Saki's mind seems to have been on the wilder parts of Eastern Europe and Asia. During a short leave from the army, in June 1916, he stayed with his brother, Charles, and sister, Ethel, in London. Ethel Munro was later to say that he then revealed his plan to buy some land in Siberia after the war. "'I could never settle down again to the tameness of London life,' he told me. [. . .] It would have been a remarkable life, wild animals beyond the dreams of avarice, at our very doors, and, before long, inside them." (E. E. Munro, 108–9.)

Sandie Byrne

Works Cited

Langguth , A.J. Saki. *A Life of Hector Hugh Munro.* London: Hamish Hamilton, 1981.

Munro, E. E. *Biography of Saki, in Saki, The Square Egg.* London: The Bodley Head, 1924.

Saki, A. J. *The Interlopers, in The Complete Saki.* Harmondsworth: Penguin, 1982.

Spears, George James. *The Satire of Saki: A Study of the Satiric Art of Hector H. Munro.* New York, 1963.

Discussion Questions

1. Why do you think Ulrich von Gradwitz decides to give up the quarrel and offer friendship to Georg Znaeym?
2. What makes Georg Znaeym change his mind about accepting Gradwitz's offer?
3. If the figures hurrying towards von Gradwitz and Znaeym had been one of the two parties of men rather than wolves, what do you think would have happened? Would the two have remained friends as they imagine?
4. Do we get any sense of the two protagonists of the story having different personalities?
5. We might wonder why von Gradwitz, whom we have been told has a rifle, doesn't fire a shot to frighten away the wolves. Is it a weakness of the story that it does not specify that the weapon is beyond his reach?
6. Why is the story called "The Interlopers" and who do you think are the interlopers?
7. How does Saki create atmosphere in the story?
8. How does the narrator of the story give us the sense that the men's quarrel is pointless?
9. "The Interlopers" is a short story, but does it contain enough plot line, characterization, or other matter to have been developed into a novella?
10. Is the story about justice? If so, is justice done?

Essay Ideas

1. Write about Saki's satire using "The Interlopers" as your example.
2. Compare "The Interlopers" to another Saki "nemesis" story such as "The Hounds of Fate" or "The Easter Egg."
3. Compare the twists in Saki's tales to those of another short story writer such as O. Henry.
4. Discuss wolves in Saki's short stories taking as your examples "The Interlopers," "The Wolves of Cernogranz" and "The She-Wolf."
5. Compare the ending of "The Interlopers" with those of "The Hounds of Fate," "The Open Window" and "The Forbidden Buzzards."

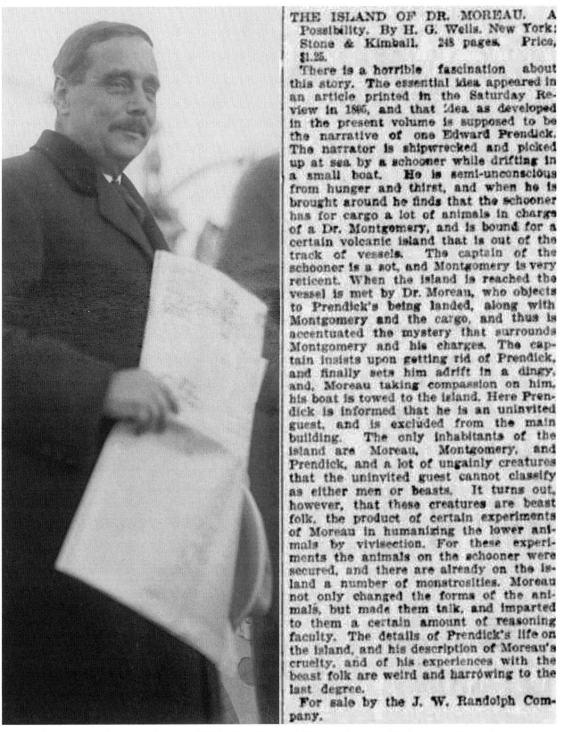

THE ISLAND OF DR. MOREAU. A Possibility. By H. G. Wells. New York: Stone & Kimball. 248 pages. Price, $1.25.

There is a horrible fascination about this story. The essential idea appeared in an article printed in the Saturday Review in 1895, and that idea as developed in the present volume is supposed to be the narrative of one Edward Prendick. The narrator is shipwrecked and picked up at sea by a schooner while drifting in a small boat. He is semi-unconscious from hunger and thirst, and when he is brought around he finds that the schooner has for cargo a lot of animals in charge of a Dr. Montgomery, and is bound for a certain volcanic island that is out of the track of vessels. The captain of the schooner is a sot, and Montgomery is very reticent. When the island is reached the vessel is met by Dr. Moreau, who objects to Prendick's being landed, along with Montgomery and the cargo, and thus is accentuated the mystery that surrounds Montgomery and his charges. The captain insists upon getting rid of Prendick, and finally sets him adrift in a dingy, and, Moreau taking compassion on him, his boat is towed to the island. Here Prendick is informed that he is an uninvited guest, and is excluded from the main building. The only inhabitants of the island are Moreau, Montgomery, and Prendick, and a lot of ungainly creatures that the uninvited guest cannot classify as either men or beasts. It turns out, however, that these creatures are beast folk, the product of certain experiments of Moreau in humanizing the lower animals by vivisection. For these experiments the animals on the schooner were secured, and there are already on the island a number of monstrosities. Moreau not only changed the forms of the animals, but made them talk, and imparted to them a certain amount of reasoning faculty. The details of Prendick's life on the island, and his description of Moreau's cruelty, and of his experiences with the beast folk are weird and harrowing to the last degree.

For sale by the J. W. Randolph Company.

H. G. Wells, pictured above, was born in 1866 in Kent, England. His experiences with the inequalities of the class system and his knowledge of science, which he studied at the University of London, are evident in *The Island of Dr. Moreau,* opposite. Other works by Wells featured in this volume appear on page 41, *The Country of the Blind;* and page 47, *The Door in the Wall.* Photo: Library of Congress.

The Island of Dr. Moreau

by H. G. Wells

Content Synopsis

Herbert George (H. G.) Wells' 1896 novel "The Island of Dr. Moreau" tells the fantastic tale of a shipwrecked man who stumbles onto an isolated island in the South Pacific where a once-respected scientist named Moreau conducts cruel and unnatural experiments on live animals, in an attempt to transform beasts into humans. The story is told in the form of a manuscript of the shipwrecked man, Edward Prendick, as found by his nephew long after the deaths of all the principal characters in the adventure. In the introduction, Prendick's nephew establishes that his uncle was a passenger on the "Lady Vain" in 1887, when that ship collided with a derelict vessel and sunk. Prendick was picked up eleven months later, at sea in an open boat, with an incredible story to tell. After this introduction, the nephew allows Prendick to tell the story.

One of the major themes of the text is the bestial nature of civilized man, and Wells sounds this theme at the beginning of Prendick's story. Prendick relates that after the "Lady Vain" sunk, he was adrift in a lifeboat with two other survivors. As food and water supplies became depleted, one of the other survivors proposes that the men draw lots and resort to cannibalism to survive. Although Prendick initially resists, believing that it would be better to die together than sacrifice one of their numbers to such a gruesome fate, on the seventh day, he agrees. However, the unfortunate sailor who is odd man out refuses to sacrifice himself. Prendick's fellow survivors begin to fight on the fragile dinghy, and both tumble overboard and sink "like stones" (Wells 3).

Horrified, but relieved, Prendick is picked up days later by the schooner "Ipecacuanha" and is nursed back to health by a secretive physician named Montgomery. The "Ipecacuanha"—named for a South American shrub that has purgative properties—is carrying a cargo full of live animals to Montgomery's as-yet-unnamed employer. After Montgomery restores the badly dehydrated Prendick to a semblance of health, Prendick notices that Montgomery's attendant M'Ling has a strange, dark, and bestial appearance that unsettles man and animal alike on board the ship. The schooner's captain is a drunken, brutish man who dislikes Montgomery, M'Ling, and the dirty, agitated cargo he is carrying. He soon takes a violent dislike to Prendick as well, and when the ship lands at Montgomery's home island to deliver its living cargo, the captain orders Prendick off the ship, to whatever fate awaits him. Prendick appeals to Montgomery's employer for help, but the mysterious man refuses to accept the castaway.

Prendick is put to sea in a decrepit dinghy, and seems to face certain death until Montgomery's employer, Moreau, relents and comes back to rescue Prendick. Once again, Prendick notices the peculiar physiognomy of the boatmen in Moreau's service. They are dark, strangely built, and have a savage, inarticulate manner that is unlike anything Prendick has ever encountered. Prendick is admonished with vague warnings, and installed in a room at the perimeter of Moreau's compound. Moreau, who is described as "white-haired and broad-shouldered," is not unfriendly, but he is preoccupied and perplexed by the nuisance of an unexpected "guest" on his island.

One of the animals delivered to Moreau is a puma, and, judging from the screams of agony that issue forth from the labs, Prendick surmises that whatever is happening within Moreau's laboratories requires painful experiments on the puma. Prendick, who has had a dim awareness of having heard Moreau's name before, suddenly recollects a sensational news story from eleven years earlier. Moreau, Prendick recalls, was the name of a notorious vivisector who was investigated by an undercover reporter. The subsequent lurid account of Moreau's experiments outraged the public, and the scientist Moreau, rather than cease his experimentation, left England altogether. Prendick reasons correctly that the man on the island and the vilified scientist must be same man.

After thus identifying his host, Prendick is driven from the safety of his room by the constant screaming of the tortured puma. Prendick ventures out onto the island, where he encounters more unsettling creatures. He is stalked by a "half-bestial" man, whom he observes drinking from a pond on all fours; discovers the bloody, mutilated body of a rabbit; and watches three swinish creatures conferring in the woods.

It is while watching these creatures that Prendick realizes what has disturbed him about all of the "distorted" men on the island: they possess the unmistakable animal characteristics of dogs, horses, pigs, and other beasts. He perceives that somehow, Moreau has "created" these men. Prendick narrowly escapes the increasingly threatening woods as night falls. He retreats to his room, horrified by what he has discovered, only to make the awful discovery that, rather than the animal screams of the puma, he now hears the tormented cries of a human being.

Prendick believes that Moreau is turning men into beasts, unaware that what is really happening is the reverse. Panicked, he flees, and stumbles onto an enclave of Beast People and learns of a "Law" that requires very specific things of them. The Law admonishes them "not" to go on all fours, suck up drinks, eat flesh or fish, chase other men, or otherwise behave like beasts. To do so would ensure a return to Moreau's "House of Pain." Prendick is followed to the enclave by Moreau, Montgomery, and M'Ling, and, after a great deal of coaxing, he calms down enough to hear the real story from Moreau. The doctor explains that he is interested in the "plasticity of living forms" (68). He dismisses Prendick's objections to the wanton cruelty of his experiments, saying that he has never troubled himself about the "ethics of the matter," (72) arrogantly believing that scientific discovery is its own justification. He confirms that the Beast People are beast/human hybrids created by Moreau. Moreau confesses that, after twenty years of experimentation, he has yet to be satisfied by his results, claiming that the beastly nature of his subjects always returns, sometimes dangerously, to overcome whatever humanity he has infused in them.

Conditions on the island degenerate when the predatory Leopard Man reclaims his taste for blood. In his wanderings over the island, Prendick has seen evidence that someone or something—he suspects the Leopard Man—is hunting for bloody sport. He has further observed that at least some of the Beast People do travel on all fours, and do drink, as animals will. When he shares his observations with Montgomery, Montgomery immediately realizes the gravity of the situation, for if these Beast People disregard the respect for the Law (and the fear) that Moreau has instilled in them, no human or beast on the island is safe.

Moreau confronts the Beast People with their transgressions and during this confrontation, he shoots and kills the Leopard Man, but not before the creature has attacked Moreau, drawing blood. Significantly, the Beast People realize that Moreau can be injured. Later, as Moreau continues his experiments on the puma woman, she pulls loose her fetters and escapes the compound, pursued by the doctor. The puma and Moreau are found dead in the woods by Prendick, Montgomery, and, in an unfortunate turn of events, some of the Beast People. The Law slowly loosens its grip on the inhabitants of the island. Montgomery and Prendick soon grow to loathe each other's company, and Montgomery, whom Prendick perceives to be an alcoholic, leaves the relative security of the compound to drink with M'Ling and other companionable Beast People. This, of course, leads to the death of Montgomery and M'Ling.

Prendick is left alone on the island with the Beast People, who inexorably revert to their animal natures. After Moreau's compound burns to the ground in an accidental fire, Prendick is without shelter or protection. He is befriended by a St. Bernard Man and a tiny sloth creature, and he manages to keep the more aggressive Beast People at bay by manipulating what remains of their fear of man and of Moreau. Although Prendick realizes that Moreau is dead, the Beast People cannot easily accept that Moreau, who has created them and held supreme power over them, is truly gone. Prendick exploits this confusion by telling the Beast People that Moreau, though apparently dead, does see their actions and will return to punish them. For a time, he lives in relative safety among the Beast People.

When Prendick's St. Bernard Man is killed by a brutal Hyena-Swine, Prendick shoots and kills him, ridding the island of its most dangerous predator. Prendick is eventually able to leave the island when a small boat, apparently carrying the decomposed body of the captain of the "Ipecacuanha," washes ashore. Prendick casts off in this boat and is picked up at sea. He recounts the tale to his rescuers, who attribute it to dehydration and temporary madness. Prendick realizes that he must keep this story to himself, for no one will believe it to be the tale of a sane man. The last chapter of his account describes his unease among men and women, and the recurring sensation that all of the human beings he encounters are merely more refined specimens of the Beast People of Moreau's island. Although he knows, logically, that this is not true, he is unable to live happily and peacefully in the company of men, and lives out his life a relative recluse, far away from the cities of men.

Historical Context

One significant historical dimension to "The Island of Dr. Moreau" that may be lost on modern readers is its place in the late Victorian anti-vivisection controversy. Throughout the latter part of the nineteenth century, the Royal Society for the Prevention of Cruelty to Animals (RSPCA) expressed concern over the use of animals for scientific and medical experimentation. Vivisection, or invasive scientific experimentation on live animals, was often performed without the use of anesthesia, and the RSPCA and groups like it abhorred the suffering engendered by the practice. The Cruelty to Animals Act, passed 1876, imposed stiffer restrictions on practitioners of vivisection. Key provisions of the Act required that any such experimentation be scientifically necessary and justifiable, and that every means, including anesthesia, be employed to mitigate the animal's suffering during experimentation. Moreau tells Prendick that he arrived on the island eleven years prior to 1887, thus placing Moreau's arrival on the island in the same year as the passage of this act. The effect of anti-vivisection sentiments on Moreau is clear—a public angered by his stubborn refusal to cease animal experimentation has chased him out of England.

In light of this long-standing social and scientific controversy, many reviewers read Wells' story of Moreau through the filter of the anti-vivisection movement. One reviewer describes Moreau as "a cliché from the pages of an anti-vivisection pamphlet" (Mitchell 44). Another expresses the opinion that Wells has created a picture that will "render vivisection unpopular" more effectively than the many societies formed to oppose the practice (Hutton 46). However, Wells' text is ambiguous regarding the actual practice of vivisection. Moreau's experiments are horrors because of the utter gratuitousness of them. Moreau seeks no cure, nor does he aim for a humanitarian scientific breakthrough, and Prendick is repelled by the cruelty of this, but not by the idea of vivisection and animal experimentation itself.

Another significant, but subtle, reference in "The Island of Dr. Moreau" is its acknowledgement of the power of the popular press in Victorian England. The latter part of the nineteenth century saw a tremendous increase in newspapers, cheap periodicals, and broadsides. These publications fed the public taste for sensational stories. The press had the power to fuel interest in a good story—the media circus surrounding the "Jack the Ripper" Whitechappel murders in the 1880s give evidence of this—and Moreau's self-imposed exile from England comes as a result of a sensational journalistic "expose."

Societal Context

The morality and even the efficacy of Empire were being questioned in the late nineteenth century. In general, there were two distinct ways of thinking about Empire: it was a means to pursue and acquire wealth for England or it was an opportunity to civilize the savage and "unchristian" (usually brown or black) races who occupied colonial holdings. Some critics have suggested that "The Island of Dr. Moreau" can be read as a parody of this latter attitude. The Beast People are described as racially different, often dark, as well as bestial. In trying to make these beasts men, Moreau has only drawn out their unsavory qualities, taken them far away from what nature has made them, and given them an empty religion that is the mere chanting of the "Law" with no real understanding or faith. For many in Great Britain, this could also be a description of the effects of imperialism on indigenous people through the British empire. Prendick's repeated comparison of the Beast People to "savages" he has encountered only serves to reinforce this connection.

At the same time, the despotism of both the captain of the "Ipecacuanha," and of Moreau suggests a ruthless brutality in the treatment of colonial subjects. Both men are portrayed as the ultimate authority and the final word of law in their small fiefdoms. Yet, while the captain of the "Ipecacuanha" is clearly a brute and a drunkard who doesn't even rate a name in the text, the characterization of Moreau is ambiguous and more complicated. Moreau's physical appearance is distinguished and powerful, and he is clearly an educated and thoughtful man, suggesting that the oppressive despot can come with a fine appearance. At the same time, Moreau's iron grip on the Beast People is tenuous but necessary to the peace and stability of the island. When his "rule" is ended, the island descends into chaos.

Thematically, "The Island of Dr. Moreau" is often compared to Swift's "Gulliver's Travels" (1726) and Kipling's "Jungle Book" (1894). It offers a dark view of the qualities of the beast in man, as does Swift's satire, rather than a more ennobling and less misanthropic examination of the civilized qualities of beasts found in Kipling. Wells' conventions of the "lost island" and a society that exists apart from the mainstream also place "The Island of Dr. Moreau" in a utopian tradition dating back to Thomas More's 1516 "Utopia." Utopian novels create a society that is apart from the familiar, yet familiar enough to have resolved many of the problems facing humankind in contemporary society. "Moreau" belongs in the sub-genre of "dystopia," in that it suggests that human society is not capable of improvement, but will inevitably descend into chaos, repression, and ruin. Other dystopian novels include Huxley's "Brave New World" (1932) and Atwood's "The Handmaid's Tale" (1985) as well as "Gulliver's Travels."

Religious Context

Religion and evolution, or more specifically, the notion of survival of the fittest has historically had an uneasy relationship. Victorians sometimes found that their respect for science and a rational understanding of the world was at odds with their need to believe in a caring, attentive Creator. The troubling implication for some, including poet laureate Alfred Lord Tennyson, was that survival of the fittest meant that nature was "red in tooth and claw" (56:14) and that survival of one species inevitably meant the extinction of another. How could God set in motion a process that seems to ensure that individual suffering means little, and that death is both inevitable and without discernment. Man is simply another species and no more protected from suffering than any other animal. In other words, humanity is not the favored child of God. Wells' contemporaries found "The Island of Dr. Moreau" shocking, perverse, and perhaps even blasphemous (Parrinder 9). Suvin calls Moreau a pitiless "demonically inverted God of Genesis" whose Beast People are counterparts of humanity (27).

The notion of man's barely contained animal nature was also troubling for many Victorians, and Wells makes this relationship explicit at several points in "The Island of Dr. Moreau." As Prendick opens his tale, he recounts the danger of savagery and cannibalism among the three survivors of the wreck of the "Lady Vain." In their danger and their panic, the men fall back on animal instincts for survival, even if it means killing one of their number in order to live; like the Beast People on Moreau's island, the shipwrecked men are reverting to their beastly nature. The captain of the "Ipecacuanha" is described as a wicked man who would callously send Prendick to his death. Montgomery, in Prendick's estimation, had become "half akin to these Beast People, unfitted for human kindred" by the time of his death (109). Finally, Prendick cannot help but recognize the Beast People's kinship with humanity even when they are at their most animals. When Prendick corners the Leopard Man after its attack on Moreau, he is shocked to see that even though it is crouched in an "animal attitude," its distorted and deformed human face nonetheless reveals the irrefutable "fact of its humanity" (93).

Prendick notes significant changes in himself, as well, not the least of which is the heightened alertness and brightness of his eyes that others note when he returns to civilization (125). Most explicit and suggestive is Prendick's description of the city and its inhabitants in the final chapter of his journal:

> I would go out into the streets to fight with my delusion, and prowling women would mew after me, furtive craving men glance jealously at me, weary pale workers go coughing by me, with tired eyes and eager paces like wounded deer dripping blood. . . . I would turn aside into some chapel, and even there, such was my disturbance, it seemed that the preacher gibbered Big Thinks even as the Ape-Man had done (132).

Wells' conviction that evolution doesn't necessarily mean improvement or progress set him apart from many others of his era who wanted, even needed, to believe that all of the suffering and loss implied in evolutionary theory had a purpose, and that purpose was to raise up the species. Rather, evolution simply means change, and adaptation to the environment is not necessarily a noble, clean, or enlightened thing. This premise is perhaps most clearly evident in Wells' "The Time Machine" (1895), in which humanity has evolved into two separate species, one industrious, misshapen and cannibalistic, the other beautiful, slothful, and essentially useless.

Scientific & Technological Context

"The Island of Dr. Moreau" was one of Wells' early "scientific romances." In this instance, the term romance signifies a heroic, adventurous, or mysterious tale that is remote in time or in place. "War of the Worlds" (1898), "The Time Machine," and most of Wells' early works fall into this category. In addition to the consideration of the possibilities and limits of science found in "The Island of Dr. Moreau," his scientific romances offer a glimpse into the coldly rational culture of a technologically advanced race in "War of the Worlds" and speculate on the future of humankind at the hands of time- and labor-saving technologies in "The Time Machine." Other nineteenth century speculative writers who wrote about science, like French writer Jules Verne, saw science as illuminating and bright. Wells' early science fiction takes an opposing, darker view. Science, perhaps like Nature itself, is indifferent at best, cruel at worst. "The Island of Dr. Moreau," written as it was at the end of nineteenth century, reflects a growing distrust of science, and the idea, introduced as a result of evolutionary thought, that the universe was essentially amoral, was a shock to Victorian systems.

In addition, the study of human psychology became increasingly scientific over the course of the nineteenth century, and by the latter part of the century, theories about the intersections of biology, physiology, and psychology were becoming more sophisticated. The belief that it was possible to understand the human mind through science is extended to Moreau's surgical manipulation of the brains and emotions of the Beast People. The human mind became something that could be understood— and perhaps changed—by rational scientific applications. Further, the murderous nature of the Beast People as they devolve reflects the late Victorian

preoccupation with the lower, bestial nature of man, an idea perhaps most clearly examined in Robert Louis Stevenson's "The Strange Case of Dr. Jekyll and Mr. Hyde" (1886). Wells' depiction of the struggle for mastery over animal impulses in the Beast People, and its eventual failure, reflected the belief of many nineteenth century scientists and psychologists that man's nature is essentially wild, and maintaining the veneer of civilization is a constant, and not always winnable, struggle.

Biographical Context

Born September 21, 1866, in Bromley, Kent, England, H. G. Wells came from a lower middle class background. His father was a shopkeeper and part-time cricket player and his mother was "in service" in an upper class home. Wells' determination to rise above this beginning marked his early life. His mother had ambitions for him to become a draper— a dry goods dealer—but Wells wanted to prove to her that he could better his lot in life through education. He first became a teacher-pupil at Midhurst Grammar School and later attended Normal School of Science in London, studying under biologist and eloquent Darwin-apologist, T. H. Huxley. He did complete the program, although he failed the final examinations; he received a degree in Science from the University of London in 1891 and spent the next few years teaching. Wells' scientific background informed the style as well as the content of his writing. His experience writing for scientific journals gave him a clean, spare prose style and an eye for scientific detail and its ethical conundrums.

Wells' early experiences with the cruelties and inequities of the class system profoundly shaped the rest of his life and his writing. First, as a product of the lower classes, he had a deep, and not especially flattering, understanding of the British class system and he had a serious appreciation for, and knowledge of, science. Both of these circumstances are evident in "The Island of Dr. Moreau." Recognizing the inequities and brutalities of men inherent in the class system may well have allowed the depiction of the arrogantly "superior" and well-educated Moreau as contrasted with the ignorant Beast People. The symbiotic and ultimately destructive master-servant relationship between Montgomery and M'Ling is also informed by Wells lower class origins. Montgomery's eventual "slumming" with M'Ling and the Beast People becomes a parody of the crossing of class lines in Victorian England, as does Prendick's rather priggish revulsion to the notion.

Wells' background in science also fueled his imagination and his art. Science is a "demonic master" in Wells and leads its practitioners to dark and destructive ends (Suvin 24). Moreau, in his pointless pursuit of creation, holds no moral authority. The indifference to ethics that Moreau professes offers a glimpse of the scientist, not as a romantic Promethean hero, but as an inhumane vivisectionist. Unlike Mary Shelley's tragic Victor Frankenstein, Moreau is not driven by any noble purpose or high ideal. Science, as Wells makes clear, is only as good and altruistic as its practitioners, and that is often a particularly discomforting thought.

Anita R. Rose, Ph.D.

Works Cited

Graff, Ann-Barbara. "Administrative Nihilism": Evolution, Ethics and Victorian Utopian Satire. *Utopian Studie*s 12:2 (2001): 33-52.

H. G. Wells. *The Island of Dr. Moreau.* 1896. New York: Barnes and Noble, 2004.

Hutton, R. H., Rev. of "The Island of Dr. Moreau." Rpt. in *H. G. Wells: The Critical Heritage.* Patrick Parrinder, ed. London: Routledge, 1972. 46–48.

Mitchell, Chalmers. Rev. of "The Island of Dr. Moreau." Rpt. in *H. G. Wells: The Critical Heritage.* 43–46.

Parrinder, Patrick. Introduction. *H. G. Wells: The Critical Heritage.* 1–31.

Philmus, Robert. *Into the Unknown: The Evolution of Science Fiction from Francis Godwin to H. G. Wells.* Berkeley: U of California P, 1970.

Suvin, Darko. "Wells as the Turning Point of the SF Tradition." in *Critical Essays on H. G. Wells.* John Huntington, ed. Boston: G. K. Hall, 23–33.

Tennyson, Alfred Lord. *In Memoriam: Tennyson's Poetry.* Robert W. Hill, ed. New York: Norton Critical Edition, 1971. 119–195.

Discussion Questions

1. At one point, the island's landscape is described as "sulphurous," suggesting perhaps a hellish environment. How do Prendick's physical descriptions of the setting affect your reading of the novel?
2. How do animal characteristics rise to the surface in the Beast People?
3. Where do you think Prendick's sympathies lie?
4. Why does the captain of the "Ipecacuanaha" take such a dislike to Prendick?
5. What do you know of Montgomery's history, and how does it affect his character and his conduct?
6. Examine class structures in the novel. Which humans and which creatures are at the top, and why?
7. Do you approve of Prendick's actions on the island?
8. Why does Prendick remain frightened for the rest of his life? What makes him so uneasy?
9. Discuss Wells' view of human nature.
10. Discuss Dr. Moreau as a father figure. Who are his different "children" and what is his relationship to them?

Essay Ideas

1. Compare and contrast Wells' view of science with that of other early science fiction writers?
2. Analyze the ways in which the novel parodies "civilized society."
3. Think about different kinds of law (natural, human, laws of nature, religious law, etc.) and consider how each kind of law functions in "The Island of Dr. Moreau."
4. Consider gender in this novel; it's not a prominent issue, but there are some very telling descriptions of females. How is "the feminine" portrayed?
5. Research the idea of "liminal space" and liminality. How does the novel's unnamed island location exemplify this idea of "in between space"? What two worlds or modes of existence does this space bridge? What does it mean that it is something of a garden?

Jane Eyre

by Charlotte Brontë

"Conventionality is not morality."

Currer Bell (Charlotte Brontë)
Preface *Jane Eyre,* 2nd ed.

Content Synopsis

"Jane Eyre" is a retrospective narrative told by a now adult Jane, who relates the experiences of her childhood in the first person with an occasional summary comment that signals her adult status to her readers. Jane Eyre is a ten-year-old orphaned child living in the home of her Aunt Reed and cousins Eliza, John, and Georgiana Reed at Gateshead Hall. Mrs. Reed is the widow of Jane's uncle, whom she is certain, would have treated her kindly had he been alive. While she does not perform household service like a common maid, like Cinderella, her cousins and aunt in fact, treat Jane abusively and resentfully. The young Reeds are coddled by their mother, whose cruel disregard of Jane's needs and feelings they emulate. On a cold November afternoon, defying one of John Reed's many attempts to bully and humiliate her, Jane flies at him after he strikes her with a book and she in turn falls against a door, bleeding from the scalp. For this retaliation, she is locked in the dead Mr. Reed's former upstairs bedroom, a room whose predominant furnishings are as red as the blood flowing from her wound, and left there alone through the night. Terrified by what she believes to be a ghostly light in the room, Jane begs to be released, but is refused by her aunt and falls unconscious, awakening later to discover herself being tended by a kindly physician who realizes the desperate nature of Jane's situation with her aunt and cousin. At the same time, Jane overhears the servants speak of her parents, a poor clergyman, and a young woman from a wealthy family who marries him against the wishes of her own parents; both have died of typhus, caught from serving the poor in a large manufacturing town.

Anxious to be rid of Jane, who refuses to be broken by her isolation and alienated treatment in the Reed home, Mrs. Reed arranges for Jane to go to Lowood School, a Christian boarding school run by the odious Mr. Brocklehurst. He questions Jane at length about her reading of the Bible and pronounces that humility and mortification are 'consistently' impressed upon his pupils there as chief virtues of the Christian life. Passionate and defiant, Jane bids good riddance to Gateshead Hall and its inhabitants.

Lowood School is a place where children are cowed by physical and psychological abuse, scarce food of poor quality, and crowded, unheated dormitories. Female students and staff under Brocklehurst's patronage experience an education involving rigid discipline, unyielding expectations of conformity in thought and behavior, and indifference to their developmental or emotional needs. Jane's two shining stars become Miss Temple, a teacher whose gentleness and compassion mark her difference from all the rest, and Helen Burns, an older girl who is unjustly the focus of the staff's disapprobation, but who accepts with dignity and humility her situation as scapegoat in the school. Passing a winter with insufficient clothing and forced into the snow with no boots, Jane is soon singled out by Mr. Brocklehurst to be shunned by the other girls, and her relationship with Helen is sealed in this moment. As an outcome of their living conditions, by spring many girls develop a fever, apparently infected with typhus, and Helen Burns dies in Jane's arms as the two sleep in Helen's sick bed. So many deaths draw attention to the deplorable conditions at the school, and it is taken in hand by men of true charitable intent, who create a "noble institution" where Jane resides for eight more years—six as a pupil and two as a teacher.

When Miss Temple leaves the school to marry, Jane feels compelled to seek a new position. She advertises her services as governess, and goes to work at Thornfield Hall at the behest of the housekeeper, Mrs. Fairfax. Her pupil is Adele, the 'ward' of the master, Mr. Rochester, who lives most of the year abroad. On the third floor where Jane lives is also the servant Grace Poole, whose appearances are infrequent but whose echoing laughter Jane frequently hears behind closed doors.

One January afternoon while Jane is walking outdoors, she comes upon a man and his dog, his horse having fallen on the icy drive and thrown him off. She helps him to remount, and returns to Thornfield Hall only to discover that she has assisted the master of the house, Mr. Rochester. Gradually, Rochester and Jane are drawn into conversation; he explores her intelligence and background and reveals that Adele is the daughter of his French sometime-mistress. Although he denies paternity, when her mother abandoned the child, Rochester brought her to his home and is raising her as his ward. Jane's attraction for the man, grows even though she has bluntly been told he is not handsome.

One evening, hearing a noise in the hall—perhaps the laughter she associates with Mrs. Poole—Jane leaves her bedroom to discover smoke billowing from Rochester's room and his bed afire. Unable to wake him from sleep deepened to unconsciousness by smoke inhalation, she throws water from the bedside pitcher on the flames and extinguishes them. Rochester awakens to find Jane beside the bed and the sheets soaked. He swears her to secrecy and expresses his fervent thanks for saving his life. Their attraction deepens as they bid each other goodnight.

Rochester leaves for a week on a neighboring estate and Mrs. Fairfax tells Jane that it is the home of the beautiful and accomplished Blanche Ingram, less wealthy than he and fifteen years his junior, but clearly a rival for Rochester's affections, nonetheless. Jane's hopes are crushed, and she makes a fantasized drawing of her imagined rival to remind herself of the hopeless affection she feels for Rochester. When Rochester returns with the Ingram family and friends in tow, Jane and Adele are invited to the drawing room after dinner, where the ladies speak about their various tutors and governesses as though she were not present. Rochester finds Jane as she tries to slip away, and commands that she appear each night in his drawing room while the guests are in his home. While Jane clearly feels Miss Ingram is not the right wife for Rochester, she recognizes that he will probably make Blanche his wife. Despite this understanding, Jane still has eyes only for him.

One evening, in Rochester's absence, Mr. Mason, who identifies himself as an old friend of Rochester, comes to the house. That same evening, an old fortuneteller knocks at Rochester's door, and is admitted to entertain the guests at

Blanche's insistence. Blanche's face suggests that her fortune, unknown to the others, causes her great disappointment and distress. Jane agrees to a reading before a blazing fire in the drawing room. The gypsy speaks of marriage and draws Jane out to reveal her feelings about the absent master of the house. Rochester reveals himself to her from underneath the gypsy's cloak. They talk, but when Jane reveals that Mason has arrived from the West Indies, Rochester staggers as if under a blow, and he sends Jane for wine to fortify him. Extracting from her a pledge of loyalty to him, he asks that she bring Mason to him.

That same evening, the household is awakened by a female voice shrieking from somewhere in the house followed by silence. When Rochester reassures the guests and they return to their rooms, he fetches Jane. Together, they find Mason in one of the third story rooms, his side and arm soaked with blood from an apparent knife wound. Behind another door to this chamber, now closed and locked, Jane hears gurgling and the laughter of Mrs. Poole. A physician arrives, treats Mason, and takes him away from Thornfield Hall, but in the interim, Rochester and Mason speak of "her," a person unknown and unexplained to Jane, who has harmed Mason. Jane and Rochester walk in the garden at dawn, and he, while asking for her support, suggests that he will marry Miss Ingram, leaving Jane to her own thoughts and going to breakfast with his guests.

Jane is summoned to Mrs. Reed's deathbed, and she informs Mr. Rochester that she must seek employment elsewhere, since he has suggested that he will marry Blanche Ingram. Jane departs after promising Rochester that she will not advertise for a position, but allow him to find her one. She finds Mrs. Reed consumed by fear of her son's gambling, their debts, and their impending impoverishment, as well as by a deep guilt at her treatment of Jane. She shows Jane a letter from an Uncle John Eyre in Madeira who had wished to adopt her, which she has kept from Jane for three years. Despite her guilt, she is unable to relent from her bitter hatred of Jane, and dies in that state.

Jane returns to Thornfield Hall and to Rochester, whom she has begun to call "my master." Their love grows, and they quickly move toward marriage. But as they prepare to say their vows, Mason's solicitor comes to the church and denounces Rochester as already married to Mason's sister, Bertha, the real source of the mad laughter and murmurings Jane had so frequently heard in Rochester's house. Rochester explains to Jane how he had been duped into marrying the mad and alcoholic Bertha, long confined in the attic of Thornfield Hall, and begs her to go away with him despite their inability to marry.

Heartbroken, Jane flees on foot and then by coach to a distant town; she wanders aimlessly for several days until, starving and exhausted, she is rescued on the doorstep of a clergyman, St. John Rivers, and his two sisters. Jane remains with the Rivers until she is able to take a job as the schoolmistress of a neighboring village. Meanwhile, Jane's Uncle John dies, and she is left an independently wealthy woman; at the same time, it is revealed by their connection to Jane's benefactor that St. John and his sisters are her cousins. She shares her generous inheritance, making them each independently wealthy. St. John, soon to depart on a missionary journey to India, expresses his wish that she accompany him. He is stunned when she refuses his marriage proposal, but presses her relentlessly over the succeeding weeks.

Just as she is about to give in to a felt duty to marry St. John, Jane mysteriously hears Rochester calling her name. Jane answers without a moment's hesitation that she will come to him. She returns to the neighborhood of Thornfield Hall to discover that Bertha has set fire to the house before leaping from the roof to her death, and that Rochester has survived, maimed and blind. Jane rushes to him at the neighboring Ferndean Hall; they profess their love for each other, and they marry.

Jane reveals at this point that the story is told ten years into her marriage to Rochester. Two years into the marriage, Rochester began to recover the sight of one eye, and was able to see his son when he was born. The novel ends with a letter from St. John Rivers, facing death, and affirming the providence of God.

Metaphors of fire and fever alternate with metaphors of ice and icy self-control, which in turn alternate with outbursts of angry denunciation, 'fits' of madness and conversational double entendre. Sandra Gilbert and Susan Gubar, two feminist critics argue that Bertha Mason Rochester, the madwoman in the attic of Thornfield Hall who burns it down as she leaps to her death on the stone courtyard below, is in fact the chief metaphor both of the novel and the situation of women in Brontë's time. Moreover, they assert, she was a double for Jane herself. The interpenetration of natural and supernatural, from the ghost that visits Jane in the blood red womb/room of her imprisoned imagination, to Rochester's cry for Jane toward the novel's close, suggests a profoundly repressed passionate self and life that Jane must bring to fruition through her stubborn independence and fulfilled passion for Rochester. Her marriage to a man largely blind and maimed reverses the typical dependencies of women upon men in marriage and in the larger society. In addition, Jane's many successful flights from places that threaten to contain her imagination and stifle her passion make her a most atypical Victorian spouse. Like many Victorian novels, "Jane Eyre" ends in a marriage. More than once in the novel, Jane steps back from a madness akin to Bertha's, but she never withdraws from the demand that her own passion be fulfilled on her own terms.

Like many novels of the Victorian period, names in "Jane Eyre" resonate with meaning. Jane meets and begins her relationship with Rochester in the proverbial thorny field, and returns to him in a green-forested world—Ferndean Hall—whose surroundings she immediately connects to Rochester himself: "You are no ruin, sir—no lightning-struck tree: you are green and vigorous. Plants will grow about your roots, whether you ask them or not, because they will lean towards you, and wind round you, because your strength offers them so safe a prop" (433). Thus does the "plain" Jane Eyre triumph over the "beautiful" Blanche Ingram, as does the darkly chiseled Rochester, phallic, jealous, and vaguely dangerous, over the blue-eyed, emotionally unavailable, controlling St. John Rivers (the latter's gospel is clearly not the Word for Jane, nor is his river her road to happiness). And so, in a towering wood far from Lowood School, Jane's pilgrimage is over, and her 'calling,' to use the dutiful Calvinist term—i.e. her spiritual and corporeal fulfillment—is found.

Historical Context

Charlotte Brontë's novel was published under a male pseudonym as was common of women writers of her day. It records her knowledge of the abuses of the poor in the guise of charity, and her anger at the hypocritical religious practices of the men directing the institutions responsible for their care and education. Schools upon which the fictional Lowood School was based abounded in England during Brontë's lifetime, as did the cruelly dependent situations of the young women and girls who taught and resided in them. While their ostensible goal was to assure the modicum of literacy that might be required for the limited if inevitable participation of the poor in the coming democracy, the larger value involved protecting the membership of the particular religious denomination sponsoring the school and maintaining the unquestioning conformity of pupils. Women might never vote, but they might teach, bear, and raise a subset of the working class male voter; they needed to be kept in their places and to educate the next generation of their peers to do the same. When government subsidies became available in the thirties, the incentive became even greater to feed, clothe and house pupils at the absolute minimum cost, as a profit could be had at their expense.

Despite its popular success, critics of the book responded to popular fears about the blurring of class lines modeled by Jane's marriage to Rochester. These critics also articulated mid-century fears of class unrest exacerbated by the Chartist movement's agitation for working class voting rights, and by reform bills that were increasingly expanding the electorate by enfranchising the middle classes.

Societal Context

For a young unmarried woman of a certain class, but without the economic means generally attributable to that class, or a father, a brother, or an uncle upon whose care she might depend, the life of a governess was the only respectable option. With a smattering of French, a bit of Art and Music, some poetry, Scripture and good penmanship, a fortunate young woman might advertise for a position as governess to young ladies in a wealthy household, thus earning herself food, shelter, and a modicum of social protection and respectability. Those less talented or less fortunate might end up on the staff of charity schools like Lowood. Those more fortunate might make marriages to men of sufficient means, allowing them to have a home and children of their own. Thus, while some critics chastised the author of "Jane Eyre" for creating in Jane a vulgar social climber (Newman, "A Critical History of Jane Eyre" in her edition of the novel, 445–58). Most would have recognized a character who successfully negotiated the limits of her orphaning, her femaleness, and of her limbo between an impoverished if genteel middle class existence and the inheritance of real wealth, to gain a personally and socially successful outcome. Jane earned for herself independence and marriage, a spiritually virtuous and a passionately satisfying relationship that could be both dutiful and self-fulfilling; hers is a Cinderella story with a twist.

At the same time, this audience could cheerfully accept the existence of the Bertha Masons of the world, and the unwitting naïveté of the young men who were their dupes. While not aristocrats, landed gentry like Rochester, and those who made their fortunes in land and trade like Jane's uncle, were a part of a growing class of men outside of cities who could take advantage of opportunities offered to them both by inheritance and by a developing capitalist entrepreneurial spirit. A man like Rochester might be both sexually profligate and respectable as long as his profligacy occurred outside the conventional bounds of English society. British imperialism offered new playgrounds for the wealthy, and the Caribbean marketplace was of interest not only for raw materials but also for the proverbial "dark" women it offered. The racial undertones of this novel go largely unexplored, but they demonstrate the beginnings of the theme of race as a complication in the themes of class and sex/gender in the nineteenth century novel.

In Brontë's novel, Rochester redeems himself with Jane first by confessing his youthful indiscretions and by his provision for Adele, presumably his illegitimate child, which of course brings Jane both employment and proximity to him. He is further redeemed by Bertha's madness, a condition that a nineteenth century English readership would find easy to accept in light of the general belief that women's weakness, their tendency toward fainting fits and hysteria, and their generally inferior intellect and temperament, alternated with their native ability to seduce even the most abstemious man to act upon his uncontrollable desire to possess them. Consequently, Rochester's story of his deluded love for Bertha that so quickly turned to revulsion, and the need to imprison his suddenly mad wife, would have been believable despite its extremity.

Thus British imperial politics, economics, sexual and racial prejudices, gendered expectations and class relations as well as religion and the supernatural in nineteenth century Victorian society form a complex, interwoven network in Brontë's love story, "Jane Eyre."

Religious Context

Critics of "Jane Eyre" also represented the voice of a self-righteous and self-satisfied group comfortable with its own class prejudices and convinced of its own class-bound and religion-bound superiority. In her angry preface to the second edition, Brontë answers her critics in scathing terms: "Conventionality is not morality. Self-righteousness is not religion. To attack the first is not to assail the last. To pluck the mask from the face of the Pharisee is not to lift an impious hand to the Crown of Thorns. . . . appearance should not be mistaken for truth; narrow human doctrines that only tend to elate and magnify a few should not be substituted for the world-redeeming creed of Christ" (17).

That Jane, the daughter of a poor clergyman, should marry Rochester (never mind her mother's wealthy roots) offended the Christian sentiments of those who believed that their God's plan determined some to be rich and others poor. Some readers objected to the smoldering passion with which Jane's and Rochester's relationship is described and developed, while still others objected to the supernatural elements that the character of Jane experienced throughout her life and upon which pivotal parts of the plot turn.

The impoverished piety of Jane's clergyman father, whose death is attributable to his service of the poor in a large manufacturing town in England, the opposition of Jane's mother's wealthy parents to their daughter's marriage to a poor if pious man, the portrait of Brocklehurst and the religious aspects of Lowood school, as well as the later calling of St. John Rivers to the missionary life, even the death of the ever-humble Helen Burns—all give Brontë an opportunity to explore the uses and abuses of religious belief and its pious applications in the everyday life of many classes of people. Repeatedly in the novel, a supposed faithfulness

to tenets of religious belief justifies behavior that involves exploiting and imposing the power of class, race, and sex/gender upon those who are unable to defend themselves. At Lowood School, the least appearance of non-conformity brings a thundering Brocklehurst and his wealthy family in a parade of silks and satins to classrooms of children who eat burnt porridge, shiver in threadbare clothes and freezing schoolrooms, and cough with the illnesses of the poor and impoverished. The Bible is cited to threaten, justify corporal and psychological punishment, and extinguish any flicker of self-affirmation and independence. Brontë remains apparently ambivalent about Helen Burns' modeled Christian humility: while at one level Helen models a genuine Christian pacifism, her self-effacement and acceptance of Brocklehurst's punitive scapegoating in the name of the Christian scriptures clearly contributes to her death, a fate that Jane will resist with every willful, independent breath and bone in her body.

In St. John Rivers, British imperialism in India and the Christian onus of the "white man's burden" offers yet another opportunity for a man who does his best to dominate and control Jane in the name of God: he loves another, but would have Jane for a wife because he perceives her to be more able to be a dutiful missionary's wife. However, Rochester's call to Jane clearly resounds more profoundly than any calling she might feel as a missionary's wife, and her sexual passion for Rochester is contrasted to the bland coldness of St. John Rivers' religious piety. In the distinction between spirituality and sexuality, Brontë's Victorian readers perceive a cavernous gap, but her character finds the two to be compatibly wedded in her own life. The novel ends with both the passionate expression of Jane's love for the maimed Rochester, and with St. John's words reported—in the narrator Jane's fervent recounting—of the final line of the New Testament from the Book of Revelations: "Amen; even so, come, Lord Jesus!" (441).

Scientific & Technological Context

"By the middle of the nineteenth century records showed that women had become the majority patients in public lunatic asylums" (Showalter 3). And so it might be said that if unprotected girls survived the physical privations, disease and psychological torment of the charity schools at the beginning of their lives, the strictures of the adult life that faced them might well lead to their institutionalization in madhouses at the end.

It is hard for most contemporary readers to imagine the grit and ego with which Brontë invested Jane as she courageously faced her orphaning, the abuse at the hands of her foster family and at Lowood school, making her way to and from employment at Thorncliff Hall, defining her relationship with Rochester on her own terms, rejecting the security of a relationship with St. John Rivers, and facing down Mrs. Reed both as a child and as an adult. The strength of her character flies in the face of what Brontë knew was the typical socio-medical opinion of the day: that women were physically and psychologically defective. Besides the physical manifestations of unfitness that were a direct by-product of embodied femaleness, madness itself was perceived as "a female malady" (Showalter 4).

Many feminist critics argue that the kinds of confinement and constriction by law and custom that women faced in their physical lives, choices, might well be the prelude to madness. But others are quick to point out that the labels "mad," or even the more insidious "hysterical," whether used in the medical or popular literature, were a means to discredit women's resistance to roles and descriptions of their behavior that kept them docile and uncomplaining. Definitions of women as inherently irrational in the Western philosophic tradition helped to feed the psychiatric "science" of nineteenth century English society. This is coupled with a larger, curiously nation-specific notion that England itself is a hotbed of insanity. Showalter offers substantial evidence that "The English have long regarded their country, with a mixture of complacency and sorrow, as the global headquarters of insanity" (7).

And so readers might come to a fuller understanding of the argument that Bertha and Jane are meant by Brontë to be doppelganger figures—doubles for each other. With her fits, claims of ghostly visitation, premonitions of death and loss, and her long-distance response to the wild cry of Rochester's grief, in different circumstances, without the economic means to return to him, Jane might well have ended up in a version of Bertha Mason's confinement. Mason's madness was all fire. Jane's would most likely have been ice (ironically, in the heat of the Indian subcontinent), as the cold and controlling St. John's missionary wife, her independence, rebellion and passion stifled by his rigid definitions of whom he needed her to be. Her rebellion—and his repressive reaction—would seem to have been inevitable. While her marriage to Rochester is the ostensible triumphant climax of the novel, Brontë may well have meant Jane's escape from Bertha's fate to be her most important statement on the conditions of women at the hands of nineteenth century medical science.

Biographical Context

Charlotte Brontë was one of three sisters who wrote under the pseudonym Bell: Anne (Acton), Charlotte (Currer), and Emily (Ellis). They were born in the north of England and spent much of their lives in a remote parsonage on the Yorkshire Moors where their father was a minister. Their mother's death after Anne's birth (she was the last of six children) was deeply felt. All the children, including the girls, had free access to their father's considerable library of literature and to the contemporary political and social journals he read. Their exposure to writers like Byron, a favorite of Charlotte's even at the tender age of thirteen, and others of the Romantic poets inspired their own writing and performance. Their entertainment, undertaken with their brother Branwell, was imaginative "plays"—fantastic yarns spun and performed with and for each other. By the time she was thirteen, Charlotte was writing and hand sewing her own books of poetry and prose, also manifestations of an intensely felt fantasy life.

Numerous events in Charlotte's life and in the life of her sisters inspired aspects of "Jane Eyre." Her sisters Maria and Elizabeth died from illnesses contracted at the Cowan Bridge Clergy Daughters School where their well-meaning father hoped they might receive the only kind of formal education he could afford. Charlotte, herself, had teaching experiences both as a private governess and at girls' school. She was shy and uncomfortable with her lack of acceptable 'beauty.' Rochester is often cited as a quintessential 'Byronic' hero of the kind Jane so admired in his poetry.

Despite her shyness, Brontë gained the courage to seek publication of her work. There was an unsuccessful book of poems under the three sisters' pseudonym, and then a first, equally unsuccessful novel. But "Jane Eyre" (1847) was an instant success, going into a third edition within a year of its publication. Subsequent novels ("Shirley" 1849 and "Vilette," 1853) also had some success but never gained the circulation or the fame of "Jane Eyre." Profoundly affected by the loss of her two sisters, Anne and Emily, to tuberculosis, and of her brother to alcoholism, Brontë married in 1854. But she, too, was dead of tuberculosis in nine months.

Deborah A. Dooley, Ph.D.

Works Cited

Altick, Richard. *Victorian People and Ideas*. New York: W.W. Norton & Co., 1983.

Brontë, Charlotte. *Jane Eyre Case Studies in Contemporary Criticism*. Newman, Beth, Ed. Boston: Bedford Books of St. Martin's Press, 1996.

Gilbert, Sandra M. and Gubar, Susan. *The Madwoman in the Attic: The Woman Writer and the Nineteenth Century Imagination*. New Haven: Yale University Press, 1979.

Showalter, Elaine. *The Female Malady*. New York: Penguin Books, 1987.

Discussion Questions

1. From the time she is a child, Jane's gendered behavior is unique among her peers. Describe the characteristics that make Jane who she is, and attempt to account for how and why she becomes the woman we see by the novel's end. Compare her to other female characters to help make sense of your arguments.

2. Despite her preface, which expresses profound anger at religious hypocrisy, Charlotte Brontë ends her novel with St. John's very religious affirmation: "Amen; even so, come, Lord Jesus!" Why would she choose this ending to a very passionate novel whose themes are far more about human relationships than about spiritual ones?

3. Look carefully at the language and situations that Brontë develops around Helen Burns; is Helen a character that Brontë means us to admire, pity, or feel ambivalence? Is Helen a character who, like Jane, resists, or is she a character who gives in for what she perceives to be a "higher good?"

4. Jane comes to her marriage with Rochester only after he is blind and maimed. Why does Brontë choose this as Jane's final marital relationship?

5. Look carefully at the language Rochester uses in his tale of his courtship and marriage to Bertha Mason and of her incarceration in the attic at Thornfield Hall. How is she determined to be mad, and why does Rochester make the decision to imprison her when and where he does?

6. Brontë develops many of her characters as doubles or "foils" for each other. Compare and contrast the characters of St. John Rivers and Edward Rochester.

7. Compare and contrast the Reed daughters with the Rivers' sisters.

8. Compare and contrast the characters of St. John Rivers and Mr. Brocklehurst.

9. Mrs. Reed is a particularly odious example of Victorian class-consciousness and religious hypocrisy, but she is not simply a stereotype. Analyze her character and attempt to assess how Brontë uses her in this novel.

10. Why does Brontë use a first person retrospective narrative in lieu of an omniscient narrator to tell the story of "Jane Eyre"?

Essay Ideas

1. Follow the color red as image and symbol throughout the novel.
2. Follow the interpenetrating images of fire and ice as Brontë uses them in "Jane Eyre."
3. Define the psychological concept of the doppelganger and explore it in relation to Jane and Bertha Mason, and to Rochester and St. John Rivers.
4. Explore the literature on madness in the nineteenth century and study how Brontë uses figures of mad behavior throughout her novel connected to the characters of Jane and Bertha.
5. Explore the literature on education of the poor in nineteenth century English society, and consider how Brontë uses her understanding of opportunities and conditions offered by charity schools in England in her novel.
6. Look at studies of the classic villain figure in the nineteenth century English novel. How does Brocklehurst fit this stereotype? Are there other characters in the novel whose characteristics touch on the villainous?
7. Is "Jane Eyre" a Gothic novel?

King Solomon's Mines

by H. Rider Haggard

Content Synopsis

"King Solomon's Mines" (1885) is the story of an excursion to an isolated region of southern Africa by three Englishmen. The protagonist is Allan Quatermain, an English hunter and guide who has lived in Africa for many years. He meets Sir Henry Curtis and Sir Henry's companion, Captain John Good, aboard a ship traveling from Cape Town, South Africa, to Natal. The three become friends; Quatermain is especially struck by Sir Henry's powerful physique and forthright English manner. Both Sir Henry and Good impress Quatermain as honorable, decent men. They in turn are equally pleased to know Quatermain, as his reputation as a top-notch hunter and man of great discretion has preceded him.

Although Quatermain doesn't realize it, he is just the man Sir Henry has hoped to find on his journey to Africa. Sir Henry is seeking his younger brother George, who disappeared two years earlier on an expedition to discover the fabled diamond mines of the Biblical King Solomon. Sir Henry is particularly anxious to find his brother, since they had quarreled rather bitterly before George Curtis departed England. Sir Henry means to find his brother and mend the rift between them. As it happens, Quatermain was the last white man to have encountered George (going at that time by the name "Neville") before he disappeared to cross the desert to reach the Suliman (Solomon) Mountains.

Sir Henry has come to Natal in the hopes of finding Quatermain and enlisting his aid in the search for George Curtis.

This situation is made more interesting by an encounter Quatermain had had several years before meeting George Curtis. Quatermain, while recovering from a bout of fever, met a Portuguese man named Jose de Silvestre bound for the Suliman Mountains. Dismissing the man's quest as imprudent and dangerous, Quatermain thought nothing more of it until the man returned, near death. Just before he died, Silvestre told Quatermain a fantastic story about a Portuguese ancestor, also named Jose de Silvestre, who found a map to King Solomon's mines and disappeared during an attempt to find the mines and their riches. His descendant possessed a copy of the map to the mines, and had hoped to complete successfully what his ancestor began.

However, the brutal desert sun was too much for de Silvestre, and he managed somehow to return to the village where Quatermain still rested. Before he died, he gave the treasure map to Quatermain. On the back of the map was a cryptic note from Silvestre's ancestor that supplemented the map's directions, confirmed the existence of the diamonds, and warned of a dangerous person named Gagool. Quatermain has since been keeping the secret of the map until he reveals it to Sir Henry and Good. He tells Sir Henry that he passed some of the information about the route to the mines to George Curtis before he departed, but that he has no idea what may have happened to Curtis after he took leave of Quatermain.

Sir Henry convinces Quatermain to accompany him and Good on an expedition to find George Curtis. Quatermain is at first reluctant, because he sees such a foolhardy journey as certain death, but he gains assurance from Sir Henry that Quatermain's son, Harry, back home in England, will be well cared for in the event of Quatermain's death. He is assured also that any "ivory or other valuables" they find in the course of searching for Sir Henry's brother will be divided between Good and Quatermain (Haggard 62). Most important to Quatermain, however, is his sense that both Sir Henry and Good are men of honor and integrity. Satisfied with the terms of their agreement, Quatermain assents to organize the trek and assumes responsibility for equipping the expedition and engaging the services of five men: a driver, a leader, and three servants, among them a mysterious Zulu named Umbopa. Quatermain finds Umbopa an unsettling personality, because he offers to join the expedition without pay, and because he is not particularly deferential to the white men. Umbopa, however, is tall, handsome, and dignified—a suitable Zulu counterpart to Sir Henry. Curtis takes an immediate liking to the African, and so Umbopa completes the party of adventurers.

Quatermain writes that their adventures were "many and various, but as they were of the sort which befall every African hunter," (71) he declines to weary the reader. The one exception that he narrates in detail is an elephant hunt that ends tragically when one of the Zulu servants is killed saving the life of Good.

The men all nearly die near the end of the desert crossing. They discover water to sustain them until they reach the mountains. As they press on, Quatermain recognizes two hilltops in the distance that de Silvestre described in his map as "Sheba's Breasts," which mark the gateway to the land containing the mines of Solomon, and he knows that they are on the right path. However, having escaped death by dehydration, they are now in danger of starvation. They find a cave, also described by de Silvestre, and enter to gain shelter for the night. The temperatures are below freezing, and in the course of the night, the second servant dies of exposure. The next morning, when the men discover the servant's body, they discover another body, that of a long-dead white man, who appears to be the ancient de Silvestre himself. They emerge on the other side of the cave to find a lush landscape, well populated by a rare species of antelope, and thus they escape starvation. They locate, from the map, Solomon's Great Road, a "sort of Roman road in this strange land" (106) and they follow it.

They are surprised by a group of "tall and copper-coloured" (110) men who seem to mean them harm. Quatermain and Umbopa find that they speak a dialect of Zulu, and are able to communicate with them and thereby deflect a conflict. They further learn that the name of this land is Kukuana. Good, who has been surprised in mid-shave, presents quite an eccentric and comic figure, for he has his pants off, half of his beard shaved, and his single eyeglass intact. He is so unusual, and possesses such unusually white legs, that it is easy for Quatermain to convince the scouting party that Good, Quatermain and Sir Henry are spirits. Quatermain "magically" shoots an antelope to confirm his magical powers.

The four men, Quatermain, Sir Henry, Good, and Umbopa, are taken to the king of this hidden land by Infadoos, an honorable old warrior. The king, Twala, is a despot who has apparently usurped the throne by killing his elder brother and banishing his sister-in-law and her infant son, most likely to their deaths. Twala is grudgingly respectful to these "spirits" and their Zulu manservant, but clearly does not trust them. At his side is a "wizened monkey-like figure" whose appearance bears further description. This figure is:

> a woman of great age, so shrunken that in size it was no larger than that of a year-old child, and was made up of a collection of deep yellow wrinkles … [t]here was no nose to speak of; indeed, the whole countenance might have been taken for that of a sun-dried corpse had it not been for a pair of large black eyes, still full of fire and intelligence … [the] wrinkled scalp moved and contracted like the hood of a cobra (133).

The old woman is Gagool; she is a sorceress and an advisor to the corrupt king. Incredibly, the name Gagool was mentioned in the 300-year-old document that has come to Quatermain from the first Jose de Silvestre.

The Englishmen soon learn that Twala, with the help of Gagool, rules Kukuana with an iron fist. Twala is brutal and Gagool is cunning, and between them, they conspire to kill and discredit any of Twala's potential opponents. Many noble warriors and politicians have grown weary of Twala's oppressive rule, and Umbopa, much to the astonishment of the Englishmen and Infadoos, reveals himself to be Ignosi, the rightful king of Kukuana. He reveals that it was his father who was murdered by Twala and Gagool. His mother did not die as believed, but with the help of loyal friends, managed to escape to the south with her infant son, Ignosi. Although many good men in Kukuana want to believe Ignosi/Umbopa, they need a sign to tell them that he is telling the truth. Quatermain realizes that a solar eclipse is imminent, and tells the warlords that this will be the sign that Ignosi is the true king, and they can, with confidence, stage a rebellion against Twala. The eclipse occurs, a bloody civil war ensues in which Sir Henry distinguishes himself as a superior warrior, and Twala is vanquished. Ignosi is recognized as the true king of the Kukuanas.

As a reward, the Englishmen are guided to the site of Solomon's mines. Gagool, who has survived the war and is as malicious as ever, is the only person in Kukuana who can show them the way. Quatermain, Sir Henry, Good, Gagool, and Foulata, a beautiful young Kukuana woman, set out for the mines. Foulata is devoted to Good because he saved her life prior to the rebellion. Gagool leads them past ancient Phoenician colossi, through the hall of the royal dead, to Solomon's treasure chamber.

Once in the chamber, Gagool treacherously returns to the huge stone door that guards the chamber and activates the mechanism that will imprison the Englishmen and Foulata in the treasure chamber forever. However, Foulata, ever loyal and protective of Good, struggles with Gagool at the door. Foulata is mortally wounded in the fight, and Gagool is crushed beneath the massive stone door. Gagool is dead, but the men and the dying Foulata are trapped in the chamber along with the astonishing, but now useless, caches of diamonds and gold. As the men gallantly attempt to make her last moments comfortable, Foulata declares her love for Good even as she acknowledges the unsuitability of their union, gasping that "the sun cannot mate with the darkness, nor the white with the black" (219).

As grim as things appear, the men do find a way out of the mines, leaving behind them the bulk of the fortune. Quatermain does manage to stuff his pockets with enough diamonds to make himself and Good wealthy for life. Sir Henry, of course, has no need of this wealth, as his objective on this journey was to find his brother, an objective that apparently will not be met, since no one in Kukuana has seen a white man in the region. The men leave Kukuana as much honored heroes. Ignosi implores them to stay and expresses regret at their decision to leave. He assures Sir Henry, for whom he has a great regard, that he will be a more humane ruler than Twala, but he also tells the Englishmen that he will not allow any white men into his kingdom; he wants no "praying-men to put fear of death into men's hearts, to stir them up against the king, and make a path for the white men who follow" (234).

Infadoos tells Quatermain, Sir Henry and Good of another, easier way across the pass that leads to the desert, and, in taking it, they at last find Sir Henry's brother living at an oasis in the desert. George Curtis tells his brother and his companions that he had made it across the desert but had been so lamed in an accident that he was unable either to return to civilization or to go ahead with his expedition. Quatermain, Sir Henry, Good, and George Curtis return together to Natal, and all but Quatermain sail for England.

In a postscript to the adventure, however, Quatermain indicates that, at Sir Henry's invitation, he plans to return to England, perhaps permanently, and reunite with his son Harry and his boon companions, Sir Henry Curtis and Captain John Good.

Historical Context

"King Solomon's Mines" is of historical interest for a number of reasons. It allows the modern reader insight into late Victorian British imperialism and the subsequent economic exploitation of Africa, as well as insight into European attitudes and ideas about Africa and what Africa came to symbolize in the European imagination.

Diamonds and diamond mining were of tremendous significance to nineteenth century England. Diamonds were first discovered in Africa in 1867, and the British-controlled south of Africa was rich in the resource. Cecil Rhodes, an Englishman, founded the De Beers Company in 1880 and by 1888, De Beers had a near monopoly of the diamond industry (Langer 888). The cache of diamonds described in "King Solomon's Mines" would have seemed fabulous to Victorian readers, but not incredible. Britons would have recognized Africa as an exotic locale rich in diamonds and other treasures.

Haggard provides a perspective that both perpetuates and subverts prevailing European images of Africa. The character of Ignosi is indeed noble, and is compared favorably to the heroic Sir Henry Curtis, both in physical stature and courage. He is, however, nonetheless, a noble savage, who resists the imposition of civilized European values onto his people. The text contains a romantic and patronizing cultural imperialism, as well. Solomon's mines and the once-fabulous ancient ruins around them are engineering wonders, but they are not of African origin. Rather, Quatermain notes great antiquities that are of Roman, Hebrew, and Phoenician origins, and it is clear that the Kukuanas, or indigenous native people, do not have the skills to create such wonders. They have merely appropriated the fantastic places for their own use.

It is also clear in the text that, while Africa may afford the men great adventure and wealth, England is the standard by which all other cultures and civilizations are measured. Key among these English values in a savage land that is not fit for European women is male friendship. The unprecedented culture of all-male boarding schools for middle- and upper-class boys made relationships among men a very real indicator of a man's worth (Adams 5). As products of this culture, Quatermain and his companions come to rely on one another. This male bond, overlaid by the bond of Englishness, sees the men through their journey and allows them to survive their hardships.

Societal Context

Although there are virtually no women in Haggard's text, gender is a significant element in "King Solomon's Mines." The three main characters, Quatermain, Curtis, and Good, all represent different "types" of Englishmen. Quatermain is the colonial adventurer, at home in the wilds of Africa, Curtis is a model of English masculinity, and Good is a fastidious dandy. Indeed, Haggard's text sets the pattern for subsequent adventure stories, reaching all the way forward to the Indiana Jones films. The three Englishmen's interaction and loyalty to one another reflects a strong late Victorian value placed on male friendships and manly virtues and beauty. Sir Henry particularly is representative of these manly virtues, being "one of the biggest-chested and longest-armed men [Quatermain] ever saw. [Sir Henry] had yellow hair, a big yellow beard, clear-cut features, and large grey eyes set deep into his head." Quatermain goes on to remark that he never saw a "finer-looking man" (44).

The African landscape is very clearly gendered female, and as such, it is ripe for conquest. The rising sun causes the east to "blush like a girl," (88), the hidden land of Kukuana is beyond twin mountains known as "Sheba's Breasts," and the terrain beyond these hilltops is "snowy," "rich" and "undulating," and shines with a "luminous beauty" (105–07). Just as the land is valued for its beauty and fertility, so are the African women in the novel. Quatermain initially tells the reader that there are no "petticoats" (i.e., European women) in the tale, but there are two African women, one of whom hardly counts, in Quatermain's estimation, as a woman at all. Gagool is described as unspeakably old, infertile, and evil, and the implication is that feminine power that radiates from a source other than procreative ability and a pleasing aesthetic is quite sinister. Early in the novel, as Quatermain sets up the story, he writes that Gagool was "a hundred at least, and therefore not marriageable, so I don't count her [as a woman]" (42). On the other hand, Foulata is young, beautiful, and slavishly devoted to Good. When Foulata realizes her impending death, just before she is rescued by Good, she laments "Oh, cruel, and I so young! What have I done that . . . no lover shall put his arm around me . . . nor shall men-children be born of me!" (155). Foulata herself recognizes youth, beauty, and promise of fertility as the qualities that give her life meaning and purpose. To be murdered before this promise is realized is tragic indeed.

Religious Context

Although he is a great friend of the white men who have helped him regain his kingdom, Ignosi makes it clear that the white man's religion is not welcome in his kingdom. In his final speech to Quatermain, he recognizes that Christianity's values subvert the values of Ignosi's warrior culture and undercut the people's loyalty to the King. Throughout "King Solomon's Mines," the clash between African tribal values and Christian European values is evident. Indeed, at the end of the novel, Christianity represents the inevitable erasure of African culture.

The manliness of Sir Henry Curtis resembles in many ways a type of Victorian manhood often characterized as "Muscular Christianity" or "Christian manliness." Although Sir Henry is not represented as an especially devout man, his religion and his conduct are very much in line with values defined by Christian manliness. The very words that Quatermain uses to describe Sir Henry—honorable, athletic, noble, simple (as in uncomplicated), and absolutely trustworthy—define a kind of stoic and steady virtue that defines the ideal Victorian male.

Scientific & Technological Context

British technological superiority, particularly in weaponry, is an important, though subtle, subtext in the novel. Quatermain relies on that superiority to dupe the more primitive Kukuanas at crucial moments in the story. The first is the moment of the white men's initial meeting with the Kukuana. Quatermain has included "express" rifles, Winchester repeating rifles, and Colt revolvers in his list of essential supplies, and it is lucky that he has. The range, accuracy, and speed of these weapons are enough to convince the isolated Kukuanas that the Englishmen are minor gods.

A scientific understanding of natural phenomena also plays an important role. Later in their Kukuanan adventure, the men search for a sign to give the warlords that Ignosi/Umbopa is indeed their returning king, Quatermain consults an almanac to discover that there will be a total eclipse of the sun at midday. Scientific and technological innovations serve in the novel to underscore the superiority and sophistication of European civilization.

Biographical Context

Henry Rider Haggard was born in 1856 in Bradenham, Norfolk, England, the eighth of ten children. In 1875, when Haggard was 19, he left England for Natal in South Africa. He served in various civil service capacities in Africa until 1881. Although the time Haggard lived in Africa was relatively brief, he was witness to a great deal of unrest and conflict, both between Africans and Europeans, and among African tribes (Whelan 126). Africa captured Haggard's already active imagination, and many of the characters who came to populate his novels, including Allan Quatermain and the Zulu king Ignosi of "King Solomon's Mines," were modeled after people he met while living there. Haggard began writing full-time following the success of "King Solomon's Mines." In 1889, he began a life-long friendship with Rudyard Kipling, another English author who wrote popular fiction informed by his experience as a colonial civil servant. He continued to travel throughout his life, visiting, in addition to Africa, Egypt, Denmark, Iceland, and Mexico. Haggard was knighted in 1912 and died in 1925.

"King Solomon's Mines" was originally written as a boys' adventure tale following the success of Robert Louis Stevenson's "Treasure Island" (1883). Literacy rates in Great Britain had reached unprecedented levels following the passage of the Education Act of 1870, which established and funded mass public education. In the latter part of the century, the phenomenon of the "best seller" gave evidence of the general reading public's appetite for accessible, exciting stories. Haggard's exotic locations, thrilling stories, and heroic protagonists made him one of the most popular writers in late Victorian England (Whelan 135).

Anita Rose, Ph.D.

Works Cited

Adams, James Eli. *Dandies and Desert Saints: Styles of Victorian Manhood*. Ithaca, NY: Cornell UP. 1995.

Haggard, H. Rider. *King Solomon's Mines*. Gerald Monsman, ed. Toronto, Canada: Broadview. 2002.

Haggard, H. Rider. *Twentieth Century Literary Criticism*. Vol. 11. 1983.

Langer, William L. ed. *An Encyclopedia of World History*. Boston: Houghton Mifflin, 1968.

Sally Mitchell, ed. *Victorian Britain: An Encyclopedia*. New York: Garland. 1988.

Whelan , Peter T. *H. Rider Haggard. Dictionary of Literary Biography*. Vol. 156. 1996. 124–136.

Discussion Questions

1. Discuss the characterizations of Sir Henry, Good, and Quatermain. How do they represent a manly ideal?

2. How does Umbopa conform to the model of male virtue presented, and how does he differ?

3. How does Quatermain represent himself as different from both Sir Henry and Good? That is, as the narrator, he is in control of how the reader views different characters, including his own. How do you think he sees himself, and how does he want the reader to see him?

4. Discuss friendships among men and the way that women are a disruptive force.

5. Examine the ways that Foulata and Gagool function as positive and negative examples of the power of the feminine.

6. Discuss descriptions of the African landscape and how the Englishmen respond to, and relate to, it.

7. How is patriarchy associated with civilization, and how is it set up in opposition to matriarchal power? How does Gagool distort feminine power?

8. How does the text address imperialism? How are Africa and Africans represented in the text? Are there different representations (i.e., are there "good" Africans and "bad" ones? Is there a "good" image of Africans in opposition to a "bad" one)? If so, what does each representation seem to suggest about good and bad in this context?

9. This text was initially conceived and published in the context of the popularity of Stevenson's "Treasure Island" as a "boy's adventure story." What characteristics make this a good adventure tale? What might have been appealing to young male readers? What values or character traits are admired or encouraged?

10. What can popular fiction, or "best–sellers," tell us about the era that produced them? What is the good of studying this kind of literature? What can we gain from it? Does popular fiction reveal cultural values in ways that more "canonical" literature might not?

Essay Ideas

1. Examine the treatment of "otherness" in the novel. This could include race, gender, cultural difference, or simply the description of Africa itself.

2. Examine the various examples of patriarchal rule and influence in the novel. You may want to look at Sir Henry's background and story, the way that Quatermain obtained the map to Kukuana, or other instances of patriarchy.

3. Discuss Allan Quatermain as a narrator. Does he seem to be at odds with either Africa or Europe? Consider what he seems to value, and whether or not that is at odds with his own culture. Consider why Quatermain is in Africa, and why he stays for as long as he does.

4. Examine the meanings of masculine and feminine in the novel.

5. Compare the image of Africa in "King Solomon's Mines" with that in Joseph Conrad's "Heart of Darkness." Include in your consideration descriptions of landscape, African culture, European values, and women. Any one of these would yield an interesting essay.

6. Watch several film versions of the novel, and compare to Haggard's text. What significant differences do you notice, and what is the source of this difference? That is, how does each iteration of the tale reveal something about the era that produced it?

The Man Who Would Be King

by Rudyard Kipling

Content Synopsis

"The Man Who Would be King," one of Kipling's most critically acclaimed stories, is a sardonic examination of imperialism. It concerns two vagabonds, Peachey Carnehan and Daniel Dravot, who go out to make a name for themselves in the wilds of Afghanistan at the time of the British Raj in India. An un-named newspaper reporter who witnesses both the beginning and the end of their grand adventure narrates the story in cryptic fashion. Peachey meets the narrator by chance on a train journey and asks him to deliver a message to Dan on another train. The narrator does this and thinks nothing more of it until several weeks later when the two turn up at his office on a stifling summer night. They reveal their dissatisfaction with life in British India and make the startling announcement that they 'are going away to be Kings' (Kipling 252) in Kafiristan, a remote part of Afghanistan untouched by the forces of modern civilization and government. The narrator is instantly cynical but looks out maps of the area for them and at their suggestion goes to the Kumharsen Serai, a trading station, the next day. Here he finds Dravot disguised as a priest and Carnehan as his servant, firmly bound for Afghanistan. He sees them off, surprised at their ingenuity but maintaining his doubts about the whole enterprise.

After two years have elapsed, Carnehan unexpectedly returns to the narrator's office, on another oppressive summer night, but he is now such a wreck of a man, both physically and mentally, that he is unrecognizable. The narrator is naturally mystified but Carnehan, in a rambling incoherent way, proceeds to relate the story of what happened in Kafiristan.

To begin with, he and Dravot found it easy enough to establish their authority among the natives, and increased it little by little until Dravot was able to proclaim himself and his companion as the kings of the whole of Kafiristan and dreamt of going even further to build an empire. All continued to go well until Dravot decided to take a native wife and to make her his queen. Carnehan cautioned against this, reminding Dravot of a 'Contrack' they had drawn up earlier between themselves, to keep clear of both wine and women in order not to jeopardize their grand plans. However, Dravot, carried away by the success of their exploits up until then, refused to listen and arranged to choose a bride in a native wedding ceremony. The girl in fear bit him as he tried to embrace her and the priests, seeing him bleed, realized that he was not the divinity he had claimed to be, but only another human being. In an instant, their fortunes were reversed; the people rose up against them and Dravot was put to death by being flung into a ravine. Carnehan was crucified, but, as he survived, was eventually released. The climax of Carnehan's story comes as he opens up a bag he is carrying to reveal Dravot's head, which Carnehan still insists on grotesquely adorning with a crown.

Having recounted his terrible story, Carnehan leaves the office, but a little later, the narrator comes upon him outside, still wandering around aimlessly, and arranges for him to be placed in an asylum where he dies two days later.

On one level, the story of Dravot and Carnehan appears to be a straightforward example of a nineteenth-century colonial adventure tale, with two Englishmen traveling out to a remote land and establishing their superiority over gullible natives. However, all is undone by their sudden and spectacular downfall; and furthermore the method of narration complicates things considerably from the start. In the first instance, Kipling chooses to present the two adventurers through the highly critical lens of the narrator's cynicism. Furthermore, the actual events in Kafiristan are conveyed through the broken Carnehan, a man who has lost his wits. In view of all this, it is difficult to get a proper handle on the story of Dravot and Carnehan, which is both begun and ended in the most abrupt, offhand manner by the narrator, and readers are left to make what they will of these two adventurers and their audacious bid to become "Kings."

Historical Context

"The Man Who Would Be King," appeared at a time when the British Empire was covering a quarter of the globe. India was its particular prized possession, and had been for many years, and Kipling, who was born in the country, used it as fruitful material for many of his early short stories. However, he was far from being the unreserved apologist for empire that he is often assumed to be. The British empire may have been at its height when he began his writing career in the 1880s (with other European nations similarly jostling for territorial gains around the world) but it was also a time when doubts were being raised about colonialism, its effects on both conquered and conqueror. European expansionism was particularly aggressive in nature at this time, as witness, for example, the rapacious activities of the Belgians in the Congo which inspired Joseph Conrad's scathingly anti-imperialist novella "Heart of Darkness." Kipling did ultimately believe in empire, but he too had misgivings, and his Indian stories nearly all show the terrible toll that the Indian climate and working conditions take on ordinary British men and women living in the country. Moreover his 1897 poem "Recessional," commemorating Queen Victoria's Diamond Jubilee, instead of being celebratory as might be expected on such a momentous occasion, sounds a note of extreme caution as to imperialist responsibilities and even includes a vision of a ruined empire. In addition, Daniel Dravot, the would-be emperor in "The Man Who Would Be King," experiences a shattering downfall.

Kipling does not condemn Dravot and Carnehan outright: they are seen to fulfil their dreams of conquest for a time (at least, if Carnehan is to be wholly believed), like the real-life Colonel James 'Rajah Brooke' referred to in the story, who set up a kingdom in Sarawak (Malaysia) in the 1840s. (The tale may also have been inspired by the American adventurer Josiah Harlan, who traveled to Afghanistan earlier in the century.) Nevertheless, we only ever get a second-hand account of their exploits, and this perhaps has the effect of increasing their air of unreality; these are events taking place in a far-off region far removed from ordinary life. Perhaps Kipling is making the point that such conquest as Dravot and Carnehan dream of is not really a practical option any more; the days of such adventures properly belong to the past, as when military commander Robert Clive annexed Bengal in the eighteenth century, thus laying the foundations of the British Raj. By the close of the nineteenth century, however, the work of empire in India was no longer a matter of war and conquest but of administration, represented here by the press office and elsewhere in Kipling's fiction by engineers, civil servants, and soldiers languishing in barracks rather than out fighting glorious battles. Against such a prosaic background, Dravot and Carnehan, two larger-than-life characters full of grandiose schemes, appear distinctly out of place.

Societal Context

As is typical of Kipling's tales, the characters that feature in "The Man Who Would Be King," are of the working class, rather than those in the higher echelons of government and decision-making. Dravot and Carnehan, in fact, occupy a position even lower than this. They have tried many professions in their time, but, having failed to establish a proper role for themselves in Anglo-India, they first turn to an alternative society—that of the Masonic order—and finally decide that India isn't big enough for them. It might be more accurate to say that they are more or less squeezed out of the country, and therefore their actions in setting out to conquer Kafiristan may not be as ridiculous as might first appear. Existing on the periphery of Anglo-Indian society, they literally have to try to find space for themselves elsewhere.

To move on to the issue of race, Kipling seems to share many of the racist assumptions of European superiority of his day in his depiction of the Kafiristan natives, who fall easily under the sway of the two Englishmen, accepting their claims of divine kingship. Dravot and Carnehan do not rule from a distance however; they feel quite at home with these people, bestowing colloquial nicknames on their chiefs. Of course, this sense of kinship seems largely to stem from the fact that the Kafiristan natives are white-skinned (it is speculated that they are descendants of Alexander the Great).

However, Kipling shows that even when the natives are European, indeed, "English" (Kipling 265), in appearance, this sense of connection can only go so far. Kipling stops well short of endorsing inter-racial marriage. Unlike, for example, Rider Haggard's romantic picture in "King Solomon's Mines" in which the heroic English gentleman Sir Henry Curtis marries the queen of an exotic African people, and becomes their ruler, Dravot's attempt to take a native wife and queen ends in sheer catastrophe. The two races can live in harmony only up to a point: the two Englishmen can live among the native people only as gods and not as fellow human beings. Kipling often went further than many of his contemporaries in humanizing natives; he was willing and able to enter into imaginative sympathy with native characters as several of his short stories, and his famous novel "Kim," demonstrate. In spite of this, however, different races generally remain segregated in his fiction.

Religious Context

The picture "The Man Who Would Be King," presents of non-European races worshiping heathen idols is a standard one in nineteenth-century colonial literature. In such a system, Dravot and Carnehan find it easy to set themselves up as living idols. Kipling, who was not an orthodox Christian believer, does not explicitly denounce idol worship. However, Dravot and Carnehan are punished for their presumptuousness. There may not be much sense of an overarching Christian order in this tale (or in Kipling's writings generally) but all the same there does seem to be some unseen force at work which eventually casts down the two adventurers for their sin of hubris.

Scientific & Technological Context

In the manner of many a colonial adventure tale of the period, Dravot and Carnehan are seen to assert their supremacy over the natives in the first instance by means of their guns, against which Kafiristan bow and arrows are, naturally, no match. However, although Dravot goes on to build his claims of kingship upon this, he and Carnehan do not get much further in terms of technological advancement. In leaving British India they leave the modern world far behind and deliberately retreat to a primitive land, untouched by the forces of scientific progress, and hope to make it their own. Instead, it consumes them.

Biographical Context

Born in Bombay in 1865, Rudyard Kipling remains the literary name most readily associated with the British Empire. After spending the first six years of his life in India, he returned to England, a disorienting experience that left a life-long impression on him. He returned to India in 1882 and later worked on a newspaper in Lahore. In 1886, he published his first literary work, the poems known as "Departmental Ditties." His first collection of short stories, "Plain Tales from the Hills," appeared in 1888 and he was hailed as a new and exciting literary talent. More collections about life in India followed, including "The Phantom Rickshaw" (1889) in which "The Man Who Would Be King," was first published. After leaving India once more in 1889, he traveled widely and lived in America for a spell before finally settling in Sussex, England. Other works with an Indian theme include "The Jungle Book" (1894–96) and the novel "Kim" (1901). Although in later years he began to concentrate more on stories with an English setting.

Kipling, who died in 1936, enjoyed outstanding literary success in his own day, his acclaim as a writer being cemented with the award for the Nobel Prize for Literature in 1907. He perhaps did more than any other writer to popularize the short story as an art form in England, with his unconventional narrative methods, taut, elliptical style, psychological penetration, and use of colloquial idioms – all of which are abundantly evident in "The Man Who Would Be King." He has also enjoyed considerable vogue as a poet, but he will perhaps always be best known for his vignettes of Indian life in the heyday of the British Raj. He was, by no means, as naively trusting as many post-colonialist critics would have us believe.

Gurdip Panesar, Ph.D.

Works Cited

Cornell, Louis. *Kipling in India*. London: Macmillan, 1966.

Kipling, Rudyard. *The Man Who Would Be King and Other Stories*. Harmondsworth: Penguin, 1987.

Mallett, Phillip. *Rudyard Kipling: A Literary Life*. Basingstoke: Palgrave Macmillan, 2003.

Paffard, Mark. *Kipling's Indian Fiction*. Basingstoke: Macmillan, 1989.

Discussion Questions

1. What kind of characters are Dravot and Carnehan? Do you think they can be called heroic? Why or why not?
2. How does the narrator's outlook compare with that of the two adventurers? How does this affect the telling of the story?
3. Do you think that the narrator is altogether trustworthy? Why or why not?
4. Do you agree that up to the point of Dravot and Carnehan's sudden downfall, the story is a conventional type of colonial adventure narrative? Why or why not?
5. Do you agree that Kipling's portrayal of "natives" in the story is simplistic? Why or why not?
6. What are the implications of the suggestion that the people of Kafiristan are descendants of Alexander the Great?
7. Why does the narrator indulge in such lengthy descriptions of the monotonous life in the press office?
8. What is the effect of Carnehan suddenly flourishing Dravot's severed head at the close of his tale? How well do you think this fits in with Kipling's overall purpose?
9. What is the effect of the story ending so abruptly? Do you also feel that it is inconclusive? Why or why not?

Essay Ideas

1. Examine Kipling's portrayal of race in "The Man Who Would Be King."
2. Analyze Kipling's method of narration in "The Man Who Would Be King."
3. Examine the idea of the unreliable narrator in relation to "The Man Who Would Be King."
4. Analyze Kipling's critique of imperialism in "The Man Who Would Be King."
5. Analyze the notion of heroism in "The Man Who Would Be King."

H RIDER HAGGARD

ISTINGUISHED English Novelist

SAN FRANCISCO SUNDAY CALL

He had a strong inclination toward literature, and after much labor he succeeded in presenting to the public, partly through his own financing, a book entitled "Cetewayo and His White Neighbors," which represented a loss of 50 pounds to him. The glimpse of a fair face which he caught in a little country church gave him the idea for his brief story of "Dawn," on which his net gains were 10 pounds. His inclinations were drawn to the occult, and in 1885 he composed "The Witch's Head," from which his revenues rose to 50 pounds. Haggard was thus 10 pounds the gainer on his three literary efforts. On his being admitted to the bar in 1885 he almost decided to abandon literature. He clung to it, however, as a pastime, and, availing himself of the leisure of the evenings, he wrote "King Solomon's Mines," his first popular success, for he awoke, as did the author of "Childe Harold," to find himself famous.

AWOKE TO FIND FAME

His great success came to him in "She," a story of such vivid fancy, of such moving action, of such a well constructed plot, that it instantly caught the approval of the fiction reading public. It shocked some of the staid English novel readers, who were accustomed to assimilate mild pabulum of the two volume style.

"Really," exclaimed one estimable woman, "the imagination of this man Haggard is simply lawless."

Others objected because the author made the heroine too beautiful and alluring.

The story of "She" is an old myth under a new garb. It will be recollected by those who followed its manifold thrills and surprises that it concerned the romance of a beautiful white woman who seemed to have immortal life and had lived for centuries in the fastnesses of the mountains of Africa as the queen of black savages who knew her as Ayesha, or "She who must be obeyed," whence the title of the book is derived.

She believes that she recognizes in a young Englishman the reincarnation of a youth whom she had loved centuries before and for whom she had waited all these years. The book comes to a tragic end, for She, in endeavoring to induce her reincarnated love to enter the fire of immortality, goes into the flames herself, where the effect is precisely the opposite from what it would have been had this not been the fiery baptism. She becomes a wrinkled hag and dies in the presence of the English youth. Here is much the same motive as pervades William Morris' "The Well at the World's End," although the language has none of the archaic form of the English socialist.

BECOMES PROLIFIC WRITER

"She" was hailed as a queen in the United States, and it is told that an American, desiring to impress Haggard with the popularity of the work, declared that he had actually counted 60 women at one American summer resort reading it.

"I am very glad to hear that," was the response of Haggard, "although every one of those books was pirated. I never got a cent of American revenue from 'She.'"

H. RIDER HAGGARD

MARCH 26 1911

Author H. Rider Haggard, pictured above in the *San Francisco Sunday Call,* March 26, 1911, is known primarily as an adventure writer. He wrote and published more than 60 works, his most successful being *King Solomon's Mines,* featured on page 129. Also in this volume is Haggard's *She,* on page 175. Photo: Library of Congress.

Midnight's Children

by Salman Rushdie

Content Synopsis

"Midnight's Children" (1981) begins with the birth of Saleem Sinai, born at the stroke of midnight on August 15, 1947, the exact time when India won independence following two centuries of colonial rule by Britain. The novel is about the mingling of the personal and the public, the birth of an individual conflated with the birth of a nation. Writing in the first person, the narrator states that "handcuffed to history, my destinies [were] indissolubly chained to those of my country" (9). Saleem Sinai's story seems to be the story of "postcolonial" India, though Rushdie has said that it is only meant as a comic novel. Thus, the several allegorical and direct references to real, historical events and people are tempered by the use of 'magic realism'—a mix of realism and fantasy. The narrator, Saleem Sinai, is bilingual, and uses a mix of Urdu, English, and English spoken in the Indian dialect—written in a style accessible to a reader of English.

Having announced the birth of Saleem Sinai, in the way much like Laurence Sterne's "Tristram Shandy," the narrator begins by recounting the story of his grandfather Aadam Aziz. Aadam Aziz has returned from Germany to Kashmir in 1915, and experienced a cultural strain between the East and the West. The Boatman, Tai, disparages him as a "foreign returned" doctor who would have little or no respect for his own culture. Praying one day on his prayer mat, Aziz happens to hit his nose too hard and decides to forgo Islamic faith. He simultaneously develops a hole where a heart should have been, representing his loss of faith.

Shortly after his arrival in Kashmir, he is called to examine the daughter of the landowner, Ghani. However, as Islam discourages unfamiliar men looking at women, Aziz's patient is shown through a hole in a sheet through which the ailing body part can be seen. Ghani's daughter, Naseem develops several illnesses and Dr. Aziz views several parts of her body including a "celestial rump" (26) which blushed. These fragmented parts, which did not include the face, exercise their influence on Aziz's imagination and he falls in love with Naseem, which is eventually realized by their marriage to each other. They move to Amritsar in Punjab.

Naseem remains a staunch Muslim, while her husband is broadminded and liberal. Naseem is now referred to as the "Reverend Mother," with her self-enforced silences as a form of rebellion, and her powerful dramatic performance in the kitchen. They have five children: Alia, Mumtaz, Hanif, Mustapha, and Emerald.

Nadir Khan, an associate of a Muslim political figure, alluded the Hummingbird' is in hiding, and Dr. Aziz hides Nadir in his cellar, where his second daughter, Mumtaz, attends to his needs. Naseem protests against Nadir Khan's stay by a vow of silence, but Mumtaz and Nadir fall in love and decide to marry. However, notwithstanding a very happy two years in love, the father-in-law is shocked to discover that his daughter is still a virgin even after two years of marriage. Meanwhile, the youngest sister divulges the secret of Nadir's stay to her politician fiancé Major Zulfikar, and Nadir deserts the house leaving a note that reads "Talaq! Talaq! Talaq!" (62); a note of divorce for his wife.

After the divorce, Mumtaz happens to meet Alia's boyfriend, Ahmed Sinai, and they eventually marry, making Alia a bitter and jealous woman. Mumtaz changes her name to Amina. Amina is pregnant with Saleem Sinai. Amina decides that she will give birth to her baby on the midnight of August 15 as the newspaper "The Times of India" announces an award for any child born at the precise moment of the nation's independence.

Amina lies in at the Narlikar Nursing home, along with Vanita, a neighbor. A son is born to each, but the nurse, Mary Pereira, switches babies and changes fates. Vanita dies in childbirth, but her child goes to the rich Sinai family, while Amina's real child stays uncared for. Though Vanita is married, her child is actually the result of a liaison between herself and a British colonist, William Methwold. Thus, Saleem Sinai's blue eyes are mistaken to be Kashmiri, whereas they were inherited from a British man. Amina is thrilled with her baby with blue eyes, who also receives the award from the newspaper as well as a letter from the first prime minister of India, Jawaharlal Nehru, equating the destiny of the baby boy with that of the new nation. The idea that he is responsible for all that happens to the nation, will haunt Saleem throughout his life.

A few years later, Ahmed learns that his financial assets have been frozen. Such a shock leads him to lose his sexual powers as well—the narrator tells us that Ahmed's testicles freeze with the freezing of his other assets. Driven by need, Amina now goes to the racetracks (much against her Islamic faith) and wins money to help with her husband's financial court case. Mary Pereira, the nurse, becomes a servant at the Sinai household, and she looks after Saleem. One night, Mary's earlier lover, Joseph d'Costa, is caught planting explosives in the watchtower, and is condemned to death.

Meanwhile, the young Saleem discovers his mother receiving strange phone calls. Saleem is hiding in a laundry tub in the bathroom, his favorite haven of privacy, when he hears his mother enter and close the door. Amina, spurned by her spouse and his 'frozen assets' is caressing herself, but with the name of 'na-dir'. The child in the laundry tub wants to keep still and quiet so that he is not discovered. The cord of a pajama in the dirty laundry gets into his nose. His nose had always been oversized, but now with the cord tickling his nostrils, it is as if it activates a new telepathic power in him. He is surprised to discover that he can make a connection with other people—he can now hear other people's thoughts! His family does not believe him when he tells them, and his new talent remains a secret.

One day, Saleem follows his mother and witnesses a rendezvous between Nadir and herself. However, Amina soon breaks up with Nadir after hearing a newspaper story of murder and infidelity. One day Saleem is chased by other boys and in his rush, he slams a door. Unfortunately the door closes on his finger severing it. At the hospital his blood type does not match that of his parents.' There is a commotion within the family, and Saleem is temporarily sent to live with his Uncle Hanif and his sexy wife, Aunt Pia. Meanwhile, Saleem forms the Midnight's Children Conference, the MCC, with his telepathic powers. He eventually goes back to the Sinai household.

At this point, his sister, whom he calls the Brass Monkey, is introduced in the novel. Mary Pereira, consumed with guilt, divulges the secret to the family that she had switched babies. However,

Saleem remains accepted and they do not attempt to find their biological child. As Amina's marriage deteriorates, she decides to move to Pakistan with her children, where her sisters Emerald and Alia are also residing. Saleem hates it in Pakistan and misses Bombay terribly. The Brass Monkey in Pakistan is found to have a beautiful voice, and growing famous as the "Jamila Singer," she is celebrated as the patriotic singer of Pakistan. She sings publicly, but with the chadar, or a piece of cloth, held in front of her. Jamila Singer, now apparently a devout Muslim, sings through a round hole in the chadar. As her fame spreads, she is known as 'the Voice of the Nation,' the 'Bulbul e din' or nightingale-of-the-faith (313).

Amina's husband develops heart trouble in Bombay (now Mumbai), and recalls his wife and children from Pakistan. Their marriage improves. Saleem is protective about his nasal powers, but one day Saleem is taken to a clinic to cure his constant sniffing and sneezing. As a result of an operation on his nose, his telepathic powers are forever lost. The entire family moves to Pakistan. During this time, Saleem also realizes that he is in love with Jamila, who is a sister, and yet not a sister. The confession horrifies Jamila. With Amina's new love for her husband, whose icy testicles seem to have thawed, Amina becomes pregnant again. In the Indo-Pakistani war, a bomb kills Amina, her husband, and sister Alia.

In the course of the unrest, either by war, or by violence done to him, Saleem loses his memory. He joins the Pakistani army. There are vivid pictures of the Bangladesh war of independence in which Pakistan attempts to crush the rebellion, and India supports East Pakistan, which successfully breaks away and becomes Bangladesh. In the killing fields of Bangladesh, Saleem meets one of his old MCC friends, Parvati-the-Witch, who not only helps his memory, but also brings him back to India, hidden in a wicker basket, with magic.

Back in India, Saleem goes to live with his civil servant brother Mustapha, and his wife, Aunt Sonia. He eventually leaves their place after a row. Here Saleem also learns of his mother's death. In the Magician's Ghetto, where he lives, Saleem refuses a match with the willing Parvati pretending that he is impotent—in reality Jamila Singer's face comes to haunt him. Parvati the witch then calls Shiva—the child belonging to Vanita—magically, and is impregnated by him. Her unmarried state and the resultant scandal eventually forces Saleem to marry her. Saleem sees his own fate being dramatized again—a baby being born in a family with the wrong father. The narration consciously repeats the same lines as the new baby Aadam Sinai is born.

Saleem was born at the stroke of midnight of freedom, baby Aadam emerged with Prime Minister Indira Gandhi's announcement of a state of national emergency that curtailed all civil rights in the country. Birth is a trope that is not only repeated, but is invested with political eventualities:

> . . . when the three contortionists had washed the baby and wrapped it in an old saree and brought it out for its father to see, at exactly the same moment the word emergency was being heard for the first time, and suspension-of-civil rights, and censorship-of-the-press, and armoured-units-on-special-alerts, and arrest-of-subversive-elements; something was ending, something was being born, and at the precise instant of the birth of the new India and the beginning of a continuous midnight that would not end for two long years, my son . . . came out into the world (419).

The baby has long ears, but he does not speak—an allegory of the demonic censorship of the Press during the emergency. Comparing himself and his son, the first and the second generation in free India, Saleem Sinai says, "We, the children of

Independence, rushed wildly and too fast into the future; he, emergency-born, is already more cautious, biding his time; but when he acts he will be impossible to resist. Already, he is stronger, harder, and more resolute than I am . . . " (425).

The novel ends on a wry note, as Saleem is made to be a victim of the Widow's forcible sterilization program. During the emergency, Indira Gandhi, the then Prime Minister of India conducted her often-forced mass sterilization program to contain India's booming population. Saleem states that the government of the Widow and her "labia-lipped" son—Indira Gandhi and her son Sanjay Gandhi rob him and the country of all hopes and optimism. Cracking up, as his grandfather did, Saleem can feel his imminent death. Padma, the earthy listener, to whom Saleem had been narrating the story, now proposes marriage to Saleem. The novel ends on the note that aged thirty-one, midnight's child Saleem smells death and destruction on the one hand, and on the other, finds and accepts a haven in the familial refuge that Padma offers.

Historical Context

"Midnight's Children" is a fictionalization of history. It captures the period from 1915 to the late 1970s in India. However, Rushdie, a graduate in history from Cambridge University is under no mistaken assumption that a single history is true. History is appropriated by various ideologies for various reasons. Rushdie's fictionalization of pre and post independent India is told from Saleem Sinai's perspective, thus it is a history recalled through individual memory, and is admittedly fragmented and incomplete. Magic realism also contributes to constructing this version of history. With many gaps and glaring omissions, "Midnight's Children" remains fiction, interspersed with history. The novel has been dubbed pessimistic, but Rushdie insists on the closing being optimistic as baby Ahmed Sinai is cautious, wary, and strong willed.

India was granted independence from colonial rule on August 15, 1947. Such freedom came with a price—the breaking up or the partition of India—into India and Pakistan. (Pakistan would further break into two as East Pakistan would break away, becoming Bangladesh in 1971). Indira Gandhi (1917–1984), the daughter of the first Prime Minister of India, Jawaharlal Nehru, remained Prime Minister of India for several years. Her role is especially important in the writing of "Midnight's Children" as the novel was conceived in the years of a national emergency.

India has always celebrated its status of democracy, being 'the largest democracy in the world'. This is the more significant as it is surrounded by military rulers in its neighboring countries. In 1977, Prime Minister Indira Gandhi was found guilty of party campaign malpractice. While politicians and the public across the country cried for her stepping down, Indira Gandhi proclaimed a state of national emergency suspending all "civil rights," including habeas corpus, freedom of the press, and grounding air flights over Delhi. With zealous participation by her son, she enforced strict policy of family planning and sterilization to control the gigantic population of India. Sanjay Gandhi's slum-clearance, without any adequate settlements for those rendered homeless, was ruthless and arbitrary. Rohinton Mistry's novel "A Fine Balance" dramatizes such atrocities.

Rushdie painstakingly points out repeatedly that Indira's second name comes from her husband, Feroze Gandhi—who had no relation to Mahatma Gandhi, the saintly political leader of India. Interestingly, Indira Gandhi's libel suit against Rushdie and the first edition of "Midnight's Children" hinged on the idea that Mrs. Gandhi hastened her husband's early death by a heart attack. In the novel, Mrs. Gandhi is referred to as 'The Widow'—a misogynist portrayal given India's dark tradition of treating widows as inauspicious non-persons. Mrs. Gandhi, the 'Widow' in "Midnight's

Children" is a terrifying picture painted in dark colors, "no colour except green and black."

If Rushdie is criticizing Mrs. Gandhi, he satirizes her rival no less. Morarji Desai, (1896–1995) was a rival to Mrs. Gandhi's claim to the office of Prime Minister. Desai was an austere orthodox, yoga-practicing Hindu, a strict vegetarian and teetotaler; he also daily happened to "[imbibe] some of his own urine as part of his personal 'yoga-therapy' (Wolpert, 407). In "Midnight's Children" he is unceremoniously referred to as the "urine-drinking Prime Minister."

Several historical events are dramatized in the storyline of "Midnight's Children." Events such as the division of the Bombay State, and the preceding violence in Bombay are intrinsically related to the story. China's war with India in 1962, as China almost invaded India over border disagreements, is poignantly and succinctly voiced by the Reverend Mother. She fears that they would have to learn Chinese, as Chinese soldiers would be stalking the streets of Mumbai. The Pakistani army ruthlessly quashing its own people in East Pakistan, and East Pakistan's birth into nationhood as Bangladesh, is dramatized in gory details in the third part of the novel.

There are several historical references in the narration. Aziz sees the face of his patient Naseem for the first time the day World War I ends. The narrator refers to the Jallianwallah Bagh massacre in which a British General opened unprovoked fire on innocent Indians killing about a thousand people. However, repeatedly, Saleem Sinai is shown to be the unreliable narrator, not only in claimed relation with several momentous events of history, but also with dates, facts, and references. Rushdie admits those gaps, as some being intended and some being unconscious. There is an absence of reference to Gandhi, in the discussion of the new nation. Known as the 'Father of the Nation,' Mahatma Gandhi's role was pivotal in gaining the independence of India. In the novel Saleem confuses the date of Gandhi's assassination. Rushdie validates the remembered history of Saleem Sinai in "Imaginary Homelands":

> . . . what I was actually doing was a novel of memory and about memory, so that my India was just that, 'my' India, a version and no more than one of all the hundreds of millions of possible versions (Imaginary Homelands, 150).

Thus. "Midnight's Children" may be about history, but it is not history per se. In a certain way, however, remembered individual memories, even in spite of magical realism, does critique the grand narrative of official history. In that sense, it is valid, and Rushdie himself confesses to being part of the history he was writing—the pessimism in the novel, he noted, derived from the period of Emergency, when it was conceived.

Societal Context

A discussion of societal contexts in "Midnight's Children" is by necessity varied. Rushdie's own cultural life is influenced by his experience in India, Pakistan, and Britain. Further, the nations have different dominant religions: Hinduism, Islam, and Christianity. This is more important as Rushdie time and again admits to being a cultural hybrid, against fundamentalism, against 'purity,' "Midnight's Children" dramatizes events from the 20's of India, with hindsight of almost three quarters of a century.

The narrative style of "Midnight's Children" has been linked to oral storytelling, especially the 'seemingly endless and digressive Indian epics of the Mahabharata and the Ramayana' (Cundy, 27). This style is superimposed on the western form of the novel. Rushdie admits to the influence of Sterne and Garcia-Marquez. The oral form of narrative implies an audience, stressing community, as opposed to solitary, intellectual introspection. In the novel, true to the subcontinent fashion, the family is large, involved, and extended.

Replacing the myth of the passive women of the East, the women in "Midnight's Children" are powerfully portrayed. This is especially true of the Muslim women, who are often stereotyped as confined, restricted, and oppressed. Ghani's daughter, to whom the reader is not given access just as Ahmed Aziz can only look at her in disembodied parts, turns out whole and larger than life after marriage. She wants to cover her face as her faith dictates, and refuses to budge from her decision. In the clash between Eastern values and Western, symbolized within her relationship with her husband, she refuses to give in passively. Her portrayal as "the Reverend Mother" is dramatic, full of energy, and most certainly matriarchal. Saleem's mother, Amina Sinai, goes to the racecourse and wins money (something Islamic faith does not allow) keeping it secret from her husband. She saves the family from penury in the process. While Saleem Sinai turns out to be a nobody, his sister, The Brass Monkey, or Jamila, becomes a famous singer in Pakistan. Pakistan dictates her fundamental Islamic outlook of covering her face so that strangers may not defile her with their glances. This is overturned in the novel at the end, as she finally becomes a Christian nun owing to her irresistible attachment to bread.

If storytelling is one cultural narrative in "Midnight's Children," the other, more modern aspect is references to Hindi films. Bollywood is more than a social institution in India. The largest film Industry in the world, Bollywood—films made in Bombay, in the 'National language,' Hindi—have effected more for the national consciousness than any ideology of political parties have been able to. Filming terminology invades "Midnight's Children," and several ideas are borne across through famous songs in Hindi films. For example, the cultural hybridity that is quintessential to the novel and its medium, is highlighted in the quote from a Hindi film song:

Mera joota hai Japani
Ye patloon Inglistani

Sar pe lal topi rusi
Phir bhi dil hai Hindustani

This roughly translates to:

O, my shoes are Japanese
These trousers are English, if you please
On my head, red Russian hat -
My heart's Indian for all that (IH, 11)

Rushdie states that it "could almost be Saleem's theme song" (IH, 11).

The Bombay Talkies or Bollywood—the prolific film industry of India with its exaggerated sense of broad comedy—conflates with the European avant-garde filmmakers such as Godard, Truffaut, and Brunel. Surrealist tendencies of such filmmakers contribute significantly to the genre of magic realism that Rushdie uses.

The metaphor of 'leaking' and 'pickling' in the context of cooking, has socio-cultural overtones in "Midnight's Children." Eventually Rushdie resists any cultural 'purity' that does not leak into, or mix with, other cultures and ideas. Rushdie's language itself is a mix of English and Hindi/Urdu. Saleem himself has many surrogate and apparently real fathers in the novel. Saleem is Muslim, yet Saleem's alter ego is Shiva, the name of a ubiquitous Hindu God. In a broad sense, it reflects the secular ideal that the nation of India was built upon, with the Congress Party rule since Independence.

In "Imaginary Homelands," Rushdie states that, "the English language ceased to be the sole possession of the English some time ago" (70). Rushdie's skillful use of English and Urdu represents his cultural hybridity. The disruption of English, or the "Indianization" of English, may be interpreted as the classic gesture of defiance against western imperialism. The English language or "the instrument of subservience" can become "a weapon of liberation"—the "decolonizing pen," as

Rushdie stated in an interview (Salman Rushdie, The Empire Writes Back With a Vengeance, *The Times*, 3rd July, 1982).

Religious Context

The cliché that 'whatever is true in India, the opposite is true as well,' comes in handy in a discussion of religion in India. India has a long past and tradition both of secularism and communalism. India's population is dominantly Hindu but the Muslims and other religious people form a substantial percentage.

While the Congress, the almost dynastic party of Nehru and Indira Gandhi, have always validated a secular tradition, The "Bharatiya Janata Party" (BJP) or the Indian People's Party, and other Hindu-first parties such as the "Rashtriya Swayam Sevak Sangh," (National Self-Help Association); or the "Vishwa Hindu Parishad" (World Hindu Council) market the idea of India as an all-Hindu state.

In an interview, Rushdie stated that:

"My view is that the tradition of India is a mixed tradition, and that it is wrong to start seeing as Indian tradition as being pure in any way, as many people try and do these days, to try and create a kind of pure Indian tradition—which in fact is a pure Hindu tradition—and to say that that is Indian culture is a kind of alien graft . . . seems to me to be first of all rubbish, and secondly, quite dangerous rubbish . . ." (Excerpts from a Conversation with Salman Rushdie)

"Midnight's Children" is best read as a healthy mish-mash of religious faiths in India. The characters portrayed in the novel are mostly Muslim. The difference, however, is that the book discourages fundamentalism and encourages cosmopolitanism. Rushdie's deliberate choice of the Dr. Aziz has echoes of Forster's Dr. Aziz in "A Passage to India." While Dr. Aziz in Forster's India dreams of the Islamic Mughal glory, Ahmed Aziz is cosmopolitan. He is westernized, but he opposes the colonizer's rule in India.

The partition of India was not only a nation being driven into two, it was also a religio-socio-cultural trauma. With the partition, communal fears and insecurities inflamed as the respective religions were asked to leave and reside in the country allotted to them. Several Hindu people moved from the part now known as Pakistan, to India. Thousands of Muslims left their homes and property in India to build a new home in Pakistan from scratch. The Sinai family moves to Pakistan, but Saleem misses the city of Bombay in India. His sister becomes a famous religious singer in Pakistan, but even her religious identity is left as vague and indistinct as she reportedly joins a nunnery.

Religion dictates cultural habits. In one curious incident, Pakistani soldiers are enthused jingoistically that meat eaters will attack vegetarians: identities metonymically formed around food habits. They are shocked to find that they are required to fight their own people, in East Pakistan. Both national and religious identities are incomplete in the storyteller's world of "Midnight's Children." Ahmed Aziz decides to forsake his religious beliefs. This decision, the lack of faith, left a permanent hole where his heart should have been. While Ahmed Aziz does not have abiding faith, his wife is conservative and believes in purdah, or covering herself. Christianity, Hinduism, and Islam are mixed together quite like a pickle. Saleem Sinai, the child of a Muslim family is actually fathered by a Christian. Saleem's alter ego within the novel is called Shiva, the Hindu all powerful god. Saleem is Muslim and yet he often compares his sensitive nose to the one of Ganesha, the Hindu God of success, who has an elephant's trunk for a nose. Saleem's lover in the novel is Padma, a Hindu girl as evidenced by the name. (Padma is named after the Hindu goddess of wealth). The reference to "the blue Christ" or the "Krishna-Christ" suggests Jesus adopting the blue color of the Hindu god of love, Krishna.

Scientific & Technological Context

The second half of the twentieth century has been dominated by research in bio-medical, and genetic sciences. In 1953 James Watson from America and Francis Crick of England developed the double helix model of DNA which explained the way in which this massive molecule could carry and transmit the hereditary model of DNA. By 1959, Japanese scientists made a discovery that would be vital in the development of genetic engineering. The scientists found resistance to antibodies in shigella dysenteriae, which is passed from one bacterium to another by circles of DNA known as "plasmids," separate from the normal DNA. This would finally lead to the marketing of the first human insulin made by bacteria as a result of genetic engineering. By mid-seventies genetic engineering was well in the news, and some scientists were calling for a halt in the development of genetic engineering until implications of what it might lead to were better understood. By 1981, the Chinese had cloned a fish.

Another revolution that touched the lives of people directly was that of communication. New satellites were laboriously thrown into space, and on Earth, news began to travel quickly, and so did personal communication.

It is possible to see these two strands of scientific thought, invention, and discovery playing a role in the making of "Midnight's Children." Human fate (as an extension of the deciding DNA), as well as human biology and parentage are contested and explored in "Midnight's Children." Saleem Sinai is the child of many dubious fathers. Like the metaphor of the double helix, he feels his fate is intertwined with that of India. Modes of communication, made possible by imagination and science, are echoed by Saleem's power to communicate, through his nose, with the other children of midnight. Rushdie aims at scientific explanation at the occurrence, how certain wavelengths may have been established by the pajama cord getting into Saleem's nose, which finally went away after his sinus operation.

The opposing pull between science and religion, scientific outlook and cultural opinions are beautifully depicted in the character of Dr. Ahmed Aziz. Choosing to embrace the western rational mode of thinking, he develops a hole in the place where the heart should have been. His loss of faith creates a vacuum in his life. By giving in to the rational way of thinking, he has lost faith forever.

Biographical Context

Ahmed Salman Rushdie (1947–) was born in Bombay (now Mumbai), the only son of a professional Muslim couple. His schooling was done in English, as is common with the educated classes in India. At home he spoke Urdu. From Bombay, the family moved to England where Rushdie studied at Cathedral School, Rugby. Rushdie studied history at King's College, Cambridge, where he also joined the Cambridge Footlights Theater Company.

After Cambridge, Rushdie went to live with his parents in Pakistan, where he worked with a television company for a short period. He came back to England to work as a copywriter in an advertising company. For a while he also worked as an actor in London. In both places Rushdie experienced censorship as a result of government policy or racism. In 1975, he published "Grimus," his first novel that was not a success. His second novel however, created waves as the new voice of the subcontinent. "Midnight's Children" (1981) won numerous awards including the Booker Prize, and the James Tait Black Memorial Prize. It was also judged to be the "Booker of Bookers"—as the best book among the Booker winners in the twenty-five years since the Booker Prize was founded.

Rushdie's third novel, "Shame" (1983) also dealt in history allegorizing the political situation in Pakistan, the struggle between military and civilian rule. His next novel, "The Satanic Verses" became notorious as many Muslims read blasphemy of Islam in the text. The book was publicly burnt in Bradford in England, India and Pakistan. In Iran, the fundamentalist Islamic premiere Ayatollah Khomeini issued a fatwa, a sentence of death, against Rushdie. Rushdie was forced to go into hiding under the protection of the British Government.

Rushdie also published "Haroun and the Sea of Stories" (1990) in which the storyteller's voice is stifled by the enemy of storytelling Prince Khattam-Shud. "Imaginary Homelands," a collection of journalism and criticism was published in 1991. Rushdie's other works include "East, West" (1994), and "The Moors Last Sigh" (1995), "The Ground Beneath her Feet" (1999), and "Fury" (2001). "Shalimar the Clown," was published in 2005.

Rushdie had been married to Clarissa Luard in 1976. In 1988, he married the American writer Marianne Wiggins. After a third failed marriage, Rushdie the Midnight's Child, wedded his Padma in 2004—Padma Lakshmi, an Indian born model and actress whom he met in 1999.

Rushdie's works are deeply involved with the concept of cultural hybridity. Having lived the life of a migrant and an exile in India, Pakistan, and Britain, Rushdie is influenced by all three cultures. Like many other postcolonial writers, he resists the term "Commonwealth Literature" finding it exclusionary and peripheral.

Searching for an identity is a constant theme in "Midnight's Children," both in history as well as in geography—the will to belong to the partitioned countries either of Pakistan or India. While in spirit Saleem belongs to Bombay in India, his religion (as well as the conventional extended family) dictates choosing Pakistan. Thus, the language of "Midnight's Children" is English, suffused with phrases in Urdu—Pakistan's national language, as well as the several regional languages of India.

There is a connection between Saleem Sinai, the first person narrator of "Midnight's Children," and Salman Rushdie. Rushdie admits in an interview that Sinai is an extended translation of his own name. Saleem in the novel is born on the exact moment that India gained independence. Rushdie closely enough was born on the same momentous year, about eight weeks before Saleem Sinai. In his book of essays, "Imaginary Homelands," Rushdie recognizes himself as a midnight's child, and confesses in real life to have set about looking for other 'midnight's children,' i.e. children born in 1947, much in the manner of MCC. Saleem Sinai's looking for an identity, the conflation of the individual and national in the novel is very similar to Rushdie's own thoughts on identity and national or cultural belonging as sketched out in his essays on critical journalism, "Imaginary Homelands."

Suchitra Choudhury, Ph.D.

Works Cited

Cundy, Catherine, Rushdie, Salman, Contemporary World Writers Series. Manchester: Manchester University Press, 1996.

Rushdie, Salman. *Imaginary Homelands: Essays and Criticism 1981–91.* London: Granta, 1991.

Wolpert, Stanley, *A New History of India.* Oxford: OUP, 1977.

Discussion Questions

1. What is magic realism? How significant is its usage in your reading of "Midnight's Children?"

2. Attempt a character sketch of Padma. How different is her personality from Saleem Sinai's?

3. How much of "Midnight's Children" is autobiographical?

4. Discuss how the language of the novel is connected to theme of the novel.

5. What is 'hybridity'? Why does Rushdie call himself a hybrid novelist?

6. What role does memory play in the storytelling?

7. Write an essay on Saleem's search for a father in "Midnight's Children."

8. Enumerate the oral techniques and qualities in the narrative of "Midnight's Children."

9. Discuss the single primary quality in "Midnight's Children" that makes it an interesting read.

10. What are the ramifications of the Midnight's Children's Club, or the MCC?

Essay Ideas

1. The Vintage cover of "Midnight's Children" states that, "'Midnight's Children' sounds like a continent finding its voice." How far is this comment justifiable?

2. Do you think Saleem Sinai a credible character? Discuss the layers of significance in his portrayal.

3. Discuss "Midnight's Children" as a search for a nation's origins.

4. Write an essay on the representation of Islam in "Midnight's Children."

5. Write a brief essay on the history of India, as represented/misrepresented in "Midnight's Children."

Oliver Twist

by Charles Dickens

Content Synopsis

Charles Dickens' novel "Oliver Twist" combines rich melodrama and scathing social comment in relating the fortunes of its young titular hero. Oliver is born into a workhouse in 1830s England to an unidentified young woman of obvious good breeding who dies in childbirth. After several years of being raised among other orphans under the charge of the unsympathetic Mrs. Mann, he is turned over to an adult workhouse where he continues to endure hardship and near-starvation.

One day, Oliver is goaded by the other boys to dare to ask for a second helping of gruel. Outraged, the overseer, Mr. Bumble, determines to get the boy off his hands by selling him off to the highest bidder. In this way, Oliver ends up apprenticed to Mr. Sowerby, a lugubrious undertaker. Oliver runs into more trouble when he attacks an older boy there, Noah Claypole, who insulted his mother, and is locked up in a vault. However, he escapes and runs away to London where he falls in with another orphan boy, the roguish Jack Dawkins, better known as the Artful Dodger. The Dodger belongs to a pick pocketing ring and takes Oliver home to the gang's hideout, which is presided over by the elderly Fagin. Other members of the gang include the ruffian Bill Sikes (and his ill used dog Bulls' eye) and Bet and Nancy, two prostitutes.

Oblivious at first to the criminal activities of the gang, Oliver is soon forced to join in when Fagin sends him out with the Artful Dodger and another boy, Charley Bates, on a pick pocketing raid. They target an elderly gentleman in a bookstall, but Oliver panics and is caught while the other two flee. However, the elderly gentleman, Mr. Brownlow, takes the terrified Oliver home with him. Oliver finds peace and comfort in Mr. Brownlow's house, but before long Sikes and Nancy re-capture him and return him to Fagin. The miserable Oliver is then dispatched to help Sikes burgle a grand house in the country. One of the servants is roused and shoots Oliver while Sikes, having left the wounded boy in a field, makes good his escape. Fortunately for Oliver, he is taken in and sheltered by the women in the house, Mrs. Maylie and Rose, her beautiful young adopted niece. Oliver once more embarks upon a contented life.

Back in London, however, Fagin remains intent on getting him back, and is now aided in this by Monks, a strange young man who has suddenly appeared on the scene. Monks appears extremely interested in Oliver and questions Mr. Bumble about him, and Mrs. Bumble, who has possession of a locket that once belonged to Oliver's mother. Monks gets rid of the locket by throwing it in the river.

Oliver then comes to London with the Maylies for a brief stay. By chance, he glimpses his former benefactor Mr. Brownlow, in the street, and they are happily re-united. Despite the presence of both Mr. Brownlow and the Maylies, Oliver is still in danger from Fagin and Monks. Nancy, who fears for Oliver, tells Mr. Brownlow and Rose of this, in a secret meeting one night on London Bridge. Although they implore her to give up her old life and start anew, she is not willing to forsake the gang, particularly Sikes, whom she loves. Unknown to her, however, this meeting has been overheard by Noah Claypole, now in London and acting as a spy for Fagin. Fagin and Sikes are incensed at this betrayal of their plans, and Sikes, in a passion, beats Nancy to death. He is stricken with guilt immediately afterwards, flees to the country, and then, tormented by his conscience, returns to London and eventually meets his death in the course of being pursued by a blood-thirsty mob.

Fagin, meanwhile, is arrested, summarily tried, and condemned to hang (his young protégé, the Dodger was also earlier committed to trial and sentenced to transportation) and so the gang is broken up for good. As for Monks, Mr. Brownlow, mindful of Nancy's warnings, seeks him out and confronts him as to his design on Oliver. Monks is therefore forced to reveal his secret, in which the whole truth of Oliver's parentage comes out. Monks is actually Oliver's half brother; their father Edwin Leeford—coincidentally, a one-time friend of Mr. Brownlow—had an affair with Oliver's mother, Agnes Fleming. Monks' interest in Oliver is less than brotherly, however: he wanted to cheat him out of his share of the family inheritance. After being compelled to sign over Oliver's rightful share to Oliver, it is clear that he can do Oliver no more harm (and we are told that he eventually goes abroad and dies there). Furthermore, it transpires that Rose is Agnes' younger sister and therefore Oliver's aunt. Following all these startling revelations about Oliver's family background, Mr. Brownlow decides to adopt him and they leave London to live in the countryside near the Maylies. Rose is married to her young suitor Harry and the book ends on a most hopeful note, in idyllic surroundings far removed from the urban squalor in which Oliver has spent so much of his young life.

With the possible exception of "A Christmas Carol," "Oliver Twist" remains Dickens' best known and best-loved work. However, it is generally perceived as having a number of flaws. Although the stirring plot has engaged generations of readers, some may feel that it indulges in excessive melodrama (for example the lurid murder of Nancy), a trait it shares with the 'Newgate' school of novels of the time. Named for the notorious London prison, this school dealt in sensationalist material involving criminals and their exploits; "Oliver Twist" was often counted among this group. Moreover, the basic story is improbable, being of the reversal-of-fortune type common to many a folk or fairy-tale, as the orphaned Oliver is initially cast into the dregs of society before being rescued and restored to his rightful place. In addition, Oliver himself is a generally passive and very much idealized character, who suffers because of, but is never tainted by, his sordid surroundings (and incongruously expresses himself in a refined upper-class idiom from the start). However, this bloodless portrait of Oliver is in keeping with Dickens' stated purpose to show 'the principle of Good surviving through every adverse circumstance, and triumphing at last' (Dickens 3), and is typical of his work as a whole. In Dickens' fiction, it is generally the villainous characters rather than the good that really come to life. While Monks, it is true, remains a rather uninteresting and shady figure of intrigue, the brutish Sikes (who yet harbors a conscience), the glib and wily Fagin, and the impish Dodger have taken their place amongst the best known characters in all of literature.

Historical Context

First published serially in 1837 and then in book form a year later, "Oliver Twist" appeared at a time of social and economic unrest in Britain. The country was still feeling the effects of the Napoleonic Wars that had resulted in increased taxes and disruption of European trade. An even more important factor was industrialization, which was rapidly transforming the face of Britain. Industrialization had a profound impact on geographical, social, and economic structure of the land, precipitating the move from a primarily agricultural nation to a largely urban one, and hastening the ascendancy of the middle class at the expense of the old landed aristocracy. Furthermore, it helped give rise to a vast new underclass of the urban poor, whose struggle to survive amidst scenes of crime and vice is powerfully reflected in "Oliver Twist." Dickens was one of the first great urban novelists, and this novel is replete with images of sordid streets, seedy drinking places, and criminal dens. (See also Societal and Scientific & Technological Context.)

However, "Oliver Twist" is concerned not just with painting a vivid picture of urban deprivation but also with attacking government policies of the time, specifically the Poor Laws of 1834, which stipulated that public assistance would be given to the poor only if they lived and worked in established workhouses. This move was due to the view of the increasingly powerful middle classes who put an emphasis on the value of hard work leading to wealth (as opposed to the leisured aristocracy who drew their wealth from their great landed estates). In this austere scheme, economic failure was virtually equated with sin. Therefore, the workhouses were deliberately designed as a deterrent, the theory being that anyone who had once experienced them would be encouraged to go and make themselves useful elsewhere, and generated a system whereby the most vulnerable individuals—the very young, the old, and the infirm—served as scapegoats for society's ills. The early chapters of the novel fully expose the cruelties inherent in the government welfare system and the failings of its enforcers (like the negligent Mrs. Mann and the odious Mr. Bumble). It also opened contemporary readers' eyes to the grim realities of the kind of degraded employment available to a boy in Oliver's position (he only just escapes being apprenticed to an inhuman chimney sweep, Mr. Gamfield). This opening section of the novel runs in an almost unbroken and bitterly satirical vein (before giving way to the more sustained melodrama of Oliver's later adventures).

Societal Context

Society in "Oliver Twist" is sharply divided. While the upper classes live in their comfortable large houses, the lower orders are seen to lead generally wretched lives, driven to crime and vice by hunger and deprivation, although they might retain some particle of a better nature. Certainly, this is true of Nancy, the 'fallen' woman who yet displays a basic goodness of heart, which Dickens believed to be "woman's original nature" (266). This is something, at least, which she shares with Rose (who, like several other women in Dickens' work, appears as a largely abstract figure of beauty, kindliness and virtue). Nancy's exchanges with Rose and Mr. Brownlow are telling: although implored by them to give up her old life of sin and start anew with their help, she declares that she cannot. The setting for their meeting, London Bridge, can be taken as symbolic; despite being explicitly urged to do so, Nancy does not—cannot—cross over to the other side. In "Oliver Twist," there appears to be an unbridgeable gulf between the upper and lower classes; they are two distant, and seemingly irreconcilable, worlds.

Mention should also be made of Dickens' treatment of race and class in this novel, as Fagin, one of the most prominent characters, is a Jew. It is easy to accuse Dickens of anti-Semitism in his portrayal of this figure that is not only criminal but also animal-like, likened to a dog or rat, or to some unholy phantom (Dickens 311–312). However, it should be noted that Dickens rarely, if ever, makes reference to any specifically 'Jewish' characteristics that Fagin may be assumed to have. Dickens had to defend himself against the charge of anti-Semitism and did so by pointing out that the other 'wicked' characters in the book are Christian. He had to explain that in referring to Fagin regularly as 'the Jew' he was merely highlighting the character's background as "it unfortunately was true of the time to which that story refers, that that class of criminal almost invariably was a Jew" (Dickens 378). In any case, Fagin is such a potent creation that many readers in the end will probably overlook any taint of racism there might be in his portrayal.

If the upper and lower classes are polarized in the novel, rural and urban living is also seen to be antithetical. Fagin's 'lair' (Dickens 311) and the squalid London riverside community known as Jacob's Island could not be further removed from the genteel and gracious country home of the May-lies. In the countryside, even the poor 'are neat and clean' (Dickens 215). Dickens paints the country-side in a glowing, unrealistic light; he takes no account of the actual situation of the time, when a protracted agricultural decline was driving people to work in the industrial towns. Dickens views the countryside as a place of refuge from the miasma of urban life. Oliver is lucky enough to find this permanent refuge.

Religious Context

"Oliver Twist" makes a plea for Christian compassion while savaging Christian hypocrisy. Nominally a Christian society that shows no pity to the weak and destitute, it harshly condemns individuals like Oliver's mother who has a baby out of wedlock. The novel ends with a solemn pronouncement: 'without strong affection, and humanity of heart, and gratitude to that Being whose code is Mercy and whose great attribute is Benevolence to all things that breathe, true happiness can never be attained' (Dickens 360). Mercy and humanity of heart are generally seen to be in short supply in the novel; Dickens' wish is for a society that actually puts Christian principles into practice instead of emptily mouthing them.

On a different note, Dickens, after the fashion of other Victorian novelists, is concerned to uphold the tenets of Christian morality when showing the ultimate fate of his characters. The seemingly incorruptible Oliver is richly rewarded after many trials while Monks, Fagin, and Sikes are all soundly punished. Nancy too has to die, although she comes to repent of her sins and her death is an utterly shocking event. (In fact, the only one of Fagin's gang who is seen to prosper eventually is Charley Bates—after he decides to go straight).

However, Sikes and Fagin, two of Dickens' most compelling characters, are not just summarily cast aside. Instead, the author chooses to take us deep into their minds during their final hours: Sikes in full flight and haunted by the memory of his victim's eyes, and Fagin sitting alone in his cell in a state of such terror and misery that "few . . . would have slept but ill that night, if they could have seen him" (Dickens 354). The psychological acuity of these passages evokes pity in the reader and makes it hard to dismiss these two characters simply as villains who have met their justified ends.

Scientific & Technological Context

In the time and place that "Oliver Twist" was written, the forces of technological progress were continuing apace in the form of industrialization, bringing about tremendous and often bewildering changes. Though industrialization is not explicitly referred to in the novel, its more unpleasant effects certainly influence the whole picture. One of its worst aspects was the appalling working conditions in mines and factories and the slum conditions in which the workers generally lived. Many of these workers, and the ones that suffered most, were children. Child cruelty is of course one of the foremost themes in this work, and recurs in many of Dickens' other novels. This, along with government incompetence and the completely dark seedy atmosphere of urban poverty and hardship, is vividly brought to life in "Oliver Twist."

Biographical Context

Charles Dickens, the most widely read and studied of English novelists, was born in Portsmouth, England, in 1812. At the age of twelve he was sent to work in a blacking factory when his father was cast into a debtors' prison and this experience of acute poverty and hardship left its mark on him for life. He later became a reporter, and the journalistic concern with political and social issues of the day is prominent in his novels. In 1834, he had his first story published and thereafter his career as a writer steadily grew. His first novel, "The Pickwick Papers," was warmly received. Even greater success came with his second, "Oliver Twist," which first appeared serially in the journal "Bentley's Miscellany," of which he himself was the editor. (He went on to form his own journal, "Household Words," in 1850.) Publishing in this form meant that he had to shape his story to the demands and expectations of a large audience, and he did just that, producing a strong plot-line full of action and dramatic twists and turns, and finally a happy ending for the young hero. His novels—all of which have become a cornerstone of English literature—also include "David Copperfield," "Great Expectations," "A Christmas Carol" and "Bleak House." He traveled widely and gave popular readings from his own works (the most famous being the story of Nancy's murder in "Oliver Twist"). He died in 1870, while working on his final novel, "The Mystery of Edwin Drood." Dickens' readiness to engage with the issues of his time, his instinct for a good story, his humor (often grotesque or scathing, as in "Oliver Twist") and above all his ability to create unforgettable, larger-than-life characters ensured that he was lionized in his own day; and well over a hundred years later the popularity of his novels has not diminished in any degree.

Gurdip Panesar, Ph.D.

Works Cited

Chittik, Kathryn. *Dickens and the 1830s*. Cambridge, England: Cambridge University Press, 1990.

Collins, Philip. *Dickens and Crime*. London: Macmillan, 1962.

Dickens, Charles. *Oliver Twist*. Norton: New York & London, 1993.

Paroissien, David. *A Companion to Oliver Twist*. Edinburgh: Edinburgh University Press, 1992.

Discussion Questions

1. Dickens' villainous characters are often more successful creations than his virtuous ones. Which characters in "Oliver Twist" do you think are the most convincing, and why?

2. How do the two main female characters in the novel, Nancy and Rose, differ? What (if anything) do they have in common?

3. What does Fagin's gang initially appear to represent to Oliver? How does this compare with the treatment he received earlier from authorities supposedly in charge of his welfare?

4. Do you agree that the portrait of Fagin is anti-Semitic? Why or why not?

5. What (if any) redeeming features do the book's two main villains, Fagin and Sikes, display?

6. How do child characters in this novel (Oliver, the Artful Dodger, Charley, and little Dick) compare and contrast with one another?

7. How effective do you find Dickens' portrayal of mid-Victorian London in this novel?

8. Discuss Dickens' portrayal of rural life in "Oliver Twist." What might the countryside be said to represent?

9. What particular demands does serialization have on the writing of a novel? How is this reflected in "Oliver Twist?"

10. Discuss Dickens' use of different narrative tones in this novel.

Essay Ideas

1. Analyze the notion of evil in "Oliver Twist."
2. Analyze the role of class in "Oliver Twist."
3. Examine the theme of identity in "Oliver Twist."
4. Analyze the child as symbol in "Oliver Twist."
5. Examine Dickens' social and political agenda in "Oliver Twist."

Pamela

by Samuel Richardson

"But, O sir! my soul is of equal importance with the soul of a princess; though in quality I am but upon a foot with the meanest slave."

—Samuel Richardson, *Pamela*, 197

Content Synopsis

"Pamela" is an epistolary novel, which means that it is written in letters. It opens with a teenage servant girl, Pamela, writing home to her parents from the house where she works. Pamela's mother and father are poor and lower class, although they are quite literate. For the last few years, Pamela has been employed by Mrs. B, a rich gentlewoman who has taken her in and trained her as a lady's maid. It was common for children at this time to be taken "into service" in this manner. But Pamela, instead of being made to scrub or cook, has been taught to read, write, and do fine embroidery—all accomplishments appropriate to a lady or a lady's companion, but not necessarily to a servant. Pamela has also been given her mistress's cast-off clothes to wear—even second-hand, these clothes would have been much finer than ordinary servants' dress. At once, then, the problematic issue of Pamela's class position arises: she is lowborn and she is a servant, but she dresses and acts like a lady.

When the novel opens, we learn that Pamela's beloved mistress and mentor, Mrs. B, has just died. Pamela grieves for her, but she is also concerned about her own position—she has effectively lost her job, but she has not been trained as a normal servant, so it may be difficult for her to find another position. To complicate matters, her dead mistress's son, the young Mr. B, now Pamela's master, has inherited and taken possession of the house. He has been paying Pamela unwanted attentions for some time, but had previously been restrained by the presence of his mother. Now, however, there is little to stop him making sexual advances. Oddly, in spite of this, Pamela seems inclined to linger; her rather unconvincing excuse is that she has to finish embroidering a waistcoat for Mr. B before she returns home to her parents.

Finally, after a series of increasingly sexually charged scenes with her master, Pamela is ready to leave his house in Bedfordshire in the south of England and return home. When Mr. B kindly offers her the use of his carriage so that she does not have to make her own way, she accepts. After a few hours' journey, however, she realizes that she does not recognize any of the scenery. Mr. B's carriage is not in fact taking her home; it is taking her to Mr. B's Lincolnshire estate. Pamela has been kidnapped and the coachman is in on the plot—there is little she can do. On overnight stops, they stay with some of Mr. B's Lincolnshire tenants, who adore their landlord and refuse to believe that he is trying to harm Pamela. Finally, they arrive at his Lincolnshire house, where Pamela is put under the direction of the "mannish" Mrs. Jewkes, Mr. B's Lincolnshire housekeeper, a bawdy and rude woman who will act as Pamela's jailor.

At this point, Pamela's letters to her parents turn into a journal, which she writes in the hope that one day they will be able to read it. Of course, she is not allowed to send them letters and her freedoms are increasingly restricted: Mrs. Jewkes tricks her into giving up her little stash of money by pretending that she wants change and also deprives Pamela of her shoes. Locked up on a country estate, she has little hope of getting away. She is able to communicate secretly with the local clergyman, Mr. Williams, who is young and dependent on Mr. B but willing to risk his position to help Pamela. He tries to interest more powerful locals in her cause—specifically, another, older clergyman, Mr. Peters, and the magistrate, Sir Simon Darnford. Both of these refuse to help on the grounds that they do not wish to interfere in their "neighbour B's" affairs—and besides, Pamela is only a servant. This provides Richardson with an opportunity to comment satirically on the self-interest of those whose public function is to help or protect others; it also establishes a setting where Pamela's survival is dependent only on her.

As Pamela remains immured in Mr. B's house, her state of mind slowly deteriorates. She has contact with no one except Mrs. Jewkes, a few of Mr. B's other servants, and Mr. B himself, as he writes to her, attempting to persuade her to become his mistress. Pamela shows her intelligence and integrity by confuting his specious arguments, copying out the "articles" of proposition he sends her and including her own commentary on why they are morally unsound. In spite of such a display of spirit, though, her position is becoming

more and untenable, until finally she contemplates suicide. Sitting by the pond on Mr. B's estate, she seriously considers drowning herself. Finally, however, her religious faith and native strength of mind save her from this decision.

Eventually, Mr. B (after increasingly blatant attempts to rape Pamela) is sufficiently impressed by her ability to hold onto her beliefs that he declares himself in love with her and proposes marriage. She accepts, and it is now clear that in spite of his immorality, she has been in love with him all along. This is not the end of her problems, though: after their private marriage, Pamela must contend with Mr. B's proud, aristocratic sister, Lady Davers, who is infuriated to think that her brother has disgraced the family name by marrying their mother's former maid. Lady Davers behaves in an outrageous manner to Pamela until finally Mr. B becomes so angry that he threatens to break off contact with his sister. At this point, she capitulates and comes to admire Pamela for her virtue and for her ability to reform the rakish, loose-living Mr. B. The novel closes with Pamela happily married, although a slightly jarring note occurs when Mr. B presents his bride with a long, new set of "articles," this time spelling out the way his wife must behave in order to please him.

Samuel Richardson's "Pamela; Or, Virtue Rewarded" was first published on November 6, 1740. It immediately caused a sensation. Its pioneering subject matter of a virtuous lower-class woman defending herself against a predatory aristocratic male made it one of the best-selling and most provocative novels of the eighteenth century. It generated a phenomenon referred to in our own time as the "'Pamela' media event" and brought its author—hitherto a staid, middle-aged London printer—to the attention of such literary greats as Alexander Pope. It even inspired one of the first promotional merchandising campaigns (readers could buy Pamela fans, handkerchiefs, and teacups).

Yet it was also deeply controversial. The novel inspired a flurry of imitations, parodies, and diatribes—so much so that recently, a six-volume collection of responses to "Pamela" in the ten years following its publication has been released. These ranged from an opera to a mock epic in heroic couplets to a semi-pornographic piece masquerading as a moral tract. Most famously, "Pamela" partly inspired Richardson's fellow—novelist Henry Fielding to write his parody "Shamela," supposedly intended as a mockery of Richardson's heroine's hypocrisy and upward mobility.

Historical Context

Richardson's novels often do not contain very obvious social commentary or satire (unlike, for example, "Gulliver's Travels" or "The New Atlantis," to take two of "Pamela's" predecessors). For this reason, it is easy to view them as isolated from historical contexts. If, however, we look more closely, it is possible to see a number of ways in which the examination of historical realities is essential to understanding Richardson's novelistic project.

It is an awful cliché to say that any historical period was "a time of great change." Essentially, though, early-eighteenth-century Britain was transforming into the sort of society we know today. Modern financial structures such as the Bank of England (founded in 1694) were introducing the idea of a credit-based economy. It seemed very strange to contemporaries that paper could represent monetary value, but credit became, increasingly, a symbol of the new prosperity that was sweeping England. The country, although involved intermittently in foreign wars, was a lot more settled and peaceful than during the civil and religious tumults of the previous century. Agricultural practices were improving, and commerce was booming. (In the late 1730s, when "Pamela" was written, the bitter disputes about enclosure of land and about the decline of wages in real terms had not yet surfaced—these would come in the later

eighteenth and early nineteenth centuries.) As more money circulated, general standards of living rose, and literacy increased. Successful businesses and the rich employed more and more people; many young people made their way to the cities, especially London, to seek new opportunities for themselves. Many of them, of course, would not make it, and would end up swelling the ranks of the urban poor, prostitutes, or petty criminals. It is against this background that we can start to understand Pamela, a lower-class but literate young woman who dares to judge her betters, to set a value on herself as a person, and to assert her right to decide with whom she has sex and when.

This brings us to another big theme: the value of Pamela's literacy. One reason that "Pamela" was so revolutionary was that it not only told the story of a poor young girl resisting seduction, but it used her voice to do the telling, thus privileging her interpretation of events. Ian Watt's classic study of the novel has reminded critics of the role of increasing literacy rates and the growing popularity of the novel as a genre during the eighteenth century. Although by the eighteenth century there was a strong demotic (or native-language) tradition of literature in England, ideas of "the literary" were still very much informed by classical, that is to say Latin and ancient Greek, literature. Having classical languages (generally) marked a man out as someone who had been to university—a gentleman. In this way, reading and writing in (or simply making allusions to) classical literature could have class and gender implications. The literary giants of the hundred years preceding Richardson—men such as Milton, Dryden, Swift, Addison, and Pope—were all classically educated and their knowledge of the classics informed their work, often to a significant extent. These are the writers that we generally have in mind when we talk about neo-classicism, or (in the case of the early-eighteenth-century ones) the "Augustan age." What was different about the novel was that it did not rely on classical literary predecessors. It told "realistic" stories of English men and women falling in love, falling out, getting married, making choices. Such stories had great appeal for the increasingly literate working classes—servants were reckoned to be some of the most voracious readers of novels (it should be noted that at this time, servants were a relatively large segment of the working population). Additionally, having more disposable income meant that more people could afford to buy books, which were becoming less of a luxury and more of a common commodity. Richardson did not learn Latin or Greek (although he probably read English translations of many of the classics), and often his novels poke fun at "pedants" who parade their learning. Study of the classics was supposed to discipline the mind and lead to better argumentative and rhetorical skills. But in "Pamela," a woman writes in English, defying a university-educated man (Mr. B has been to Oxford), arguing against him—and winning.

Other historical-literary contexts of note are the importance of romance narratives and the idea of the rake. "Romance" was something of a contentious term at the time; nowadays, we distinguish between more "realistic" novels and old romances, which often take place in an exotic location or distant time, and which feature princesses, sorcerers, dashing heroes, improbable coincidences, exciting revelations, and so forth. People in the eighteenth century did not make this sharp (retrospective) distinction. As the novel was quite new, critical vocabularies for discussing it as literature did not necessarily exist. Often, the novel was satirized as being trashy and leading to immorality (Richardson himself often inveighs in his works against young girls reading novels and being led astray by them). We can perhaps understand why this is so: at the time, the strong literary novelistic tradition that we have now did not exist, and many novels were churned out by sleazy printers simply to make money. Most do not have enduring literary interest

or merit. Richardson conceived of his project as introducing "a new species of writing." Obviously, he was not in a position to see himself as one of the first of the great English novelists ("Selected Letters" 41). People who rewrote Richardson's plot often introduced "romance" elements. Richardson himself was not interested in writing romances; nevertheless, the fact that Pamela manages to get her aristocratic man and earn the respect of all the gentry around her does have something of a fairy-tale air to it.

Finally, it is necessary to mention the idea of the rake. For students who are reading "Clarissa" (Richardson's next novel, published in 1747–1748), this concept will be particularly important, but it is also relevant to understanding "Pamela." The "rake" was a specific type of aristocratic masculinity. Urbane, witty, powerful, dissolute, and above all, sexually predatory, he represented an alluring and yet dangerous species of manhood. Probably the most famous rake at the time was the seventeenth-century court poet, John Wilmot, the Earl of Rochester. Rochester's amusing and often-obscene poetry, together with his sharp wit and (long) list of sexual conquests were the stuff of legend in Richardson's time (Richardson would draw on Rochester's published letters when he wrote the character of Lovelace in "Clarissa"). Conversely, however, the rake could be represented as corrupt, diseased, and dangerous—in contrast to "virtuous" middle-class womanhood. In "Pamela," Mr. B is a young rake who has not yet become utterly debauched. Pamela, with her beauty and strict moral standards, is instrumental in reclaiming him. In this way, although Pamela is very definitely marrying up, we can also read this marriage as a moral promotion for Mr. B, from vice to virtue.

Societal Context
One important societal context that needs to be considered when approaching "Pamela" is the increased social mobility of the eighteenth century.

The eighteenth century is often considered the period that witnessed "the rise of the middle class." In many ways, this is simplistic; however, it is true that more and more, people were making money from commerce and not just inheriting wealth. Such people often "married up" into the gentry or aristocracy. Others developed a sense of themselves as a hard-working, domestically oriented class apart from the aristocracy. Tradesmen and merchants were often called, in derision, "cits," short for "citizens," or members of the City, the financial area in London (as opposed to St James's or one of the aristocratic areas of London). In any case, there were cultural anxieties around the ideas of class membership and of possible mobility between classes. It is noteworthy, once again, that Pamela is allowed to dress up in her mistress's clothes and to pursue pastimes more suitable for a young lady than for a servant. It is almost as if Pamela is "naturally" of a higher class than might first appear. Certainly, after her marriage to Mr. B, the other characters in "Pamela" insist (almost too frequently) that no one would ever be able to tell that Pamela had not been born a lady. It is also worth remarking that many of those mentioned above who adapted Richardson's novel, changed Pamela's family history so that she unexpectedly turned out to be the daughter of aristocratic parents. One good example is Carlo Goldoni's operatic version, in which Pamela's father suddenly reveals himself to be a Scottish earl who is conveniently carrying around the title deeds to his estate and two character references to prove his claim. Richardson avoids such absurdities, but for a twenty-first-century reader, Pamela's identification as "lower-class" may be complicated: for one thing, few real-life working-class women would have been able to write like her.

Generally, although "Pamela" radically privileges the voice of a servant, it can be regarded as a work with a "middle-class" bias. As mentioned, Pamela often seems to have qualities associated with the middle classes. Mr. B, too, although he is nominally a member of the gentry, in fact subscribes to many ideas associated with the middle classes. For example, he does not wish to obtain a title, although it is hinted that he will be offered the rank of baronet. Equally, Richardson's work generally was criticized by members of the upper classes for presenting an unrealistic take on aristocratic life. For instance, Richardson was accused of giving titles to too many of his characters in an effort to make the novel seem "genteel." In later editions of "Pamela," many of characters who were originally entitled "Lady" become "Mrs."

Religious Context

Richardson's ideas about Christian morality pervade all his novels—for example, Pamela's religion quite literally saves her life when she decides not to commit suicide on the grounds that it would be a sin. Understanding the religious background to Richardson's work is often crucial to appreciating why his characters behave and think the way they do.

As mentioned above, novels in the mid-eighteenth century were often regarded as propagating (specifically sexual) immorality. Richardson wrote his novels with the idea that he would provide instruction in Christian morality under the guise of an entertaining fiction. Underneath the absorbing storyline and characters is a serious concern with expounding moral and religious lessons. In our often secular world, this can be hard to appreciate, but it is essential to understanding how Richardson conceived of his own work.

Historically, then, England at the time of "Pamela's" publication was an Anglican country; Anglicanism had split off from the Catholic Church in 1529, becoming a Protestant church. Still, many aspects of Anglicanism remained similar to aspects of Catholicism; types of Anglicanism or Anglican practices that strongly recalled Catholicism were referred to as "High Church" ("Low Church" practices were closer to evangelicalism). During the Civil Wars (1642-6; 1648), Anglicanism was debated hotly. The republicans who governed the country during the Interregnum ("time between kings," 1649-1660), wanted to "disestablish" the Anglican Church, or remove it from its position as the official national religion. Ultimately, they were unsuccessful, but they left behind them a legacy of religious schism, which often involved distrust of non-Anglicans and certainly of Catholics. For example, Catholics were popularly blamed for the Great Fire of London of 1666 and into the eighteenth century, they suffered significant civil disabilities, such as not being able to go to university or live within ten miles of London. Other religious groups such as Dissenters (non-Anglican Protestants, like Presbyterians or Methodists) and Jews similarly suffered from religious prejudices.

Richardson himself was solidly Anglican, and probably more High Church than anything. For all this, however, he was not prejudiced in religious terms—in fact, by the standards of his time, he was remarkable for his relativism. He expressed tolerance towards Jewish people in his private correspondence and his last novel, "The History of Sir Charles Grandison," has an extended, sympathetic treatment of a Catholic family.

In spite of his sympathy for the faiths of others, though, Richardson was secure in his own Anglicanism and used his novels in part to expound his interpretation of that religion. Pamela has a very personal investment in her religious faith: she privileges her soul as her highest concern, and considers it a duty to be as cheerful and selfless as possible in the face of whatever trials God may send her. For example, she describes how she and her parents faced poverty before she went into service with the B family; often, she remembers, they would not have enough to eat, but they were still thankful that God had given them the opportunity to be together. Pamela reads the Bible intensively

and comes up with her own interpretations of the scriptures (as well as of popular fable). Most importantly, of course, the whole plot revolves around the fact that Pamela will not give up her "honesty" (read: virginity) to Mr. B because she believes that would be an offense against God. Pamela boldly declares that no matter what her "quality" (social status) is, her soul has exactly the same worth as that of a "princess." Using an accepted reading of religion, Pamela thus makes potentially radical social statements. By centralizing the voice of a servant undergoing a religious trial, the novel enacts the idea that a lower-class woman's thoughts and experiences are indeed as important as those of a "princess."

For Richardson, religion and morality are inextricably linked. This is shown by the fact that Pamela's religious faith is a mainstay of her ability to value herself and to retain control over her own body and sexuality. Additionally, religion is involved in Mr. B's reformation. About eighteen months after the publication of "Pamela," Richardson issued a continuation entitled "Pamela in Her Exalted Condition" (nowadays generally referred to as "Pamela II"). It is not widely read these days (it is notably inferior to the original in terms of plot) but it does show Mr. B's full reformation, which is couched in explicitly religious terms. Generally, Pamela shows her moral worth by structuring her life around religion; she "meditates" often and when she is married, prays with her servants in order to provide them with a good example.

However, religion can also be used in "Pamela" to comment sharply on circumstances or people. For example, when she is imprisoned in Lincolnshire, Pamela rewrites one of the psalms as a pastime. She does this in such a way as to position herself as a virtuous, suffering biblical character and her jailors as evil. Here, then, a religious text is used to create or represent moral superiority. Similarly, religious expectations can be used to comment negatively on others. Whilst Richardson valued clergymen and their social roles, he was also not averse to criticizing them when they failed to fulfill those roles. For example, Mr. Peters, a local clergyman, refuses to help Pamela when Mr. Williams asks him to. Mr. Peters is shown as selfish and worldly for not performing his religious duty of helping the innocent. The fact that he is a clergyman makes this even worse. It is not enough simply to profess religious beliefs—one has to act up to them.

Scientific &Technological Context

Superficially, none of Richardson's novels have overt or important connections to scientific and technological issues (although an argument might be made that "The History of Sir Charles Grandison," contains comment on agricultural reforms). Richardson himself was not at the center of scientific debates, nor did he have any particular expertise in related areas. He was, however, a good friend of the famous eighteenth-century doctor George Cheyne, who was Richardson's personal physician as well as correspondent and confidante. Richardson suffered from nervous ailments in the latter part of his life (when he wrote "Pamela" he was already fifty-two, no longer a young man) and Cheyne was an expert in nervous diseases. Cheyne prescribed a vegetarian regime for Richardson, as well as regular walks and a home exercise device.

Nerves and nervousness in the mid-eighteenth century were often connected to "sensibility," that is, to the ability to empathize or enter into others' feelings, particularly suffering or distress. This also often implies the capacity for personal emotional experience. Sensibility related to the physical manifestation of symptoms of emotion at another's feeling or at one's own internal state (for example, tears, blushing, fainting, increased heartbeat as a result of sympathetic emotions). Richardson's heroines, including Pamela, are in many ways heroines of sensibility; Pamela responds physically to emotionally distressing situations. For example, when Mr. B tries to rape her, she faints in such a dramatic manner that he believes he may have killed or seriously injured her. Pamela's "sensibility" functions in at least two ways in the novel. Firstly, it serves to position her as delicate and feeling and thus, by implication, "naturally" of higher class than one might expect of a servant girl. Secondly, sensibility, with its attendant display of physicality, can be a discreet way of introducing sexual feeling into a narrative like "Pamela."

Biographical Context

Richardson is supposed to have come up with the idea for the novel whilst writing a book of model letters (such books became increasingly common in the eighteenth century as literacy levels increased and people wanted to know how to communicate effectively in writing). In his own private letters, he claimed also that he had once heard a story from an acquaintance about a servant girl who married her master and that this provided part of his inspiration. Apparently, whilst he was writing his book of model letters—now known generally as the "Familiar Letters"—the idea for "Pamela" sprung into his head and took hold of him. He put aside the "Letters" for the time being and wrote frantically, using every spare moment. Richardson was also a successful and busy printer (he was an official publisher of the records of the Houses of Parliament), so the writing of "Pamela" was crammed into whatever time he had left over.

Critics have often found it odd that someone like Richardson should have written the novels he did (his other three novels, "Pamela II," "Clarissa," and "Sir Charles Grandison" are also mostly told from the perspectives of young women). When "Pamela" was published, he was a fifty-two-year-old man of humble beginnings, twice married, and now running a lucrative printing business. Why would he feel the need to write as a teenage girl in danger of being seduced by an aristocrat?

The disparity between Richardson and his heroines has led to some extremely dubious critical speculations: that Richardson was "effeminate," that he was a pervert of some description, and that he was some sort of "natural genius" who wrote through inspiration rather than conscious thought. In reality, of course, it is almost impossible (and pointless) to try to understand why a particular person might have felt compelled to write a certain text. That said, it is possible to trace some meaningful biographical contexts for his work.

As mentioned above, Richardson was already involved in composing a text made up of fictional letters. Nor was this his first experience with the epistolary (letter) format. He recalled how, as a clever and literate young apprentice, local girls would get him to help them write love-letters to their sweethearts. We have no way of ascertaining the truth of Richardson's memories (nor do we have reason to question them) but if they are accurate, this experience must certainly have informed Richardson's ideas of young women's epistolary styles and concerns. After he published "Pamela," Richardson became involved in correspondence with a wide range of women (some of whom, like Sarah Chapone and Elizabeth Carter, were literary figures in their own right). Even before this, however, Richardson was evidently able to imitate a young woman's epistolary style convincingly. As one detractor remarked, Richardson wrote not like a man of sense, but like a young girl. The commentator obviously intended this as a criticism, but it could well serve as the highest sort of compliment to Richardson's achievements in characterization.

Bonne Latimer

Works Cited

Carroll, John, ed. *Selected Letters of Samuel Richardson*. Oxford: Clarendon Press, 1964.

Keymer, Tom and Peter Sabor, eds. *The Pamela Controversy: Criticisms and Adaptations of Samuel Richardson's Pamela,* 1740–1750, 6 vols. London: Pickering & Chatto, 2001.

Kimpel, Ben D. and T. C. Duncan Eaves. *Samuel Richardson: A Biography*. Oxford: Clarendon Press, 1971.

Richardson, Samuel. *Pamela; Or, Virtue Rewarded* (1st ed., 1740; 14th ed., 1801) Margaret Anne Doody and Peter Sabor, eds. Harmondsworth: Penguin, 1985.

Watt, Ian. The *Rise of the Novel: Studies in Defoe, Fielding, and Richardson*. London: Chatto & Windus, 1957.

Discussion Questions

1. After having read "Pamela," look back at its full title, which is "Pamela; Or, Virtue Rewarded." In what do you think Pamela's "virtue" consists? Is it appropriately rewarded in this novel?

2. Richardson wrote this novel avowedly as a didactic piece of literature, that is, one that is supposed to inculcate a moral. What do you think this moral is? Are you convinced by it?

3. Satire was one of the dominant literary modes in the eighteenth century. Do you find "Pamela" satirical in places? Give specific instances.

4. Think about the transgression of gender boundaries in relation to Mrs. Jewkes and to Mr. B. In what ways do these characters sometimes cross gendered lines? How does their transgression comment on Pamela's character?

5. How do you think the fact that this is an epistolary novel affects the presentation of viewpoints? Do you ever find it too one-sided? Is it fair to say that the element of "correspondence" falls apart after Pamela has been imprisoned?

6. Discuss the idea of deception versus honesty with relation to this text. What kinds of deceptions are practiced? Are they ever justified? Think about characters in this novel who dress up in new clothes or in someone else's clothes. Is this practice a type of deception—or not necessarily?

7. Consider displays or articulations of sexual desire in this text. Who feels such desire? How is it signaled—or hidden? How can it be talked about?

8. In the mid-eighteenth century, class was one of the most important social markers (along with gender, wealth, religion, amongst others). How is class used to construct character? Look at the characters of Mr. B and Lady Davers. Does Richardson have anything good to say about the upper classes?

9. "Pamela" was satirized in its own day for its supposed preoccupation with the physical: we hear all about Pamela's clothes, the work she is doing, how much money she has. How are physical objects important to the novel? Think about letters as an object; how does the fact that they can be read, destroyed, stolen, wrongly sent, and hidden, inform the narrative? How is writing as a physical process important?

10. Think about the power politics of sex in "Pamela." How is sex or the threat of sex used in this novel? How does Pamela herself confront it? Reading this novel in modern terms, does it ultimately offer a "feminist" statement—or not?

Essay Ideas

1. Examine different kinds of violation in "Pamela."
2. Writing, reading, and control: who really holds power in "Pamela?"
3. Is religion merely a tool of self-assertion in this novel?
4. Can "virtue" be bought?
5. Does trickery ever work in "Pamela?"
6. To what extent is epistolary a fiction in this novel?

The Remains of the Day

by Kazuo Ishiguro

Content Synopsis

Set in 1956, "The Remains of the Day" (1989) is the gap-packed tale of an almost retired British butler named Stevens who works for Mr. Farraday, the wealthy American owner of Darlington Hall, a majestic mansion located in the English countryside. Dedicated to his lifetime occupation, working night and day like a galley slave, Stevens is contemplating a breakaway on the advice of his master and finally embarks on a journey in the West Country. This "expedition," as he calls it, is an opportunity for him to meet up again with Miss Kenton, a retired housekeeper whom he formerly met under Lord Darlington's initial occupation of the mansion. As Stevens is short of staff, he intends to coax her into taking up a job again at Darlington Hall. By means of a mnemonic and therefore patchy account of his glorious days under the reign of Lord Darlington, Stevens recounts the early decades of the twentieth century by chronicling his daily chores, the master-servant relationship, the political concerns of the time, the historical impact of unofficial and allegedly important conferences, to name a few.

"The Remains of the Day" typifies what Tzvetan Todorov termed "a plot of predestination," which he defines as a story in which the narrator reveals the plot from the outset, as illustrated by the incipit of the novel's prologue. In it, the narrator-cum-protagonist Stevens states that he will embark on a journey. This leisurely journey will turn out to be equally geographical and psychological, using roundabout ways to reach the heart, of a butler, of a mind, of a country, of a culture and of the past. In a sense, "The Remains of the Day" are the excavations of Stevens' archaeology of the past. A sense of the past chiefly transpires through the numerous analeptic leaps and a lexical field of varied expressions and terms related to memory. Stevens' memories are punctuated by major events that belong to the private and public spheres: his father's fall; the death of his master Lord Darlington; the secret meetings of prominent political figures, to name a few. Nevertheless, recollections are far from being reliable and the narrator's faulty memory on many occasions is a giveaway of his knowledge gaps resulting from inaccurate reminiscences together with a sense of confusion. Because he is backward looking and keeps harping on the good old times, Stevens has trouble living in the present.

The narrative complex structure draws on post-modern strategies of embedding, narrative shifts, fragmentation, discontinuous timeline, and unreliable narrators. Skillful and insightful characterization allows Kazuo Ishiguro to show his protagonist caught in the web of a persisting mental maelstrom. Largely, Stevens also somewhat embodies the archetypal antihero who, far from being a dull character, stands out because of his failures and inaction but is irritating and therefore deserves no more sympathy than empathy.

Stevens' professional part, which requires him to be omnipresent and to show some virtually round-the-clock availability, makes him an acute and privileged discreet observer of life at Darlington Hall. To be sure, his stance as a homodiegetic narrator gives him storytelling credence thanks to his ability to record facts from an insider's perspective. However, by relying too heavily on the memory of an aging focalizer like Stevens, this stimulating account automatically addresses the issue of unreliability with its thematic nexus of privacy, mendacity, mystery, secrecy, dissimulation, transformation, transposition, deception, and omission. For David Lodge, unreliable narrators are invariably homodiegetic. Commenting on "The Remains of the Day," he further asserts that "The point of using an unreliable narrator is indeed to reveal in an interesting way the gap between appearance and reality, and to show how human beings distort or conceal the latter" (Lodge 155). Contributing to that effect is the novel's self-conscious narrator whose occasional comments within the text alluding to the storytelling process: "But I am digressing," emphasize the gap between fiction and reality (53).

Historical Context

"The Remains of the Day" was a timely publication which coincided with the international popularity of cosmopolitanism in literature. More specifically, it came in print when editors, in an attempt to establish the World fiction genre, ferreted among unsolicited manuscripts and authors with a migrant or postcolonial background.

The novel possesses an undeniable postcolonial dimension which challenges the Eurocentric perspective on power relationships. Kazuo Ishiguro is a novelist standing at the crossroads of two imperialistic cultures, experiencing the in-betweenness felt by most postcolonial writers. As both an outsider and insider, Kazuo Ishiguro has no vantage point to speak properly on behalf of either British or Japanese people. Born in Japan, he has chosen to live in England with his wife and daughter and although he seems to be concerned with Japanese identity and culture, he can hardly express himself in his native tongue. This did not deter some critics from pointing out that "The Remains of the Day" reads like a Japanese novel, the Englishness of the novel being somewhat like a coating covering a Japanese cake. In other words, they argued that Kazuo Ishiguro transposed the plight of the Japanese people on the British by pitting stringency against democratic freedom. However, readers unaware of Japanese culture would rather believe that Kazuo Ishiguro has carried things to extremes by writing a novel which reads more English than even the British could write, a successful impersonation he achieves with his highly polished style and turgid speech.

If "The Remains of the Day" has been dubbed "post-imperial" by George Landow, it is chiefly because it was composed from a once-colonizing standpoint. This fragmented narrative pays a tribute to early twentieth-century aristocratic England while being a remembrance of things past. Although the story takes place in 1956, most of its flashbacks refer to the interwar years. Among the events which purport to belong to History are: the 1923 Conference for peace talks, historical figures such as Lord Halifax, Sir Oswald Mosley, and Herr Ribbentrop, along with less explicit references which need to be inferred from the context such as Prime Minister Neville Chamberlain. In such a post World-War I context, references to the Jews inevitably crop up with the effect of creating a feeling of general discomfort as the reader realizes Lord Darlington's overt anti-Semitism.

Additionally, the novel alludes to the decline of the British Empire following the decolonizing process which has set in motion in the post-World War II era. Great Britain was losing its status of powerful master as her servants gradually walked out from her house. India and Pakistan claimed their independence in 1947 and political unrest climaxed in 1956 with the Suez Canal Crisis which accelerated decolonization. Other nations like the Gold Coast (1957, later called Ghana), Nigeria (1960), Jamaica, Western Samoa, Tobago and Trinidad (1962), Kenya (1963), Malawi and Zambia (1964) and many more would follow suit. The Americans have taken over the power to rule, like the symbolic replacement of Lord Darlington epitomizing the very influential British aristocracy and grandeur by the crushing might of Mr. Farraday personifying the superpower.

Societal Context

To some extent, the novel also draws our attention to role-playing, mimicry, and (self) deception. In this melodrama of sorts, Stevens cuts a pathetic theatrical figure, using words as a mask and memories as props to remain at all times in the limelight. His job is even challenged by Mrs. Wakefield as being part of a charade, as reports his American master, Mr. Farraday: "She even thought you were 'mock', Stevens"(130). Stevens is therefore 'not' acting 'as' a butler, but rather 'like' a butler. This lack of authenticity certainly throws charges of fakery. Adding to the theatrical dimension, is that most of the action takes place indoors with actors making their entrances and exits, not to mention the personal reflections in the guise of asides.

British imperialism, together with the master-servant relationship which he fully explores in the novel, are at the core of the postcolonial dialectics between the colonizers and the colonized, between the imperial centre and its peripheral countries. Yet, Ishiguro's status as a postcolonial writer needs to be qualified as he does not originate from a former British dominion.

The psychological dimension is of prime importance in "The Remains of the Day" as the narrative is best read between the lines. The subtext is therefore more important than the text proper, in the sense that the story serves as a mask to hide the narrator's inner thoughts and feelings which, following the British tradition, must be contained. As a central character, Stevens—a stiff-upper-lipper to the backbone—will linger in the reader's mind thanks to his phlegmatic demeanor, characteristic of stereotypical British behavior. Because he is steeped in social conventions and in a deeply entrenched sense of formalism which transpires in his stilted narrating style, the distinguished butler is sentimentally-challenged. His strong focus on his career has also contributed to the eclipse of his sentimental life, Stevens' libido being a major gap in the narrative. As David Lodge remarks: "The same mystique of the perfect servant rendered him incapable of recognizing and responding to the love that Miss Kenton was ready to offer him when they worked together" (156).

In line with this thinking, it has been posited that avoidance is one of the keywords in "The Remains of the Day":

> . . . the true type of avoidance which the tale both reflects and masks is the avoidance of desire, of feeling, of anything that pertains to emotions. The avoidance of main arteries speaks volumes for Stevens' avoidance of feelings. Avoidance—for which possible synonyms would be coyness, shyness, fear, anxiety, undue reluctance to face up to the reality of man's flesh and blood—materializes for instance in the ellipsis between Day Four and Day Six. The encounter, at once longed for and deferred, is avoided, postponed, delayed" (Porée, 17–8).

Kazuo Ishiguro's statement about his use of language seems to confirm such hypothesis: "I am interested in narrators who are trying to evade certain truths about themselves and about their past. They are actually dealing with the language of self-deception and so I have to employ a language which is forever flinching from facing up to something." (Bigsby, 28).

Rich in psychological implications, "The Remains of the Day" can be pertinently assessed with psychoanalytical concepts, especially Freudian theories. Stevens' speech does not represent his surmised modest charisma in "The Remains of the Day." A rapid survey of his verbal bombast designed to enshrine his grandeur while inflating his ego, will record frequent use of hyperbolic adjectives. As Marc Porée cogently points out, Stevens' attempts at self-persuasion are germane to what Freud termed 'Verneinung' (i.e. negations), "implying the very opposite of what is immodestly claimed or denied" (Porée, 83). Interestingly enough, language, apart from capturing the world in the tradition of realistic fallacy, is often at variance with its signifiers. One word has to be substituted for another one, since the most truthful meaning is chiefly found 'Obliquo ductu' (in an oblique way). Let there be no misunderstandings, Kazuo Ishiguro does not question the age-old problematic relationship between words and things, nor is he on a quest for using the most accurate word, the novelist only wishes to highlight the discrepancy between telling and thinking, the gap between consciousness and unconsciousness.

Religious Context
Metaphorically speaking, this introspective novel could be read as a religious allegory, starring Stevens as a pilgrim of sorts facing a series of trials and progressing not on foot but by car. However, such interpretation might be judged as too far-fetched because religion is a minor concern in the novel. At best, one can say that Stevens is epitomizing one of the seven Deadly Sins, namely pride, which is responsible for his emotional downfall. To be sure, there are issues about Good and Evil (embodied by Nazism), but they would be most aptly dealt with on a moral level.

Scientific & Technological Context
The Ford which Mr. Farraday kindly lends to his butler in "The Remains of the Day" is both a token of wealth, of the ruling class, and the symbol of American hegemony, in terms of cultural, political, and economic influences. With such a gift, the master gives his "slave" the means to emancipate and break away: "It seems increasingly likely that I really will undertake the expedition that has been preoccupying my imagination now for some days. An expedition, I should say, which I will undertake alone, in the comfort of Mr. Farraday's Ford; an expedition which, as I foresee it, will take me through much of the finest countryside of England to the West Country, and may keep me away from Darlington Hall for as much as five or six days" (3). However, readers will read between the lines the implications of Mr. Farraday's generosity. The master is willing to free his slave as long as he is assured that his servant will be back as soon as he requests it. Indeed, Stevens can be asked at any time to return the car and fall back into subservience.

Biographical Context
Born in Nagasaki on November 8, 1954, Kazuo Ishiguro migrated to England at the age of five. He graduated from the University of Kent (B.A. with honors) where he studied English and Philosophy, then completed an M.A. from the University of East Anglia. Most of his novels, which won many literary accolades, had been shortlisted for the Booker Prize—England's most prestigious literary award—which he finally obtained on his second nomination with "The Remains of the Day" which met both a critical and a popular success. From then on, his reputation was established worldwide thanks also to the countless translations of his books. In 1993, James Ivory's adaptation

of "The Remains of the Day," starring Anthony Hopkins and Emma Thompson, has contributed to increasing his stature. A recipient of many distinctions, Kazuo Ishiguro has all the makings of an international bestseller writer: he was awarded an OBE in 1995 and was made Chevalier de l'Ordre des Arts et des Lettres (France) in 1998. Married, he currently lives in London with his family.

Jean-François Vernay, Ph.D.

Works Cited

Bigsby, Christopher. "An Interview with Kazuo Ishiguro." *The European Messenger*. Norwich, Autumn 1990.

Ishiguro, Kazuo. *The Remains of the Day*. London: Faber and Faber, 1989.

Lodge, David. *The Art of Fiction*. London: Penguin, 1992.

Porée Marc. *Kazuo Ishiguro, The Remains of the Day*. Paris: Didier Erudition/CNED, 1999.

Discussion Questions

1. What are the two reasons which prompted Stevens to undertake his expedition?
2. What word is obsessively repeated in the "Day One" section? What use of repetition is made here?
3. Why did Miss Kenton leave Stevens' staff in section 3 of the book?
4. What other relationship is there between Stevens and his father?
5. What does the communication between Miss Kenton and Stevens reveal about their personalities, following their second clash when Stevens mentions her "great inexperience"? What is the parallel episode to that one in the novel?
6. What are the two outlooks on the world which are mentioned in section 4? Could you elaborate on that?
7. What is Mrs. Wakefield's appreciation of Darlington Hall? How does it affect readers in regards to the narrative content?
8. Does Stevens condone or condemn Lord Darlington's attitude towards Jews? Why?
9. Explain why the incident involving Miss Kenton barging into Stevens' pantry uninvited is "a crucial turning point." How revealing could that be to readers?
10. In what circumstances did Lord Darlington pass away? How could you relate this to question 2 (above)?

Essay Ideas

1. One would read in Philip Salom's "Toccata and Rain" (2004, 162): "We define ourselves a lot through episodes from our life—hence "episodic memory," as we call it. Like a big book. We're just very slow, tedious books. Except the stories change the more we tell them. Some are dramas, others are factual, and some are trivial. Most are trivial." Discuss this statement in the light of "The Remains of the Day."
2. To what extent is Kazuo Ishiguro a postcolonial writer?
3. In "The Art of Fiction," David Lodge argues that Stevens' life "has been based on the suppression and evasion of the truth, about himself and about others." Discuss.
4. In a sense, "The Remains of the Day" are the excavations of Stevens' archaeology of the past. Discuss this novel in terms of an assessment of the central character's life.
5. Write an essay on the sense of "dignity" in "The Remains of the Day."

She

by H. Rider Haggard

Content Synopsis

Haggard's (1856–1925) "She," categorized both as a quest and romance narrative, is also a commentary about the nineteenth century African colonization and the mysterious and compelling figure of the female racial "Other." Historically, critical readings of "She" have emphasized the depiction of Ayesha, the central and powerful female ruler of Kor, as a response to the threat of the 'new woman' (Murphy). Ayesha or "She," a shortened version of She-Who-Must-be-Obeyed, is a powerful and threatening unnaturally beautiful woman who exudes mesmerizing sexuality. Her power, however, is undercut by the misogynistic tone of the tale, a tone epitomized by the statements and behavior of Holly and Job, two of the three main male characters. Holly even openly admits, "Job, like myself, is a bit of a misogynist" (88). While the men in the story are configured as active participants, tellers and thinkers, "She" is little more than an objectified presence, the most obvious evidence of this provided in the shortened version of her name from its specific proper form (Ayesha) to a generalized pronoun (She).

The main narrator, Ludwig Horace Holly, is a fiercely independent and isolated teacher with no living relatives. Seemingly content in his isolation he states, "[I] felt a sort of grim satisfaction in the sense of my own loneliness; for I had neither father nor mother, nor brother" (8). Unlike to take a wife with whom he could relieve his solitary existence, Holly admits to experiencing intense anxiety in the presence of women: "I was set apart by nature to live alone, and draw comfort from her breast, and hers only. Women hated the sight of me. Only a week before I had heard one call me a monster when she thought I was out of hearing" (8).

The story opens in Holly's rooms in Cambridge when he is visited by a dying student named Vincey. The man requests that after his death, Holly takes over as guardian of his son, Leo, and directs his specifically designed courses of study. The last offspring of one of the oldest families in the world, Leo is a direct descendant of a priest named Kallikrates. The father explains that upon his twenty-fifth birthday, Leo is to be provided with an iron box, the contents of which, once displayed would present Leo with a choice: follow or deny the challenges it contains. Leo reaches his twenty-fifth birthday without any incident and opens the box. After removing three layers of covering, a potsherd (fragment or piece of pottery) is unveiled. A history of love and revenge is revealed after the language of the potsherd is translated, the writer exhorts the remaining descendant (Leo) to go after a woman who caused the death of his ancestor Kallikrates and "slay" her. The woman is revealed as residing somewhere in Africa. Leo immediately takes up the challenge and Holly and Job, Holly's servant, accompany him on his quest to find the great and terrible queen.

The search for a hidden tribe, ruled by an ageless and powerful 'White' woman is concluded when an African native, Billali, saves the group. He acts upon orders from Ayesha herself, that no white man should be harmed in her domain. Billali guides Leo, Holly and the rest of their group to his tribe, and thus to Ayesha herself. Once in the Amahagger settlement, the social structure of the tribe both excites and horrifies the English men. The excessive sexuality of the women shocks all the visitors and Job becomes particularly unhinged at the sexually aggressive behavior of the women who "have a way of looking at one . . . which I don't call respectable" (135).

Within the tribe, the women practice cannibalistic rituals, and their victims are usually male. Ustane, a woman who dares to show interest in Leo, who Ayesha has set her sights upon, is the only female in the story ever in any mortal danger and is murdered by The Amahagger Queen. The women appear to control completely the men of the tribe, a false impression eventually corrected by one of the male tribesmen. Billali discloses, "In this country the women do what they please. We worship them, and give them their way because without them the world could not go on; they are the source of life" (114). The real power of men is then explained: "We worship them. . .up to a certain point, till at last they get unbearable which. . .they do about every second generation. . .[then] we rise, and kill the old ones as an example to the young ones, and to show them that we are the strongest" (114).

Even though Ayesha has ordered that Holly and his men not be harmed, another Amahagger woman subverts her authority by provoking an attack on Mohamed (one of their guides) in retribution for Job's snubbing of her. During a banquet, a ritual then is performed in which a woman approaches Mohamed with sinister intent.

Mohamed recognizes the attention of this woman as different from the others who sexually accosted him as he "had been seated, shivering, and calling on Allah" (96). The woman then begins to "fondle him, patting his cheeks, calling him by names of endearment, while her fierce eyes played up and down his trembling form. . .the caressing was so snakelike" (235). Here the connection of woman and snake is illustrative of a desire to connect women to both bestial tendencies and cunning manipulation. The Amahagger swiftly attempt to "hotpot" Mohamed (a mode of death in which a gigantic heated pot is slipped over a person's head, trapping and cooking them). Holly responds to the threat by launching an attack on the tribe, shooting both the woman in question, and regrettably, Mohamed. The death of the female Amahagger results in a mass retaliation by the tribe who come after them "mad with fury" (101). Even though outnumbered, Holly knows he will prevail as "they were strong men, but I was mad with rage, and that awful lust for slaughter which will creep into the hearts of the most civilized of us" (235). Leo is seriously wounded during this battle.

Billali then takes the group to Ayesha herself. Her inner sanctum exists within a womb-like mountain which they enter "the bowels" through a "canal." The most central point of the mountain cave holds the Pillar of Life through which Ayesha was able to transform herself into her present incarnation. A significant portion of the later sections of the novel is devoted to describing Ayesha, who is noted as having unnatural beauty and is compared to a mummy, snake, and sibyl. Her beauty is reportedly so powerful that she must veil herself in a gauzy white material (like both a burial shroud and wedding veil). While the mythological medusa's gaze turns men to stone, men who gaze upon the equally mythologized Ayesha feel an undying lust after which the man may as well die for he is sure to "eat his heart out" with longing (191). Ayesha appears to cast a spell over both Holly and Leo, but

Leo is the real object of her affection, as in him she sees the vestiges of her long lost love Kallikrates one night while he is sleeping. "Human" torches are lit (specially embalmed bodies made to burn for long periods) within the passages of Ayesha's dwelling. Ayesha plans to bring Leo to the pillar of life so that he too may enjoy immortality, living out his days by Ayesha's side.

Leo hesitates in entering the pillar, causing Ayesha to enter it once again, hoping to prove that it will do no harm. The effect, however, is not increased youth and beauty, but rather a change in which she becomes a dehumanized and shrunken version of herself. "Smaller she grew, smaller yet, till she was no larger than a baboon" upon whose "shapeless face" was stamped "unutterable age" (294).

The two remaining members of the group (Job had died after witnessing Ayesha's pillar transformation) Holly and Leo return home after their three week journey during which time Leo's youthful locks have turned white.

Historical Context

Like many novels published during the nineteenth century in England (*Dracula, Heart of Darkness, Frankenstein, The Time Machine*), this tale is presented as a "truthful history." Probably influenced by the flood of extremely popular travel narratives, missionary accounts and anthropological studies published in England in the 1800s, the story also replicates the early problems of objectively and faithfully representing a foreign culture.

The narrative strategy of contextualizing the story as a 'found' manuscript, which at many points is reiterated as truthful, is first exemplified as "the most wonderful history as distinguished from romance" (4). Aside from the text's assertions of historical "truth," "She" is peppered with signs of its relationship to 'real' historical fact. It is heavily footnoted and includes drawings as well as extensive passages in foreign language in various states of translation.

Letters also add to the overall impression that the text is not only historically accurate but also offers a view into an historical 'secret,' instantly piquing the curiosity of its Victorian audience whose interest in secrets of any kind was intensified by their repressive social environment. Holly, the internal narrator and writer of the text that finds its way to the editor who publishes it, explains "I have recently read with much interest a book of yours describing a central African adventure. I take it that this book is partly true and partly an effort of the imagination" and continues, explaining that he is "offering a real African adventure, of a nature so much more marvelous than the one which you describe, that to tell you the truth I am almost ashamed to submit it to you for fear that you should disbelieve my tale" (3). The troubled relationship between fact and fiction, history and His Story is highlighted in one scene in which Holly visits the embalmed bodies of previous inhabitants of Kor: "Let him who reads forgive the intrusion of a dream into a history of fact . . . [but] who shall say what proportion of fact, past and present, or to come may lie in the imagination?" (186).

Societal Context

The social position of women in the nineteenth century was one in flux. Women were beginning to see that there were, in fact, more opportunities than previously imagined for them. The "New Woman" emerged as one who crossed the boundaries from objectified to autonomous subjective presence, owning her experiences and asserting and inserting herself into the workplace, the literary salon, and the political sphere. However, Westfahl argues, "while modern feminists have chastised Haggard's Ayesha . . . as an unflattering and stereotypical portrait from a man horrified by the Power of Women, his novels actually feature a wide variety of female characters, including some who share Ayesha's intelligence and resourcefulness without her aura of manipulative evil" ("H. Rider Haggard").

The social hierarchy in Kor, the isolated and primitive "Matriarchy," is presented as one in which women appear to have utter control over "their" men. Unnatural and at times excessively violent, these women are finally characterized as being controlled by the very men they appear to rule. In this sense, even an imagined community ruled by a powerful woman is undercut. Aside from the statements about women from both Holly and Job, other men express a negative estimation of the female Amahagger tribe. Billali, who is described as the "father" of the tribe, warns about women: ". . . flee from them, for they are evil, and in the end they will destroy thee" (110), which advice the narrative action repeatedly supports. Job is particularly hateful of women, especially Ayesha for whom he held "the most distrust and horror, being by no means sure that she was not an animated corpse." (209). Billali explains to Holly and Leo the power structure of their society is not what it seems on the surface, although as Holly notes, the women are "upon terms of perfect equality with the men" they "are not held to them by any binding ties" (81). The generational genocide is another example of the not-so-subtle misogyny in the text as well as an example of the blurring of appearance and reality.

Holly's morbid fear of the tribal women reflects a general anxiety at the time that women were in fact evolutionarily inferior to men by their very nature, and that if not careful, they would drag men down via their regressively sexual yearnings into a spiral of devolution ultimately fatal to the race (Dijkstra). Holly notes that Ayesha's "diablerie" both "horrified and repelled, attracted in an even greater degree" (159). Holly notes, "I could not say why, but I know their appearance filled me with a sick dread of which I felt ashamed" (77).

Kor is a society in which cannibalistic rituals are practiced, often with a sexual element. Representative of not only social fears about women actively moving from a passive to active social existence, these women are unnaturally sexual and perverse. They threaten the established 'order' and their civilization is one in which all the norms of 'correct' behavior are turned upside down.

Religious Context

The religious elements of "She" are more a study of ancient ritual and primitivism than they are a reflection of contemporary faith. Ayesha leaves her native land to establish herself as a Goddess worshipped by a foreign tribe. Westfahl points out that Haggard's dislike for modern society and civilization in general was translated into his works where "he crafted his lost worlds as attractive antitheses of European culture: often dominated by women, not men, their power derived from ancient magic, not modern laws and customs" ("H. Rider Haggard: An Overview").

Scientific & Technological Context

As many other Victorian texts, Haggard's "She" engages with Darwinian theories of evolution. Holly, for example, notes that a woman made the comment "I had converted her to the monkey theory" (8). The monkey theory to which he alludes refers to Darwin's theories of evolution, which, hardly universally accepted at the time, nonetheless were explored in most literature of the nineteenth century in at least a tangential way. The idea that Holly was not as 'evolved' as other men, a fact which seems to be predicated solely on his external appearance, not only reflects other pseudo-sciences of the day like the study of physiognomy, but also serves as an historical grounding for contemporary obsessions with appearance and eugenics in which scientists, politicians and laypeople alike toy with or even attempt to intentionally breed a higher order of human. The monkey theory appears again later in the text as Ayesha transforms into a monkey-like creature; a woman whose physical appearance finally mirrors what the men feel is her internal psychological primitivism. Women in the text are usually associated with dangerous sexual allure; if a man submits he will be manipulated by the woman who entices him and reduced in faculties to little more than a zombie, as in the case of Leo, who is unable to resist Ayesha's tempting advances.

The connection of external beauty with internal evolutionary superiority is undercut by Holly's statements about the Amahagger women who "not withstanding their beauty . . . on the whole, I had never seen a more evil looking set of faces" (77). Appearance and reality are thus called into question as much as the objectivity of a narrator thoroughly, by his own admission, found repulsive by the women he meets.

Biographical Context

Henry Rider Haggard, who reportedly "thought himself to be the reincarnation of a Zulu warrior ("H. Rider Haggard: An Overview") is known primarily as an adventure writer. Using first-hand experiences collected via his world travels, Haggard's texts reflect detailed accounts of foreign lands that his reading public so enjoyed. Haggard married in 1879 and published his first book three years later. "King Solomon's Mines" (1885) was the book that definitively launched Haggard's career, affording him "immediate and spectacular success" ("H. Rider Haggard"). Most of Haggard's texts are set in Africa, a place he was familiar with due to his living there for many years and serving various governmental positions. Haggard was knighted in 1922.

Haggard's "She" is, as described above, an example of the blurred boundaries of fiction and fact, reflecting a problem experienced by Haggard himself. John Koetze, a magistrate who worked with Haggard in the Transvaal "remembered

Haggard as 'emotional and much given to romancing' a young man who sometimes described 'as fact what was mere fiction'" (Harris 48).

Of Haggard's influence on fantasy and romance fiction, Westfahl argues: "The extent of Haggard's influence on modern fantasy is almost incalculable. Many fantasies, from Victorian fairy tales to modern homage's to J. R. R. Tolkien, can seem Eurocentric, domesticated and comforting; Haggard insisted on fantasies that were more exotic, unfamiliar and disturbing" ("H. Rider Haggard: An Overview"). Even though Haggard wrote and published more than sixty works, he could never equal the success that "King Solomon's Mines" garnered.

Tracy M. Caldwell. Ph.D.

Works Cited

Auerbach, Nina. *The Woman and the Demon: The Life of a Victorian Myth*. Massachusetts: Harvard University Press, 1984.

Bram Dijkstra. *Idols of Perversity: Fantasies of Feminine Evil in Fin-de-Siècle Culture*. New York: Oxford University Press, 1988.

Haggard, H. Rider. *She*, Daniel Karlin, ed. New York: Oxford University Press, 1991.

Harris, Michael. *Outsiders and Insiders: Perspectives of Third World Culture in British and Post Colonial Fiction*. New York: Peter Lang Publishers, 1992.

Murphy, Patricia. "The Gendering of History in She." *Studies in English Literature*, 1500–1900 39.4 (1999).

Westfahl, Gary. "H. Rider Haggard." *Cyclopedia of World Authors*. MagillOnLiteraturePlus. EBSCO. 12 Sept. 2005.

————. "H. Rider Haggard: Overview." *St. James Guide to Fantasy Writers*. David Pringle ed. St. James Press, 1996. Literature Resource Center. Thompson Gale. 23 Sept. 2005.

Discussion Questions

1. Discuss the narrative structure of the story. Do you feel the 'editor' adds authenticity to the texts?

2. Do you like Holly as a protagonist? Why or why not?

3. Do you feel Leo is fully developed as a three dimensional character?

4. What is your feeling about the fact that Haggard created She as a White woman ruling over an African tribe?

5. How do you explain Haggard's desire for the narrative to appear 'real'?

6. Do you see Ayesha as a strong female lead or role model, or a weak and ultimately dominated woman?

7. What are each character's fatal flaws?

8. In what ways are relationships between men and women explored in the story? Which is figured as more important or essential: male/female relationships or male/male relationships?

9. What do you think readers liked so much about Haggard's style and content?

10. Watch one of the film adaptations of the story and discuss whether it faithfully represents the plot and characterization of the book.

Essay Ideas

1. Write an essay that explores at least three ways in which the conflict of appearance versus reality is presented in the text.

2. Write an essay that compares and contrasts the main male characters in the story: Leo, Holly, Job, and Billali.

3. Explain the ways in which the novel reflects historical and scientific events of Haggard's day.

4. Explore the meaning behind the major symbols in the text and how they help develop the theme of the novel.

5. Analyze the various settings in the story and what each symbolizes.

Skin and Other Stories

by Roald Dahl

Content Synopsis

Dahl's biographer, Jeremy Treglown has perhaps best described Dahl's stories as irritants and provocations. "Fantastic as Grimm, neat as O. Henry, heartless as Saki, they stick in the mind long after subtler ones have faded: incredible (literally), unforgettable and vengefully funny."

The stories in "Skin" are plot-driven works featuring memorable characters, unique situations, and crisp dialogue. All of the stories deal with some of the baser elements of human nature—most notably the elements of greed, suspicion, cruelty, jealousy, obsession, and desperation. Descriptive passages are used sparingly, though Dahl often finds creative and highly evocative ways to describe certain characters or situations.

Dahl's stories are also notable for a dark sense of humor used as a way of adding levity to what are otherwise grim narratives.

The following are brief plot descriptions of the eleven works that comprise "Skin and Other Stories":

In "Skin," a down-and-out old man discovers that the unknown artist who tattooed his back decades ago has since become a very famous painter, and that his skin has suddenly become a very valuable—and very coveted—commodity.

In "Lamb to the Slaughter," a pregnant, devoted wife uses an unorthodox weapon–a frozen leg of lamb—to kill her husband after he tells her that he's leaving. Her method of getting rid of the evidence is even more unusual.

In "The Sound Machine," an eccentric inventor builds a machine that is able to detect sounds being made at very high frequencies. When he listens in, he hears unsettling screams that are coming from a most unusual source—the roses being cut next door.

In "An African Story," an old farmer living in Kenya attempts to solve the nightly disappearance of milk from his cow, while also plotting revenge on an oafish farmhand for beating his dog to death.

In "Galloping Foxley," a highly regimented English businessman has his carefully structured commute thrown for a loop when an intrusive stranger appears on his train platform. Could this stranger be the same boy who used to torment him at prep school some 50 years ago?

In "The Wish," a young boy decides that in order to ensure his birthday wish of a new puppy, he must challenge himself by walking across a multicolored carpet using only the yellow spots.

To make the game more interesting, the boy assigns deadly properties to the other two colors on the carpet—the red spots will burn him alive, while the black spots are poisonous snakes that will strike him dead. It's a tricky task, but it's only a game, right?

In "The Surgeon," an unassuming middle-class doctor is the recipient of a tremendously valuable diamond given to him as a gift by a thankful patient. With the banks closed for the weekend and a two-day vacation already in the plans, how can he keep the diamond safe while he's away?

In "A Dip in the Pool," a man traveling on a steamship bets his life savings on the low number in a lottery that's based on estimating how far the ship will travel each day. When a patch of rough weather unexpectedly clears up, the man desperately hatches a new plan for slowing the ship's progress.

In "The Champion of the World," an ambitious poacher named Claud and his reluctant accomplice Gordon try to break Claude's father's record for poaching pheasants by feeding drugged raisins to 200 birds. However, is there a critical flaw in the plan that escapes them both?

In "Beware of the Dog," an English fighter pilot is badly injured in a dogfight over Europe during World War II and is forced to bail out. He miraculously ends up in a friendly British hospital. The pilot's suspicions start to mount, however, when first his ears and then his eyes start to suggest he's being lied to.

In "My Lady Love, My Dove," well-to-do Pamela bullies her meek husband Arthur into bugging their guest room prior to the arrival of weekend houseguests that she finds detestable. But, when she gets a chance to hear what the couple has to say behind closed doors, she suddenly finds them a lot more interesting.

Symbols & Motifs

There are a number of symbols and motifs in the stories of "Skin." As noted above, Dahl is very interested in exploring the darker aspects of human nature—greed, jealousy, resentment, cruelty, and obsession. His literary world is filled with people who are nasty in both big and small ways.

Dahl seems to be particularly interested in the consequence of greed. In both "The Champion of the World," and "A Dip in the Pool" the greed of the main characters leads to an unfortunate and unexpected ending.

Both "Skin" and "The Surgeon" deal with the threat that greedy people pose to those who stand in the way of them getting what they want.

In fact, it is somewhat telling that the only truly sympathetic main character in the collection is Robert Sandy, the notably un-greedy doctor in "The Surgeon." "Unlike many of his colleagues, he did not hanker after fame and riches. He was basically a simple man utterly devoted to his profession" (95).

Many of the characters in the stories of "Skin" demonstrate some form of obsessive behavior. There is Klausner, the eccentric inventor in "The Sound Machine" who is so obsessed with listening to the unearthly sounds of plants screaming that he is compelled to keep cutting them.

There is also Claud, the ambitious poacher in "The Champion of the World" who is so obsessed with shattering his father's poaching record that he is willing to overlook the practical difficulties that his plan presents.

Examples of obsessive/compulsive behavior can also be seen in Pamela's meek husband Arthur in "My Lady Love, My Dove." Pamela plays on

Arthur's compulsion to snoop on other people to get him to go along with her plan to spy on their houseguests, even though he objects to it initially.

Dahl also has a talent for finding highly evocative ways to describe people, particularly when he is trying to emphasize their negative aspects. In "Skin," he focuses on the facial features of a greedy art dealer to emphasize his corrupt nature. "It was a flabby face with so much flesh upon it that the cheeks hung down on either side of his mouth in two fleshy collops, spaniel-wise" (15).

In "Galloping Foxley," it is a handsome face that draws the narrator's ire. "It was really an intolerable face, vulgarly, almost lasciviously handsome, with an oily salacious sheen all over the skin" (75).

Dahl also enjoys depicting battles of will between strong and weak-minded individuals. In "Skin," the old man Drioli, allows himself to be convinced that his new benefactor is telling the truth in promising him a lavish lifestyle at a seaside resort because he wants to believe it so badly.

In "An African Story," the old man is able to manipulate his much larger and more dangerous farmhand into dangerous situations using nothing more than shouts, threats, and bluster.

In "My Lady Love, My Dove," Pamela is able to convince Arthur to go along with her plan by the sheer force of her will and her intimidating size. As Arthur explains in the story; "You understand, she was a big woman, with a big white face, and when she looked at me hard, as she was doing now, I became—how shall I say it—surrounded, almost enveloped by her, as though she were a great tub of cream and I had fallen in" (200).

While Dahl has been accused by some critics as being misogynistic in his writing, it is difficult to see examples of this in "Skin."

As Treglown writes in a Guardian newspaper article on Dahl's legacy, "…the claim that Dahl's work is misogynistic has to contend with the fact that while there are some awful women in the tales, there are still more awful men, and his most technically accomplished plots involve victories by wives over bad husbands."

Historical Context

The majority of Dahl's stories have a timeless nature to them, and can be read and enjoyed without the need for any particular historical context.

Several stories are tied to a particular time and place, however. "Beware of the Dog" deals with a fighter pilot who was shot down during World War II, and the reader needs a basic familiarity with the circumstances of the war in order to understand the implications of the plot twists in that story.

It is also important to note that one of Dahl's tasks for the Royal Air Force during World War II was to drum up American support for the war. In its depiction of the enemy as a sneaking threat, "Beware of the Dog" can be seen as a subtle but effective work of British propaganda.

The plot of "Galloping Foxley" is tied into the social structure and disciplinary practices of English boarding schools during the early 20th century. The type of corporal punishment described by Dahl has been discontinued.

Societal Context

Many of Dahl's stories are about class struggle. He writes about characters who are struggling to gain wealth and respect, characters who resent those who have wealth, and wealthy characters that disdain those who are below them in the social order.

Mr. Barbitol, the ambitious gambler in "A Dip in the Pool," takes enormous personal and financial risks simply so he can show up his wife by arriving home in a brand new Lincoln convertible. Claud, the poacher from "The Champion of the World," so greatly resents the wealthy brewer who stocks his land with pheasants that he tries to take all 200 pheasants in one great score.

There is also Drioli, the destitute old man in "Skin," who does not realize the dangerous situation he is putting himself in when he reveals the expensive tattoo on his back.

There are also characters like William Perkins in "Galloping Foxley, the rigid solicitor who is personally offended by anyone who does not match his meticulously structured approach to life.

Pamela, the wealthy wife in "My Lady Love, My Dove," is clearly disdainful of her houseguests because they come from a lower social station, and because they are so seemingly untroubled by it.

Religious Context
Religion is not a major topic in the short stories comprising "Skin."

Scientific & Technological Context
Science and technology does not play a major role in the stories of "Skin," though Dahl does show an interest in using technology to eavesdrop on forbidden, threatening, or unseemly information.

This can be seen in the character of Klausner, the eccentric inventor obsessed with high-frequency sound waves in the "Sound Machine," and Arthur, who uses his knowledge of sound technology to bug the guest room in "My Lady Love, My Dove." Peter Williamson, the convalescing pilot in "Beware of the Dog," also uses his knowledge of the sounds made by airplane motors to deduce that the hospital staff is not being truthful with him.

While Dahl is not necessarily commenting on the use or impact of technology on everyday life, he is happy to use it to further a story.

Biographical Context
Dahl incorporated many of his real-life experiences into his writing. The author was born in Llandaff, Whales in September of 1916. He was the son of immigrant parents from Norway. The family experienced tragedy early on when his older sister died of appendicitis in 1920 and his father died shortly thereafter.

According to Kristine Howard's "My Dahl Biography," Dahl was sent to St. Peter's Preparatory School in Weston-Super-Mare at the age of nine, where he was first subjected to the physical and mental abuse that he chronicled in short stories like "Galloping Foxley" and "Lucky Break," and in his autobiography "Boy."

At the age of 13, he was sent to the Repton Public School, where he continued to suffer at the hands of older students.

After graduating from Repton, Dahl got a job with the Shell Oil Company and spent two years in training before being sent to Africa to supervise the East African territory.

In 1939, Dahl joined the Royal Air Force and began training as a fighter pilot during the buildup to World War II. In 1940, he crashed his plane in the Libyan Desert after being given the wrong coordinates while en route to joining his squadron. He fractured his skull and was temporarily blinded by the accident. It took him nearly a year to recover.

Dahl was unable to fly again until 1941, when he joined his squadron in a campaign in Greece, engaging in a number of dogfights against German planes. When he was forced out of active duty due to the lingering effects of the crash, he was sent to the United States as a British military envoy. One of his duties was to drum up American support for the war effort.

To further this goal, Dahl began hanging out with a high-society group of friends in Washington, D.C. He also wrote his first published story, a factually questionable retelling of his plane crash titled "Shot Down Over Libya," which appeared in the *Saturday Evening Post*.

Dahl returned to England after the war ended in 1945 and continued writing, though he did not find considerable success until he came back to the United States in the early 1950s. He moved to New York and once again fell in with a high-society crowd. It was here that he met and married the actress Patricia O'Neil.

Dahl wrote the majority of his short stories for adults in the 1950s and early '60s, before turning to children's books when he began to run out of ideas for adult fiction. He wrote only a handful of adult-themed works during the last three decades of his life.

Several of the stories in "Skin" make clear biographical references to Dahl's life. As previously noted, the abuse suffered by the narrator in "Galloping Foxley" is very similar to the real-life abuse suffered by Dahl.

The British pilot who retells the old man's story in "An African Story" has crashed in the desert as Dahl did, though his crash was the result of accidentally clipping a giraffe with his plane.

Peter Williamson, the pilot in "Beware of the Dog," is also forced to make a crash landing after he is injured in a dogfight. While recovering from his injuries, Williamson thinks that he hears the distinctive sound of German Ju 88 planes, the same planes that Dahl fought against during World War II.

Brian Burns

Works Cited

Dahl, Roald. *Skin and Other Stories*. New York: Viking/Penguin Books, 2000.

Howard, Kristine. *My Roald Dahl Biography*. RoaldDahlFans.com, 26 Feb. 2008. http://www.roalddahlfans.com/mydahlbio.php

Talbot, Margaret. "The Candy Man." *The New Yorker* 11 July 2005: Online. http://www.newyorker.com/archive/2005/07/11/050711crat_atlarge?currentPage=1

Treglown, Jeremy. "The Height of Fancy." *The Guardian* 9 Sept. 2006: Online. http://books.guardian.co.uk/review/story/0,,1867703,00.html#article_continue

Discussion Questions

1. Describe the relationship between Soutine the painter and Drioli, the tattoo artist in "Skin." Are they friends? How does Drioli's wife fit into the equation?

2. Who is the more sympathetic character in "Lamb to the Slaughter," Mary Maloney or her husband Patrick?

3. What descriptive terms does Dahl use to characterize the unearthly sounds made by the vegetables screaming in "The Sound Machine"? Are they effective?

4. How does the physical appearance of Klasuner, the inventor of "The Sound Machine," mirror his personality?

5. Why does Judson so willingly follow the old man's commands in "An African Story"?

6. What does the identity of the intrusive passenger in "Galloping Foxley" suggest about the narrator's state of mind?

7. How does Dahl view the boy in "The Wish"? Is he sympathetic to his plight? Critical? Apathetic?

8. Are the snakes real or imagined in the "The Wish"?

9. What do you think about the ending of "Beware of the Dog"? Does it come too soon in the story, or is it just right?

10. What subtle methods does Dahl use to suggest Arthur's compulsion toward snooping in "My Lady Love, My Dove"?

Essay Ideas

1. Name several stories in "Skin" that deal with the idea of greed and describe the circumstances of each. What do the stories suggest about how Dahl feels about greed?

2. Both "Lamb to the Slaughter" and "My Lady Love, My Dove" deal with husbands and wives who want the opposite things. How does Dahl's depiction of the argument between Mary and Patrick Maloney differ from that of the argument between Arthur and Pamela? Is one more convincing than the other?

3. Of all the characters depicted in the stories in "Skin," who is the most reprehensible? Why?

4. What makes Dr. Robert Sandy such a likeable character? Does he have any flaws?

5. Dahl has been accused by some critics of being a misogynist. Discuss Dahl's depiction of several female characters in the stories in "Skin." Does he treat them differently than his male characters?

The Strange Case of
Dr. Jekyll and Mr. Hyde

by Robert Louis Stevenson

Content Synopsis

Perhaps one of literature's most pervasive stories, "The Strange Case of Dr. Jekyll and Mr. Hyde" is the tale of one man who finds a way to release the dark side of his nature. By drinking a potion of his own making, the respectable Dr. Henry Jekyll is able to transform into the evil Mr. Edward Hyde and so indulge his most base desires. However, the strong cautionary tone of the story teaches us that such indulgence can only lead to tragedy, and so it is for Dr. Jekyll.

Initially, the book does not follow the Doctor and his alter ego, but instead is told in the third person, through the eyes of one of Dr. Jekyll's old friends and colleagues, a lawyer named Gabriel Utterson. As his name suggests, Utterson is the mouthpiece through which the story is told, he is our everyman providing a rational viewpoint to such a fantastical story. Stevenson gives him a rather non-descript nature describing him as "undemonstrative at best" (29) and as the "last reputable acquaintance and last good influence in the lives of down-going men" (29). As such, we are made aware that we are traveling through this story in the company of a trustworthy, if slightly dull, man who will show us the truth of the story. In this way, Stevenson grounds what comes after and uses Utterson to lend truthfulness to what unfolds.

As the book opens, Mr. Utterson is taking one of his customary Sunday walks with his cousin, Richard Enfield. They pass by a lone door upon which Enfield comments, "'Did you ever mark that door?'…'It is connected in my mind…with a very odd story'" (30–31). Therefore, we are told the 'Story of the Door' that gives the first chapter its name. In this story, Enfield tells us of witnessing an appalling event in which, late one night, he saw a man trample a young girl "like some dammed Juggernaut" (31). He apprehended this man and sought some reparations for the injuries caused to the girl. This resulted in the man leading Enfield and an assembled crowd of onlookers and family to the door in question, whereupon he disappeared inside and re-emerged with a check for the requested amount. Not trusting this man—for he had taken an immediate dislike to him, as had all of the others who had gathered—they waited until dawn for the man to cash the check. Enfield refuses to disclose the name on the check—a man who "is the very pink of proprieties [and] celebrated too" (33) but names the man who trampled the girl as Mr. Hyde (34).

Through his story, Enfield informs Utterson of more than he intends, for Utterson knows that the door in question is a back door to Dr. Jekyll's property. He also provides us, the reader, with our first intimation that not all is as grounded in reality as it might seem. His initial revulsion at seeing Hyde—something that could easily have been caused by seeing him trample the girl with so little concern—does not dissipate and seems to be a product of Hyde himself. This is borne out by the reactions of the others in the crowd which gathers, including those of the doctor whom Enfield describes as being "about as emotional as a bagpipe" (31). This is our first intimation of Hyde's nature and the reaction he provokes in others continues throughout the story with character after character feeling angered or sickened by nothing more than his physical presence. This is not to suggest that he is ugly, but he exudes some evilness that affects the people he meets.

Returning from his walk with Enfield, Utterson removes a document from his safe that is revealed to be Jekyll's will. The terms of this will cover the transfer of all of Dr. Jekyll's possessions to Edward Hyde should the former die, or in the case of his "disappearance or unexplained absence for any period exceeding three calendar months" (35). Utterson re-reads this will with disquiet, especially following the story he has heard of Mr. Hyde. He pays a visit to a mutual friend of his and Jekyll's, Dr. Hastie Lanyon. There he seeks more information about Mr. Hyde, but Lanyon has never heard of the man. In fact, he tells Utterson, he has had little to do with Jekyll at all since they fell out over Jekyll's "unscientific balderdash" (36). This is our first major clue to the reality of the relationship between Jekyll and Hyde.

In response, Utterson decides to spend his time watching the door that initially prompted Enfield's story, in the hope of meeting this Mr. Hyde. Eventually, the meeting takes place and Utterson feels the same disquiet previously reported by the onlookers in Enfield's story. Utterson starts to believe that Jekyll is in trouble and being blackmailed by Hyde.

Some weeks later, following a dinner at Jekyll's, Utterson raises the subject of Mr. Hyde. Jekyll assures Utterson that there is no problem and asks for his forbearance. Utterson reluctantly agrees.

A year later, Utterson is called to assist the police after the brutal murder of Sir Danvers Carew is attributed to Mr. Hyde. He helps the police search the man's lodgings and all the indications are of a man who has taken flight. He says nothing to the police about Hyde's connection to Dr. Jekyll, but pays a visit to the doctor later that day. Jekyll is huddled in his room, looking sick. He and Utterson talk and Jekyll confesses that Mr. Hyde had a hold over him, but is now gone and will not return. Jekyll gives Utterson a letter purporting to be from Mr. Hyde to this effect. Utterson leaves with it in his possession after discovering from the butler that the letter did not come via the usual route, leading Utterson to believe that Hyde had been to the house that day and had written the letter in Jekyll's presence. Utterson returns home where his clerk compares the handwriting of this letter with the handwriting on a dinner invitation from Dr. Jekyll. Utterson is appalled to discover that they were written by the same hand and that it is his interpretation that Jekyll has been covering up for his protégé Again, we are given clues to Hyde's real nature.

From this point, things turn to the worse very quickly. Following an evening dinner at Jekyll's with Lanyon, both doctors are taken ill. Utterson tries to visit Jekyll but is denied admittance. He visits with Lanyon who tells him he has received a shock that will kill him. He refuses to say more and refuses to talk about Jekyll at all. Shortly thereafter, Lanyon dies. Again, Utterson's attempts to visit Jekyll are met with refusal. Shortly after this, during another Sunday walk with Enfield, the two men are in the square that Jekyll's house overlooks. They see the doctor at the window and speak to him, but he quickly changes in manner and slams the window, retreating from view.

Finally, some time later, Utterson is called from his house by Poole, Jekyll's butler, to attend to his master. He fears that his master has been murdered and replaced by Hyde. Utterson accompanies him back to Jekyll's house where they break down the door to Jekyll's room only to find Mr. Hyde dying on the floor, a bottle of poison still in his hand.

All that is left for Utterson are two letters; one bequeathed him by Dr. Lanyon and one left in his room by Dr. Jekyll. These two letters form the rest of the book.

'Doctor Lanyon's Narrative' tells the story of the night after the dinner at Dr. Jekyll's. He receives a message from Jekyll asking him to retrieve a drawer from his workshop and to await a messenger at midnight. The messenger is Mr. Hyde who concocts a potion from the contents of the drawer and drinks it. Following convulsions and contortions, he transforms into Dr. Jekyll. The shock of this is what killed Dr. Lanyon. This is our great moment of revelation at which Hyde is revealed to be part of Jekyll. In turn, Jekyll's narrative provides the explanation behind the revelation, working in much the same way as a mystery story.

'Henry Jekyll's Statement of the Case' tells how Dr. Jekyll had dark and base passions that he could not indulge as a reputable member of society. As a result, he found a chemical way to transform those passions into the physical form of Mr. Hyde. He tells of adventures undertaken in the guise of his 'protégé' and of the dreadful murder he committed in a fit of rage. Finally, he tells how, despite having foresworn his evil side, the change from Jekyll to Hyde started to come upon him without the help of the potion. He eventually found himself in a public place needing to take the potion in order to change back. This is why he sent the message to Lanyon requesting the chemicals he needed. Following this, the change came over him with more and more frequency.

The end came when one of the chemicals required for the potion ran short and none of the trial replacements were effective. Jekyll could only conclude that it was an "unknown impurity which lent efficacy to the draught" (96). And so, with no chemical left, Jekyll wrote his statement and waited for his final change to take him. He wonders, as his statement draws to a close, whether Hyde will wait to be arrested and hanged for the murder of Sir Danvers, or whether he will take his own life. This, of course, has already been revealed to us, and lends truthfulness to Jekyll's account, bringing "the life of that unhappy Henry Jekyll to an end" (97).

Historical Context

This novella was written at the end of 1885 and published in 1886. This was a period before Sigmund Freud and his analysis of the human psyche, but the story foreshadows these ideas. Lettice Cooper's comment is that "Stevenson's ego feared his id" (55), that he was worried about his own capacity for unconscious evil. The fact that the story came to him in a dream, and all twenty five thousand words were written in only three days (by hand, this was a time before typewriters were common) bears this out. In a letter in early March 1886, he confided that "'Jekyll [& Hyde]' is a dreadful thing" (310) a feeling he seems to have continued to hold for this story for the rest of his life.

Likewise, despite being published too early to be considered part of the traditional modernist canon, this tale is often included in studies of that movement. With its attention to the city, rather than the countryside, and with dealings of the lower classes and the inner workings of the mind, it examines many of the areas which modernism sought to uncover. Perhaps most apparent is the low level of respect which Stevenson obviously felt for the overtly middle-class protagonists of his story. The only character who emerges well is the butler, Poole.

This was also a period when arguments were still raging about Charles Darwin's book on evolution: "The Origin of Species." Stevenson's attempt to enter these arguments can be seen in the way in which Jekyll's potion (representing science) can be seen to show how modern man's civilized presentation is just a facade to hide his primitive side.

Societal Context

One of Stevenson's concerns in this book was the double standards adopted by the middle-classes. All of the main characters are middle-class, middle-aged professional men in positions of responsibility: Utterson is lawyer; Jekyll and Lanyon are both doctors. Even Utterson's cousin, Richard Enfield, is described as a 'well-known man about town,' (29) thus providing him with an elevated status. As such, the story can be seen as much as a critique of these men in their high positions as it is of Hyde and his degenerate nature. These men meet for dinners and sit over drinks in front of fires discussing their work while the rest of London continues around them. The only glimpses we get of life outside this polite enclave come from the occasional interruptions of the servants and, of course, Hyde's excursions into the seedier side of London. These, however, are mostly alluded to rather than shown so we are forced to imagine them based purely on Stevenson's treatment of the more bourgeois characters.

Having seen the life of these characters so clearly displayed, the degeneracy of Hyde comes to act as a commentary on them. Although ultimately a part of the very middle-class Jekyll, Hyde decides to take his lodgings in the lower-class area of Soho, thereby associating himself with this other section of society. In this way we can see Stevenson commenting that it is at least as likely for higher members of society to succumb to perversion and degeneracy as for the lower members. And this commentary is emphasized when Hyde's rooms in Soho are found to contain wine, silver plates and other fineries, marking him as a gentleman with base tastes rather than the lower-class figure that might have been presumed. This is a figure who would have been quite familiar to readers of the time thanks to other characters such as Duc Jean Floressas des Esseintes ("A Rebours" by J.K. Huysmans, 1884) and Dorian Gray ("The Picture of Dorian Gray" by Oscar Wilde, 1890), both also rich and decadent.

The criticism of the social isolation of the characters is confirmed during the final stages of Mr. Utterson's portion of the story when a maid is shushed after crying out in fear. Poole, the butler, seeks to protect Utterson from the fears and worries of those he would see as lower than him.

Religious Context

The religious connections are all too clear in a story which seems to suggest that evil is more powerful than good. Stevenson was fascinated by the portrayal of evil in the Calvinism that had informed his upbringing. In this religion, the presence of evil was always disguised in 'the shape of devils and spirits' (Calder 10). Stevenson's fascination concerned what happened when evil adopted a human face. This is the concept that Calvinism is so set against, with its doctrine of abstinence and self-control being in place to prevent such an occurrence from happening.

It is clear that Stevenson was interested in these principles of self-denial so prominent in Calvinism, but also in the reverse: the attractive power of what is forbidden purely because of its disallowed status. While Jekyll's narrative imparts to us the horror he feels on discovering how much of a monster Hyde is and the fear of losing himself, which eventually comes true, it also shows us the joy he feels in letting go of that part of himself. This sums up the battle that religions like Calvinism have to wage when faced by human nature. The fact that Utterson, Lanyon, and Jekyll himself are shown as religious, church-going folk, merely makes the latter's slide into the darkness all the more stark a criticism.

Scientific & Technological Context

The late 19th Century was a time of vast growth in medical areas with the likes of Louis Pasteur and Joseph Lister making great strides in anti-bacterial protection and making operations much more likely to succeed. In addition, recent discoveries had shown living beings to be made up of small building blocks, cells, organized into larger organs and then organisms. Add to this Darwin's book on evolution, "The Origin of Species," and the time seemed to hold almost limitless potential. The medical profession was just starting the process of splitting into specialties, and it seemed that the possibilities for medicine and scientific advancement were infinite.

This was the period that gave us the first real works of science fiction, of which "Jekyll and Hyde" can be seen as just one. Jules Verne was a contemporary of Stevenson's and writers such as H. G. Wells came soon after. It was a time when the possibilities of science were being grasped for the first time, which powered the imaginative faculties of scientist and writer alike.

It is, of course, unlikely that a potion such as that taken by Dr. Jekyll could have the effects described to change him physically. However, in an age where people were still coming to grips with the concept of being descended from apes, it must have seemed at least reasonable. It is certain that Stevenson would have seen the way in which alcohol, laudanum, and opium would have acted on the human personality to effect dramatic changes.

Biographical Context

Robert Lewis Balfour Stevenson was born on November 13, 1850 in Edinburgh to Thomas Stevenson, a successful lighthouse engineer, and Margaret Balfour. They were both devoutly religious and brought their son up to be the same. However, he later decided to renounce his religion while he was studying at Edinburgh University. This was also the time when he changed his middle names to become Robert Louis Stevenson.

Having contracted tuberculosis as a child, he had poor health for most of his life, finding problems with breathing which eventually led to his moving to Samoa, where the air better agreed with his lungs.

His first major literary success—"Treasure Island"—was published in 1883 as his second book. His first had been the story collection, "The New Arabian Nights" published in 1882. These were followed by "The Black Arrow" in 1884 and "The Body Snatcher" in 1885. His next books, "Kidnapped" and "The Strange Case of Dr. Jekyll and Mr. Hyde" were both published in 1886. These were followed by "The Wrong Box," (1892), and "The Master of Ballantrae" (1888). His final book, "Weir of Hermiston" was left unfinished by his death in 1894.

Despite spending his final years in the South Sea Islands, his writing was still grounded in Scotland and he always considered himself a Scottish writer. In true Stevenson fashion, his final, unfinished, book, "Weir of Hermiston," was about the strong-willed Scottish Lord of Hermiston and his son, and once again dealt with the duality of human nature.

Calum A. Kerr, Ph.D.

Works Cited

Calder, Jenni. *Dr. Jekyll and Mr. Hyde and Other Stories*. Introduction London: Penguin Books, 1979.

Cooper, Lettice. *The European Novelists Series — Robert Louis Stevenson*. London: Arthur Barker Limited, 1967.

Hennessy, James Pope. Robert Louis Stevenson. London: Jonathan Cape, 1974.

Lindsay, Maurice. *History of Scottish Literature*. London: *Robert* Hale, 1977.

Mehew, Ernest (ed.). *Selected Letters of Robert Louis Stevenson*. New Haven: Yale University Press, 1997.

Robert Louis Stevenson. *Dr. Jekyll and Mr. Hyde and Other Stories*. London: Penguin Books, 1979.

Discussion Questions

1. For most of the story, Utterson believes Jekyll and Hyde to be two different men. What information does he base this belief on? Could he be expected to guess the truth from the information he receives before he reads the final letters?

2. Stevenson claimed that Hyde is 'no more sexual than another'. In what form does Hyde's nature manifest itself?

3. What is the physical layout of Dr. Jekyll's house and laboratory? How does this symbolize the nature of his relationship to Hyde?

4. How does the nature of the relationship between Jekyll and Hyde change during the course of the story?

5. How does Utterson's personality (or lack thereof) serve the story by making it more or less believable?

6. The story is told in first and third person and in chronological order and flashback. How do these narrative devices enhance the story?

7. Why do you think that Stevenson also included Lanyon as a first person voice?

8. The character names used in the story are often symbolic. Discuss their significance in relation to the themes of the story.

9. This story is often seen as an allegory of 'good' and 'evil'. Discuss the motifs within the story that highlight these aspects.

10. Poole seems to be a central voice in the story, yet he does not say very much. What is his role in the narrative?

Essay Ideas

1. Jekyll is the cause of his own downfall and this story fits in the category of 'classical tragedy'. Discuss.

2. "Jekyll and Hyde" is a story written by a man about men together. Examine the ways in which the story excludes women. How does this represent the society if late-nineteenth century London?

3. The city seems to play as large a part in the story as any of the individual characters. To what extent is this a story about urban life?

4. Although the story is set in London, Stevenson is thought of as a particularly Scottish writer. How is this reflected in "Jekyll and Hyde?"

5. Stevenson destroyed his first draft of the story in order to rewrite it as an allegory. What is the allegory in the story and how well do you think Stevenson brings it out?

The Subtle Knife

by Philip Pullman

"Anything that was associated with human workmanship and human thought was surrounded by Shadows . . . There was a cut-off point about thirty, forty thousand years ago. Before that, no Shadows. After that, plenty. And that's about the time, apparently, that modern human beings first appeared."

The Subtle Knife

Content Synopsis

The first book of this trilogy, "The Golden Compass," left its heroine, Lyra Belacqua, about to follow her father into the Northern Lights (the Aurora Borealis), from one universe to another, in her search for the mysterious Dust particles that she believes are good, and her father wishes to destroy. "The Subtle Knife" opens in our own universe, in Winchester, in the south east of England, as twelve year-old Will Parry is delivering his mother Elaine to the best safe haven he can think of, the home of Mrs. Cooper, his piano teacher. Since she was left alone with Will when her husband, John Parry, disappeared on an expedition to Alaska, Elaine Parry is distracted, confused, and afraid. For years, she

has believed that unnamed enemies are tracking her down. Believing her to be suffering from mental illness, Will has looked after her since he was seven, protecting her from inquisitive neighbors, police, and social services, determined to keep the family together. They made her fears a game. However, when men came to question her, and searched the house, Will realized that it was not a game.

Having left his mother in Mrs. Cooper's puzzled but kindly care, Will goes home and systematically searches the house for a writing case containing his father's letters, accompanied only by Moxie, his cat. Exhausted, he falls asleep in the early hours of morning and wakes a few hours later, knowing not only where the case is, but also that two men have broken in. Will retrieves the case, and as one of the men enters the room, attacks him. The man trips over Moxie, falls down the stairs, and crashes against the hall table. Will runs out, and by the following night, he has reached Oxford, forty miles away. In the suburbs, heading north, pausing to befriend a cat, he sees her suddenly disappear, and he follows her through a "window" opening into another world.

Will finds himself in the warm Mediterranean-like night of a harbor town with cafés, bars, hotels, and houses, all silent and apparently entirely empty. Looking for food, he explores a small restaurant and encounters Lyra and her demon, Pantalaimon. After mutual shock and initial suspicion, they team up. They discover that the town they are in is not entirely deserted—some children remain, who tell them that it is called Citàgazze and that its adult inhabitants have been attacked by "Specters." Specters are invisible to children and have no interest in them, but cluster around adults and drain them like spirit vampires, leaving a living, but empty, husk. They agree to cross back though the window because Lyra learns it leads to Oxford, where she will finds scholars who can tell them more about both the linked universes and Dust.

In Oxford, Will learns a little more about his father. John Parry's hunt for an "anomaly" led him to one of the windows to other worlds, but the alleged academics on the expedition with him were not all that they seemed. Powerful forces in his own world were after the same thing, and are now after Parry's wife to find out whether he told her the gateway's location. Lyra reads the alethiometer, the truth-telling device she was given in "The Golden Compass," and is told both where to find a scholar who will tell her about Dust, and direct her to help Will to find his father. The scholar, Dr. Mary Malone, is studying what she thinks of as "dark matter," but her research is running out of funding. She has discovered the existence of something she calls "shadow particles." She tells Lyra that these are "particles of consciousness." Lyra realizes that these are what her world calls Dust.

In Lyra's world, Lee Scoresby, a Texan hot-air balloonist, and Serafina Pekkala, a witch queen and her clan, are searching for Lyra. The witches enter the world of Citàgazze and learn about the existence of both Specters and angels. The angels take one of the witches to the world to which Lord Asriel crossed at the end of "The Golden Compass," and where he is building a citadel and collecting an army. Stanislaus Grumman, now a revered shaman of a Tartar tribe in Lyra's world, asks Scoresby to fly him north to the gateway Asriel has opened. He wants to find and take to Asriel the bearer of

the Subtle Knife. Scoresby agrees, provided that Parry "will use the Subtle Knife to help Lyra." The Subtle Knife is a powerful and dangerous tool for which many would give fortunes, and others would kill. One edge of the Subtle Knife will cut though any material in the world—the other will cut an opening out of the world into others.

In Will's Oxford, the alethiometer is stolen by an elderly man, Sir Charles Latrom. When Lyra and Will go to get it back, Will notices that although he pretends to come from this world, Sir Charles has a concealed demon. Sir Charles promises to give back the alethiometer in exchange for something in the possession of a man living in the Torre degli Angeli (Tower of Angels) in Citàgazze— the Subtle Knife. The two return to the city of Specters. In a tower, the children find an old man, Giacomo Paradisi, bound and beaten by a young man who has stolen the Subtle Knife. The young man attacks Lyra and Will. In the fight, Will is hurt, losing two fingers of his left hand, but getting the Subtle Knife. The young man flees the tower and is attacked and drained by Specters. It becomes clear that, knowing he was reaching adulthood, he was trying to use the Subtle Knife to cut his way out of that world. Paradisi tells Will that he is now the new bearer, and shows Will his own left hand, from which the Subtle Knife had cut two fingers, making its mark. Will must learn to feel for the other universes that the Subtle Knife can open with his mind, and must follow the rules of the Guild that made the Subtle Knife: never open a gateway without closing it, never allow anyone else to use the Subtle Knife, and never use it for a "base" purpose.

Will and Lyra return to Will's Oxford to retrieve the alethiometer, and find Lyra's mother, the ruthless Mrs. Coulter, arriving with Sir Charles. Unaware that her mother, or the Church she works for, had discovered the gateways between worlds, Lyra is horrified. Then she remembers where she has seen Sir Charles before. In his own world, he is called Lord Boreal. In spite of Mrs. Coulter's vicious demon, the children escape with the alethiometer back into Cittàgazze. They are not out of danger, however. Will is losing blood. They are attacked by a mob of children led by the brother and sister of the young man who fought Will and was drained by Specters. Just in time, the witches arrive and drive away the mob. They weave a powerful spell to heal Will's wound, but it is only temporarily successful.

In our world, Sir Charles visits Dr. Malone, and issues barely veiled threats to close down her lab if she doesn't hand over her findings, and Lyra, to him. Working against time, Dr. Malone tries to contact the Shadow particles/Dust, and finds that she can communicate with them through the equipment she has been using in her research. When she asks "But what are you?" the reply is "Angels" (260). Angels are structures or "complexifications" of Shadow-particles/Dust. They tell Dr. Malone that they interfered with human evolution in order to seek vengeance. Dr. Malone guesses: "Vengeance for—oh! Rebel angels! After the war in Heaven—Satan and the Garden of Eden—but it isn't true, is it? Is that what you—but why?" (261) she is told, "Find the girl and the boy. Waste no more time. You must play the serpent." She destroys the equipment and, as instructed, goes to the gateway.

In Cittàgazze, three parties are converging—Lyra and Will with the witches, Lee Scoresby with John Parry, and Lord Boreal/Sir Charles with Mrs. Coulter. Scoresby and Parry are attacked by zeppelins. The shaman magically destroys three but has no more strength left to bring down the fourth. In a shoot-out, Scoresby is killed. Before Mrs. Coulter kills Lord Boreal, she finds out he has been seeking the Subtle Knife: "Some people call it "teleutaia makhaira," the last knife of all. Others call it æsahættr" (326). Earlier, Serafina Pekkala has said that the word æsahættr can mean "god-destroyer." Mrs. Coulter makes a witch tell her the truth about Lyra, learning that "She will be the mother—she will be life—mother—she will disobey [. . .] Eve! Mother of all! Eve, again! Mother Eve!" (328). In pain from his wound, Will leaves the witches' campfire, and is grabbed by an unseen assailant. They fight, and Will overcomes his opponent. Realizing Will is the bearer of the Subtle Knife, he smears healing blood-moss on to the stumps of his fingers. He tells Will that a great war is coming, the second such war: "We've had nothing but lies and propaganda and cruelty and deceit for all the thousands of years of human history. It's time we started again, but properly this time" (334). The Subtle Knife, he explains, is the one weapon in all the universes that can defeat "the tyrant. The Authority. God." Will must take it to Lord Asriel. During the last war, the man explains, the "rebel angels fell because they didn't have anything like the knife." When the two see each other properly for the first time, Will realizes that the man is his father. In the same moment, John Parry dies, shot by the witch whose love he had refused in order to stay faithful to his wife. Will returns to the gully where he had left Lyra, and finds two figures—angels. Lyra is gone, and the witches guarding her have been attacked by Specters. The angels tell Will that he must go with them to Lord Asriel, but Will, overcome by the knowledge that Lyra has been captured, does not hear them.

Historical Context

The scenes in Winchester and Oxford show that the story is set in our own time, though other universes are not necessarily synchronized to this one. Cittàgazze, as Will notices, seems to be old-fashioned, though modern enough to have refrigerators, canned food, and soda. Writing in the *Sunday Times*, critic Peter Kemp notes the "teasing" setting of "The Subtle Knife" in our own world and time. In "The Golden Compass," he finds that "[s]uspense, surprise and eerie poetry coalesce into a terrific tale flickering with allegoric significance, (it's no accident that Lyra's most valuable possession is a device for deciphering symbols) but "The Subtle Knife" opens as though it were a contrasting kind of fiction: in the real world of today, 12-year-old Will, sturdy and sensible, worries about how to help his ill, depressive mother. However, what follows: "has all the narrative excitement and ingenuity you'd expect from Pullman [. . .] Marvels and monsters, tragedies and triumphs are unrolled with a lavishness typical of this prodigiously gifted author" (11).

Societal Context

In "The Golden Compass," Lyra discovers the hideous purpose of the church's General Oblation Board: to learn more about the nature of Dust and its relationship to children by "intercision," severing children from their demons. The child Lyra meets, who has been put through this process, is less than half a person. Half dead when Lyra finds him, he dies, but working at the Board's Arctic experimental station are adults who have undergone the process and survived. They are unfeeling, unimaginative, and unquestioningly obedient, and their demons are similarly docile and dull. In "The Subtle Knife," we encounter other kinds of half-death brought about by different causes. Will's mother has been driven out of her mind by anxiety for her husband and fears for the safety of herself and her son. She has periods of mental instability in which she cannot function as a full person. In Citàgazze, the Specters drain the spark of life from their victims and leave them without interest, curiosity, or volition. Even when it is a world of children, ignorance, false knowledge and superstition breed cruelty and violence. Lyra is appalled to find that children could be capable of tormenting and trying to kill a harmless cat, and that they become a mob intent on murder. Each society is in its way flawed and dysfunctional. In Lyra's society, the Church seeks to repress intellectual curiosity and knowledge in order to support the power of The Authority and therefore of itself. In Citàgazze, the Guild's quest for knowledge, and perhaps the power that knowledge would bring, has brought about a catastrophe that will mean the end of that

society. In Will's society, other authorities (Special Branch and agents of various governments) seek knowledge of the other worlds for, we infer, their own dubious purposes.

Lyra and Will have only a short time together, but each learns something about his or her own society from learning about the other's. Will is shocked to learn that gender roles are so rigidly fixed in Lyra's world that it is inconceivable to her that she could wear trousers. Lyra learns that Will's world has many easily available pleasures such as hamburgers and films, but also that its people have no demons, and reflects that they must be terribly lonely. The reader learns more about the society of the witches, who own no possessions, will give anything another witch needs without question, and love one another like sisters, yet whose clans are divided by politics. Though they can feel cold, they do not mind it because with the chill of the upper air comes the joy of experiencing the sky and the stars. Repeatedly, the trilogy emphasizes the futility of life half-lived, and the importance to both the individual and society as a whole of retaining a child-like curiosity, and zest for life.

Religious Context

"The Subtle Knife" continues the themes of "The Golden Compass." It explains further the significance of the quotation from John Milton's "Paradise Lost" used as an epigraph to the first volume. Several characters refer to the god of Lyra's world as "The Authority" and we hear of a war in Heaven in which the ancient, but un-aging, angels we meet had fought. If the outlook of Pullman's narrative voice is closer to that of his other major source, Blake, then he is "of the devil's party," that is, against blind obedience to the figure of a patriarchal god, or to the church that exercises power in that god's name. In Blake's writing and engravings, the characters who challenge god or the church, or authority represent humanity's curiosity, imagination, independence of will, and daring. If Lord Asriel is to lead the forces of opposition against the Authority, then he is like Blake's Satan, and the champion of humanity. The witch tortured by Mrs. Coulter reveals that Lyra is to be a new Eve—she will "disobey." Dr. Malone is told that she must be the serpent. The elements are gathered for the story of the fall.

Beppie Keane finds that the trilogy is concerned with "resisting existing social codes and practices, particularly those linked with the practice of organized religion," Pullman's secular humanist story "strives to recuperate [. . .] mythical Judeo-Christian figures traditionally associated with 'evil'" (such as Lord Asriel, the "Satan" figure in the stories, and the "Eve" figure of Lyra), and does so in a way different from and more daring than other recent writing for children and young adults. Pullman's writing, "assigns a defining role to the resistance of conservative social practices," and puts secular humanist texts in opposition to the teachings of religions such as Judeo-Christianity (50).

Interestingly, Pullman's writing seems to have sent readers back to Milton's, and Oxford University Press' "Paradise Lost" includes a general introduction and introductions to each book by Philip Pullman.

Scientific & Technological Context

Lyra's world, measured in terms of technology, seems to be in an earlier period than our own, but not one for which we have an exact parallel. There are no refrigerators, computers, cinemas, televisions, or automobiles. There are, however, electric ("Anbaric") power and gas-engine boats, and knowledge of magnetic fields, firearms, archaeology, and geology. Science and technology are both relatively sophisticated, though they co-exist with magic powers such as the witches' spells, but they are forced to work within the confines of approved theology and to further the interests of the church, and scientists are subject to persecution for heresy if they forget either.

Biographical Context

Philip Pullman studied English at Exeter College, Oxford, on which he loosely based his Jordan College. While he was writing the trilogy, he was living in Oxford, working in a shed at the back of his garden. Before becoming a full-time writer, he was a schoolteacher for a number of years and later taught trainee teachers at Westminster College in Oxford. He was, therefore, very well acquainted with contemporary and classic children's literature before he began writing it. He has been the awarded several prizes, including the Carnegie Medal, the Guardian Children's Book Award, the Astrid Lindgren Award (with illustrator Ryoji Arai), the *Publishers' Weekly* Best Book of the Year Award, and the Whitbread Book of the Year Award (for "The Amber Spyglass," the third in the "His Dark Materials" trilogy). This was the first instance of that prize going to a book classified as for children (though read by many adults). Pullman produced illustrations for the first two volumes of the trilogy and small pictures as running heads for the second, to indicate which world the characters are in at the time. These were not printed in the first US editions of the novels, but are present in the 2002 editions published by Knopf.

Sandie Byrne

Works Cited

Gribbin, Mary and John Gribbin, *The Science of Philip Pullman's His Dark Materials.* New York: Knopf, 2005.

Keane, Beppie. "Of the postmodernists' party without knowing it: Philip Pullman, hypermorality and metanarratives" in *Explorations into Children's Literature*. Thompson Gale. Vol. 15 (1 March 2005) 50–9.

Kemp, Peter. "Master of his Universe." Books Section, *The Sunday Times* (19 October 1997) 11.

Milton, John, *Paradise Lost, introduced by Philip Pullman*. New York: Oxford University Press, 2005.

Pullman, Philip. *The Subtle Knife*. London: Scholastic, 1997; Reprint 1998.

Discussion Questions

1. When Lyra first meets Will, she is hostile and afraid. What reassures her about him and why does this seem strange to the reader?

2. Does Lyra change in personality as well as appearance from the girl we first encounter in "The Golden Compass?"

3. Both Will and Lyra are deeply suspicious of Sir Charles (Lord Boreal) because of his appearance, his car, his house, and his possessions. What does that tell us about their attitude about money and class?

4. In what ways does Hester, Lee Scoresby's demon, differ from Pan, and what does this tell us about the characters of demons?

5. Is John Parry, Will's lost father, the kind of person we expect from what we learn of him in our own world—his military background, his career as an explorer, and his letters to his wife?

6. A number of characters in the novel, even sympathetic characters, die, and one of the two central protagonists kills a man. How surprising is that in a series often classified as children's fiction?

7. Does it seem strange that while Lyra is self-sufficient enough to endure the journey to Svalbardto escape from Mrs. Coulter and the experimental station, and to lead the children across the arctic, she doesn't know how, and doesn't want to know how, to cook, clean the dishes, or wash her own hair?

8. What is the significance of Dr. Malone having been a nun as well as a scientist?

9. Why is Lyra so upset when she first comes to the Oxford of Will's world?

10. By the end of the novel, do we have any idea of where the story is likely to go from here?

Essay Ideas

1. Lyra is the vocalizer of "The Golden Compass." The reader sees almost everything through her eyes and empathizes or even identifies with her through a long series of adventures. At the end of the novel, we leave her following her father across the bridge he has created between worlds. Discuss the effect of "The Subtle Knife's" opening on our own world seen through the eyes of a new protagonist.

2. How does Philip Pullman create "cliff-hangers" in the episodes of "The Subtle Knife" and to what extent does the novel have a "cliff-hanger" ending?

3. "The Subtle Knife" cuts between several different worlds and plot-streams. How does Pullman enable his readers to keep track of when and where they are, and how well are the strands of the story interwoven?

4. A number of critics have compared Philip Pullman's writing in the "His Dark Materials" series to that of Tolkien. How useful is that comparison?

5. Compare Pullman's descriptions of his angels with the figures in illustrations of his own poems by William Blake.

Tom Jones

by Henry Fielding

Content Synopsis

Henry Fielding published "Tom Jones" in 1749, as a 'comic epic in prose,' i.e. a concave pattern of the hero's fortunes changing from ordinary to low, and eventually to high fortune. The definition also involves a journey undertaken by the hero, which ends with marriage.

The novel begins with Squire Allworthy, who lives in Somerset with his seemingly priggish sister Bridget. Allworthy has been away for about four months from home on work. On the evening of his return, he finds a small baby wrapped up and lying in his bed. The Squire's sister Bridget, and her maid Mrs. Deborah Wilkins, suspect that the schoolmaster Partridge and his wife's maid Jenny Jones are the parents of this baby. They subsequently give a long harangue against the sexual waywardness of lower class women. Jenny admits to the crime later but refuses to name the father, and Squire Allworthy adopts the infant, naming him Tom Jones.

Jenny and Partridge soon leave the neighborhood after this incident. A few years later Bridget marries Captain Blifil, whose actual interest lies not in Bridget, but in her money. However, Captain Blifil soon dies, leaving their only child, a son who is also named Blifil. The junior Blifil and Tom are brought up and educated together in Squire Allworthy's household. The two boys share little in common: Blifil is self-righteous, hypocritical, and manipulative; Tom is a happy-go-lucky fellow, with generosity of heart and one who is often irresponsible and forgetful. Their mean-minded teachers, Thwackum and Square, prefer the well-mannered Blifil to the reckless Tom.

Though Tom is brought up as a gentleman, he is an illegitimate child, a 'bastard' with no recourse to money. According to popular belief at the time, being conceived in passion, and not in cold matrimonial beds, bastards were supposedly more sexually vigorous, and more passionate by nature.

Tom falls in love with the sweet and gentle Sophia, the neighboring Squire Western's daughter. Sophia begins to like Tom. However, in spite of his love for Sophia, Tom engages his attentions with Molly Seagrim, the gamekeeper's daughter. He is even mistakenly said to be the cause of Molly's pregnancy. Sophia's father and her aunt misunderstand Sophia and prefer the young Blifil for her marriage. Meanwhile many false reports against Tom make him lose Allworthy's favor and he is forced to leave home, giving up his hopes of marrying Sophia. In an ungrateful moment, Molly's father, who is known as Black George, steals the money given to Tom by Allworthy as a parting gift.

Once on the road, Tom decides to go to the sea. On his way, he meets The Redcoats, the army against the Jacobite rebellion and he abandons his plans. By chance, he meets Partridge, his supposed father, now a barber-surgeon. In another consequent adventure, Tom rescues Mrs. Waters, a physically attractive woman being waylaid, and he eventually goes to bed with her at the inn of Upton.

Meanwhile Sophia, rebels against her father's choice of Blifil, and starts on her own with her maid Honor looking for Tom on her way to London. Unfortunately, she comes to Upton Inn, and discovers Tom in bed with Mrs. Waters. Tom, devastated, pursues Sophia to London.

In London, Sophia boards with her kin Lady Bellaston. Much older than Tom or Sophia, this dangerously manipulative lady coerces Tom to have a sexual relationship with herself. She even gives him £50. She then advises her friend Lord Fellamar to violate Sophia so that she will agree to marry him, thus allowing him access to her wealth. Fortunately, Squire Western arrives to save his daughter. Meanwhile, Partridge reveals to Tom that Mrs. Waters is Jenny Jones, Tom's supposed mother. Tom's fortune at this point is at its lowest. He has lost Sophia, has possibly slept with his own mother, and is in an unhealthy relationship with Lady Bellaston.

However, at this point the reversal begins. Jenny confesses that Bridget Allworthy is Tom's real mother, and Jenny Jones has been paid to act the part. Blifil had been aware of this since reading his mother's deathbed letter. A letter from Squire Western also brings Allworthy to London, who is now aware of Blifil's sustained machinations against Tom since childhood. Tom is established as being Bridget's son (though illegitimate), and he is therefore related to Allworthy by blood as his nephew. Fielding hints that Tom is also a possible heir to Allworthy's estate, Paradise Hall, as Allworthy has never married. Allworthy now rekindles his love for Tom and repents for having ever doubted him. Tom apologizes to Sophia for his sexual infidelities and Sophia forgives him. Tom proposes to Sophia who accepts his proposal, and Squire Western is indeed happy with the match. Tom forgives all, which is the consistent hallmark of his character.

Fielding's organization of the plot is meticulous. The eighteen books are thematically divided into three sections. Each section (of six books), is dedicated to events in the country, road, and London. The events at the Upton Inn form the center of the novel. In the first half, Sophia pursues Tom. In the second, Tom pursues Sophia. On either side, there is a tale: in the first half, the man-of-the-hill tale, and the other—Mrs. Fitzpatrick's tale. Counterpoints are provided to compare and contrast each character. Tom contrasts with Blifil, Sophia with Molly, and Mrs. Deborah Wilkins with Sophia's maid of honor.

Fielding's "fictionality," or the fact that he is always drawing attention that it is a story, and not real life, emerges in his relationship with his reader in the novel. Fielding's addresses to his reader are constantly present in the novel in the form of comment, intrusions, and suspense. The chapters are always pre-judged by him as 'common' 'grave' 'surprising', 'low', etcetera. Fielding's long digressions from the main storyline might seem like obstacles, but critics point out that the narrator's voice is as much part of the plot as Tom is. It is the narrator's voice that helps keep surprises, and keep the reader from knowing the truth, such as Tom's parentage. In this sense, the narration is 'ironical'—seemingly saying one thing, but actually referring to something other than the apparent.

Fielding's characters are flat characters, and their names may be said to derive from a 'ruling passion', or a type. Thus Allworthy is indicative to be 'all worthy,' and Sophia to mean wisdom. The types can fall into black or white characters, good or bad. The complexity of the characters themselves is limited.

Historical Context

Fielding was a political man, and historical events of the day contributed significantly to his novel, in spite of his constant reminder to the readers that it is only a story. The historical situation has connections since the last century. The Stuart King James II was Catholic and was overthrown in the 'glorious revolution' (1688). His Protestant daughter, along with her husband William, was invited over to rule. Neither Mary nor her sister and successor as queen, Anne, left any heirs. After Queen Anne's death in 1714, George I was brought over from Hanover to rule England. He was brought in through an indirect succession on the sole reason that he was of Protestant faith. He was succeeded by George II subsequently.

Meanwhile, James II of the Stuart line, who had fled to France after the "glorious revolution," had a son, and later a grandchild who came to be known historically as "the Old Pretender," and "the Young Pretender" respectively. They were thus named as both of them 'pretended' to monarchical claims being in direct descent from the Stuart line—but never ruled.

In 1745, "Young Pretender" Charles Edward mobilized Highlanders, and with the implicit support of the French, organized the Jacobite Rising (Jacob, the Latin of James, suggesting Catholic), with claims of a direct descent for monarchy. Many British people had support for the Stuarts. However, though the rising advanced as close as the south of England, it failed. The 1745 Catholic rising was a common topic of discussion regarding claims to monarchy, and a concern with divine rights of kinship—undermined by the Bill of Rights (1689) and Act of Settlement (1701) which upheld the supremacy of the Parliament over the monarch.

"Tom Jones" is thematically connected with this historical issue, concerning itself with birth and legitimacy. There is also a connection between Rebellion and the claim to the seat of power or wealth. Tom is of the right lineage being Allworthy's nephew, though throughout the novel Tom remains a bastard, and there is no discovery about a secret marriage between Bridget and her lover. Fielding's discussion of politics also emerges in small instances of conversation in the novel. Squire Western's sister is Hanoverian, while Squire Western toasts "the king over the waters"—James II having fled to France in legend.

References to historical situation are more direct in Tom's meeting the Redcoats (soldiers marching to Scotland to defeat the rebellion). Partridge is a Jacobite, and he mistakenly thinks that Tom is on the way to support the Young Pretender. In the story of the man-of-the-Hill, the man supported Monmouth's rebellious army against James II's accession; and Tom steadfastly supports the Constitution in his conversation with him.

Fielding also makes his political position clear in his narrative mode, saying, "I am . . . the Founder of a new province of Writing . . . . Readers, whom as I consider as my subjects are bound to believe in and obey . . . I am, indeed set over them for their own Good only, and was Created for their Use, and not they for mine" (68). Fielding would not support the historical issue of divine rights and lineage.

The eighteenth century was the heyday of imperialism. It was not only a matter of trade, but it was also a matter of survival of the fittest with rivals such the French, Dutch, and Portuguese. England was thinly populated compared to its rival nations, and needed a powerful Navy not just for the frequent wars, but also for its imperial aggression. Tom is forced to join the navy, a common occurrence in the times. Earlier Tom plans to go to sea, and he starts for Bristol, as it is from Bristol that a substantial number of imperial and slaving ships started their voyage from this port.

Societal Context

Eighteenth-century England was hardly a stable society. Many revolutions, direct and indirect, affected its people. Eighteenth century novels famously portray a mingling of classes, aristocracy and the new trading middle classes. In these novels, women enjoy better validation, even though they still lived under restrictive conditions. Commercially, and with imperialistic trade, England's markets were flooded with foreign goods. In the contemporary literature, leisure and luxury are both celebrated and denigrated. The eighteenth century newspapers, printed in London, and other cities, made a connection between the rural and the urban, and gave the sense of a new patriotism.

Women lead restricted lives in the eighteenth century. They were barred from education and opportunities. A woman lost her rights to money and property to her husband after her marriage. The law stated, "By marriage the very being or legal existence of a woman is suspended" (Colley, 238). Thus, Captain Blifil marries Bridget for money; and Lady Bellaston advises Lord Fellamar to rape Sophia, so that he can marry her later "to make amends." Fielding's portrayals of women are stereotyped. Sophia is sweet, feminine, and kind, represented in synecdoche by a feminine item of adornment, her muff. She forgives Tom's various infidelities by a sweet moral instruction. Bridget is called an "old maid," though not truthfully. Lady Bellaston, the lady with money and power is represented as the manipulative lady, with insatiable sexual appetite and bad breath. Conduct literature of the times is replete with instructions to adhere to the private sphere of life and to maintain female domesticity, chastity, and passivity.

With women living under restrictive roles, bearing children out of wedlock was enough to reduce a woman to "ruin" and prostitution. The illegitimate child was a responsibility of the parish, as Mrs. Wilkins mentions (35). Interestingly, a whole host of hospitals and orphanages came up during this century, including the first lying-in hospital at St. James's Infirmary (1739), The Foundling Hospital (1741) and, The Dispensary for the sick poor

in Holborn (1769)—the first children's dispensary in Europe. Linda Colley points out that this had also to do with producing the nation's canon fodder for wars, as England had much less population than France or Spain.

The moral tide against single mothers was vehement. As Mrs. Wilkins suggested to Squire Allworthy: " . . . take up the hussy its mother…and I should be glad to see her committed to Bridewell and whipp'd at the cart's tail. Indeed such wicked sluts cannot be too severely punished." The illegitimate children themselves were disowned by society. Briget's husband, Captain Blifil objected Tom's being brought up with his son. He reminded Allworthy that "tho' the Law did not positively allow the destroying such base born children, yet it held them the children of no body; that the church considered them as the children of no body; and at best, they ought to be brought up to the lowest and vilest offices of the Commonwealth". Contemporary law books described the bastard as being, "he that is born out of marriage. He shall never inherit or be heir to anyone . . . in law he is 'Quasi nullius Fillius,' and no Man's issue." He is also quoted to be sometimes "fillius populi"—'son of the people. Homer Obed Brown remarks that Tom's being " 'fillius nullius'—son of no one-or 'fillius populi'—son of the people—would seem to support the now common notion of Tom as a novelized version of the allegorical Everyman" (203). It is important to remember that though Tom is rewarded with good birth towards conclusion, he remains being born out of wedlock until the end.

Though Fielding wrote in the 'popular' genre of the novel, his sympathies were with the ruling class. He exhibits his preference of high classicism and Augustan values through his usage of the form and content. The form of his novels suggests a highly developed classical architecture highlighting balance and regularity. The theme of the novel, which deals with 'history of a foundling' does not empower figure of the 'bastard' in its scheme. In

"Tom Jones," the history of a 'foundling', he does not empower the figure of the bastard in the scheme of the novel. By a fictionally contrived ending, he makes Tom an insider - by birth. Tom does not earn the rewards in the practical sense; he is merely rewarded by the novelist.

Religious Context

England was united with Wales and Scotland by the Act of Union in 1707. The defining feature of this act purported that it was that a Protestant King now ruled the "United Kingdom." England's religious situation in the eighteenth century was dominated by the interaction between Catholicism and Protestantism, both inside and outside the country. It was also influenced by the various subgroups within Protestantism, such as Anglicans and Protestant non- conformists, Presbyterians and Episcopalians in Scotland, and Congregationalists, Baptists, Quakers, and Methodists.

The threat of Catholicism came from England's Catholic enemy nation, France, with whom England had intermittent wars throughout the century. Scotland was also suspect as Jacobite risings gained strength with Scottish Highlanders in 1708, 1715, and 1745. Several patriotic ideologies, such as freedom and masculinity were in opposition with French Catholicism. Britain was 'free' and masculine' as opposed France with its despotic ruler, fashion, and 'effeminacy'. In "Tom Jones," there are several reminders that it supports "the glorious cause of liberty and of the Protestant religion" (321). Tom ticks off Partridge's discussion of "Popish" prophesies by saying, "With what stuff and nonsense hast thou filled thy head? This too, I suppose, comes from the Popish Priest" (381), and does not support the Catholic uprising.

Fear and hatred for Catholics were fueled by sixteenth century texts such as John Foxe's "Book of Martyrs," which graphically described Protestants tortured at the hand of Catholics through the ages. This text with provocative illustrations was kept along with the Bible in many an eighteenth-century church. Catholics in England were denied many rights such as formal education, freedom of worship, or possession of firearms. The Act of Settlement (1701) prohibited anyone Catholic, or married to a Catholic "forever incapable to inherit, possessor enjoy the crown and government of this realm', a law that still stands" (Colley 46). Catholics were barred from owning any property near the city of London. They were persecuted and were held responsible for everything that went wrong, and rumors fanned the fire of hatred.

Though Fielding supported Protestantism, in "Tom Jones" we do not see any denigration of Catholics. Partridge is not portrayed maliciously, if only as a little queer and superstitious. Hypocrisy in Christianity is virulently attacked. Deborah, the maid, says of the infant Tom, "Faugh, how it stinks! It doth not smell like a Christian" (35). She suggests Mr. Allworthy leave it at the churchwarden's door, " it is a good night, and if it is wrapped up and put in a warm basket, it is two to one but it lives till it is found in the morning"(35) discharging her Christian duties. The overtly materialistic Captain Blifil is "well read in scriptures" (69). The "pious" Blifil quotes the Bible, and yet is shown to be evil. The Reverend Mr. Thwackum is rigid, cruel, and self-seeking. In contrast, Tom does not quote the Bible, but is always generous, good, willing to forgive, and truly repentant. Fielding's portrayals of religious people are suspect and overtly negative, and directly contrasted with the less religious and good at heart.

Scientific & Technological Context

The eighteenth century is referred to as the "Enlightenment," and the time of the origin of the science of man, the "new Man"—referring to its scientific, philosophic, and rational thoughts. This "scientific revolution" of the early modern period especially thrived on Isaac Newton's discovery of theories of gravity and light: "Philosophiae

Naturalis Principia Mathematica" (1687), "Opticks" (1704), and "Arithmetica Universalis" (1707). Newton, popularized and circulated by writers like Pemberton, captured the imagination of the day by demonstrating the apparent orderliness of a vast universe. As science was not a segregated discipline in those days, philosophy, science, and arts were in close contact. Thus, Descartes, Newton, and the German mathematician Leibnitz were all philosophers as well as mathematicians.

The Royal Society (founded in 1662) had individuals who contributed to science, but as an institution, it was not very effective. Writers like Swift and Pope made oblique criticisms of the Society. Fielding himself published "Some Papers Proper" to be read before the Royal Society concerning Chrysipus, Golden-Foot or Guinea, collected by Petrus Gualterus, but not published till after his death in 1743, satirizing the ineffectuality of the institution.

Physician and philosopher John Locke (1632-1704) in his "Essay Concerning Human Understanding" (1690) stated the child's mind being a 'tabula rasa' or a blank slate—bereft of their godliness, and open to change and transformation. Locke accepted that most scientific writing proposed a harmonious wedding of science and religion. Robert Boyle (1627-91), formulated 'Boyle's Laws', and published on religion simultaneously. However, scientific temper and writing successfully diffused the earlier metaphysical tradition in religion and thought.

It was not out of the ordinary that Newton's friend, Desaguliers, insisted that mathematical discoveries of the "Principia" should be applied to all branches of human life. The scientific premise of cause and effect celebrated to reason in literature and society. This aspect deriving from Newtonian quantification can also be detected in "Tom Jones" in its impeccable structure. The ending especially conforms to Leibnitz's 'harmonious whole'—the idea of a hierarchical universe celebrating order and status quo,

rather than any change. The cause-and-effect philosophy is exemplified in "Tom Jones" as the ending is explained away in terms of facts superseding the overall tone of the novel. The scientific claim to objectivity, and the premise that science increases control over nature for the benefit of man, is adopted by the narrator's persona of the novel.

As an offshoot of scientific thought in the seventeenth century, reason was celebrated as the eighteenth-century ideal—the foundational quality that differentiated us from beasts. It was only toward the end of the eighteenth century that gentler feelings were recognized and validated, the Romantics in the nineteenth century highlighted spontaneity and feeling as the touchstone of their identity.

Biographical Context

"Tom Jones" by Henry Fielding (1707-1754) was published in 1749. It is one of the most influential of novelistic narration as Fielding was the first one to address his readers directly, and to temper their judgment and viewpoint. The theme of the 'bastard,' and legitimacy is, in many ways, connected to Fielding and his art. The novel itself was a 'bastard' genre with mixed parentage of the romance, epic, comedy, tragedy, journalism, and conduct literature. Fielding's parentage was also mixed, on his mother's side there were meritorious people who were even 'reputed' to be connected with dubious aristocracy. Henry's father was an army officer who settled in Somersetshire, much like Allworthy himself.

Henry was sent to Eton, when after being widowed his father re-married. At Eton, Henry enjoyed his classical studies, an aspect that shows itself in the meticulous classical structure of his novels. The bluestocking Lady Mary Wortley Montague was his cousin and she encouraged his literary gifts. Fielding turned a dramatist, and among others, "Love in Several Masques" was performed in Drury Lane theatre in 1728. He also went to Leiden in Germany to study classical literature.

Fielding came back to write some 25 dramas. However, his dramatic career came to a stall with the licensing Act of 1737.

He married in 1734 and both Sophia of "Tom Jones" and the eponymous heroine of his novel "Amelia" are based on his adored wife Charlotte's character. Fielding was drawn to novel writing by Richardson's "Pamela," whom he satirized in his spoof, "Shamela," and later going on to write "Joseph Andrews," the supposed brother of Pamela. Fielding mocked "Pamela's" hypocrisy and the same attack on hypocrisy and deceit can be seen in "Tom Jones." Fielding's sister Sarah Fielding also made a name for herself with her best-known work, "The Adventures of David Simple."

Though we know Fielding more for his novels today, his career had always been closely connected with politics. Fielding's dramatic works written early in his career had been political. Fielding had also edited "The True Patriot," for six months defending the Constitution and supporting the Hanoverian monarchy. He studied the law and made a living by his public office of a magistrate and was known for his honesty and willingness. He also wrote influential legal enquiries and pamphlets. Although he's not against giving the death sentence, Fielding wrote vigorously in favor of abolishing public hangings. The description of Tom's imminent hanging may have been connected with his ethical beliefs.

After the death of his wife, Fielding managed to impregnate his wife's maid and eventually married her causing a scandal. In Tom's fictional life, one is reminded of Molly Seagrim's pregnancy, and Tom's agreeing to stand by her.

Fielding died in Lisbon, after going to Portugal with his daughter and wife in hopes of recuperating his failing health. His "Journal of a Voyage to Lisbon" was published posthumously. The social and political issues raised in "Tom Jones" were a part of Fielding's life, not just as an observer but being there socially and professionally.

Suchitra Choudhury, Ph.D.

Works Cited

Brown, Homer Obed. Tom Jones: The "Bastard" of History, *Boundary* 2, Vol. 7, No. 2, (1979), 201–234.

Colley, Linda. *Britons: Forging the Nation 1707–1837*. New Haven and London: Yale University Press, 1992.

Fielding, Henry. *Tom Jones*. John Bender and Simon Stern, eds. Oxford: Oxford University Press, 1996.

Discussion Questions

1. In what ways are good and bad characters portrayed in Fielding's novel, "Tom Jones?" Are they 'flat' or multi-dimensional?
2. "Tom Jones" is narrated by a voice that unfolds the story to us. How far can we rely on this omniscient narrator? To what extent does he hide information from us?
3. "Tom Jones" provided us with several portrayals of servants. Discuss their relationship with their masters.
4. How far does Tom conform to the figure of the hero? On what grounds do you think he is fit to be a hero of a novel?
5. The ending of the novel has a lot to say on 'poetic justice,' as against its being closer to life. Comment on the ending of the novel.
6. The structure of "Tom Jones" is said to be perfect. Elaborate on the various themes and counter-themes that contribute to this balanced structure.
7. To what extent is sexual morality in "Tom Jones" indicative of 'character'?
8. What route does Tom follow in his journey? How is it connected with the people in the novel?
9. Discuss the system of "property marriages" as shown in the novel.
10. If you were the author of "Tom Jones," how would you end the novel, and why?

Essay Ideas

1. Compare the figure of the 'bastard' vs. the legitimate son in "Tom Jones," and any other literature you may have studied.
2. Analyze the narrative voice in the novel, and his persona.
3. Explore the literary technique of irony in Tom Jones.
4. Illustrate stereotypes of women evidenced through Bridget, Sophia, Molly, and Lady Bellaston's actions and speech.
5. Discuss the Jacobite Rebellion of 1745, and its connections with "Tom Jones."

The Unlit Lamp

by Radclyffe Hall

Content Synopsis

The novel opens with a portrait of the Ogden family living in the British seaside town of Seabourne. Colonel Ogden, although physically weakened by ill health, is the patriarch of the household, ruling over his wife, Mary Ogden, and their two daughters, Joan and Milly, aged 12 and 10, respectively. Joan and Milly are "poles apart in disposition" (11) and while Milly is her father's favorite, Mrs. Ogden relies on the support of Joan in her role as wife and mother.

Despite the family's financial difficulties, Mrs. Ogden insists that her children must be educated at home, in the tradition of her own ancestry. The Colonel consequently engages Elizabeth Rodney, the 26-year-old sister of the local solicitor, as governess. Orphaned at only one year old and brought up by her mother's cousin, Elizabeth is "obliged to study to earn her living" (39) when her guardian dies. Ralph, her older brother, was adopted by their Uncle John before the death of their parents. He invites Elizabeth to live with him in Seabourne following their Uncle's death. Elizabeth quickly becomes frustrated with life in Seabourne. Her only salvation is Joan, with whom she finds an immediate kinship. The relationship, which blossoms between Joan and Elizabeth, causes tension between Joan and Mrs. Ogden. While Mrs. Ogden is jealous of her daughter's friendship with Elizabeth, Elizabeth resents Mrs. Ogden for stifling Joan's potential. As the years pass, Joan herself begins to recognize that she is growing apart from Mrs. Ogden, and finds herself caught between her love for her mother and her love for Elizabeth.

The arrival of the Benson family in Seabourne intensifies Joan's desire to study. Her friendship with Richard Benson allows her access to his family library and the medical books that he studies. Like Elizabeth, Richard encourages Joan to go to Cambridge to study, while Mrs. Ogden becomes increasingly anxious about Joan's intellectual pursuits. When the Colonel's sister dies, she leaves her estate to Joan and Milly, giving Joan the opportunity to fund her own studies. Nevertheless, the opportunity is lost—Colonel Ogden, trustee of his daughters' inheritance until they come of age, reveals he has borrowed a substantial amount of money from the estate to meet his own medical costs. In an attempt to recover these funds, he makes an unsound investment in a mine in Rhodesia. The Colonel's death shortly afterwards leaves the family financially shaken, and his daughters are forced to abandon their hopes of independent scholarships.

Two years after the Colonel's death, Mrs. Ogden has become the hysterical grieving widow, even more emotionally dependent on Joan while also embracing a newfound religious favor. Elizabeth continues to tutor Joan in her studies, despite the fact she is no longer employed to do so, and puts their names down on a waiting list for a flat in Bloomsbury. However, Joan's plans to leave Seabourne are delayed once more when she discovers that Milly is having a secret affair with the local tradesman, Mr. Thompson. Joan convinces her mother that Milly must be sent away to London on her scholarship in order to end the affair and rescue her reputation. Joan remains at home to see to the needs of her mother and the household in the face of increasing financial pressure. Joan fears she is becoming a "fixture" at Seabourne, but refuses to leave. She rejects Richard Benson's repeated marriage proposals, and when the flat Elizabeth has reserved becomes available, Joan refuses to leave Seabourne. Elizabeth goes to London alone.

A year later, however, Elizabeth returns to Seabourne and to Joan, claiming she has "come back to wait with her a little while longer" (183) and the two become constant companions. Milly also returns to Seabourne due to illness and Joan stays to nurse her sister. Despite the family doctor's insistence that the condition is not serious, Joan fears that her sister has been misdiagnosed. Mrs. Ogden refuses to listen to Joan's concerns, and Milly eventually dies of consumption at the age of nineteen.

Following Milly's death, Mrs. Ogden strengthens her emotional hold on Joan. While outwardly accepting Joan's insistence that she is leaving Seabourne, Mrs. Ogden manipulates Joan into believing she cannot cope without her. On the day that Joan is to depart with Elizabeth, she decides she cannot leave her mother. Once again, Elizabeth departs alone, sending Joan one final letter informing her of her intention to marry Richard Benson's brother, Lawrence, and leave for South Africa. Joan never sees Elizabeth again.

The novel then moves forward 20 years. Still living in Seabourne and caring for her mother, Joan is bland and lifeless. She is now plagued with minor physical ailments and appears old before her time. Joan has abandoned her studies, having locked away the books she and Elizabeth studied. During their annual holiday in North Devon, Joan and her mother bump into Richard Benson, with whom Joan had lost contact many years previously. Joan has long given up on her dream of a medical profession. Richard, by contrast, is now an eminent surgeon on Harley Street. Richard informs Joan that Elizabeth is still in South Africa with Lawrence, devoting much of her time to charity work, and Joan mourns the loss of her former friend. She refuses Richard Benson's final marriage proposal and returns to Seabourne with her mother.

Mrs. Ogden is struck down by flu, and Joan is forced to sell the family's remaining investments to cover her medical costs. Shortly afterwards, Joan discovers Mrs. Ogden dead in her bed. Left with little over £50 a year, Joan must sell the family home and work for a living. Now 40 years old, troubled with varicose veins, and unqualified for any contemporary occupation, Joan finally leaves Seabourne to care for her mentally ill cousin, Rupert Routledge. Even with her mother gone, Joan is forced to live the same life, in a place, which is "Seabourne with a new name, with Cousin Rupert to take care of instead of her mother" (314).

Themes & Motifs
A lesbian subtext runs through "The Unlit Lamp." Joan is an unfeminine figure, "lanky as a boy" (11) and sporting a cropped haircut. The novel follows her relationship with Elizabeth, from pupil and tutor, to two women both stifled by the domestic sphere to which they are confined. Their affinity is such that they increasingly appear as two halves of the same whole. When Lawrence Benson tells Elizabeth she looks beautiful, she smiles "across at Joan, as though in some way Lawrence's

compliment concerned her" (207). Their friendship arouses an almost sexual jealousy in Mrs. Ogden as she declares "I'll tell [Joan] how I want her [. . .] that I can't, simply can't, live without her [. . .] [S]he knew that in her tormenting jealousy she might lose Joan altogether" (55). While lesbian desire is never consummated, or even made explicit, passions run high in Joan and Elizabeth's friendship. When Elizabeth writes to Joan to tell her she has left Seabourne forever, she writes with the pathos of a rejected lover—"I must go away from you, tear you out of me, forget you. You have had too much of me already" (259). The triangular relationship between the three central female characters creates problems with the patriarchal order.

This order is also destabilized by a crisis of masculinity in the text. Colonel Ogden may be "master of the house" (9) who "bullies" his wife and daughters (13), but his authority is undermined by his physical weakness. His death in the first half of the novel means there is an absence of a central patriarch for much of the story. Other men in the novel are similarly problematic in their relation to masculinity. Elizabeth's brother, Ralph, is a "confirmed bachelor" and a "sentimentalist" (40), and Joan's cousin, Rupert, is child-like in his mental incapacitation. The novel resists the conflation of man and masculine, woman and feminine, to unsettle gender conventions.

The potential transgression of these characters is countered in the text by the failure of Joan and Elizabeth to realize their independence. Both remain as fixtures in the domestic sphere: Elizabeth marries Lawrence Benson although she does not love him, and Joan is trapped as a nurse to her various ill relatives. The novel may pose many questions about the role of men and women, but it does not offer any easy answers.

Historical Context

Literature of the early twentieth-century was undoubtedly shadowed by the impact of World War One (1914–1918). As Susan R. Grayzel notes, the war "was the first European (and ultimately global) war of the modern era to demand the full participation of both combatants and non-combatants [. . .] with millions killed or injured directly or indirectly in the participant countries" (Grayzel 2). A war of this scale left an indelible mark on the psyche of all the participating countries.

"The Unlit Lamp" alludes to the major threat which war posed to the borders of Britain, both as a nation and Empire. Published in 1924, the beginning of the novel is set in the late 1880s. The text prefigures the upcoming war in its depiction of the British military class and the motif of Empire. The Ogden family had previously lived in India, but has left due to the Colonel's ill health. India's presence is still felt in the Ogden household with its furniture 'bleached by the suns of many Indian summers' (9). Colonel Ogden is 'authority personified', instructing his wife and his daughters in the running of the house, but his authority is undermined by the family's financial problems and the Colonel's own physical weakness. The Colonel belongs to an era of colonialism and military expansion, but this era is in decline. The club which is frequented by the Colonel is comprised of aging and retired military men such as Admiral Bourne and Major Boyle. Yet these men appear unable to let go of their earlier military lives. Admiral Bourne's house, the aptly named "Glory Point," has been constructed in homage to his Navy days, furnished and decorated as though it were a ship and described in nautical terms by the Admiral. By the end of the novel, however, the Empire is unable to sustain the class of men that embody it both literally and figuratively. Colonel Ogden eventually dies from the heart problems attributed to the time he spent in India, and his unsound investment in a mine in the British colony of Rhodesia, partially funded by Joan and Milly's inheritance, leaves the Ogden family struggling to make financial ends meet.

Societal Context

The early twentieth-century was a pivotal time for women in their struggle for emancipation. Diana Wallace describes how a new idea of citizenship emerged for women during wartime. Having to take over traditionally male occupations, while British men went off to fight, meant that women felt more liberated and were even more determined to establish their equality with men (Wallace 25–26). The Suffrage movement, which had begun in the late nineteenth century, had a partial respite when the government extended the vote to women over 30 (although women were not fully enfranchised until 1928). The new place for women in the public sphere meant that they became interested in gaining access to a university education. In the interwar years, however, there was an "anti-feminist backlash" (Wallace 26). The adaptation of women to their newfound role in industry, and the trauma of a bloody battle on the male psyche, led to anxieties about the emasculation of the social order. The high death rate of the war also meant that the 1920s faced a population imbalance, whereby the number of women in Britain was significantly higher than the number of men. The combination of these factors constructed an image of the single woman as not only a threat to masculinity, but also a threat to the nation itself.

Joan Ogden embodies this image of the threatening single woman: "I shall never marry anyone. I'm not a woman who could ever have married. I've never been what you'd call in love with a man in my life" (302). Shunning the conventions of society, Joan is doomed to be an outsider; the text repeatedly refers to her as 'queer' and her desire to be educated is constantly thwarted by her manipulative mother. While Mrs. Ogden has her own reasons for opposing Joan's desire to set up home with Elizabeth and go to University, she is also reflecting society's anxiety over women rejecting the domestic sphere for the public one of education and work. Joan herself recognizes how "unusual" this step is and rails against "that monster tyrant: 'the usual thing!'" (247). Joan's ultimate failure to oppose convention means she is forever confined to the domestic role, even after her mother's death.

Religious Context

After the death of Colonel Ogden, Mrs. Ogden turns to religion. Her faith becomes a new source of "emotional excitement" (180) and she embraces the rituals of Catholicism, becoming a "slave of small pious practices" (181). The text plays on Mrs. Ogden's devotion for comic effect, with Joan marveling at how her previously incapable mother manages to do the four-mile round trip to Sunday service. The supposed charity of her church is completely misguided and self-motivated:

> The poor of Seabourne were really non-existent; but since certain types of religiously minded people are not happy unless they find some class beneath them on whom to lavish unwelcome care, the churches of each denomination [. . .] invented deserving poor for themselves and visited them strenuously (272).

Religion becomes a way in which the boundaries of class are maintained It is Mrs. Ogden's endorsement of this kind of faith that brings her into conflict with her daughter, who refuses to attend Church services. Joan does not object to religion, but she does not "recognize Christ in this guise" (181). Hall was a devout Catholic, and through Joan, articulates her objection to the ways in which religion can be misappropriated. Following Victorian belief, Christianity at this time denounced homosexuality as a sin. Despite Hall's own sexual preference for women, she converted to Catholicism in her twenties, "undeterred by the Vatican's condemnation of same-sex love" (Souhami 48), and saw little contradiction in doing so.

Scientific & Technological Context

By the beginning of the twentieth century, new medical discourses on sex were emerging. The term "sexuality" came into usage in the late nineteenth century, and was brought into public consciousness by the advent of sexology, or the science of sex. Sexologists such as Richard von Krafft-Ebing and Havelock Ellis began to publish theories on the physiological drives that informed sexuality, attributing sexual preference to biology. Out of the field emerged the concept of "inversion," which defined homosexuality as an apparent malfunction in biological impulses where the object of sexual preference was of the same sex.

Building on the theories that sexology endorsed, psychoanalytic theory, led by Sigmund Freud, was established in the early part of the twentieth-century. The first international meeting of psychoanalysts was held in 1908 in Salzburg. Psychoanalysis began as a clinical practice that attempted to understand the psychic processes that informed sexuality. While Freud would later revise and refine his writings on sexuality as the twentieth-century progressed, his "Three Essays on the Theory of Sexuality" (1905) countered sexology's claim that homosexuality was 'innate' and a symptom of 'nervous degeneracy' by analyzing psychic drives. The core of Freudian thinking was rooted in the idea that sexuality developed in childhood and Freud argued that the mother was the first object of sexual desire for all children, regardless of gender.

"The Unlit Lamp" appears to be caught between these two different ideologies of sexuality. In some ways, Joan appears as a figure of inversion with her cropped hair and lack of femininity. However, the relationship between Joan and her mother relates to Freudian models. Mrs. Ogden manipulates Joan into offering her comfort and welcomes it "as if a lover held her" (13). However, Joan's relationship with Elizabeth brings her into conflict with her mother and incites jealousy. Joan recognizes the Freudian implications of growing apart from her mother 'She was terrified because she feared that if she did not love her mother, she might grow to love someone else instead [. . .] Here was a new and fruitful source of analysis; if she loved Elizabeth she could not love her mother' (68–9). Ultimately, Joan is unable to reconcile her love for her mother and her love for Elizabeth, and so remains with her mother, caring for her until her death.

Biographical Context

Radclyffe Hall was born Marguerite Radclyffe Hall in 1880. Her relationship with her family was troubled: her mother was violent and unpredictable, and her father mostly absent. She became virtually financially independent at the age of 18 when her father died, leaving his estate to her. Although she could not access the estate until she was 21, she was given a substantial allowance from it. Hall recognized her sexuality from a young age, often trying to kiss other girls. She confessed her lesbian tendencies to her mother, who labeled her "perverted" (Souhami 13). This did not discourage Hall from actively seducing other woman, and her lovers would later include Violet Hunt and Lady Una Troubridge, among others.

"The Unlit Lamp" was the first novel that Hall wrote but it was initially rejected by various publishers. After the success of her second novel, "The Forge" (1924), the publication of "The Unlit Lamp" quickly followed. The novel's characters read like figures from Hall's own life, with the manipulative and hysterical Mrs. Ogden reminiscent of Hall's own mother. The central figure, Joan Ogden, seems to be based on Hall herself; Joan and Elizabeth's plan to live in London reflects Hall's cohabitation with Una. However, Joan Ogden is a much more subtle figure than Hall's larger-than-life persona. Pictures of Hall show her as a masculine figure, a type that would later come to be identified as the mannish lesbian, dressed in suits and wearing a trademark monocle. In her adult life, she would insist on being called John. Souhami argues that Hall's inheritance meant that she could exert control over the mother that she had been afraid of as a child (Souhami 27). The financial difficulties that prevent Joan from leaving Seabourne render her a fictional version of the Radclyffe Hall who might have been, had her father not died and given her control of the family estate.

Hall courted controversy with "The Well of Loneliness" (1928), a novel that was famously banned following a trial for obscenity. The book tells of the emotional difficulties faced by the 'invert' Stephen Gordon, and was consciously written as a plea for tolerance and compassion. The work was defended by contemporaries such as Leonard and Virginia Woolf, and even Vera Brittain. The furor surrounding the book has meant that subsequent literary criticism has often seen Hall's pre-1928 fiction as a mere precursor to "The Well of Loneliness," and analysis of her other works of fiction has been rare by comparison. Hall was to publish seven novels in total, before her death in London on October 7, 1943.

Emma Sterry

Works Cited

Freud, Sigmund. "Three Essays on Sexuality". 1905. Sigmund Freud. Vol 7. *On Sexuality: Three Essays on Sexuality and Other Works*. Angela Richard, ed. Trans James Strachey. London: Penguin, 1991.

Grayzel, Susan R. *Women's Identities at war: Gender, Motherhood and Politics in Britain and France during the First World War.* Chapel Hill and London: The University of Carolina Press, 1999.

Hall, Radclyffe. *The Unlit Lamp.* 1924. London: Virago, 1981.

Souhami, Diana. *The Trials of Radclyffe Hall.* London: Virago, 1999.

Wallace, Diana. *The Women's Historical Novel: British Women Writers, 1900–2000.* Basingstoke and New York: Palgrave MacMillan, 2005.

Discussion Questions

1. Who, or what, do you see as the 'Unlit Lamp' of the novel? How might different interpretations of this affect the reading of the characters?
2. With whom do your sympathies lie in the novel? Why?
3. How is the coastal juxtaposed with the metropolitan in the text?
4. The novel begins in the pre-war period and concludes in the post-war period. What impact has the war had in the final chapters of the novel?
5. Trace the representation of Empire in the novel. How is this related to the portrayal of family relationships?
6. Discuss the text's depiction of religion. What kinds of perspectives on religion are offered in the text?
7. The text is full of characters with physically weakened or ailing bodies. Look at the different ways in which we can categorize these bodies e.g. male/female, physical/emotional, old/young. How easy is this to do?
8. Discuss how the characters are confined by their gender or class in the novel.
9. Elizabeth and Joan's relationship is initially based on a love for study. Are they emancipated through education or are they restricted by it?
10. Look at the dynamics of 'family' in the novel. To what extent do you think the 'family' is disintegrating? Why is this?

Essay Ideas

1. 'Men are no more than a narrative device' (Souhami 117). Discuss Diana Souhami's assessment of "The Unlit Lamp."
2. Examine the motif of Empire in the text.
3. Examine "The Unlit Lamp" as a lesbian love story.
4. Examine medicine and invalidism in "The Unlit Lamp."
5. "'Gentle, tyrant mother [. . .] and virgin daughter withering on her stem' (Hall 287)." Discuss Richard Benson's view of Mrs. Ogden and Joan, with reference to both the representation of femininity and masculinity in the text.

Thomas More, pictured above, was born in 1478 and educated at Oxford University. *Utopia,* featured opposite, portrays the ideal political system he had been dreaming about. It was not his only work, but the one he is most remembered for. Photo: Library of Congress.

Utopia

by Thomas More

Content Synopsis

Thomas More's "Utopia" (1516) is a classic work of the imagination, divided into two parts, which depicts a perfect world that serves as a blueprint for a better society. Located in an isolated dimension which sustains a vivid imagination for a world of otherness, More's idea-driven narrative is the founder of the utopian genre in which the individual, being part of what Fredric Jameson calls the "statistical population," is depersonalized and sacrificed to the community.

Book I opens with a lengthy title: "Concerning the Best State of Commonwealth and the New Island of Utopia: A truly Golden Handbook No Less Beneficial Than Entertaining by the Most Distinguished and Eloquent Author Thomas More, Citizen and Sheriff of the Famous City of London." The opening of Book 1 also includes a paratextual map, a woodcut image of Utopia. Raphael Hythloday's journey from Portugal to Utopia and back to England is modeled after the Socratic quest. As said in the opening pages, "his sailing has not been like that of Palinurus but that of Ulysses or, rather, of Plato" (5). While Palinurus was the careless traveler type, Ulysses learnt from his travels and Plato travelled to learn. The reader is then told how the More character met Raphael Hythloday (whose Greek name means "the nonsense peddler") who just came back from his journey. The More character invites his friends and Raphael over to his house: "There in the garden we sat down on a bench covered with turf to talk together" (6).

The More character, playing the part of the adversary, is convinced that it is the duty of a philosopher to take service in a Prince's court so that his wise counsel may benefit the commonwealth. Raphael, the satirist, has a duty to shoot down the opinions launched by the More character for the satire to work out properly. The battle of wits starts on the interaction between politics and philosophy. The conversation veers to economy, regulations, order, sartorial matters, customs, etc. and becomes an oblique critique of England which is compared to other nations tangentially related to Utopia: the Polylerites (15), "the Achorians who live off the island of Utopia towards the southeast"(21), "the Macarians, a people who also live not far from Utopia" (25). The debate on governance almost ends on a reminder: Plato had shown in the "Republic" that philosophers are right in abstaining from active politics ("Plato in a very fine comparison declares that wise men are right in keeping clear of government matters." (27). In conclusion, now that he has been toying with the subject, Raphael is urged to give a full picture of the tantalizing island of Utopia to his eager listeners (Peter Giles and the More character).

Book II is a full depiction of Utopia, starting with its geography and then switching to its urbanization, its social and economic organization, its moral values, its educational system, its hierarchy and regulations, and its foreign affairs and religious framework. While Book I is specific in its way of giving examples of imaginary societies, Book II focuses on just one imaginary society while tackling general philosophical issues. Hythloday's crossing to Utopia becomes on a symbolic level a metaphoric return to the womb, which offers nothing but the security it gets through its artificial isolation. Utopus, who conquered Abraxa (Utopia's former name), "cut a channel fifteen miles wide where their land joined the continent, and caused the sea to flow around the country" (31). This enterprise allowed the prevention of contamination from the Continent perceived as diseased. Utopia's difficult access ("the entrance into the bay is very dangerous," (31)) and man-built defense structure ("the coast is . . .so well fortified that a few defenders could beat off the attack of a strong force," (31) contribute to its isolation and image of a sealed-up space and self-contained world which is hard to penetrate. Everything is controlled, channeled, and regulated like clockwork although it bears close resemblance in form to the actual England. Both Utopia and England are islands separated from the continent by a channel. Utopia is comprised of 54 cities (England has 53 counties plus London), a tidal river called Anyder crossed by an arched stone bridge (which mirrors the London bridge over the Thames), and a walled city with its supply from a second river which runs down, within its walls to the Anyder. England has its walled city and second river, the Fleet river. In the Utopian temples, the women sit on the left side and the men on the right, similar to the way it is done in the churches of England. Houses in Utopia reflect those in England in their disposition, with glass very common in Utopian abodes just as glass was used on a massive scale in London.

Thomas More's "Utopia" has a mirror composition: Book I (1–30) known as the dialogue of counsel and Book II (30–85) which is Hythloday's monologue. The inversion comes from the fact that the second book was written prior the first one, hence the inequality of style in this bipartite structure. The mirror effect appears in the various mise-en-abyme techniques. Book I is a dialogue within the dialogue (of counsel) and comprises three mini utopias: the Polylerites, the Achorians, and the Macarians.

More's book is hard to pigeonhole, as it is a cross between a work of fiction and a philosophical essay. The content is so difficult to pinpoint since "Utopia" reads like a world of negations. Lots of Greek etymologies present in the text point to absurdity: Anyder means "waterless," Hythloday is "the nonsense peddler," Achorians means "without a place," utopia is Greek (ou-topos) for "no where," and Polylerites translates as "much nonsense."

Historical Context

When Thomas More started writing "Utopia" in 1515, there was political unrest in a Europe whose stability in the previous century was troubled by many conflicts. The Houses of Lancaster and of York were at loggerheads in the Wars of the Roses in order to gain power and governance while the young Tudor government had reduced its detractors to silence.

Humanism originated in the thirteenth century in an attempt to devote oneself to human interests through the reassessment of Greek and Roman writers. The Humanists' study of the Bible led them to contemplate the renovation of the Church. More has been said to propose a pagan commonwealth in which the four Cardinal Virtues (wisdom/sapientia, fortitude/fortitudo, temperance/temperentia, and justice/justicia) are put into practice to the detriment of Christian humanism.

More and Erasmus are perfect examples of North European humanism, as compared with Italian humanism (chiefly concerned with the governments of their local principalities. North European humanists widened this regional scope to Europe). Both men were familiar with classic authors and with both Latin and Greek languages. While logic was the bedrock of education in the Middle Ages, humanists like More wanted to reorganize it around oratory skills (mainly grammar and rhetoric, or the skillful way of writing and speaking). In 1515, Erasmus was counseling François Ier to set up the Collège de France while More was having an influence of his own on British education. The ultimate aim of such a policy was to breed a generation of learned scholars who could teach the humanities. The humanists' teaching would mainly benefit the statesmen who could henceforth govern in an equitable way.

Societal Context

Thomas More's "Utopia" is chiefly a satire, which fills in all the criteria of the genre such as established conventional roles like the encounter and battle of wits between a satirist and the adversary. The appearance of the author in the guise of a character in his own dialogue (i.e. the More character), the interlocutor acting as a mechanism to launch opinions for the satirist to shoot down; the careful balancing of the negative criticism with positive suggestion; the use of irony as a protective device, resorting to the ancient rhetorical trick of blame-by-praise; and the presence of a final paragraph winding up the debate, to name a few. Moreover, as a precaution, the author disavows his own creation by dismissing it as "poetry," in other words, "any work of the imagination." If "Utopia" is poetry, Thomas More is the poet, which is nothing as serious as being a thinker. The title of the book itself, Ou-topia might even prevent readers from accepting More's work as a serious proposal of a practicable scheme.

Thomas More's "Utopia" broaches the political issue of the commonwealth, a much-debated topic among intellectuals, like Plato in his "Republic," an allusion to which can be found in Book I of "Utopia." ("Plato thinks that commonwealths will become happy only when philosophers become kings or kings become philosophers" (20). In Book 2 of Aristotle's "Politics," the author analyses the best form of government for a political community and defines its didactic and realist method. Aristotle refutes Plato's Ideal City. For Aristotle, the distinction between being and well-being is linked to two opposing but complementary systems: firstly between the private sphere (private community) and the public society identified with the city and secondly between the free men who participate in the management of public affairs and all those who are deprived of freedom (slaves, children, women and craftsmen). In "De officis," Cicero warns us against the dangers of putting our happiness into someone else's trust. Citizens must act for themselves. Negotium is not incompatible with philosophy, as action prevails over contemplation.

Plato's Commonwealths are based on class distinction. In the "Laws," the citizens fall into four classes, similarly to what we find in the "Republic." However, for him, every man should have only one job. Plato advocates a hierarchical society, which runs counter to the notion of democracy. He pleads for a constitution in which the power to legislate, to judge and decide is not given to anyone in advance. In the private community, the head of the family rules, whereas the public society is a community of free men, all equal, in which each of them are to rule in turn.

The Middle Ages inherited the same idea of the State in which ploughmen and artisans are destined for labor, clerks dedicated to pray and study, and knights trained to fight. Busleiden, Thomas More's friend, in his introductory letter to "Utopia" tells us that the perfect commonwealth must unite "Wisdom in the ruler, Fortitude in the soldiers, Temperance in private individuals and Justice in all"; in short, the four cardinal virtues.

In a sense, utopian thinkers like Thomas More could be regarded as silent tyrants as they superimpose their models of better social systems onto the existing one to which they have to comply half-heartedly. Their utopian impulses do not appear as a straightforward spelled-out demand for change; rather they present themselves as suggested counter-models, altered blueprints for the society in which a given people live, so as to point out in a most oblique way the dysfunctions inherent in reality. Even though these are imagined worlds, it follows that Utopianism is the cement, which consolidates the foundations of their mute tyrannies under which life is ritualized, well organized, and closely controlled, forcing people into becoming overcautious and extremely regimented. Otherwise "How to account for the fact that in such confined spaces so many individuals can co-exist without killing or mortally detesting one another," (103) as Emile Cioran puts it? Happiness becomes a moral duty, the norm—a rule, companionship—a lifestyle, and seclusion from the external world —an essential requirement. In addition, when you think of it, the denial of complaint, the compliance to a norm, communitarian activity, and isolation, are all defining traits of prison life. Because utopian schemes are a response from a mind discontented with the present situation, they are hardly more than a sublimated vision of a corrupt world that makes the here and now more endurable to the utopian thinker.

Because utopias are chiefly hope-generating in their intent, the utopian dream should be attainable in the eyes of most readers. In no way should readers be under the impression that they are unable to seize their chance to carry out the dream, or worse, that they might have missed it. There lies the contradictory essence of Utopianism, which simultaneously jettisons all dawning hopes and sustains them. Indeed, anything belonging to the future is contingent (in other words, it can or cannot occur), and yet, because anticipation turns putative things into the soon-to-be-realized present, there is still hope for the project to be carried out. Paradoxically enough, utopias hinge on the possibility to be realized—through their seeming accessibility and sense of immediacy—and the impossibility to be pinned down, thus safeguarding its desirability; hence their elusiveness and allusiveness reflected in vague time markers and geographical landmarks. Interestingly, paratextual maps, which accompany utopian texts, are systematically decontextualized enlargements, which cannot be used to pinpoint the exact location of utopian societies.

Christian Marouby cogently argues in "Utopie et primitivisme" that utopia presents itself as a "structure of defense," insularity being understood as a paranoia-prone space. Fittingly enough, Thomas More's "Utopia" features an insular society located on an island whose overprotective and overprotected environment acts as a buttress against deep-seated anxieties of penetration and aggression. This fantasy of physical inviolability seeks to ward off putative dangers of invasion, contamination, and degeneration, which the openness of borders cannot prevent in the normal course of events. This defense mechanism rests on the illusion that evil has been shut out of the now sanitized enclosed and self-contained space.

Religious Context

In More's "Utopia," Utopians have been inspired by Christianity. Christ encouraged his disciples to practice the community of goods. The More character advances the classical objections to communism. According to him, it destroys initiative, encourages dependence on others (sloth), it is conducive to sedition and bloodshed, it undermines authority and it pits private interest against the public well-being.

More's enclosed island has religious overtones and recalls the Garden of Eden and milky innocence. It is the topos of the hortus conclusus: "a garden enclosed is my sister, an orchard of pomegranates" ["Song of Songs" 4: 12–13]) and the Savior appearing to Mary Magdalen in the form of a gardener in "The Gospel of John." Besides, in "Exodus" (3: 8, 17), Christ likens his heavenly Father to a farmer or gardener, who prunes his fruit-trees for a better yield. Dreams of paradise also indicate that utopian thinkers regard evil as a threat, which they keep at bay. This dread of evil with which writers are over-concerned morphs into visions of overwrought and strictly controlled societies. Such fantasies of control and domination exemplify the utopian writer's indulgence in wishful thinking. In this illusory world, the quest for the earthly paradise fulfills an ab initio fantasy, which finds expression in exaltation for beginnings. The craving to regress into a state of original bliss accounts for such exaltation while hinting at the idea that utopian thinkers are dissatisfied with and overcritical of their world which they see as fallen and imperfect.

Roger Mucchielli's definition of ideal cities in "Le Mythe de la cité idéale" (1961) refers to the utopian city as a "myth, awakened by the personal revolt against the human condition in general in the shape of existing circumstances, which meets the obstacle of impotence and evokes in the imagination an other or a nowhere, where all obstacles are removed" (Frank E. Manuel's introduction to "Utopia" xi). There is, in the minds of utopian thinkers, a feeling of impotence, which morphs into fantasized omnipotence and turns them into perfection-shapers. Paradoxically enough, the impotence of utopian writers lies less in their inability to have their ideas put into practice—time will probably tell!—than in their ability to create ideal societies. One can see these visionary dreams of perfect worlds as the overcompensation of our unalterable actual society, which writers cannot change, save by imagining flawless alternatives that alleviate frustration. However, as in the case of fantasies, utopian visions are best to remain impulses which are not to be acted out, lest they would lose their soothing effect on the thinkers' discontented minds.

Scientific & Technological Context

The journey motif was influenced by sixteenth century preoccupations with discovering the world thanks to circumnavigation. Thomas More's "Utopia" shows the journey as a delocalization of a hic and nunc (here and now) in search of otherness. Therefore, relocation is achieved in otherness. The physical journey is also symbolic of a journey of the mind. Thinking of a better world, of an alternative world, may also be seen as a form of escapism. To perceive utopia as the imagination or dreaming of another world existing on a foreign or other land implies the recognition of extra-territoriality as a distinctive feature of utopias. More has paved the way for establishing utopias as far-off locales, encapsulating otherness whose depictions either derive from imaginative tales (i.e. diegesis) or from imitations of reality (i.e. mimesis). In both instances, the mechanism of projection that underpins utopian visions—in the form of extraterritoriality (i.e. projection in space) and extra-contemporaneousness (i.e. projection in time)—is essential to disconnect and distance fantasy from reality.

Biographical Context

Born in 1478, Sir Thomas More is the eldest son of lawyer Sir John More. He was educated at Oxford University before he moved to London where he read law. He finally became a fully-fledged barrister in 1501. He decided against joining the Franciscans in order to get married in 1505 to Jane Colt, with whom he had four children. After Jane died six years later, he walked down the aisle with Alice Middleton, a wealthy older lady. He wrote his creative work in Latin and English, but he is now best remembered for his 1516 neologism, "Utopia," the eponymous ideal projection of a political system he had been dreaming about. He held many terms in public offices (he was a statesman, a London under-sheriff, a personal advisor to the King, the Speaker of the House of Commons in 1523, chancellor of the Dutchy of Lancaster), his most prominent function being that of Lord Chancellor, a position he occupied from 1529 to 1532.

He later became involved in a religious controversy by collaborating on the "Defense of the Seven Sacraments" (1521), a pamphlet that challenged King Henry VIII's title of "Defender of the Faith." More's attacks against Protestantism grew stronger and were contrasted with his staunch support of Catholicism. His constant opposition to the Pope's authority and to King Henry VIII forced the latter into beheading him on July 6, 1535. Three and a half centuries later, More was beatified by Pope Leo XIII (in 1886) and eventually canonized in the twentieth century by Pope Pius XI (in 1935).

Jean-François Vernay

Works Cited

Adams, Robert ed. *Thomas More Utopia*. New York and London: Norton, 1975.

Cioran, Emile. *Histoire et utopie*. Paris: Gallimard, 1960.

Jameson, Fredric. "Politics of Utopia." *New Left Review 25*, (Jan./Feb. 2005): 35–54.

———. *Archaeologies of the Future: The Desire Called Utopia and Other Science Fictions*. London: Verso, 2005.

Logan, G.M.. *The Meaning of More's Utopia*. New Jersey: Princeton University Press, 1983.

Manuel, Frank. *Utopia and Utopian Thought*. Boston: Beacon Press, 1965.

Marin, Louis. *Utopiques, jeux d'espace*. Paris: Minuit, 1973.

Marouby, Christian. *Utopie et primitivisme. Essai sur l'imaginaire anthropologique à l'âge classique*. Paris: Seuil, 1990.

Smith, D. Baker. *More's Utopia*. London: Harper Collins, 1991.

Discussion Questions

1. Why is the conversation taking place in a garden?
2. Who is the satirist among the characters? What is his function?
3. In what ways is Book I a critique of England?
4. Why does Raphael defer the description of Utopia itself?
5. Why do Raphael and the More character hardly agree with each other?
6. Why is Utopia an overprotected and isolated island?
7. Is "Utopia" an analysis in good statesmanship?
8. Can you describe how Raphael came to meet the Utopians?
9. How does Book II portray Utopia as an ideal world?
10. Why is Thomas More's "Utopia" a warning to the reader in the oblique way?

Essay Ideas

1. In the eighteenth century, English philosopher Jeremy Bentham stated that "The greatest happiness of the greatest number is the foundation of morals and legislation." Discuss this statement in the light of Thomas More's "Utopia."
2. To what extent is More's utopian city a "myth, awakened by the personal revolt against the human condition in general in the shape of existing circumstances, which meets the obstacle of impotence and evokes in the imagination an other or a nowhere, where all obstacles are removed," as Roger Mucchielli has it?
3. Is Thomas More a truth-seeker in his depiction of "Utopia" or is he simply a consciousness-raiser?
4. Give a humanistic interpretation of Thomas More's "Utopia."
5. Study the fictionalization of Thomas More's "Utopia."

The Vampyre: A Tale was written by John Polidori. When the manuscript arrived in 1818 at London's *New Monthly Magazine* unsigned and resembling scientific content written by Lord Byron, it was credited to Byron. This makes sense, since Polidori was, for a short time, Lord Byron's personal physician. Photo: Wikipedia

The Vampyre: A Tale

by John Polidori

Content Synopsis

"The Vampyre" begins in London, during the fashionable winter social season. A mysterious nobleman, Lord Ruthven, makes his entrance into high society, a man "more remarkable for his singularities, than his rank" (3). Stimulating and fascinating the jaded London socialites with his peculiar character, Lord Ruthven becomes quite popular. Though he dismisses women of questionable reputation, he often socializes with "those females who form the boast of their sex from their domestic virtues" (4). During this time, another gentleman, young Aubrey, arrives in London. An "orphan left with an only sister in the possession of great wealth, by parents who died while he was yet in childhood" (4), Aubrey joins Lord Ruthven on a European tour, during which the younger man is surprised "at the apparent eagerness with which his companion sought for the centres of all fashionable vice" (6). Aubrey is also disturbed by what appears to be Lord Ruthven's malign influence upon all those whom he encounters.

While in Rome, Aubrey receives a letter from his guardians instructing him to leave Lord Ruthven, whom they expose as a "dreadfully vicious" reprobate who uses his "irresistible powers of seduction" to ruin the innocent women he meets and to cast them "from the pinnacle of unsullied virtue, down to the lowest abyss of infamy and degradation" (7). Accordingly, Aubrey notifies Lord Ruthven by note

of his decision to part with him. Aubrey then foils his erstwhile companion's plot "to work upon the inexperience of the daughter of the lady at whose house he chiefly frequented" (8) by warning her mother of the scheme. Aubrey departs from Italy and travels to Greece, where he meets a young woman, Ianthe, and is struck by her "innocence, youth, and beauty, unaffected by crowded drawing rooms and stifling balls" (9). She recounts for him "all the supernatural tales of her nurse," including one of a "living vampyre, who had passed years amidst his friends, and dearest ties, forced every year, by feeding upon the life of a lovely female to prolong his existence for the ensuing months" (9). Though Aubrey tries "to laugh her out of such idle and horrible fantasies" (9), when Ianthe describes "the traditional appearance of these monsters" he is horrified to hear "a pretty accurate description of Lord Ruthven" (10).

After meeting Ianthe's parents, Aubrey terrifies them by announcing his decision to "pass through a wood, where no Greek would ever remain after the day had closed," for it was feared as "the resort of the vampyres in their nocturnal orgies" (10). He promises Ianthe to return "ere night allowed the power of these beings to be put in action" (11), but he becomes so absorbed in his antiquarian research that he finds himself in the wood at nightfall. Approaching a hut, he hears "the dreadful shrieks of a woman mingling with the stifled exultant mockery of a laugh" (11). He enters and struggles with an unseen assailant of "superhuman" strength who abruptly leaves the hut after being disturbed by "the glare of many torches" (12). The men with the torches search for the woman who had screamed, and Aubrey is appalled when they enter the hut with Ianthe, now dead. In a state of shock, he holds "almost unconsciously in his hand a naked dagger of a particular construction, which had been found in the hut" (12). When her parents are informed of her demise they are "inconsolable" and themselves die "broken-hearted" (13). Meanwhile, in Athens, Aubrey is gripped by a powerful fever and sinks into delirium. Lord Ruthven arrives in the same city, and after being informed of Aubrey's condition becomes "his constant attendant" (13). When Aubrey regains mental lucidity he is "startled at the sight of him whose image he had now combined with that of a Vampyre," but by showing him "attention, anxiety, and care" Lord Ruthven soon soothes his fears (13). The younger man recovers but is "now as much a lover of solitude and silence as Lord Ruthven" (13), and he proposes to his companion, to whom he holds himself "bound by the tender care he had taken of him during his illness, that they should visit those parts of Greece neither had yet seen" (14).

Though they hear "much of robbers," the travelers ignore the advice of the locals and thus find themselves "with only a few guards, more to serve as guides than as a defence" when they are attacked in a "narrow pass" (14). Lord Ruthven is shot in the shoulder, and through "promises of a great reward," Aubrey convinces the robbers "to convey his wounded friend to a neighbouring cabin" (15). While Aubrey and Lord Ruthven await the arrival of the ransom, the latter rapidly declines until his demise appears imminent. On his deathbed, he asks Aubrey to "swear for a year and a day" not to tell anyone of his "crimes or death" (15). Aubrey so swears, and Lord Ruthven dies, "laughing upon his pillow" (15). The next morning, Aubrey discovers that his companion had asked the robbers to

move his corpse "to the pinnacle of a neighbouring mount," so that it would "be exposed to the first cold ray of the moon that rose after his death" (16). Aubrey searches for the corpse but cannot find it. He then travels to Smyrna and examines Lord Ruthven's personal effects. When he finds among them "a sheath apparently ornamented in the same style as the dagger discovered in the fatal hut" (16), he sheaths the dagger and recognizes Lord Ruthven as Ianthe's murderer. On his way home, Aubrey stops in Rome and inquires about "the lady he had attempted to snatch from Lord Ruthven's seductive arts," only to discover that her "parents were in distress, their fortune ruined, and she had not been heard of since the departure of his lordship" (16). His psyche "almost broken under so many repeated horrors" (17), he arrives in England and seeks comfort with his sister.

Miss Aubrey, being "yet only eighteen [. . .] had not been presented to the world; it having been thought by her guardians more fit that her presentation should be delayed until her brother's return from the continent" (17). When she makes her debut in a "drawing room" (18), Aubrey recalls that "the first time he had seen Lord Ruthven was in that very place" (18). He is then seized by the resurrected nobleman, who whispers in his ear, "Remember your oath" (18). Horrified, Aubrey withdraws from society—only to rejoin it, "anxious to forewarn, in spite of his oath, all whom Lord Ruthven approached with intimacy," and persuaded "by the idea that he left by his absence the whole of his friends, with a fiend amongst them, of whose presence they were unconscious" (19). Unfortunately, under the burden of his secret he quickly declines in appearance and health, until at last he is "confined to his chamber" (20) by his guardians.

Months pass, and as the year draws to its conclusion his spirits begin to rise. Finally, "on the last day of the year," he learns that his sister is to be married to "the Earl of Marsden" (20). He believes her fiancé to be "a young earl whom he had met with in society" (20) and congratulates his sister upon her engagement; but he is horrified to discover in her locket a portrait not of this gentleman but of "the monster who had so long influenced his life" (21). When he destroys the portrait and asks her to "swear that she would never wed this monster" (21), he is judged by his physician and guardians to be insane. Confined to his chamber, Aubrey writes to his sister and implores her to delay her wedding for a few hours; however, his letter is intercepted by the physician. On the morning of the wedding day when Aubrey hears carriages outside, he panics, flees the house, and arrives at the wedding—only to be confronted by Lord Ruthven, who tells him, "Remember your oath, and know, if not my bride today, your sister is dishonored. Women are frail!" (22). In his rage Aubrey breaks a blood vessel, collapses, and is taken to his bed. His sister and Lord Ruthven are married and leave London. After midnight strikes and his oath expires, Aubrey calls his sister's guardians, relates to them Lord Ruthven's story, and dies. The guardians hurry to help Miss Aubrey, but they discover that her husband has vanished and that she has "glutted the thirst of a VAMPYRE!" (23).

Symbols & Motifs

Romance and reality: In his "Introduction," Polidori discusses vampires in literature, folklore, and history, archly describing at one point "a curious, and of course credible account of a particular case of vampyrism" in 1732 (241). The story proper likewise links and even conflates romance and reality, particularly with regard to vampires. Aubrey is naïve and romantic, mistaking "the dreams of poets" for "the realities of life" and "cultivat[ing] more his imagination than his judgment" (4). He thus "believe[s] all to sympathise with virtue, and [thinks] that vice was thrown in by Providence merely for the picturesque effect of the scene, as we see in romances" (4). He later becomes disillusioned, however, and realizes that there is "no foundation in real life" for the "pleasing pictures

and descriptions contained in those volumes, from which he had formed his study" (4). Indeed, Aubrey is "about to relinquish his dreams" (4) when he meets Lord Ruthven and becomes enthralled by him. "[A]llowing his imagination to picture everything that flattered its propensity to extravagant ideas," he fashions the vampire "into the hero of a romance, and determine[s] to observe the offspring of his fancy, rather than the person before him" (5). Ironically, Aubrey struggles to accept the vampire's fantastic resurrection: "[H]e could not believe it possible—the dead rise again!—He thought his imagination had conjured up the image his mind was resting upon. It was impossible that it could be real" (18). Too late, Aubrey recognizes that Lord Ruthven is not a character from fantasy but an all-too-real—though supernatural—threat to both him and his sister.

Innocence and experience: Upon coming of age, Aubrey "hint[s] to his guardians, that it [is] time for him to perform the [European] tour, which for many generations has been thought necessary to enable the young to take some rapid steps in the career of vice, towards putting themselves upon an equality with the aged" (5). His literal and figurative journey from innocence to experience is echoed elsewhere in "The Vampyre." Perversely, the jaded Lord Ruthven pursues only innocent women—for the sole purpose of debauching them. While "the common adulteress could not influence even the guidance of his eyes" (3), he is drawn "to the virtuous wife and innocent daughter" (4), as he "require[s]," to enhance his gratification, that his victim, the partner of his guilt, should be hurled from the pinnacle of unsullied virtue, down to the lowest abyss of infamy and degradation" (7). Like the vampire who comes to fascinate him, Aubrey too is drawn to innocent women—though his attraction has more to do with their authenticity than with their potential for debasement. Thus he "attach[es] himself more and more to Ianthe," as "her innocence, so contrasted with all the affected virtues of the women among whom he [has] sought for his vision of romance, [wins] his heart" (10).

Historical Context

In part a commentary upon early-nineteenth-century mores and behavior (particularly among members of the upper classes), "The Vampyre" is set in the period in which it was written and published. That some of the story's action takes place in Greece is significant, since the Greek Revolution or War of Independence (1821–1831) would begin shortly after its publication. When Aubrey travels to Greece, he studies "the faded records of ancient glory upon monuments that apparently, ashamed of chronicling the deeds of freemen only before slaves, had hidden themselves beneath the sheltering soil or many coloured lichen" (8). This passage emphasizes how the Greeks had fallen from their "ancient glory" as citizens of a democracy to their contemporary status as "slaves" under the Ottoman Empire, which had ruled most of Greece since conquering the Byzantine Empire during the fourteenth and fifteenth centuries. When "The Vampyre" appeared in 1819, however, the Ottoman Empire was in decline and Greek nationalism—stimulated by the French Revolution of 1789—was on the rise. Western Europeans sympathized with the Greeks, Christian people seeking to liberate themselves from an Islamic power. Among these sympathetic foreigners was Polidori's former employer and companion, the poet Lord Byron. Leaving Italy for Greece in 1823, Byron offered the Greeks money and supplies to equip their fleet. The world-famous figure's participation in the Greek Revolution—and, more significantly, his death from fever at Messolonghi in 1824 while in service to the cause—helped move the European powers to involve themselves in the struggle.

Societal Context

The term "lady-killer" had come into vogue during Polidori's lifetime (Morrison xx), and he literal-izes this metaphor in the figure of Lord Ruthven. Polidori's noble vampire is often considered the prototype for the aristocratic bloodsuckers that follow him—most notably, Bram Stoker's Count Dracula—but he is more fundamentally and obviously a variation on a common figure in eighteenth- and early-nineteenth-century fiction: the "rakehell" or "rake" (Morrison xix). This gentleman—for he is typically a member of the upper classes—is a libertine who indulges in dissolute pastimes such as drinking, gambling, and seducing women. In gothic tales he is sometimes used as an object lesson, as readers are cautioned to avoid "his example and his fate" (Morrison xviii). "The Vampyre" may be viewed as a warning against both rakes in general and one famous libertine in particular: Lord Byron.

Religious Context

Though a story of the supernatural, "The Vampyre" is not interested in religious rituals or totems. That said, in this tale superstition conquers skepticism, and events appear to be predestined. Ianthe's parents are aghast when Aubrey dares "to mock a superior, infernal power" (11), especially since in the past "those who had dared to question" the existence of vampires "always had some proof given, which obliged them [. . .] to confess it was true" (9–10). Aubrey recognizes the reality of these monsters in "the fatal hut" (16) wherein Ianthe is killed by Lord Ruthven—which is doubly fatal insofar as it is both deadly and linked to the workings of fate. Likewise, it is "fate" that draws young men "within the reach of this fiend" (6), and the vampire seduces Aubrey's sister either because "he [knows] so well how to use the serpent's art, or such [is] the will of fate" (22).

Scientific & Technological Context

John Polidori was, for a time, Lord Byron's personal physician; thus, it makes sense that science appears in "The Vampyre" in the form of Aubrey's doctor, who attends more to his patient's mind than to his body. This individual ministers to Aubrey after the young man realizes that Lord Ruthven is stalking his sister—which realization is wrongly assumed by those around him to be a sign of madness. Aubrey's guardians, "fearing that his mind was becoming alienated," and "[d]esirous [. . .] of preventing him from exposing to the general eye those marks of what they considered folly," hire "a physician to reside in the house, and take constant care of him" (20). Frenzied, Aubrey writes to his sister and implores her to delay her impending marriage to the vampire; but when "the physician" is given this letter by the servants he "[thinks] it better not to harass any more the mind of Miss Aubrey by, what he considered, the ravings of a maniac" (22). As a result of this physician's ineptitude, the supernatural defeats science, Aubrey's sister is destroyed, and the reader is left pondering Polidori's view of his own profession.

Biographical Context

John William Polidori was born in 1795. His father, who left Italy for England, was a scholar and a translator; his mother had served as a governess. He studied first at Ampleforth, a Catholic college in England, and then at the University of Edinburgh, where he wrote a dissertation on sleepwalking and earned his degree in medicine at the remarkably early age of nineteen. In April of 1816 Polidori became the personal physician to Lord Byron, with whom he also traveled throughout Europe. Byron's publisher, John Murray, had commissioned Polidori to record his journeys with Byron. The resulting "Diary" was published in 1911.

Both Polidori and his protagonist Aubrey are enthralled by and accompany a dissolute nobleman on a European tour; indeed, "The Vampyre" contains many echoes of Polidori's own experiences with the larger-than-life and self-indulgent Lord Byron. Like Ruthven, Byron became infamous for his sexual dalliances—most notably, with Lady Caroline Lamb, who called him "mad,

bad, and dangerous to know," and who portrayed him as Clarence de Ruthven, Lord Glenarvon, in her novel "Glenarvon" (1816). Seeking to escape his notoriety, Byron left England in 1816. In the summer of that year, he was in residence with Polidori at the Villa Diodati on Lake Geneva, where they were joined by Percy Bysshe Shelley, Mary Wollstonecraft Shelley, and Claire Clairmont for the ghost-story competition. This competition would give rise not only to Polidori's "The Vampyre" but also to Byron's "Augustus Darvell" and Mary Shelley's "Frankenstein." Polidori based his complete tale upon Byron's fragment, and there is some overlap between the two texts (for instance, before dying both Darvell and Ruthven elicit oaths from their companions not to reveal their deaths). That said, certainly "The Vampyre" is Polidori's own creation—though it would not be recognized as such upon its publication.

After being dismissed by Byron, Polidori traveled throughout Italy, returned to England in 1817, and established a medical practice in Norwich. In the autumn of 1818 the London *New Monthly Magazine*, which was edited by Henry Colburn, acquired a package of documents including "The Vampyre." The unsigned confessional tale resembled Byron's work in many respects, and Colburn, anxious to improve his magazine's flagging sales, published the story in April of 1819 as "A TALE BY LORD BYRON." It proved quite popular and began the *New Monthly Magazine's* success as a venue for macabre tales—despite the fact that Byron immediately denied having written "The Vampyre" and published "Augustus Darvell" to show the contrasts between the two works—while Polidori announced himself as the true author of the tale.

Although Polidori had introduced the European reading public to the vampire (thereby beginning a fascination with the creature that continues to this day), his life after "The Vampyre" was neither successful nor happy. He followed the story with a novel, "Ernestus

Berchtold or, The Modern Oedipus," which was fairly well reviewed but sold poorly. When "The Fall of the Angels: A Sacred Poem" appeared, Polidori was depressed, in debt, and disappointed with his medical and literary careers. He committed suicide by poisoning himself on August 24, 1821, in his father's house.

Jamil M. Mustafa, Ph.D.

Works Cited

Macdonald, D. L. *Poor Polidori: A Critical Biography of the Author of The* Vampyre. Toronto: U of Toronto P, 1991.

Polidori, John William. *"The Vampyre."* In *The Vampyre and Other Tales of the Macabre*, Robert Morrison and Chris Baldick, eds. *The World's Classics*. Oxford: OUP, 1997. 3–23.

Discussion Questions

1. "The Vampyre" is told from a limited-omniscient point of view. How would the story change if it were told in the first-person by Aubrey? by Lord Ruthven? by Ianthe?
2. Given his interest in poetry, his "exalted imagination," and his sense that the mystery surrounding Lord Ruthven might stem from "something supernatural" (7), why does Aubrey seem so skeptical about the vampire lore he encounters in Greece?
3. What role does travel play in "The Vampyre"?
4. Why is Aubrey interested in Ianthe and not in the women of his own class and country?
5. Why does Lord Ruthven prey only upon innocent young women?
6. What is the significance of Lord Ruthven's noble status? How does the story link vampirism and aristocracy?
7. Is Lord Ruthven actually a vampire? Why or why not?
8. Why is Ianthe in the forest after dark?
9. Why does Aubrey make his oath to Lord Ruthven? Why does he keep it?
10. Why does the story end as it does? Are Aubrey's guardians searching for a murderer, a vampire, or both?

Essay Ideas

1. "The Vampyre" features characters from various socioeconomic levels. Discuss the role played by class in the story.
2. Analyze the relationship between Aubrey and Lord Ruthven, paying particular attention to the ways in which the characters are similar to and different from each other.
3. Explore how Aubrey matures during the course of "The Vampyre."
4. Discuss the role of women in the story. Are they simply victims?
5. Compare this story to any text mentioned above in terms of theme, character, figurative language, or other literary elements.

W. M. Thackeray, pictured above, top, was born in Calcutta, India in 1811. *Vanity Fair*, featured opposite, was first published in book form in 1848. The subtitle of the original illustrated story in installments was "Pen and Pencil Sketches of English Society." Photo: Library of Congress.

Vanity Fair

by William Makepeace Thackeray

"Ah! Vanitas Vanitatum! Which of us is happy in this world? Which of us has his desire? Or, having it, is satisfied? — Come children, let us shut up the box and the puppets for our play is played out."

—W. M. Thackeray, *Vanity Fair*

Content Synopsis

The main plot of "Vanity Fair" concerns the rise and fall of Rebecca (Becky) Sharp on the ladder of early nineteenth-century English society. Becky begins on a low rung, daughter of a French opera-girl who has died before the story opens and an impoverished artist. That she will rise by virtue of her energy, determination, daring, and intelligence, is however, clear. We come upon her first near the end of her time as part-pupil, part drudge at Miss Pinkerton's school. Before taking up a post as a governess she is to make a visit to the home of her school friend, Amelia Sedley, a kind-hearted but naïve girl from a comfortable middle-class background. Becky's talent for infiltrating the circles higher than her own by making herself agreeable to one of their members is shown in the relationship she has established with Amelia. That talent is quickly put to use again when she finds that Amelia's brother, Joseph (Jos) Sedley, has come home from India unmarried and, if not rich, at least secure. She evinces fascination with Jos' interests and makes him feel that he is not the fat dullard every one else sees. She also meets Amelia's fiancé, George Osborne, and his friend, William Dobbin. George affects the lifestyle and manners of a gentleman, the more so because his father's fortune derived from trade, but it is clear that Dobbin, in spite of being the son of a grocer, is truly a gentleman. Kind, loyal, thoughtful and generous, Dobbin is obviously in love with Amelia but would never betray his friend by courting her. George suggests that he could not ally himself with a family which included so low-born a woman, and ridicules Jos' bungled attempts at a proposal, so that Jos gives up and Becky has to take up her post as governess to the two daughters of Sir Pitt Crawley.

At the run-down and shabby Queen's Crawley Becky becomes indispensable to the eccentric Sir Pitt, particularly during a visit from the rich elderly Miss Crawley, whom each member of the family wishes to please in the hope of obtaining a legacy. Becky pleases Miss Crawley so well that she is invited to London for a visit. There she meets Miss Crawley's favorite nephew, Sir Pitt's younger son, Captain Rawdon Crawley. Though Rawdon has expectations from his aunt, he has very little ready money. A rake, gambler, and drinker, he is nonetheless dashing, handsome, and engaging, and above Becky on the social scale. Becky maneuvers Rawdon into proposing to her and they are secretly married. When Lady Crawley dies, Sir Pitt proposes to Becky. She has to confess that she is already married, and is devastated to think that she made an only fairly advantageous marriage when she could have made a better one. Miss Crawley cuts Rawdon out of her will, making the elder brother, Pitt, her heir. Becky and Rawdon establish themselves in London, living on credit and Rawdon's gambling winnings, and they have a son, young Rawdon. Sir Pitt Crawley the elder dies and Rawdon's elder brother, young Pitt, inherits the title, Queen's Crawley, and his aunt's fortune. The new Sir Pitt's wife, Jane, young Rawdon's aunt, shows far more kindness to young Rawdon than his own mother, Becky, who shows little interest in him until he inherits Queen's Crawley later in the novel.

Among a party of men brought back to their house by her husband, Becky meets the Marquis of Steyne, a licentious and nasty aristocrat who hopes to make her his mistress. Her liveliness, wit and charm ensure that she is a social success, particularly with men, but by now the reader is also aware of her ruthlessness and her utter lack of maternal feeling for young Rawdon. As she has risen socially, so Amelia has fallen. Her father has been bankrupted during the economic collapse brought about by panic upon Napoleon's escape from Elba. The Sedley's house and goods are auctioned off. Dobbin buys Amelia's piano and sends it to her, but Amelia believes it is from George. George's father, John Osborne, is one of Mr. Sedley's most brutal creditors, and he insists that George break off the engagement and marry an heiress of his choosing. George is revolted by the heiress, however, and bowing to Dobbin's persuasion, honors his engagement. He and Amelia marry, and are cut off by John Osborne.

The three soldiers, George, Dobbin and Capt. Rawdon all leave England to join the army of the Duke of Wellington in Belgium. Amelia and Becky accompany them to Brussels, where the cream of English society has gathered on the eve of Waterloo. Although George considers himself to be made for greatness, he is not a social success, and Amelia is made miserable by the rudeness of the aristocrats she encounters. Becky is similarly snubbed by some matrons, but is assiduously courted by those who recognize her as a rising star. When the British army is reported (falsely) to have suffered defeat, and the rest of the panic-stricken city flees, Becky is one of the few to have horses with which to make an escape, and is delighted to be able to refuse to sell them to those who previously snubbed her. She sells the horses to Jos for a fabulous price, but remains in Brussels. Rawdon and Dobbin return from the battle intact, but George has been killed. Amelia is left to bring up her son, young George, in dire poverty. Back in England, Becky continues to shine and to extract social advancement and money from Lord Steyne, who hopes for sexual favours in return. She hides this from Rawdon, who is imprisoned for debt even though she has the means to pay his creditors, and it is Lady Jane Crawley, Rawdon's sister-in-law, who rescues him by coming to the prison with the required sum. Rawdon catches Becky in a compromising position with Lord Steyne and realizes that he has been blind to Becky's true nature, and living in a delusion, just as Becky, seeing her husband anew, begins to value him. "She stood there trembling before him. She admired her husband, strong, brave, and victorious" (676). Leaving young Rawdon in the care of the boy's aunt, Lady Jane, Rawdon goes into the exile arranged for him by Lord Steyne, the Governorship of Coventry Island, knowing that the fevers brought on by its swamps and unhealthy climate will soon kill him.

Dobbin tries to persuade John Osborne that he should offer financial support to his daughter-in-law and grandson, but Mr. Osborne will not see Amelia. He offers to make provision for young George, but only if the boy's mother will give him up to the Osbornes entirely. Amelia is reluctant, but finally agrees on the persuasion of her mother, who points out that she is otherwise condemning George to a life of poverty and hardship. Becky, for whom Steyne has made life in London society impossible, leaves for the continent. She gradually descends into a vagabond existence between boarding-house, gaming houses and the demimonde.

The characters meet again some years later in a German inn. Amelia and her son, reunited, are traveling in the company of Dobbin, who has remained a faithful family friend but no more. When Dobbin tries to warn her against Becky, Amelia rejects his advice. He realizes that she still cherishes her illusion that George was a heroic and faithful husband to her, and decides finally to break free. He leaves to rejoin the army, and Amelia finds that she misses him. Becky reveals to Amelia that George had pestered her to have an affair with him and that he had written to her the day before he died, begging her to run away with him. Her illusions shattered, Amelia eventually realizes the worth of Dobbin, and they marry. We see Dobbin as a country squire, having retired from the army, settled near Queen's Crawley, and taken up the preparation of a history of the Punjab region. This might seem like a conventional happy ending, and Dobbin might be expected to be overjoyed, but "Vanity Fair" is not a conventional wish-fulfillment novel. Just before Amelia realizes how dependent she has become on Dobbin and how unfairly she has treated him, and agrees to marry him, Dobbin realizes that he has been wasting his life; he has been a deluded fool. The narrative voice makes it clear that when she does finally bestow her hand upon him, Dobbin finds that Amelia was not worth the wait, and their marriage is dull.

Jos remains on the continent with Becky, and Amelia hears that he has taken out a heavy insurance policy of which Becky is the co-beneficiary. Dobbin finds him in a poor Brussels lodging house, and urges him to fly to India, where Becky cannot follow, but Jos prevaricates, and begs Dobbin not to reveal their conversation to Becky, for fear that she would kill him. Although the text says nothing, an illustration shows Becky hiding behind a curtain listening to the conversation, and its caption announces that this is Becky's "second appearance" in the character of Clytemnestra (85). In Ancient Greek myth, Clytemnestra was the murderer of her husband, Menelaus, and Becky's first appearance in the part had been in a charade, in which Menelaus was played by her real husband, Rawdon. Jos dies three months later. Whether Becky has poisoned him is not revealed, but in 1848, in a playful letter describing the later life-histories of his characters to the Duke of Devonshire, Thackeray says that "the late Jos Sedley, Esq., of the Bengal Service" bequeathed Becky "two lakhs of rupees" (Pollard, 35). In a kind of after word to the story we encounter Becky years later as a respectable matron from a provincial town running a stall at a London charity bazaar.

Historical Context

The novel was written in the middle of the nineteenth century, but its story opens thirty years earlier, in 1814, in the heyday of the Regency, when high society took its lead from the extravagant, expensive and feckless Prince Regent, the future George IV. The earlier period is used as a medium for satire of the contemporary period, and of human nature as Thackeray saw it (it is significant that in Thackeray's illustrations the characters wear the dress of the 1840s, not 1814), so historical characters such as the Regent and the Duke of Wellington are never the central focus of the novel, but it does contain a wealth of vivid detail about the people, events of the time. Regency society prided itself upon being rigidly ordered, with the uppermost stratum of the "ton" (the well-born, wealthy and fashionable) being closed to outsiders, but in fact its bastions were crumbling. High society was being forced to take in some who had risen from the lower ranks via fortunes which they had made rather than inherited, and lose some of those who had inherited 'good' blood and ancestral estates but insufficient funds to maintain them. Fortunes changed hands at the gambling tables and through betting, aristocrats married 'low-born' heiresses, and naval officers earned vast sums in prize money from captured French ships. The emergent capitalist system also won and lost fortunes for investors and for the first time rather than land, capital, invested in trade and industry, was the more profitable source of income. This was also the period when the British Empire flourished. Businesses such as the East Indian Company were enormous concerns, feeding the huge demand for spices and other goods, the colorful, decorative and opulent objects with which the novel is studded: fabrics such as cotton and silk; shawls; headdresses; carpets; perfumes; exotic pets. This opportunistic age was a perfect setting for Thackeray's story of the quintessential opportunist, Becky Sharp.

The novel reminds us that social mobility can be downward as well as upward. The decade of the novel's composition and publication has been called 'the hungry forties'. Economic recession had led to unemployment, high prices, and appalling wants. Though the upper echelons of society were to an extent cushioned from its worst effects, working- and middle-class families suffered. Many women were forced to try to generate or supplement the family income by taking in washing, or sewing, or other work, and girls from relatively affluent families who might have expected to enter society as debutantes became governesses. The

period in which the novel is set had a long-lasting consequence on the period in which it was written; the Napoleonic wars so depleted a generation of young men that there was a 'surplus' of unmarried women in the succeeding decades.

During the 1840s, Charles Dickens had made popular book-length fiction published in monthly instalments with steel engravings and/or woodcut illustrations, and "Vanity Fair" was initially published in this form, in twenty monthly installments, between 1847–8, with illustrations by Thackeray himself.

Societal Context

The subtitle of the original illustrated story in installments was "Pen and Pencil Sketches of English Society." Shallow seeking after selfish desires and the hypocrisy of pretending not to, are Thackeray's versions of 'Vanity', and it is these failings on which his satire is most severe. While Becky is materialistic, the narrative voice of the novel sympathizes with her; her impoverished beginning and habitual hand-to-mouth existence are felt in some measure to excuse or at least explain her craving for security in terms of possessions and social position. There was no Welfare State in Britain until the twentieth century, and no medical insurance. The Poor Law Amendment Act of 1834 made obtaining relief difficult and the relief itself meager. Families who lost their bread-winner to accident, infirmity or death might be incarcerated in the dreaded workhouses, or at the mercy of cold charity which distinguished between the "deserving" and "undeserving" poor. For an impoverished woman, choices were very few, and many were forced into prostitution. Lord Steyne, however, as a wealthy aristocrat, has no such excuse, and the snobbery, falsity and hypocrisy of both Osborne men are condemned as inexcusable.

Williams suggests that their single-minded pursuit of ultimately empty goals (wealth, social success, fame) made these characters less than whole human beings, for Thackeray (186), which was why he refers to them as puppets, without any real control over their destinies, since vanity is puling their strings. To the first book-form edition of "Vanity Fair" (Bradbury and Evans, 1848), Thackeray added the subtitle "A Novel without a Hero" and a preface titled "Before the Curtain," which refers to a "Manager of the Performance," emphasizing the puppet-show nature of the story to come.

Religious Context

The title of the novel comes from John Bunyan's allegorical "Pilgrim's Progress," published in 1678–84, in which Pilgrim, an Everyman figure, has to make his way to the Celestial City, Heaven, through trials and tribulations, and overcome temptations and distractions. Pilgrim and his companion Faithful come to a city called Vanity, which is holding a fair, Vanity Fair. The name is taken from the Authorized Version of the Bible, and refers to the desire for earthly, superficial things of outward appearance, such as beauty and treasure, rather than for spiritual matters. The fair's stalls sell the trappings of earthly, material wealth, such as kingdoms, rich possessions, and honors. Faithful is killed in Vanity but Pilgrim passes through the fair and eventually reaches his goal. Thackeray's narrative voice urges readers not to forget the title of the novel, "and that Vanity Fair is a very vain, wicked, foolish place, full of all sorts of humbugs and falsenesses and pretensions" (95).

Ioan Williams suggests a secondary source of the title of "Vanity Fair," Thomas Carlyle's essay on Boswell's "Life of Samuel Johnson" (1791), which was published in 1832. Carlyle makes a distinction between those who are blinded by the 'mere Show of things' and those who can see into the things themselves; between those who are drawn to surface glitter and illusion, and those who look beyond to reality. Williams finds that the word "Vanity" in the novel means more than in Bunyan's biblical reference: "it suggests that those who seek it are fundamentally godless and are living their lives without directing their energies in a fruitful way," thus, "Amelia would be a creature who was seeking after Vanity because she worshipped something unreal, and Dobbin would be so because he sought for happiness and expected to find it by means of another human being" (Pollard, 186).

"Vanity Fair" contains satirical portraits of worldly clergymen, such as the Reverend Bute Crawley, who lives for hunting, drinking and gambling, and the church is shown not to be exempt from the social corruption the novel depicts. Thackeray may be making a distinction between faith and practice. In the mid-nineteenth century, the Established Church, the Church of England (or Anglican Church), was under attack from critics who pointed out that many men were ordained for the sake of the living rather than from any real vocation, and were able to appoint curates who performed their duties for, often, a fraction of their income. The establishment of dissenting and reformed churches had also weakened the hold of the Church of England on society, and many of the newer sects were attracting members from the working and lower middle classes, though the high Tory, upper-middle- and upper-classes tended to remain Anglican.

The materialistic and godless attitude of characters in "Vanity Fair" may also derive from the Victorian sense that the sea of faith was ebbing. Science, in particular theories of evolution, were challenging conventional religious belief (in for example the nature of Creation), and there was a feeling that people, at least affluent people, were becoming more interested in things—the new consumer goods available—than things of the spirit.

Biographical Context

Thackeray was born in Calcutta, India, in 1811, to an upper-middle-class professional family. The Thackerays and Bechers (his mother's family) were doctors, lawyers, civil servants, and functionaries of the East Indian Company, and his stepfather, Henry Carmichael-Smyth, was an officer in the Bengal Engineers. From his early years in India, Thackeray knew at first-hand the exploitative conditions in which "servants of empire" such as Jos Sedley made fortunes in "the colonies" (though Jos himself has not returned with a fortune). He also knew what it was to live hand-to-mouth. After leaving Trinity College, Cambridge in 1830 without taking a degree, and a short period in legal chambers in London, he spent a year in France during which he ran through most of his fortune in the same way as Rawdon Crawley spends his more slender means in "Vanity Fair." The failure of Indian banks the following year disposed of most of what remained. As well as hardship, he understood unhappiness and the absence of maternal affection. Sent away from India and his mother at the age of five, he had a miserable time at school in Southampton, and later attended Charterhouse at a point in the school's history when academic standards were low and the behavior of both teachers and pupils could be brutish. He married in 1836 Isabella Shawe, and had three daughters, one of whom died in infancy. After the birth of their third daughter, Harriet, Isabella entered what would today be called a depressed state and tried to take her own life. Several bouts of mental illness followed, and eventually she was declared incurably insane. Thackeray placed her with a keeper in Camberwell, in south-east London. While she lived he could not remarry, and contemporaries spread the rumor that he was having an affair with his daughters' governess, a rumor

evidently untrue, though inadvertently given credence by Charlotte Brontë's dedication to him in 1848 of the second edition of her novel "Jane Eyre," in which a man who keeps an insane wife locked away in the attic falls in love with the governess of his ward. The opinion Brontë expressed of Thackeray in her preface to the novel, like that of many contemporary and later critics, was high indeed:

> I see in him an intellect profounder and more unique than his contemporaries have yet recognized; because I regard him as the first social regenerator of the day—as the very master of that working corps who would restore to rectitude the warped system of things; because I think no commentator on his writings has yet found the comparison that suits him, the terms which rightly characterize his talent. They say he is like Fielding: they talk of his wit, humor, comic powers. He resembles Fielding as an eagle does a vulture: Fielding could stoop on carrion, but Thackeray never does. His wit is bright, his humor attractive, but both bear the same relation to his serious genius that the mere lambent sheet-lightning playing under the edge of the summer-cloud does to the electric death-spark hid in its womb. Finally, I have alluded to Mr. Thackeray, because to him—if he will accept the tribute of a total stranger—I have dedicated this second edition of "Jane Eyre" (36).

The frontispiece of the first edition of "Vanity Fair" has an illustration of a shabby, down-at-heel actor in a torn and patched costume peering into a cracked looking glass. This suggests that though Thackeray, actor/manager of the "puppet show" "Vanity Fair," was not afraid to look into the same glass as he held up to society. He was ruthless in mirroring the flaws and failings of his fellow-human beings, but equally willing to acknowledge his own.

Sandie Byrne

Works Cited

Brontë, Charlotte. Preface to the 2nd edition of *Jane Eyre* (1848); repr. Harmondsworth: Penguin, 1986.

Illustrations to *Vanity Fair*. Retrieved from http://www.victorianweb.org/graphics/thackeray/gallery1.html.

Thackeray, William Makepeace. *Vanity Fair*. John Sutherland, ed. Oxford: Oxford World's Classics, 1998.

Williams, Ioan. "Thackeray" (1968), reprinted in Pollard, ed., "Thackeray," *Vanity Fair: Critical Essays*, Basingstoke: Macmillan, 1986.

Discussion Questions

1. If "Vanity Fair" is "A Novel Without a Hero" is it also without a heroine?
2. How significant are wills and inheritance in the story?
3. Does the narrative voice show compassion for any of the "bad" characters?
4. Does the narrative voice judge any one character more harshly than the others?
5. The battle scenes of Waterloo which readers are led to anticipate as the climax to a section of the novel do not materialize. Why do you think this is?
6. The minor character Mrs. O'Dowd is said to be a caricature of Thackeray's mother-in-law. Is she the only stock-type in the novel?
7. Are any of the characters in entirely good or flawless?
8. The story is told by an omniscient narrator rather than by one or more of its protagonists. What effects does this allow in the novel?
9. Does Becky Sharp ever achieve happiness in the story?
10. There are many parallels in "Vanity Fair," for example, we see both Amelia and Becky and Dobbin and George at school, and both Amelia and Becky have a son. Can you find other parallels?

Essay Ideas

1. Discuss the proposition that the dominant tone of the narrative voice of "Vanity Fair" is irony.
2. Regarding the "silver fork novels," "Waterloo novels" or "Newgate novels" of the period, describe the ways in which "Vanity Fair" parodies any of these popular genres and their readers.
3. Describe how the final form of the novel betrays its origin in publication by installment.
4. Argue for or against the proposition that Becky Sharp murders Jos Sedley.
5. If "Vanity Fair" is a "puppet show," does it follow that the novel's characters are all two-dimensional or without subtle characterization?

Villette

by Charlotte Brontë

Content Synopsis

Charlotte Brontë's (1816–1855) mid-nineteenth century English novel, "Villette" (1853), opens with the fourteen-year-old Lucy Snowe's visit to the home of her godmother, Mrs. Bretton. Soon after her arrival, a young girl, Polly, comes to stay while her father, Mr. Home, travels abroad to recover from the death of his "silly and frivolous" (63) wife. Polly, a solemn and precocious child, soon forms a deep attachment to Mrs. Bretton's kind-hearted, if somewhat thoughtless sixteen-year-old son, Graham.

Lucy returns home and (with characteristic evasiveness) refers cryptically to some family calamity that, eight years later, will force her to find employment as a companion to an elderly spinster, Miss Marchmont. After Miss Marchmont's death, Lucy impulsively decides to seek employment abroad. She travels to Villette (based on real-life Brussels), where she happens by chance upon Madame Beck's school. Madame Beck employs Lucy on the strength of a physiognomy reading by the school's literature professor, M. Paul Emmanuel. Crucially, unlike all of Lucy's other acquaintances he does not see her as "grave [and] sensible" (554) or as an "inoffensive shadow" (403). Instead, he tells Madame Beck Lucy possesses a capacity for evil as well as good, and that he hopes good will predominate in her nature.

Lucy works her way from nursery maid to English teacher. Though professionally successful, Lucy's deep suspicion of Catholicism prevents her from becoming close to her fellow teachers or pupils. The only exception is Ginevra Fanshawe, a beautiful but flighty young English girl, whose suitors include the mysterious "Isidore," and the roguish Colonel Alfred de Hamal. When Madame Beck's daughter becomes ill, a handsome young English doctor, called Dr. John, attends to her. With her usual coyness, Lucy does not immediately reveal to the reader that Dr. John is, in fact, the same Graham Bretton she knew all those years ago, or that he is "Isidore," Ginevra's admirer.

Lucy remains behind at the school during the long vacation, alone but for a servant and a mentally impaired student, referred to as "the cretin." She experiences an extreme loneliness that results in a form of mental and physical breakdown. In desperation, Lucy visits a priest's confessional, after which she collapses in the street. Lucy awakes in a strange house, which she discovers to be the home of Graham and his mother, who have also endured some financial hardship. Lucy finally reveals her identity to her old acquaintances and begins her recovery. Returning to Madame Beck's, Lucy's love for Graham, though never explicitly declared, becomes increasingly apparent. Lucy also begins to see the mysterious, ghostly figure of a nun around the school and its gardens. Graham interprets these sightings as a sign of her psychological fragility and he begins to write her letters in a kind-hearted attempt to temper her loneliness. She treasures his letters, while striving to control her feelings or any romantic hope.

On a visit to the theatre with Graham to see the legendary actress Vashti, they encounter another set of old friends, Polly and her father, who is now Count de Bassompierre. There is a seven-week hiatus in Lucy's correspondence with the Brettons. When Lucy realizes she will never receive another letter from Graham, she buries his other correspondence in a hermetically sealed jar under the old pear tree in Madame Beck's garden, where once more, Lucy sees the mysterious figure of the nun.

Realizing Graham's growing love for Polly, Lucy's feelings begin to shift towards the fiery tempered, but good-hearted, M. Paul. He claims to see her nature as it truly is: not the timid creature others see, but a woman with a blazing soul who must be "kept down" (226). He becomes her French tutor and their relationship develops and deepens.

Madame Beck asks Lucy to carry out an errand to malignant, shriveled Madame Walravens. Lucy discovers M. Paul was once engaged to Madame Walravens's daughter, Justine-Marie. When her family rejected him, Justine-Marie withdrew to a convent and died. Later, her family was ruined financially, and M. Paul began to support them, making it impossible for him to marry. Lucy meets the priest from the confessional once more, Pere Silas. He is Madame Walravens's confidant and M. Paul's mentor. He confesses to spying on Lucy and presses her to convert to Catholicism. Madame Walravens, Madame Beck, and Pere Silas plan to undermine Lucy's affection for M. Paul. However, rather than shaking her faith in him, their actions strengthen it, as she realizes the constancy and kindness that lies beneath his often despotic and bullying exterior.

Lucy discovers that M. Paul must leave on a long voyage. She becomes increasingly distraught waiting for him to say farewell to her. Madame Beck slips her an opiate to calm her, but the drug causes Lucy to become more restless. She makes her way to the park at midnight, where a fete is being held. There, in a dreamlike state, she observes Graham, Polly and M. de Bassompiere as well as the "secret junta" of Madame Walravens, Beck, and Pere Silas. She discovers that the Walravens' estate in the West Indies has grown prosperous again and that they are to send M. Paul to manage it for two or three years. Lucy then returns home to discover Ginevra has eloped with de Hamal, leaving the nun costume de Hamal used for their secret trysts in Lucy's bed.

M. Paul finally meets with Lucy two days before he leaves. He takes her to a school he has established for her and promises that on his return from the West Indies she will share his life. Lucy spends three happy years building up the school's business and a pensionnat (boarding school) next door. However, the novel ends ambiguously on the day M. Paul is due to return, leaving the reader to decide whether he arrives home safely or whether he perishes at sea.

One of the most significant oppositions in the novel is that between what Lucy calls "feeling and reason." Lucy constantly strives to use her reason to suppress and control her feelings. Drawing on the gruesome tale of the Old Testament characters, Jael and Sisera, Lucy believes she must use her reason to drive a nail through the temples of her longings. Lucy's extreme self-repression (seen in the marked evasiveness of her narrative) also manifests itself in characters that function as Lucy's psychological doubles or alternative selves.

First, there is the spinster figure, Miss Marchmont, whose fiancé and true love, Frank, was killed one Christmas Eve, shortly before their wedding. Miss Marchmont's lonely fate seems to foreshadow one interpretation of Lucy's own destiny. Secondly, there is story of Miss Turner "a poor friendless English teacher," employed and then abandoned by Madame Beck, who represents another of Lucy's possible fates. Thirdly, there is the mysterious figure of the nun. The nun is associated with moments of extreme emotion. Lucy initially sees her after reading her first letter from Graham Bretton—a rare instant of unrestrained feeling for Lucy. She next encounters the nun in Madame Beck's garden just after she has buried Graham's letters—and, metaphorically, her feelings for him—in an air-tight jar under the old pear tree. Lucy's third sighting is with M. Paul. At this point Lucy is thinking about her old love for Graham, and her relationship with M. Paul increasingly becomes emotionally charged. M. Paul describes the "affinity" between himself and Lucy, while she reveals that M. Paul was the stranger who gave her the bunch of white violets on the street, which she has secretly preserved.

The figure of the nun is important for several reasons. As a symbol of celibacy, the nun represents Lucy's self-repression. However, the nun is finally revealed as Colonel de Hamal in disguise. De Hamal has adopted the costume to facilitate his romantic trysts with Ginevra. In this sense, the nun also represents Lucy's veiled sexual desire, as the final discovery of the nun costume in her bed confirms. The figure of the nun also symbolizes Lucy's ambivalent relationship to Catholicism. While Lucy claims to be repulsed by Catholicism, she is clearly drawn to the religion emotionally, as her visit to Pere Silas's confessional illustrates. Similarly, Lucy is clearly disturbed by the figure of the nun, and yet fascinated by her. Finally, the nun also represents another instance of Lucy's emotional suppression: the barrier to her relationship with M. Paul, his first love Justine-Marie, who withdrew to a convent and died.

Another important symbol in the novel is the storm. Just as the nun appears to Lucy at moments of heightened tension, so too are times of great calamity for Lucy accompanied by storms. Her own family's ruin is described through metaphorical references to storms, while the death of Miss Marchmont is accompanied by a storm. It is a storm at the end of the long vacation that prompts her breakdown, and a storm rages as she collapses on the streets of Villette after her visit to Pere Silas. A storm accompanies Lucy's visit to Madame Walravens, where she learns of Justine-Marie. Finally, Lucy suggests at the close of the novel that M. Paul dies in a storm at sea.

Lucy's doubles and the recurring storms illustrate the manner in which she constantly externalizes her feelings as a means of controlling them. Her narrative is also constantly evasive and unreliable. She often withholds information from the reader such as the identity of Dr. John, the fate of her family and, of course, M. Paul. This strategy symbolizes both her desire for control and her deep self-alienation.

Historical Context

"Villette" offers an insight into the relationship between Great Britain and the continental Europe in the mid-nineteenth century. Napoleon was defeated at the Battle of Waterloo in 1815, and the hostilities of the Napoleonic wars were still a fresh memory. Indeed, Patrick Brontë, Charlotte's father, made a point of visiting Waterloo in 1842, when he accompanied Charlotte and Emily to Brussels. The Duke of Wellington had been a special hero to Charlotte growing up, often featuring in her juvenilia, and her view of continental Europe was still shaped by these recent hostilities.

"Villette's" only direct references to the Napoleonic wars are seen in Lucy's descriptions of M. Paul, who is constantly compared to Napoleon Bonaparte. However, there is also latent antagonism or tension between the English and the continental European characters in the novel that stems, at least in part, from these earlier hostilities. M. Paul abuses England and the English "with vicious relish" (429), causing Lucy to remark "it is curious to discover how these clowns of Labassecour secretly hate England" (429). Lucy herself is extremely jingoistic. Her students, she claims, think nothing of lying, and are incapable of the same kind of hard work she would expect from an English girl. In addition, while the influence of republicanism results in "equality" being "much practiced" (146), Lucy also claims that the Labassecourians are more comfortable with despotism, like that practiced by Napoleon, than the English. Not only are young women subject to constant surveillance and observation on the continent, but according to Lucy they also "rather liked the pressure of a firm heel" (147)

The nineteenth century was also a period of colonial expansion for many European nations. These colonies touched the lives of those who stayed at home, as well as those who traveled abroad. Lucy discovers that Madam Walravens owns an estate in the French colony Guadeloupe, and intends to send M. Paul there for two or three years to manage it. In this instance, a colonial property seems to offer the possibility of freedom (working the estate for three years will release M. Paul from his obligations to Madame Walravens) as it does in another of Brontë's novels, "Jane Eyre." However, in "Villette," colonialism may also have a very detrimental impact, as it is suggested that M. Paul dies on the voyage back from Guadeloupe in a storm at sea.

Societal Context

The role of women became an increasingly important question as the nineteenth century progressed. Mary Wollstonecraft's "A Vindication of the Rights of Women" had demanded equality and proper occupation for women in the late eighteenth century. However, even by the mid-nineteenth century the proper sphere of women was still regarded as the home and the "angel by the hearth" was a familiar image.

"Villette" offers an implicit critique of nineteenth century expectations of women. Lucy reacts with derision to the painting sequence "La vie d'une femme" (277), which depicts the life of the exemplary woman as a transition from pious daughter to dutiful wife and mother to devout widow. Lucy's own experience of domestic confinement during the long vacation result in her near mental breakdown, while she describes the happiest years of her life as those she spends building the business of her own school.

As well as considering the position of women in general, Brontë was particularly keen to examine the role of the spinster in society. Given the emphasis placed on women's roles as wives and mothers, the spinster was regarded as almost superfluous in the nineteenth century. As an impoverished and unmarried woman, Lucy is treated with some carelessness by her friends, the Brettons and the de Bassompierres, who continually fail to recognize her emotional needs and desires. Brontë also explores the limited options available for the middle class single woman, driven by financial circumstances to seek employment. Such women could become companions, as Lucy does to Miss Marchmont, governesses like Jane Eyre, or endure the drudgery of school teaching, as Lucy does in "Villette." One of the few possibilities of achieving independence was to set up a school, as Charlotte and Emily planned to, and as Lucy succeeds in doing in "Villette."

Nineteenth century British society was also driven by ideas of moral management of the self. It was believed that "uncivilized" drives and desires could (and should) be controlled and quelled, as Matthew Arnold's fear of "Barbarians" in "Culture and Anarchy" exemplifies. Lucy Snowe's attitudes towards her own sexual desire and appetites reflect this belief. Not only does she suppress her desires by refusing to report them in her narrative, however, she literally buries her love for Graham Bretton in a hermetically sealed jar under the old pear tree.

Religious Context

Lucy Snowe's virulent anti-Catholicism was not uncommon in mid-nineteenth century Britain, where suspicion and fear of the Catholic Church was growing, especially among members of the Protestant Church of England. In 1850, the Pope appointed Nicholas Wiseman as the first Cardinal and Archbishop of Westminster since the English Reformation. There was a panic-stricken response among Protestants, especially Anglicans, who were suspicious of Wiseman's influence on the Oxford Movement, a High Church group within the Church of England, and his success in converting Anglicans to Catholicism. These suspicions were confounded for many when Wiseman confirmed J. H. Newman, a founder of the Oxford Movement, into the Church of Rome. Furthermore, there were rumors that Wiseman planned to reunite the Church of England with the Catholic Church, if he became Pope, by abolishing celibacy for priests.

The Brontë household in Haworth took part in public debate on these issues. Patrick Brontë argued in the "Leeds Intelligencer" that the Church of England was in danger of being seen as a "Romish nursery" instead of a "bulwark of Protestantism," while Arthur Bell Nicholl signed a resolution condemning the Pope for appointing a cardinal and archbishop in Britain (Barker 661). These events almost certainly increased Charlotte Brontë's own dislike of Catholicism, which stemmed in part at least from her lonely experiences in Brussels, and her own near conversion.

Lucy Snowe's own religious faith in "Villette" is carefully presented as non-Sectarian; she visits "indiscriminately . . . the three Protestant chapels of Villette" (513), rendering the religious conflict in the novel a simple Protestant-Catholic opposition. For Lucy Snowe, Protestantism symbolizes individual choice and freedom, while Catholicism represents an authoritarian, repressive structure, based on a culture of spying and surveillance. Confirming mid-nineteenth century suspicions of Catholicism, Lucy Snowe is subject to a campaign of conversion, orchestrated by Pere Silas: he attempts personal persuasion after her visit to his confessional, he watches her secretly, and he persuades M. Paul to leave tracts and pamphlets in her desk. But while Lucy professes an intense dislike of Catholicism, like her creator, she betrays a considerable attraction to the faith. Pere Silas states, perhaps correctly, that "Protestantism is altogether too dry, cold and prosaic" (234) for Lucy. Not only does she visit the confessional, but she is fascinated both by the nun that haunts Madame Beck's school and Justine-Marie, M. Paul's first love. Furthermore, while she may claim to dislike the attentions of Pere Silas, he and M. Paul take an active interest in Lucy Snowe, and claim to see her as she really is. By contrast, for the Protestant characters of the novel, like the Brettons, Lucy is nothing but an "inoffensive shadow" (403), whom they carelessly neglect. Protestantism may be figured in "Villette" as guaranteeing individual freedom, but it is a lonely freedom for Lucy.

Scientific & Technological Context

"Villette" is dominated by the nineteenth century "scientific" practices of phrenology and physiognomy. Physiognomy uses physical appearance, and especially the face, to judge character. This system of interpreting human nature has its roots in the middle ages. Phrenology, founded by F. J. Gall and J. K. Spurzheim in the late eighteenth century, attempts to gauge an individual's mental capacity by "reading" the bumps on the skull. George Combe helped promote phrenology in Victorian Britain, where his book, "The Constitution of Man," was only a little less popular than the Bible, "Pilgrims Progress and Robinson Crusoe" (Dames 371). The notion that human character and intelligence could be read and understood from appearance was attractive to many people in the Victorian period, and both systems were regarded as sciences and sources of entertainment.

Brontë was extremely attracted to phrenology and physiognomy and had herself visited a phrenologist, Dr. J. P. Browne, in 1851. Ideas from phrenology and physiognomy are apparent in her all her novels, particularly "Villette." Lucy Snow continually employs phrenological vocabulary in her readings of others. For example, when talking of her students' parental generosity, she states, "The Labassecouriens must have a large organ of philoprogenitiveness" (166). When she contrasts the characters of Ginevra Fanshawe and Paulina de Bassompierre, she focuses on the physical differences between the two young women. Lucy's reading of their faces supports her belief that the character of Ginevra is less sensitive and cruder than that of her cousin: "Nature having traced all these details slightly and with a careless hand, in Miss Fanshawe's case; and in Miss de Bassompierre's, wrought them to a high delicate finish" (398).

Crucially, Lucy herself is also the subject of a phrenological and physiognomic reading by M. Paul Emmanuel. Madame Beck instructs her cousin, "We know your skill in physiognomy; use it now. Read that countenance" (128). Rather than reading Lucy Snowe as a timid, insipid individual, M. Paul believes she has a capacity for good and evil. M. Paul continues to read Lucy through "Villette," offering a very different interpretation of her character from others. He believes Lucy is extremely passionate and "must be kept down" (226). Lucy's (and "Villette's") tacit agreement with his readings, signal the importance placed on phrenology and physiognomy in the novel.

In contrast to phrenology and physiognomy, the novel presents the conventional medicine practiced by Graham Bretton as unreliable. Graham's reading of Lucy's condition epitomizes the male dominated medical establishment's readings of female patients. He misinterprets her character, reading her as a woman without passion or desire, while he assumes her visions of the nun are a sign of her

hysteria when of course, they are finally revealed to be the very real and substantial presence of Colonel De Hamel.

Biographical Context

For better or worse, critics have read Charlotte Brontë's novels as heavily autobiographical since their publication. Certainly, "Villette" draws extensively on Brontë's experiences in Brussels, like her first novel, "The Professor" (written 1846, published 1857). Indeed Brontë's time in Belgium has been identified as "the single biggest influence on her life" by some biographers (Barker 412).

Charlotte first traveled to Brussels in February 1842 accompanied by her sister, Emily, and her father, the Rev. Patrick Brontë. She and Emily had enrolled for six months as students in a school in Brussels with the principal aim of improving their French and foreign language skills. The school was owned and run by Madame Claire Zoe Heger. Her husband, Constantin Georges Romain Heger was a teacher at the neighboring boy's school, who, like M. Paul Emmanuel, also gave literature lessons at his wife's school. M. Heger has long been recognized as the model for M. Paul Emmanuel. Charlotte described him as "very choleric and irritable as to temperament; a little black ugly being" (Barker 383). But as with M. Paul and Lucy Snowe, he was quick to recognize Charlotte's talents. Indeed, M. Heger also had an important impact on Charlotte Brontë's writing style, encouraging her to write tighter, cleaner prose, through successive rewrites of her essays.

The architecture and surroundings of Madame Heger's school is clearly the model for Madame Beck's school in "Villette." Madame Heger's school, like Brontë's fictional version, had an enclosed garden, with an "Allee defendue" down one side. In the same way that Madame Beck's pupils are forbidden to frequent this path, so Madame Heger's pupils were also forbidden from entering the pathway, as it neighbored a boy's school. Like Lucy, Charlotte Brontë was promoted to English teacher, while Emily became a music teacher in August 1842. Charlotte was very happy in Brussels during this period, but the death of Aunt Branwell forced them home in November 1842. Charlotte then traveled back to Brussels alone in January 1843. This experience inspired Lucy's lonely journey to Villette from London. Charlotte was now employed as a teacher and earned sixteen pounds a year. But her experience in Brussels was very different the second time around. Not only was she without Emily, but many of their English acquaintances had left the city. Furthermore, as a Protestant, she felt isolated from the other teachers, and mixed with them little. Charlotte became, like Lucy Snowe, increasingly lonely.

As a result of this loneliness, she became increasingly dependent on M. Heger's approval, and almost certainly fell deeply in love with him—as Lucy Snowe does with M. Paul. Consequently, her relationship with Madame Heger became increasingly difficult. During the long vacation, Charlotte Brontë was driven by loneliness and—presumably—feelings of guilt about M. Heger to visit a Catholic confessional. Like Lucy Snowe, Brontë claimed she almost converted to Catholicism at this moment. Instead she resolved to leave Brussels, and did so in January 1844.

Brontë did not just draw on her experiences in Brussels when writing "Villette." Graham Bretton and his mother are also based on her publisher, George Smith and his mother. Uncomfortable at the extent to which the novel reveals her feelings for Smith, Brontë was at first reluctant to share her work with him, and at one point even demanded that the novel be published anonymously.

Brontë also realized there was a good chance the Hegers would recognize her depiction of them and she tried to stop publication of "Villette" in Belgium. "Villette" eventually became available in Brussels, where Madame Heger's school was recognized—allegedly causing some loss of business as a result (Barker 787). When Elizabeth Gaskell visited Brussels to collect information for her biography of Charlotte Brontë, Madame Heger was still sufficiently piqued to refuse to meet with her, though her husband supplied Mrs. Gaskill with some of Brontë's devoirs and letters.

Anne Longmuir, Ph.D.

Works Cited

Barker, Juliet. *The Brontës*. London, Phoenix, 1995.

Brontë, Charlotte. *Villette*. London: Penguin, 1979.

Clark-Beattie, Rosemary. *Fables of Rebellion: Anti-Catholicism and the Structure of 'Villette'*. ELH 53.4 (1986), 821–847.

Dames, Nicholas. *The Clinical Novel: Phrenology and 'Villette.' Novel: A Forum on Fiction"* 29.3 (1996): 367–390.

Discussion Questions

1. Lucy Snowe was called "Lucy Frost" at one point in Charlotte Brontë's draft of "Villette." What might have prompted Brontë to change Lucy's last name? What are the different connotations of Frost and Snow? Does it change your interpretation of Lucy's character?

2. Lucy compares herself to Jael and Sisera (176), arguing that her reason must drive a nail through the temples of her longings. Where do you see her suppressing her feelings in this novel? Discuss with specific reference to plot events and characters in the novel.

3. Lucy is sometimes an unreliable narrator. Identify specific points in the text where she fails to tell the reader the whole truth. What does her unreliability as a narrator tell us about Lucy? How does it help us understand her character?

4. Graham Bretton sees Lucy as an "inoffensive shadow" (403), whereas M. Paul believes she is a passionate woman who "must be kept down" (226). Which description best fits Lucy?

5. Lucy plays a male fop opposite Ginevra Fanshawe in the school play. She wears a man's waistcoat, but refuses to wear breeches. How does this scene help us understand Lucy's relationship with Ginerva and Lucy's attitude to her own gender identity?

6. Doppelgangers and split personalities are a staple of Victorian fiction. Who are Lucy's doubles? And, in what way does she seem to have a split personality?

7. Lucy seems to be vehemently anti-Catholic, and yet she visits a confessional after her breakdown in the long vacation. How would you describe her attitude to Catholicism? Why is it attractive to her despite her bigotry?

8. Polly and Ginevra are presented as physical and moral opposites. Compare the two characters with specific reference to the text. Lucy describes their future lives. Is Ginevra unfairly punished?

9. Young women are constantly spied on, or put under surveillance in "Villette." How does this affect their characters and identity? Discuss with specific reference to the text.

10. "Villette" explores the romantic and vocational options of an impoverished single woman in the mid-nineteenth century. In what ways might it be described as a feminist novel?

Essay Ideas

1. Analyze the unreliable narration of Lucy Snowe.

2. Explore the uses of physical appearance as character: Phrenology and physiognomy in "Villette."

3. Analyze the use of doubles and doppelgangers in "Villette."

4. Compare and contrast the roles available for women in the text: Cleopatra or "La Vie D'une Femme."

5. Explore the symbolism and development of the figure of the Nun and anti-Catholicism in "Villette."

BIBLIOGRAPHY

Ackroyd, Peter. *Dickens*. New York: Harper Collins, 1990.

———. *Dickens*. London: Minerva, 1991.

Adams, James Eli. *Dandies and Desert Saints: Styles of Victorian Manhood*. Ithaca, NY: Cornell UP, 1995.

Adams, Robert, ed. *Thomas More Utopia*. New York and London: Norton, 1975.

Altick, Richard. *Victorian People and Ideas*. New York: Norton, 1983.

Atwood, Margaret. "Running with the Tigers." *Flesh and the Mirror: Essays on the Art of Angela Carter*. Ed. Lorna Sage. London: Virago, 1994. 117–135.

Auerbach, Nina. *The Woman and the Demon: The Life of a Victorian Myth*. Massachusetts: Harvard UP, 1984.

Barker, Juliet. *The Brontë*. London: Phoenix, 1995.

Batchelor, John. *H. G. Wells*. Cambridge: Cambridge UP, 1985.

Bergonzi, Bernard. *The Early H. G. Wells: A Study of the Scientific Romances*. Manchester, England: Manchester UP, 1961.

Bettelheim, Bruno. *The Uses of Enchantment: The Meaning and Importance of Fairy Tales*. New York: Knopf, 1976.

Bigsby, Christopher. "An Interview with Kazuo Ishiguro." *The European English Messenger* (Autumn 1990): 26–29.

Bloom, Harold. "Introduction." *Bloom's Modern Critical Views: Mary Shelley*. Philadelphia: Chelsea, 1985. 1–10.

Bottigheimer, Ruth B., ed. *Fairy Tales and Society: Illusion, Allusion, and Paradigm*. Philadelphia: U of Pennsylvania P, 1986.

Botting, Fred. *Gothic*. London and New York: Routledge, 1996.

Brannan, Robert Louis, ed. *Under the Management of Mr. Charles Dickens: His Production of the Frozen Deep*. Ithaca: Cornell UP, 1966.

Bridger, Francis. *A Charmed Life: The Spirituality of Potterworld*. London: Darton, Longman and Todd, 2001.

Brontë, Charlotte. *Villette*. London: Penguin, 1979.

———. *Preface to the 2nd edition of Jane Eyre*. 1848. Harmondsworth: Penguin, 1986.

———. *Jane Eyre Case Studies in Contemporary Criticism*. Ed. Beth Newman. Boston: Bedford/St. Martin's, 1996.

Brooke, Patricia. "Lyons and Tigers and Wolves-Oh My! Revisionary Fairy Tales in the Work of Angela Carter." *Critical Survey* 16.1 (2004): 67–88.

Brooks, Chris. *Signs for the Times. Symbolic Realism in the Mid-Victorian World*. London: George Allen and Unwin, 1984.

Brown, Homer Obed. "Tom Jones: The 'Bastard' of History." *Boundary 2* 7.2 (1979): 201–234.

Buickerood, James G., ed. *Masham, Lady Damaris Cudworth. The Philosophical Works*. Bristol: Thoemmes Continuum, 2004.

Burke, Edmund. *A Philosophical Enquiry into the Origin of Our Ideas of the Sublime and Beautiful*. Ed. Adam Phillips. Oxford: Oxford UP, 1990.

Butler, Marilyn. *Romantics, Rebels and Reactionaries: English Literature and It's Background, 1760–1830*. New York and Oxford: Oxford UP, 1982.

Calder, Jenni. "Introduction." *Dr. Jekyll and Mr. Hyde and Other Stories*. By Robert Louis Stevenson. London: Penguin Books, 1979.

Carroll, John, ed. *Selected Letters of Samuel Richardson*. Oxford: Clarendon, 1964.

Carter, Angela, trans. *The Fairy Tales of Charles Perrault*. Illustrator Martin Ware. London: Victor Gollancz, 1977.

———. *The Bloody Chamber*. 1981 (c. 1979). London: Penguin 1987.

———. *Shaking a Leg: Collected Journalism and Writings*. London: Chatto & Windus, 1997.

Cavaliero, Glen. *A Reading of E. M. Forster*. London: Macmillan, 1979.

Chabon, Michael, ed. "Dust and Demons." *Navigating the Golden Compass: Religion, Science and Dæmonology in Philip Pullman's His Dark Materials*. Ed. Glen Yeffeth. Dallas, Texas: Benbella, 2005. 1–14.

Chittik, Kathryn. *Dickens and the 1830s*. Cambridge: Cambridge UP, 1990.

Cioran, Emile. *Histoire et utopie*. Paris: Gallimard, 1960.

Clark-Beattie, Rosemary. "Fables of Rebellion: Anti-Catholicism and the Structure of 'Villette'." *English Literary History* 53.4 (1986): 821–847.

Clery, E. J. *The Rise of Supernatural Fiction 1762–1800*. Cambridge: Cambridge UP, 1995.

———. "The Genesis of 'Gothic' Fiction." *The Cambridge Companion to the Gothic*. Ed. Jerrold E. Hogle. Cambridge: Cambridge UP, 2002. 21–40.

Colley, Linda. *Britons: Forging the Nation 1707–1837*. New Haven and London: Yale UP, 1992.

Collins, Philip. *Dickens and Crime*. London: Macmillan, 1962.

Collins, Wilkie. *The Frozen Deep*. London: Hesperus, 2004.

Coogan, Michael D., ed. *The New Oxford Annotated Bible*. New York: Oxford UP, 1989.

Cooper, Lettice. *The European Novelists Series— Robert Louis Stevenson*. London: Arthur Barker Limited, 1967.

Cornell, Louis. *Kipling in India*. London: Macmillan, 1966.

Cornford, Stephen, ed. *Edward Young, Night Thoughts (1741)*. Cambridge: Cambridge UP, 1989.

Cundy, Catherine, and Salman Rushdie. *Contemporary World Writers Series*. Manchester: Manchester UP, 1996.

Dahl, Roald. *Skin and Other Stories*. New York: Viking/ Penguin Books, 2000.

Dames, Nicholas. "The Clinical Novel: Phrenology and 'Villette.'" *Novel: A Forum on Fiction* 29.3 (1996): 367–390.

Davis, Philip. *The Oxford English Literary History. The Victorians. Vol. 8: 1830–1880*. 1880. Oxford: Oxford UP, 2002.

Delany, Paul. "Island of Money: Rentier Culture in *Howards End*." *New Casebooks: E. M. Forster*. Ed. Jeremy Tambling. Basingstoke, England: Palgrave Macmillan, 1995, 67–80.

Dickens, Charles. "On Strike." *Household Words* 11 Feb. 1854: 196–210.

———. *Oliver Twist*. New York & London: Norton, 1993.

———. *Hard Times for These Times*. 1854. Ed. Kate Flint. London: Penguin, 1995.

Dijkstra, Bram. *Idols of Perversity: Fantasies of Feminine Evil in Fin-de-Siècle Culture*. New York: Oxford UP, 1988.

Duncker, Patricia. "Re-Imagining the Fairy Tales: Angela Carter' Bloody Chambers." *Literature and History* 10.1 (1984): 3–14.

Eaves, T. C. Duncan, and Ben D. Kimpel. *Samuel Richardson: A Biography*. Oxford: Clarendon, 1971.

Fielding, Henry. *Tom Jones*. Eds. John Bender and Simon Stern. Oxford: Oxford UP, 1996.

Forster, E. M. *Howards End*. London: Penguin, 1973.

Foyster, Elizabeth. *Marital Violence: An English Family History, 1660–1857*. Cambridge: Cambridge UP, 2005.

Freud, Sigmund. "Three Essays on Sexuality". *Sigmund Freud. Vol 7. On Sexuality: Three Essays on Sexuality and Other Works*. 1905. Ed. Angela Richard and Trans. James Strachey. London: Penguin, 1991.

Gallagher, Catherine. *The Industrial Reformation of English Fiction. Social Discourse and Narrative Form 1827–1867*. Chicago: U of Chicago P, 1985.

Gamble, Sarah. *Angela Carter: Writing from the Front Line*. Edinburgh: Edinburgh UP, 1997.

Gilbert, Sandra M., and Susan Gubar. *The Madwoman in the Attic: The Woman Writer and the Nineteenth Century Imagination*. New Haven: Yale UP, 1979.

———. "Horror's Twin: Mary Shelley's Monstrous Eve." *Bloom's Major Literary Characters: Frankenstein*. Ed. Harold Bloom. Philadelphia: Chelsea, 1985. 55–74.

Graff, Ann-Barbara. "Administrative Nihilism": Evolution, Ethics and Victorian Utopian Satire. *Utopian Studies* 12.2 (2001): 33–52.

Gray, Jennie. *Horace Walpole and William Beckford: Pioneers of the Gothic Revival."* Gothic Society Monograph Series. Chislehurst, UK: The Gothic Society, 1994.

Grayzel, Susan R. *Women's Identities at War: Gender, Motherhood and Politics in Britain and France during the First World War*. Chapel Hill and London: The U of Carolina P, 1999.

Gribbin, Mary, and John Gribbin. *The Science of Philip Pullman's 'His Dark Materials.'* New York: Knopf, 2005.

Haggard, H. Rider. *Twentieth Century Literary Criticism*. Vol. 11. Detroit: Gale Research, 1983.

———. *She: A History of Adventure*. Ed. Daniel Karlin. New York: Oxford UP, 1991.

———. *King Solomon's Mines*. Ed. Gerald Monsman. Toronto, Canada: Broadview, 2002.

Hall, Radclyffe. *The Unlit Lamp*. 1924. London: Virago, 1981.

Hammond, J. R. *H. G. Wells and the Short Story*. Basingstoke, England: Palgrave Macmillan, 1992.

Harris, Michael. *Outsiders and Insiders: Perspectives of Third World Culture in British and Post Colonial Fiction*. New York: Peter Lang, 1992.

Hennessy, James Pope. *Robert Louis Stevenson*. London: Jonathan Cape, 1974.

Hoffman, Michael J., and Patrick D. Murphy, eds. "John Barth. The Literature of Replenishment." *Essentials of the Theory of Fiction*. Durham and London: Duke UP, 1988. 273–286.

Hogle, Jerrold E., ed. *The Cambridge Companion to Gothic Fiction*. Cambridge: Cambridge UP, 2002.

Huntington, John. *The Logic of Fantasy: H. G. Wells and Science Fiction*. New York: Columbia UP, 1982.

Hutton, R. H. Rev. of "The Island of Dr. Moreau." Rpt. in *H. G. Wells: The Critical Heritage*. Ed. Patrick Parrinder. London: Routledge, 1972. 46–48.

Ishiguro, Kazuo. *The Remains of the Day*. London: Faber and Faber, 1989.

Jameson, Fredric. *Archaeologies of the Future: The Desire Called Utopia and Other Science Fictions*. London: Verso, 2005.

———. "Politics of Utopia." *New Left Review* 25 (Jan./Feb. 2005): 35–54.

Keane, Beppie. "Of the Postmodernists' Party without Knowing It: Philip Pullman, Hypermorality and Metanarratives." *Explorations into Children's Literature* 15 (1 Mar. 2005): 50–59.

Kemp, Peter. "Master of His Universe." *The Sunday Times* [Books Section] 19 Oct. 1997: 11.

Keymer, Tom, and Peter Sabor, eds. *The Pamela Controversy: Criticisms and Adaptations of Samuel Richardson's Pamela, 1740–1750*. 6 vols. London: Pickering & Chatto, 2001.

Kilgour, Maggie. *The Rise of the Gothic Novel*. London: Routledge, 1995.

Kimpel, Ben D., and T. C. Duncan Eaves. *Samuel Richardson: A Biography*. Oxford: Clarendon, 1971.

Kipling, Rudyard. *The Man Who Would Be King and Other Stories*. Harmondsworth: Penguin, 1987.

Lago, Mary. *E. M. Forster: A Literary Life*. Basingstoke, England: Palgrave Macmillan, 1995.

Langer, William L., ed. *An Encyclopedia of World History*. Boston: Houghton Mifflin, 1968.

Langguth, A. J. *Saki: A Life of Hector Hugh Munro*. London: Hamish Hamilton, 1981.

Langhorne, John. "In a review of 'The Castle of Otranto, a Story." *Monthly Review* 32 (1765): 97–99.

Lenz, Millicent, and Carole Scott, eds. *His Dark Materials Illuminated: Critical Essays on Philip Pullman's Trilogy*. Detroit, MI: Wayne State UP, 2005.

Lindsay, Maurice. *History of Scottish Literature*. London: Robert Hale, 1977.

Lodge, David. *The Art of Fiction*. London: Penguin, 1992.

Logan, G. M. *The Meaning of More's Utopia*. Princeton, NJ: Princeton UP,1983.

Lougy, Robert E. *Dickens's Hard Times: The Romance as Radical Literature in Charles Dicken's Hard Times*. Ed. Harold Bloom. New York: Chelsea, 1987.

Lowry, Nelson R. "Night Thoughts on the Gothic Novel." *Bloom's Modern Critical Views: Mary Shelley*. Ed. Harold Bloom. Philadelphia: Chelsea, 1985. 31–48.

MacCulloch, Diarmaid. *Book of Common Prayer: 1662 version*. London: Everyman, 1999.

Macdonald, D. L. *Poor Polidori: A Critical Biography of the Author of the Vampyre*. Toronto: U of Toronto P, 1991.

Malchow, H. L. *Gothic Images of Race in Nineteenth-Century Britain*. California: Stanford UP, 1996.

Mallett, Phillip. *Rudyard Kipling: A Literary Life*. Basingstoke, England: Palgrave Macmillan, 2003.

Manuel, Frank. *Utopia and Utopian Thought*. Boston: Beacon, 1965.

Marc, Porée. *Kazuo Ishiguro, The Remains of the Day*. Paris: Didier Erudition/CNED, 1999.

Marin, Louis. *Utopiques, jeux d' espace*. Paris: Minuit, 1973.

Markman, Ellis. *The History of Gothic Fiction*. Edinburgh: Edinburgh UP, 2000.

Marouby, Christian. *Utopie et primitivisme. Essai sur l'imaginaire anthropologique à l'âge classique*. Paris: Seuil, 1990.

Mehew, Ernest, ed. *Selected Letters of Robert Louis Stevenson*. New Haven: Yale UP, 1997.

Miles, Robert. *Gothic Writing, 1750–1820: A Genealogy*. London: Routledge, 1993.

———. "The 1790s: The Effulgence of the Gothic." *The Cambridge Companion to the Gothic*. Ed. Jerrold E. Hogle. Cambridge: Cambridge UP, 2002. 41–62.

Milton, John. *Paradise Lost, Introduced by Philip Pullman*. New York: Oxford UP, 2005.

Mitchell, Chalmers. Rev. of "The Island of Dr. Moreau." Rpt. in *H. G. Wells: The Critical Heritage*. Ed. Patrick Parrinder. London: Routledge, 1972. 43–46.

Mitchell, Sally, ed. *Victorian Britain: An Encyclopedia*. New York: Garland, 1988.

Munro, E. E. *Biography of Saki, in Saki, the Square Egg*. London: The Bodley Head, 1924.

Murphy, Patricia. "The Gendering of History in She." *Studies in English Literature, 1500–1900* 39.4 (1999): 747–772.

Naydor, Lillian. "The Cannibal, the Nurse, and the Cook in Dickens, the Frozen Deep." *Victorian Literature and Culture* 19 (1991): 1–24.

Norris, John, and Mary Astell. *Letters Concerning the Love of God (1695)*. Eds. E. Derek Taylor and Melyn New. Aldershot, UK: Ashgate, 2005.

Oulton, Carolyn. "A Vindication of Religion: Wilkie Collins, Charles Dickens, and the Frozen Deep." *Dickensian* 97.2 (2001): 154–158.

Paffard, Mark. *Kipling's Indian Fiction*. Basingstoke, England: Palgrave Macmillan, 1989.

Paroissien, David. *A Companion to Oliver Twist*. Edinburgh: Edinburgh UP, 1992.

Parrinder, Patrick. "Introduction." *H. G. Wells: The Critical Heritage*. London: Routledge, 1972. 1–31.

Perry, Ruth. *Novel Relations: The Transformation of Kinship in English Literature and Culture, 1748–1818*. Cambridge: Cambridge UP, 2004.

Philmus, Robert. *Into the Unknown: The Evolution of Science Fiction from Francis Godwin to H. G. Wells*. Berkeley: U of California P, 1970.

Polidori, John William. "The Vampyre." *The Vampyre and Other Tales of the Macabre*. Oxford World's Classic. Eds. Robert Morrison and Chris Baldick. Oxford: Oxford UP, 1997. 3–23.

Pullman, Philip. *The Subtle Knife*. London: Scholastic, 1997.

———. *The Amber Spyglass*. London: Scholastic/ David Fickling Books, 2000.

———. *Northern Lights*. London: Scholastic, 1995. Rpt. as *The Golden Compass*. New York: Dell Laurel-Leaf, 2003.

Punter, David. *The Literature of Terror: The Gothic Tradition*. 2 vols. 2nd ed. London and New York: Longman, 1996.

Reeve, Clara. *The Old English Baron*. Ed. James Trainer and Intro. James Watt. Oxford and New York: Oxford UP, 2003.

Richardson, Samuel. *Clarissa. Or, the History of a Young Lady (1750–51)*. 8 vols. 3rd ed. London: S. Richardson, 1751.

———. *Clarissa or the History of a Young Lady (1747–48)*. 1747–48. Ed. Angus Ross. London: Penguin, 1985.

———. *Pamela; Or, Virtue Rewarded*. 1740. 14th ed., 1801. Ed. Peter Sabor and Intro. Margaret Anne Doody . Harmondsworth: Penguin, 1985.

———. *The History of Sir Charles Grandison (1753–54)*. 1972. 7 vols. Ed. Jocelyn Harris. Oxford: Oxford UP, 1986.

Richter, Norton, ed. *Gothic Readings: The First Wave, 1764–1840*. London and New York: Leicester UP, 2000.

Robinson, Kenneth. *Wilkie Collins, A Biography*. New York: Macmillan, 1952.

Rowling,Rowling, J. K. *Harry Potter and the Sorcerer's Stone*. New York: Scholastic, 1997.

Rowling ———. *Harry Potter and the Order of the Phoenix*. New York: Scholastic, 2003.

Rushdie, Salman. *Imaginary Homelands: Essays and Criticism 1981–91*. London: Granta, 1991.

Sage, Lorna. *Angela Carter*. Plymouth: Northcote, 1994.

Saki, A. J. *The Interlopers, in the Complete Saki*. Harmondsworth: Penguin, 1982.

Schoene-Harwood, ed. *Mary Shelley Frankenstein: Essays, Articles, Reviews*. New York: Columbia UP, 2000.

Sedgwick, Eve Kosofsky. *The Coherence of Gothic Conventions*. New York and London: Methuen, 1986.

Showalter, Elaine. *The Female Malady*. New York: Penguin Books, 1987.

Slater, Michael. "Frauds on the Fairies Household Words (1 Oct. 1853)." *The Dent Uniform Edition of Dickens' Journalism, Vol. 3: "Gone Astray" and Other Papers from "Household Words" 1851–1859*. London: J.M. Dent, 1998. 166–174.

Smith, D. Baker. *More's Utopia*. London: Harper Collins, 1991.

Souhami, Diana. *The Trials of Radclyffe Hall*. London: Virago, 1999.

Spears, George James. *The Satire of Saki: A Study of the Satiric Art of Hector H. Munro*. New York, 1963.

Springborg, Patricia. *Some Reflections upon Marriage*. London: John Nutt, 1700.

———, ed. *Mary Astell. A Serious Proposal to the Ladies (1694)*. Peterborough, Ontario: Broadview, 2002.

Squires, Claire. *Philip Pullman's "His Dark Materials" Trilogy: A Reader's Guide*. Continuum Contemporaries Series. London: Continuum, 2003.

Stallybrass, Oliver. "Editor's Introduction." *Howards End*. By E. M. Forster. London: Penguin, 1973. 7–17.

Stevenson, Robert Louis. *Dr. Jekyll and Mr. Hyde and Other Stories*. London: Penguin Books, 1979.

Suvin, Darko. "Wells as the Turning Point of the SF Tradition." *Critical Essays on H. G. Wells*. Ed. John Huntington. Boston: G. K. Hall, 1991. 23–33.

Talbot, Margaret. "The Candy Man." *The New Yorker* 81.20 (11 July 2005): 92. Tennyson, Alfred Lord. "In Memoriam A.H.H." *Victorian Poetry and Poetics*. Eds. Walter E. Houghton and G. Robert Stange. New York: Houghton Mifflin, 1968.

———. "In Memoriam." *Tennyson's Poetry*. Ed. Robert W. Hill. New York: Norton Critical Edition, 1971. 117–195.

Thackeray, William Makepeace. *Vanity Fair*. Ed. John Sutherland. Oxford: Oxford World's Classics, 1998.

Wagner, Erica. "Review of His Dark Materials." *The Times* 18 Oct. 2000: T2, 12.

Wallace, Diana. *The Women's Historical Novel: British Women Writers, 1900–2000*. Basingstoke and New York: Palgrave Macmillan, 2005.

Walpole, Horace. *The Castle of Otranto*. Ed. W. S. Lewis and Intro. E. J. Clery. Oxford and New York: Oxford UP, 1998.

Watt, Ian. *The Rise of the Novel: Studies in Defoe, Fielding, and Richardson*. London: Chatto & Windus, 1957.

Watt, James. *Contesting the Gothic: Fiction, Genre, and Cultural Conflict, 1764–1832*. Cambridge: Cambridge UP, 1999.

Wells, H. G. *The Complete Short Stories of H. G. Wells*. London: Phoenix, 1998.

———. *The Island of Dr. Moreau*. 1986. New York: Barnes and Noble, 2004.

Westfahl, Gary. "H. Rider Haggard." *Cyclopedia of World Authors*. Ed. Frank N. Magill. New York: Harper & Row, 1958. 467–468.

———. H. Rider Haggard: Overview. *St. James Guide to Fantasy Writers*. Ed. David Pringle. New York: St. James, 1996.

Whelan, Peter T. "H. Rider Haggard (1856–1925)." *British Short-fiction Writers, 1880-1914: The Romantic Tradition, Vol. 156 of Dictionary of Literary Biography*. Ed. William F. Naufftus. Detroit: Gale Research, 1996. 124–136.

Williams, Ioan. "Thackeray." 1968. Rpt. as Pollard, A. ed. *Thackeray: Vanity Fair: Critical Essays*. Basingstoke, England: Palgrave Macmillan, 1986.

Wolpert, Stanley. *A New History of India*. Oxford: Oxford UP, 1977.

Zipes, Jack. *Breaking the Magic Spell: Radical Theories of Folk and Fairy Tales*. London: Heinemann, 1979.

INDEX